YOU REALLY COULDN'T MAKE IT UP

Jack Crossley spent some 40 years in Fleet Street, first as a reporter on the *Daily Mail* and later as news editor/assistant editor on the *Mail*, the *Observer*, the *Herald* (Glasgow), the *Daily Express*, *The Times* and, for two crazy months, the *National Enquirer* in Florida.

He also edited the *Sunday Standard*, a short-lived quality broadsheet in Scotland and was briefly a reporter on the Quincy Patriot Ledger in Massachusetts.

He now lives in London with his wife, Kate.

You Really Couldn't Make It Up

BY JACK CROSSLEY

You Really Couldn't Make It Up

MORE
HILARIOUS
BIZARRE-BUT-TRUE
STORIES FROM AROUND
BRITAIN

JOHN BLAKE

Published by John Blake Publishing Ltd,
3, Bramber Court, 2 Bramber Road,
London W14 9PB, England

www.johnblakepublishing.co.uk

First published in paperback in 2004

ISBN 978 1 84454 078 5

British Library Cataloguing-in-Publication Data:

A catalogue record for this book is available from the British Library.

Design by www.envydesign.co.uk

Illustrations by John Miers

Printed in the UK by CPI Bookmarque, Croydon, CR0 4TD

9 10 8

Papers used by John Blake Publishing are natural, recyclable
products made from wood grown in sustainable forests. The
manufacturing processes conform to the environmental regulations
of the country of origin.

Every attempt has been made to contact the relevant copyright-
holders, but some were unobtainable. We would be grateful if the
appropriate people could contact us.

Dedicated to my son Gary –
who brings order to
my disjointed ramblings

Contents

Chapter 1

Mixed Messages:
Signs of the Times

Lip-enhancing gloss labelled 'For external use on the oral lips only'.

'The instructions with my new steam iron include the warning: "Never steam iron the garment you are wearing."'

Christopher Bell, Sevenoaks, Kent,
The Times

'Spring Health Leisure require part-time fitness instructor able to work evenings and weekends. Must be flexible.'

Spotted in the *Hartlepool Mail* by Les Hester

Seen in a car park in Bakewell, Derbyshire, a sign saying: 'Public Toilets'. And underneath it a sign saying: 'Have You Paid and Displayed?'

Mrs Wendy Brant, *Daily Mail*

Instructions on a new digital telephone include: 'When the other person answers, speak.'

Debbie Beasley, Langdon Hills, Essex, *The Times*

Sign at King's Cross railway station – designed to help passengers with pre-booked seats on the 16.28 to Doncaster: 'Coach G is in M. M is in J. E is split between A and D.'

Mark Carter, Beverley, Yorkshire, *The Times*

Sign seen on the back window of a car: 'Caution. Driver under the influence of children.'

Sue Barnard, Altrincham, Cheshire, *The Times*

'A charity that helps dead and blind people is looking for volunteers.'

Spotted in the *Hastings Observer*
by Mrs M Tower, of Broad Oak, East Sussex

Because of a new EC directive it was felt necessary to put up a sign on the slopes of the Cairngorms in Scotland saying: 'Hazard Warning. This snow could be slippery and dangerous.'

Sunday Telegraph

Sign on the door of a repair shop: 'We Can Fix Anything. Please knock on the door, the bell is broken.'

Reader's Digest

The @ sign used in e-mails is known as 'monkey's tail' in South Africa, 'pickled herring' in the Czech Republic, 'snail' in Israel, 'maggot' in Hungary, 'little mouse' in Mandarin Chinese and 'little monkey's testicle' in Holland.

The Times

Advert in the *Glossop Chronicle & Advertiser* for a factory shop closing down sale: 'New stock arriving daily.'

Spotted by Mr L A Penny of Glossop, *Daily Mail*

A winter sports catalogue advertises: 'Ladybird £14.95. A small city backpack for girls with a padded bottom.'

Sunday Times

Britain has many weird and wonderful place names (Crackpot, Blubberhouses, Pratts Bottom, Twatt, Booze) – but the US throws up some stiff competition. 'Fearnot' and 'Rough and Ready' are neighbouring towns in Pennsylvania, which led to the headline: 'Fearnot man marries Rough and Ready Woman.'

Independent on Sunday

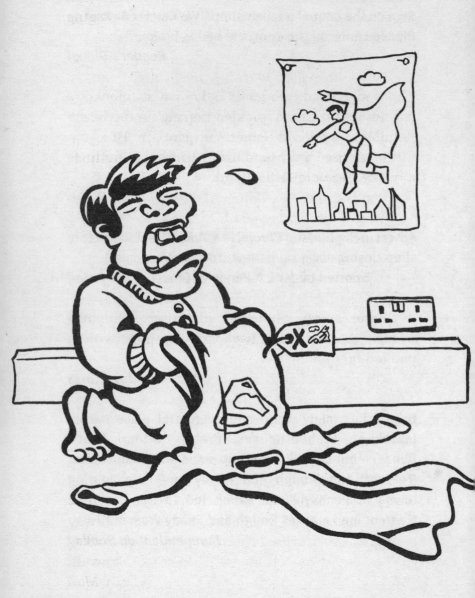

In a contest to find Britain's silliest packaging instructions the samples below were finalists:

- Nytol sleep aid: 'Warning: may cause drowsiness.'
- Tesco's tiramisu dessert: 'Do not turn upside down' – printed on bottom of box.
- Marks and Spencer's bread pudding: 'Product will be hot after heating.'
- Boot's Children's Cough Medicine: 'Do not drive a car or operate machinery after taking this medication.'
- On several brands of Christmas lights: 'For indoor or outdoor use only.'
- On a child's Superman costume: 'Wearing this garment does not enable you to fly.'
- On lip-enhancing gloss: 'For external use on the oral lips only.'

Sunday Telegraph

A box of fire-lighters warns me that they are 'Highly Inflammable'.

Duncan Heenan, Isle of Wight, *The Times*

Sign on the Truro - Falmouth branch railway line: 'Toilets are closed at Falmouth Town Railway Station due to flooding. Please use Falmouth Docks.'

Mrs A Dennant, Falmouth, Cornwall,
Daily Mail

The British affection for place names – particularly silly ones – is celebrated in the *Penguin Dictionary of British Place Names*, compiled by Adrian Room.

You can soak up Booze in North Yorkshire or Beer in Devon and then go for a Wyre Piddle in Worcester.

Members of the Loose Women's Institute in Kent may feel they have a slight edge on those at the Ugley Women's Institute in Essex.

Daily Telegraph

Mucking and Messing are two place names in Essex.

The Times

Peter Luff MP recalls 'a poem of place names in my constituency':

Upton Snodsbury, Tibberton and Crowle
Wyre Piddle, North Piddle, Piddle in the Hole.

Sadly, writes Mr Luff, modern maps omit the last of these and it now lives on only as the appropriate name of a fine, locally brewed beer.

Daily Telegraph

Imagine my delight to learn from the packaging that my Tesco Premium teabags are 'Suitable for everyday use. Throughout the day.'

Richard Arch, London NW, *The Times*

On the pack of a purchase from a garden centre: 'Kills ants for up to five weeks.'

Catherine Henderson, Lancaster, *The Times*

Found on the underside of a box of sweets: 'Do not read while the carton is open.'

Chris Spurrier, Hampshire, *The Times*

A woman writes from America to tell the *Daily Telegraph* about the Harry Potter broomstick given to her five-year-old. The packaging read: 'Caution. Broom does not really fly.'

On the handlebars of a child's scooter: 'Caution. This product moves when used.'

Martin G Sexton, Norwich, *The Times*

Sign on a farm fence in Colwyn Bay: 'Well rotted horse manure £1. Or DIY 50p'.

Daily Mail

Label on Tesco Pudding Rice: 'Ideal for rice puddings.'

Norman Braidwood, Edinburgh, *The Times*

Sign at a van sales room in Beckenham: 'All major credit cards excepted.'

Anthony Vigurs, *The Times*

Warning on an item of clothing: 'The hemp used in this garment is non-toxic and cannot be used as a drug.'

The Times

People keep stealing a street sign identifying Butt Hole Road, Conisbrough, South Yorkshire. American tourists are suspected.

Sheffield Star

Label on a glass paperweight: 'Easy to use.'
   'This I can confirm to be true,' writes Paul McLure of Exeter in *The Times*.

A sign in Musselburgh, East Lothian, points to: 'Toilets'. Underneath it another sign says: 'Free P'.

Daily Mail

Sign in a butcher's shop in the Yorkshire Dales: 'Orders may be placed by e-mail or by fax or pushed under the door.'

Reader's Digest

A book called *The Warning Label* Book includes the warning covering Ray-O-Vac batteries: 'If swallowed or lodged in the ear or nose, see doctor.' And this on the Sno-Off Automobile Windshield Cover: 'Caution. Never drive with the cover on your windshield.'

Independent on Sunday

Sign in a hotel in Great Yarmouth: 'Please fold up wheelchairs when using the ramp.'

Daily Mail

Stephen Edwards of Nottingham wrote to *The Times* about a sign he saw in India: 'The Old Ladakh Guest House – hospitalising since 1974.'

British tourists frequently steal the road signs that tell them they have arrived in the South-West France town of Condom.

Independent

Underneath the 'automatic door' sign at the TSB Bank in Bracknell, Berkshire, there is another sign saying: 'Push to Open.'

Paul Simmonds, *Daily Mail*

'I have just returned from a cruise where a Force 10 made the ship pitch. My Boots Travel Calm Tablets had an accompanying advice leaflet warning of possible side effects "which may include vomiting". Oh – joy!'

Mrs Gloria Gillot, Cambridge,
The Times

9

Sign seen outside a hotel near Blackpool by Thelma Hawes of Southampton: 'Please Be Careful When Reve Your C'. The rest of the sign has been broken off, presumably by a reversing car.

Daily Mail

Sign above a men's urinal in York: 'RELAX. Help is at hand. Please ask a member of staff if you can't find what you are looking for or need a suggestion.'

Spotted by Ian Davis, *Daily Mail*

A Wacky Warnings Label Contest produced these gems:

- On a fish hook: 'Harmful if swallowed.'
- On a toboggan: 'May develop high speed under certain snow conditions.'
- On a CD storage rack: 'Do not use as a ladder.'
- On a bottle of bleach: 'If you do not understand or cannot read all directions, cautions and warnings, do not use this product.'

Independent on Sunday

James Whitworth, of Eastbourne, noticed 'the pompous wording' on the vehicle taking away his rubbish and wondered how the songwriter would have managed 'My old man's a recycling collection operator'.

Daily Telegraph

Warning on a pamphlet about birth control: 'Reproduction forbidden without our written consent.'

Tony Rich, Bristol, *Reader's Digest*

Sign on the stairs at Gidea Park, Essex, railway station: 'Caution. Do not run on the stairs. Use the hand rail.'

E D Spink, Hornchurch, Essex, *Daily Mail*

Spotted on a package of frozen turkey breasts: 'Can be cooked from frozen. If cooking from frozen please defrost in the fridge.'

Clare Day, Northampton, *Daily Mail*

A 'Male Toilet' sign seen at Hever Castle in Kent points to a battered tin bucket.

Mrs T Holley, Kent, *Daily Mail*

Sign in a jeweller's shop in the West Midlands: 'Tight rings removed while you wait.'

The Financial Times

'At our local community refuse tip there is a sign saying: "If you can't read, please ask for assistance."'

Stuart Gray, *Reader's Digest*

There's an estate agency called Doolittle and Dalley in Bridgnorth, Shropshire.

> Spotted by R J Kerridge of Worthing,
> West Sussex, *Daily Mail*

When she was a child Catherine Pease-Watkin was always somewhat alarmed by a sign at a local hospital in Yorkshire: 'White Hart Hospital. Guard Dogs Operating.'

> *Independent*

'Marks & Spencer used to supply bags bearing the legend: "To avoid suffocation keep away from children."'

> Elizabeth Monkhouse NW, London, *Independent*

'To add to your letters on misleading signs, I certainly won't be returning in a hurry to a pub in North Yorkshire which had a notice: "Try our delicious home made pies – you'll never get better."'

> Ian Beresford, Stockport, Cheshire, Independent

Sign on a bulk carrier seen on the A23 in Sussex: 'Non-hazardous food.'

> *Daily Telegraph*

Sign outside a camping shop in Lytham, Lancashire: 'Now is the season of our discount tents.'

> Daily Telegraph

An information slip from Oxted Library:

- Easter Opening Times 2003
- Good Friday 18 April 2003 – Closed
- Saturday 19 April 2003 – Closed
- Easter Sunday 20 April 2003 – Closed
- Monday 21 April 2003 – Closed
  Tony Duckworth, Oxted, Surrey, *The Times*

Sign in a hospital waiting room: 'Books 20p each. Pay at reception as honesty box has been stolen.'
W J Brookes, Redditch, Worcestershire, *Daily Mail*

Chapter 2

Medical:
What's Up, Doc?

Man hospitalised by milk float – driven by dog ...

A man went into Leeds Infirmary for a heart by-pass. Part of a leg vein was removed to replace a blocked artery. This meant that a tattoo on his leg, which used to read 'I love women', ended up reading 'I love men'.

Independent on Sunday

Message seen on a wall at a Middlesex Hospital: 'The only difference between this place and the *Titanic* is that they had a band.'

Guardian

Health advice – Beryl Bainbridge style: 'It takes too long to get tight on champagne. On whisky it takes me only five minutes. Giving up smoking would kill me.'

Independent

'First there was a report saying that going to the pub is good for the mind. In a second blow to the health police, my dentist tells me that smoking makes your fillings last longer.'

Jeremy Clarkson's column in the *Sun*

At the age of 105 Dolly Jackson, of Hereford, said that she started smoking when she was 14 – but was giving it up to help her live longer.

News of the World

The West Country Ambulance Service received a barrage of ridiculous calls over the 2003–04 festive season, including those from:

- A woman who was lonely and wanted a cuddle.
- A couple who wanted someone to fetch logs from their shed.
- A man scared of thunder.
- Someone who had lost the TV remote control.

Western Morning News.

In one recent year almost one million people were admitted to UK hospitals as a result of unfortunate and often unusual incidents (costing the NHS some £1bn). Department of Health statistics show that:

- 51 people were bitten or crushed by reptiles.
- 22 were bitten by a rat.
- 190 had 'come into contact with plant thorns, spines and sharp leaves'.
- 369 had fallen foul of lawnmowers.
- 3,038 were injured through 'contact with a non-powered hand drill'.
- 389 were admitted after crashing their bicycle into a stationary object.
- 31 children under 14 got on a motorcycle and crashed into a car.
- 24 were burned by 'ignition or melting of nightwear'.
- 754 were scalded by hot tap water.
- 189 needed treatment after 'foreign objects' were accidentally left in their bodies during surgical and medical care.
- Lightning struck 65 times – but not in the same place twice.

The Times/Evening Standard

'As a medical student I was baffled by the abbreviation BNOR, but discovered from a nurse in the obstetric unit that it meant: "Bowels not opened regularly."'

Bernard Gaston, Hale, Cheshire, *The Times*

A 75-year-old man was treated for a knee injury in a Wirral hospital after being hit by a milk float being 'driven by a dog'.

Guardian

As a retired vet I have also come across useful acronyms. DMITO stands for 'dog more intelligent than owner'.

Mike Godsal, Aylesbury, Buckinghamshire,
The Times

To celebrate the 75th anniversary of the discovery of penicillin the Royal Society of Chemistry wants to find the most spectacular growth of grunge in a forgotten coffee mug. Staff in offices, factories and other work places are being asked to submit photos of the muckiest mugs in Britain. 'Send pictures, not the mugs,' pleads the Society.

Independent

Amid stories of unhygienic hospitals, I A Olsen of Aberdeen writes to *The Times*: 'The quest for cleanliness can have unforeseen circumstances.

Queen Victoria is reputed to have indignantly dismissed a doctor who carefully washed his hands – after he had examined her.'

Stephen Brown got a phone call when he was on holiday in Spain telling him that his mother was ill and an ambulance had been called to take her into hospital. He flew back and got to Derby General Hospital before his mother did. She had had to wait more than eight hours before the ambulance arrived.

The Times

Doctors in Leeds have told student Ashley Clarke, 18, to eat as much junk food and drink as much beer as he likes to combat a rare medical disorder – vasovagal syncope syndrome. A high-fat, salty diet of chips, crisps and chocolate helps to fur up extra wide arteries.

The Times/Sun

A Liverpool doctor accused of groping an expectant mother's breasts told her: 'You could feed a street with those.'

Sun

A man who broke a tooth filling telephoned the NHS Dentaline, in Medway, Kent, and was told he was not in enough pain to justify an out-of-hours consultation. Use Blu-tack as a temporary filling, they said. A spokesman explained later: 'Chewing gum is also acceptable as a temporary filling.'

Daily Mail

'We have black cabinet ministers, judges and doctors, but apparently only false limbs for white people.'
Black woman Ingrid Nicholls who was offered a white artificial leg because black ones were not available on the NHS,

The Times

Warning on an over-the-counter medicine: 'Do not take this medicine if you suffer from kidney disease or have difficulty urinating unless advised to do so by your doctor.'

Keith Griffiths, Wakefield, West Yorkshire,

Daily Mail

A *Times* reader suffering from slight tendonitis of the upper arm reports that the leaflet accompanying his prescription painkillers warns that possible side-effects might include: 'Blood disorders, bronchospasms, chest pain, congestive heart failure, constipation, diarrhoea, dizziness, double vision, drowsiness, faintness, fits, fluid retention, giddiness, hair loss, headaches, hearing loss, heartburn, hepatitis, hypertension, hypotension, impotence, inflammation of the colon, inflammation of the pancreas, inflammation of the tongue, jaundice, loss of appetite, loss of memory, loss of weight, mood changes, mouth ulcers, nightmares, palpitations, pneumonitis, skin rashes, sleeplessness, stiff neck, stomach ulcers, swollen ankles, tinnitus, vasculitis and vertigo.'

Still, writes Bob Papworth, of Berkshire, my arm should get better.

The Times

Readers' letters in *The Times* told of worrying warnings of possible side-effects that came with their medicines.

One – on quinine sulphur tablets for night cramp – 'concludes with the somewhat alarming possibilities of "kidney damage, changes to blood cells, low blood pressure, coma and death".'

Another, prescribed for a persistent sore throat and cough, lists possible side-effects that include: 'a mild sore throat, coughing and hoarseness.' The reader writes that her condition did not improve 'and I am at a loss to know whether the prescription is not working or I am now suffering the side-effects'.

A nurse celebrated New Year's Day 2004 locked in a lavatory at a nursing home near Bury St Edmunds, Suffolk. Friends passed a straw through the keyhole of the lavatory door to allow her to celebrate with a drink as the chimes of midnight struck. Then firemen arrived to rescue her.

Western Morning News

When Dorothy Fletcher from Liverpool had a heart attack while flying to America for her daughter's wedding a stewardess asked: 'Is there a doctor on board?' Fifteen overhead lights went on – because the flight was full of cardiologists on their way to a conference. 'They saved my life,' said Mrs Fletcher. After three days convalescing she was up and about in time for the wedding.

Daily Mirror

Gardening is the ultimate danger sport. One in five of all accidents occur in or around the garden. In 2002, 62,500 adults needed hospital treatment following a gardening mishap. The Prince of Wales needed a hernia operation after injuring himself at Highgrove.

Daily Telegraph

On Christmas Day, a Hampshire GP got a call from a patient: 'I'm on antibiotics. Can I wash my hair?'

This was among a collection of witless out-of-hours calls collected by *Pulse* magazine. Others included:

- 'Can the dog be treated on the NHS?'
- 'I'm doing a crossword. How do you spell eczema?'
- 'How many calories are there in prawns?'

Independent on Sunday

When a patient in a specialist ward in Wakefield, Yorkshire, fell ill with a chest infection, nurses had to dial 999 for an ambulance to take him to the Accident and Emergency Ward – 150 yards away. Routine procedure made it necessary to get the 80-year-old readmitted as a new patient. A hospital spokeswoman said: 'I accept it must seem quite odd, but the doctors in A&E are trained to find out what's wrong. We apologise.'

Sun

A 19-year-old asylum seeker facing deportation was granted a reprieve after claiming that he will fall victim to a witch doctor's spell if returned to Africa.

Daily Mail

A faith healer targeted his powers on a deaf woman during a 'miracle healing crusade' at Brampton Speke, Devon. Afterwards he had to shout at her repeatedly to ask if she could hear better.

Exeter Express and Echo

Twenty-six-year-old Becky Nyang from Reading almost died when lightning hit metal studs in her mouth. She reported getting blisters on her feet where the lightning bolt exited.

Daily Mail

When old soldier Bill Edwards sent his artificial leg to the repairers ... the Post Office lost it. A search through undelivered parcels unearthed two false legs. Neither of them were Bill's.

Sunday Express

A Scarborough schoolteacher went to hospital for treatment after being hit by a boot thrown by a pupil during a welly-throwing contest.

Yorkshire Evening Post

When I saw a man collapse in the street I stopped my car and ran to give him cardio-pulmonary resuscitation. A traffic warden approached and I asked him to call an ambulance – but he said that wasn't his job and gave me a ticket.

Debra Selinger W1, London, *Daily Mail*

An Essex hospital put both the arms of a two-year-old boy in plaster – because they forgot which one he had broken.

News of the World

DIY is deadly dangerous. Every year there are around 70 deaths and 250,000 serious accidents involving DIY, reports a survey. And one in ten of us has to spend over £1,000 rectifying bodged efforts.

One man dislodged guttering when retrieving his son's kite. He climbed a ladder to fix the guttering.

While he was up there the family budgie escaped through a bedroom window and distracted the DIY enthusiast. He ended up as part of the hapless 250,000.

The Times

Chapter 3

Politics:
Order, Order

Meet Miranda, Lionel and Smiling Boy – your Prime Minister. Or is he just a cult?

When Peter Mandelson asked Gordon Brown for 10p to phone a friend, the Chancellor replied: 'Here's 20p – phone all of them.'

The Times

Peter Rushton, of Hyde, Cheshire, recalled an ancient joke from the satirical puppet show *Spitting Image*: 'Margaret Thatcher's Cabinet were in a restaurant. She ordered her main course and was asked: "What about the vegetables, ma'am?"

'"They'll have the same," she replied.'

Daily Telegraph

House of Lords amendment on the Sexual Offences Bill: 'Page 32, line 1. Leave out "genitals". Insert "penis".'

Sunday Times

'There's an old and no doubt unreliable story about Churchill and Sir Stafford Cripps, socialist member of the War Cabinet. Cripps was badgering Churchill about something and sent a civil servant to him with a message. Churchill was in the toilet and sent the civil servant back with the message that he could deal only with one shit at a time.'

Andrew Marr, *Daily Telegraph*

The late Earl of Arran introduced two Private Member's Bills into the House of Lords. One was on badgers, the other on homosexuals. He allegedly told a friend: 'When I spoke about badgers no one turned up. When I spoke about buggers, the place was packed.' His friend replied: 'There are very few badgers in the Lords.'

Daily Telegraph

'The dreadful truth is that when people come to see their MP, they have run out of better ideas.'

Boris Johnson, Conservative MP for Henley,
Daily Telegraph

'Three years ago the Cabinet Office published its stultifyingly dull "Code of Practice on Written Consultation". Now the minions of the Cabinet Office have launched a public consultation of the Code. A consultation on consulting. Not even *Yes Minister* went this far.'

Observer Pendennis column

A *Sunday Telegraph* correspondent revealed that a nickname for Robin Cook was PB – after *Panurus biarmicus* (bearded tit). Reader S G Clifford of Telford, Shropshire discovered from his bird encyclopaedia that the bearded tit is a member of the babbler family.

Sunday Telegraph

'On being appointed leader of the Conservative Party, Michael Howard said that Tory MPs should not forget that the syllable at the heart of the party's name is "serve" – overlooking the fact that the first syllable is "con".'

Andrew Pierce, *The Times*

'I was standing in the hall when a leaflet dropped through my letterbox saying: "Unfortunately there was no reply when Edwina Hart, your Labour candidate called today. We hope we can count on your support in the Assembly Election."'

Lyn Thomas, Swansea, *The Times*

Tony Blair was 50 on 6 May 2003 and the *Daily Telegraph* printed '50 good things about the man'. No. 1 on their list was: 'He reads the *Daily Telegraph*.'

No. 1 on the *Daily Mail's* list of '50 facts about the Premier' was: 'His nickname at Fettes College was Miranda, because of his fresh face and long hair.' No. 30 was: 'His children call him Lionel.' No. 50 was: 'He sang in the cathedral choir during his time at Durham Choristers' Preparatory School, where he was nicknamed Smiling Boy.'

The *Telegraph* signed off their 50-good things with: 'Regular readers may be pleased to know that a list of 50 not-so-good things about the Prime Minister would be a lot harder to do – there's such a lot to choose from. All the same, Happy Birthday, Mr Blair. Tomorrow normal service is resumed.'

Responding to reports that somebody had scribbled insulting graffiti on a House of Commons table, Gordon Elliot, of Selborne, Hampshire, asked in the *Independent*: 'Are you sure that the inscription didn't read: "Tony Blair is a cult"?'

Since House of Commons committees began meeting at the new early time of 8.55 a.m., MPs are calling for a tea-trolley service. A Commons Early Day Motion states that MPs need the 'stimulation and refreshment of a reviving cup of tea'. Labour

MP Stephen Pound said: 'I like tea so strong you can trot a mouse across its surface.'

Daily Mail

At a Downing Street reception Lady Thatcher took great delight in showing visitors where she had seated Giscard when he was the French president – directly opposite portraits of Nelson and Wellington.

Independent

Former Labour leader Michael Foot was criticised for wearing a 'donkey jacket' at the Cenotaph Remembrance Service in 1981. In an interview just before his 90th birthday he said: 'It wasn't a donkey jacket. It was a perfectly respectable green coat. The Queen Mother liked it very much... I've got quite a few donkey jackets now, because lots of people send them to me in the post.'

Daily Telegraph

'Perhaps I could visit Harrogate and lounge on that beach this summer.' Thus spake Education Secretary Charles Clarke in the Commons, forgetting that the Yorkshire spa town is landlocked and 70 miles from the nearest coast.

Daily Telegraph

At the height of Victorian power and prosperity in 1851 the government employed 1,628 civil servants. In 2003 the government employed a total of 516,000.

Daily Mail

An entry in the House of Commons Register of Members' Interests from shadow foreign secretary Michael Ancram, covering his visit to China: 'The cost of my flights were met by the Conservative Party and all hotel accommodation was provided by courtesy of the Chinese Communist Party.'

Independent

'My seven-year-old niece's autograph book was sent to No.10 and she received a photograph of the Prime Minister with a facsimile signature. She read out to us the accompanying note and it came out as: "A photograph of the Prime Minister with a fake smile."'

Nigel Swann, Derbyshire, *Daily Telegraph*

As a result of his statue of Lady Thatcher being brutally beheaded, sculptor Neil Simmons has found new customers making odd requests: 'I now give people the option of the piece headless or with a head. There are two prices – with or without.'

Independent

In August 2003 Tony Blair overtook Clement Attlee as the longest continuously serving Labour prime minister. There were many fond stories about Clem, who had a reputation for modesty:

- As Roy Hattersley reminds us: 'To Clem Attlee spin was what you put on a cricket ball. He only agreed to have a telex machine at No.10 after he was told that he could get test match scores on it.'
- Attlee penned this jingle about himself: 'Few thought he was even a starter, There were many who thought themselves smarter, But he ended PM, CH and OM, An Earl and a Knight of the Garter.'
- Churchill quipped: 'He had much to be modest about.'

Keith Waterhouse's column, *Daily Mail*

Lamenting the decline of such traditional British qualities as showing a stiff upper lip in the face of triumph or disaster, Leo McKinstry recalls how the modest former prime minister Clem Attlee and his wife drove themselves around the country during election campaigns – taking their own home-made sandwiches.

Daily Mail

Once, outside a polling station, Attlee was asked if he had a message for the British people.

'No' was his wonderfully honest reply – a contrast to the self-important spin of modern politicians.

Daily Mail

'When he was prime minister, Jim Callaghan was guest of honour at a lunch in Blackpool. The waitress serving him tipped a leg of lamb with gravy into the lap of his immaculate suit. "Thank you, my dear," said the PM. "But shouldn't you have served Mrs Callaghan first?"'

Keith Waterhouse, *Daily Mail*

When Gladstone was busy saving loose women from the streets, Disraeli said: 'I wish he'd save one for me.'

John Mortimer, *Daily Mail*

Tony Benn wanted to present his voluminous diaries to the British Library, but they could not afford to have them indexed. He applied to a charity for a grant to pay for his diaries to be available at the Library. 'But you're still alive,' they objected.

Mr Benn told the Cheltenham Literary Festival: 'I wasn't prepared to make that sacrifice.'

Independent

A briefing note for US journalists covering President George W Bush's visit to Australia tells them that in 1996 'a Liberal/National Party coalition came to power under Prime Minister John Major'.

Observer

Baroness Thatcher once told Douglas Hurd that she hadn't thought much of the three people who stood for election as Tory leader after she had lost the job. She had forgotten that Hurd was himself one of them.

BBC online news magazine

Dennis Thatcher — 'the first man to be married to a British prime minister' — died on 26 June 2003. Tributes to him included:

- 'He hardly ever spoke in public and refused to give interviews, saying: 'It is better to keep your mouth shut and be thought a fool than open it and remove all doubt.' *Daily Mail*
- When asked how he liked to relax the millionaire industrialist Sir Denis said: 'When I am not pissed, I like to play a lot of golf.' *Independent*
- The received wisdom now is that he was far from being a gin-soaked old bigot ... but, as he once put it to his wife when she queried

his request for a stiff drink on a morning flight to Scotland: 'My dear, it is never too early for a gin and tonic.' Simon Hoggart, *Guardian*

- Margaret was seen going out to buy bacon for Denis and a permanent secretary said there were plenty of people who would be glad to do that for her. 'No, the bacon had to be just as he liked it, and only she knew what he liked.' W F Deedes, the 'Dear Bill' of *Private Eye's* famous satire, in a tribute to his close friend. *Daily Telegraph*

Tony Blair wanted MP Ronnie Campbell's opinion of a speech he was going to make. The speech was e-mailed by mistake to a hairdresser with the same name. Crimper Campbell replied: 'It's very good. Just go ahead with it.'

Independent

In a survey which asked people to choose which characters best represented loyalty, Winston Churchill beat the Queen to the top spot. Tony Blair scored less highly than Lassie, Jess (Postman Pat's cat), Skippy the Bush Kangaroo and Mr Darcy from *Pride and Prejudice.*

The Times

For his State visit to Britain US President George W Bush brought along 250 Secret Service men, 150 National Security Department advisers, 200 government representatives, 50 political aides, 100 journalists, his personal chef, four cooks, a 15-strong sniffer-dog team and his armoured limousines.

Daily Telegraph

Former foreign secretary Robin Cook has a stuffed stoat on his desk at the House of Commons. Apparently he has moved it around from desk to desk for years. The stoat has startled many visitors who, at first, think it is alive.

The Times

Health minister Lord Warner said that 900,000 people were on incapacity benefit because they were clinically obese, costing the taxpayer £70,965,00. The real figures were 900 fatties costing £70,965. His department apologised for an administrative error.

Daily Telegraph

The Ministry of Defence spent more than £600m settling compensation claims in 2003. Some of it was paid out on a parrot that was startled by a jet fighter. The bird fell off its perch, broke both legs and the claim included a vet's bill for supplying two splints. Fifty-one thousand pounds went to six people who fell out of bed.

Soldier Magazine

Deputy Prime Minister John Prescott has a furry gonk dangling from the computer in his office. On his desk there is a biscuit tin that calls out 'Keep away from the cookie jar' when opened. *The Sunday Times'* comment: 'You don't have to be mad to work there, but it clearly helps.'

During the row about checks on asylum seekers being too lax, opposition leader Michael Howard raised a laugh by saying that one of the tens of thousands of immigrants waved through was a one-legged Bulgarian who claimed to be coming to Britain to work as a roof tiler.

Sun

Paul Goggins, Labour MP for Wythenshawe and Sale East and junior minister with responsibility for prisons, seemed doomed to live out his political life in the shadows. But during a radio interview it was not prison policies that excited listeners. It was the minister's name. Was it possible that he had anything to do with the great Mrs Goggins, who runs the village post office in Postman Pat? Sure enough. Author John Cunliffe was a friend of Goggins' uncle Edmund and borrowed the

family name. As the *Daily Telegraph* said in a learned leader on 26 January 2004: 'Hoons and Hains may come and go. But Mr Goggins's fame will live for ever.'

Fears that Blackpool may fail to attract future party political conferences sparked a mixture of emotions. In a longish list of things he will miss, Simon Hoggart wrote in the *Guardian* of the friendliness of the resort, its sensible and convenient trams and sole Veronique and lobster thermidor served with tea and bread and butter.

His 'Won't Miss' list included its soggy fish and chips and beef sandwiches he described as hot gristle in a bun. He also wished that Yates's Wine Lodge still served champagne on draft even though 'it tasted like sparkling battery acid'.

Chapter 4

Legal:
Law and Disorder

**Scotsman's sporran detained
under quarantine laws ...**

A performance dancer in a London nightclub broke a leg when a table collapsed beneath her 13-stone weight. She had been snuffing out candles on a birthday cake with her bottom. She has claimed compensation.

Sunday Times

Police in Calderdale, West Yorkshire, are writing to criminals inviting them to turn themselves in as the cells at Halifax police station have been refurbished.

Halifax Evening Courier

Irish police are being handicapped in a search for a stolen van, because they cannot issue a description. It's a Special Branch vehicle and they don't want the public to know what it looks like.

Guardian/BBC News Quiz

After a burglar severed a testicle climbing through a window in Berkshire the 80-year-old female householder said: 'He was screaming, but I was in no mood to be sympathetic.'

The Times

A defendant explained to a court in Warrington that the reason he missed an appointment with his probation officer was that his 18-stone mother-in-law fell on him.

Warrington Guardian

A prisoner was granted legal aid to sue the Home Secretary because he was refused a second helping of rhubarb crumble in the jail canteen.

Daily Mail

Avon and Somerset police report some bizarre 999 calls:

- A man called because there were no local buses running.

- A distressed woman called to report a dead pigeon in the road.
- Another crank call came from a man who wanted the police to go to the DSS with him to make sure he got his money.
- A drunk dialled 999 because his pint had been knocked over.
- A dad wanted to know if his 15-year-old daughter had broken the law by having a tattoo.

Avon and Somerset Police website

A 22-year-old man set his house on fire attempting to destroy a wasp nest in Glen Parva, Leicestershire. He poured petrol into a wall cavity and then lit it. He caused £800 worth of damage and got a two-year community rehabilitation order for reckless arson.

Daily Telegraph

Returning to his West Yorkshire home from a holiday in the US, Dave Rogers, 31, was carted off by the FBI because they thought his toy dog was a bomb. He was held for two hours and body-searched at Norfolk Airport, Virginia. His dog was subjected to forensic tests, which revealed that the only explosive thing about the toy was its ability to fart.

Dave had bought it as a birthday present for his girlfriend.

Sun

A boy of ten who squirted a woman with his water pistol was interviewed by two officers from Dorset police. He was summonsed for assault and hauled before Weymouth youth court. The decision to withdraw the summons was criticised by the victim, who said: 'It was a calculated assault.'

Daily Telegraph/The Times

Van Thinh Lee told Barkingside magistrates that he had tucked a Canada goose under his jacket because he wanted to cuddle it – not to eat it. He said cuddling geese was a common practice in his native Vietnam. He got a conditional discharge, was ordered to pay £400 – and warned not to try cuddling geese again.

Daily Telegraph

When the use of hand-held mobile phones in cars became illegal in December 2003, Colwyn Lee, of Swarkstone, Derbyshire, wrote to the *Guardian*: 'For years I drove a large passenger vehicle across London, steering with only one hand while engaged in intense phone conversations. I was an airline pilot.'

Among excuses given by TV licence dodgers to detection squads in Aberdeen were: 'I've never noticed that TV before' and 'The set is just for the cat to have somewhere warm to sleep.' One household had their TV wrapped in tin foil in the belief that this would make it invisible to detector vans.

Independent on Sunday/Scotsman

'My wife and I were sitting in our garden when a neighbour began firing an air pistol into his apple tree – with the shots landing among us. We phoned the police, only to be told: "Call back when you've been hit."'

Rod Hewing, Bakersfield, Notts, *Daily Telegraph*

An elderly woman driver who was involved in a crash near Bridport, Dorset, was found to be wearing oven gloves.

Dorset Echo

Leeds magistrates banned a woman from dining out in her home city after she went on a three-year spree treating friends and relatives to restaurant meals – and leaving without paying. The manager of an Italian restaurant said that ten minutes after being ejected she returned saying: 'I've come back to finish my f****** Tia Maria.'

Daily Telegraph

A drunken man has been charged under the 1990 Environment Protection Act – for dropping a £5 note in the street.

North West Evening Mail

Police constable Simon McEvoy was enjoying his Liquorice Allsorts when his patrol car was called to a gas leak in Oldham. He effected a temporary repair with one of the succulent sweets, which proved to be a perfect fit.

Daily Mail

A Scotsman was questioned for hours at an Australian airport after his sporran had been detained under quarantine laws.

Independent on Sunday

Scotland Yard is seeking ways of marketing its name as one of the world's most famous brands. They include a 12in-tall toy model of a Metropolitan policeman with accessories such as flak jacket, fire extinguisher, loud hailer, telescopic truncheon, riot shield and handcuffs.

The Times

Alex Wilson, 33, put a joke advertisement on the Internet offering his boisterous five-year-old son for sale for £5. Two years later he was questioned by Strathclyde police who had received a complaint from a woman in America complaining of child slavery. Mr Wilson said: 'The police officer was quite jokey at the end, but said I would have to remove the advert.'

A thief in Suffolk stole 27 slippers from a shop – unaware they were all right-footed. A burglar in North Tyneside was caught after falling asleep in his victim's armchair.

Reader's Digest

Police are putting cardboard cut-outs of local officers in shops on housing estates in Sandwell, West Midlands – hoping they will deter shoplifters.

The Times

Members of a Neighbourhood Watch meeting in Wordsley, West Midlands, asked police for protection against stone-throwing yobs. They were told: 'Tape your windows so you won't be hurt by flying glass.'

Sun

Police received a 999 call from a husband complaining that his wife would not cook him an evening meal because she was decorating.

Daily Mirror

A girl who snatched a pensioner's mobile phone was caught when she answered a call on the phone. The call was from a police sergeant in front of her in a bus queue.

Daily Telegraph

'Could we have a Householders Handbook of Useful Phrases when confronted by a burglar?

"Hello old chap." "The money's upstairs." "Have a nice day."'

G H Ward, Middlesborough, *Independent*

North Yorkshire people who complained that they never see policemen patrolling their streets got a letter saying: 'Just because you don't see them does not mean they are not there.'

Guardian

Magistrates in Barrow, Cumbria, ordered a youth to pay £100 compensation to a policeman he had called 'fat'. They decided that the 14-stone policeman had been caused 'mental anguish'.

Daily Mail

Wiltshire police officers warned Karen McFarlane that she could be charged with carrying an offensive weapon in her car – a plastic toy sword belonging to her seven-year-old son Jake. She had to put it out of sight in the boot.

Daily Mail

Nick Fowell, 64, who uses a coffin as a coffee table, was visited by Norfolk police after social services feared there might be a body in it.

Guardian

A police patrol car, aiming a speed camera at passing motorists on the A38 near Bristol, was parked illegally – half on the pavement, half on a double yellow line and in a cycle lane. A senior police officer condemned the practice as '… appalling. We cannot be seen to break the law in order to enforce the law.'

Daily Mail

Adsworth village school, Stockport, was broken into so many times that it started leaving doors open to stop thieves kicking them in. It has also put up notices advising thieves that there's nothing left to steal.

Manchester Metro News

Police in Southampton gave away lollipops in a bid to reduce late-night violence – the theory being that sucking on a lolly would make drunks less likely to be abusive. 'With something in their hands they are less likely to wave fists around,' said the police. There was a hitch when a fight broke out after one drinker didn't get a lollipop.

Daily Mail

Judge Jeremy Roberts adjourned a kidnap case at the Old Bailey and went to watch his horse race at Ascot. It came 12th.

Sunday Telegraph

Thames Valley police refused to give a job to a man because of his three tattoos – one being a mouse sitting on a toadstool smoking a hubble-bubble pipe. The man's MP said that none of the tattoos was visible when he was wearing a short-sleeved shirt.

Daily Telegraph

Under the headline 'Open to Abuse', *The Times* reported that more than 4,000 inmates have absconded from open prisons in the past five years – and 481 who have fled since 1998 have yet to be caught.

A one-legged robber was easily identified after leaving his artificial limb at the scene of the crime. His leg came off during a struggle with the newsagent whose shop he was robbing in Dagenham. He was sentenced to three years' jail.

Independent

Sarah Colwell went to a meeting to discuss crime prevention in Cherry Hinton, Cambridgeshire, and came out to find that her moped had been stolen.

Sunday Times

Tory MP Ann Widdecombe, speaking after being granted the Freedom of London in July 2003, said she was enthusiastic about taking up the ancient right to drive a flock of sheep across London Bridge and was positively inspired by the fact that if she commits murder she now has the right to be hanged with a silken rope.

The Times

Mary Piper, 65, planted prickly rose bushes to deter burglars from her Broadstairs, Kent, home. Thieves stole the bushes.

Sun

An armed robber serving a six-year sentence confessed to three other crimes so that he could stay in prison longer to complete a catering course. Cambridge Crown Court granted his wish – jailing him for a further three years.

Daily Telegraph

When police revealed that the comedian who gate-crashed Prince William's 21st birthday party would not face criminal charges his mother said it was wonderful news. The comedian said: 'What bastards! No more free publicity.'

The Times

A man who had stolen an accordion in Alfriston, Sussex, was stopped by police. He told them he was a busker, but ended up behind bars when they discovered he couldn't play the instrument.

Sussex Express

A scarecrow made to look like a cop got its owner nicked – for impersonating a policeman. The scarecrow was placed next to a speed-check sign and police ordered it to be removed and warned the owner he might face prosecution.

Sun

A suspected teenage burglar was overpowered by the warden and the elderly residents of a sheltered home. Police were called several times, but the only bobby on duty at the local station at Machynlleth, Mid-Wales, was on crutches. Other officers were away on duty at the National Eisteddfod. A police helicopter hovered over the scene but could not help because there was no officer on board. An off-duty PC who lives nearby eventually came to the rescue.

The Times/Sun

A man faced prosecution after beating his girlfriend with a cat – for cruelty to the cat.

Sunday Times

A cyclist in York was stopped by police and accused of riding his bike too slowly.

York Star

'A police officer who attended a training session on courtroom skills was asked: "What is the difference between a sting and a fit-up?" He replied: "We video a sting. We don't video a fit-up."'

Letter from solicitor Mark Solon in *The Times*

Judge Barrington Black, renowned for his one-liners and occasionally wearing a bandana in court, backed out of a case because of the unexpected involvement of his dog Vinnie. The judge was startled to see a defence video showing a dog accused of being dangerously out of control romping harmlessly with other dogs – one of them being Vinnie. The judge stood down after declaring 'a four-footed interest'. The accused dog was acquitted by another judge.

Guardian

South Wales police upped their conviction rate by setting up a speed camera at the Rally of Great Britain. As well as fans trying to emulate their heroes, 20 of the world's top rally drivers were caught speeding. On one stretch of the B4242 in the Neath Valley 200 motorists were caught in a single day and a Belgian competitor was accused of breaking the 30mph limit seven times.

The Times

In Silloth, Cumberland, a woman rented her walk-in wardrobe for £40 a week to an accomplice who grew cannabis in it.

Cumberland News

Jailed solicitors and accountants doing jobs outside prison as part of a resettlement programme are earning up to £20,000 a year – more than the prison officers looking after them.

Daily Express

HBOS, the country's largest mortgage lender, announced it was going to use a lie detector to expose clients making false claims. *The Guardian* published some of the 'Bogus Claims You Couldn't Make Up'. They included:

- A woman claimed five times for the loss of the same eye.
- A man claiming for recuperation costs after suffering a heart attack was found to have submitted a bill from a local brothel.
- A policyholder told the police of a burglary the day before the alleged incident took place.
- A holidaymaker claimed for the cost of having his appendix taken out while on holiday. He had done so on eight previous occasions.

A burglar reported to the police that he had seen a severed human head in a jar in a flat he had broken into. Merseyside Police got a search warrant, kicked down the door of the flat – and found a face-shaped mask inside a sweet jar filled with formaldehyde. They apologised to the Damien Hirst-inspired artist who lived in the flat and said they would pay for a new front door.

The Times

Newark Crown Court, Nottinghamshire, accepted a debtor's offer to pay off £1,879 at the rate of £1 a month. It would take 156 years to clear the debt.

Lincolnshire Free Press

'The Police Federation magazine *Police* tells of thieves who raided a soccer clubhouse in Surrey. They wheeled away their haul of drink on the club's white-line marking machine – and the police tracked down the villains by following the white line.'

Tommy Wilson (PC retired), *Daily Mail*

Police arrested a man in Derby suspected of climbing on to railway diesel tankers and pumping fuel into storage tanks in his garden when freight trains stopped near his home in Derby.

Derby Evening Telegraph

'I've been arrested twice for poaching, but you're not called a poacher any more. You're called a rural criminal. It was a nice term, poacher.'

Daily Telegraph

You can never find a bobby when you need one. Neighbourhood Watch had to abandon a meeting in Danby Village Hall, North Yorkshire, because no one from the police turned up. 'We had a cup of tea and a biscuit and went home,' said one of the organisers.

Yorkshire Post

The *Sun's* associate editor Paul Field wrote an article about how there was virtually zero interest when he reported a burglary. Then hundreds of readers phoned in with similar experiences. Ann Mozdzer, of Camberley, Surrey, said she was shocked when she called to report a burglary in progress at an office block. Police turned up 40 minutes later and one of them told her: 'We don't rush. It's usually over by the time we get there.'

Sun

A Lancashire police constable avoided a speeding conviction by invoking a little-known law that allows police to ignore speed limits even if there is no emergency. Magistrates in Blackpool cleared him of driving at 36mph in a 30mph zone.

Daily Mail

On the same day *The Times* carried a story saying that 12 North Wales policemen had been fined for speeding when they had no legitimate reason for doing so. They were fined £60 and lost three penalty points each.

John Burbeck, chief constable of Warwickshire, has suggested that the answer to rural crime is for citizens to arrest criminals themselves. Said Mr Burbeck: 'People say "Isn't it a bit risky?" Yes – but it's also a bit risky to travel on the roads or play rough sports.'

Daily Mail

Tony Cassidy, 28, was charged with drink driving after police caught him riding a 12in-high micro-cycle outside a pub in Exeter. Magistrates cleared him – ruling that the miniature motorbike was not legally a vehicle after Cassidy carried it to court under his arm.

Daily Telegraph

A police motorcycling club in Somerset has withdrawn T-shirts featuring a skeleton toting a smoking Thompson sub-machine gun in one hand and the flag of St George in the other. Slogans on the shirts included: 'If it moves, shoot it. If it don't, jail it.' Anti-gun campaigners objected and the club apologised 'if the shirts caused any distress'.

Western Morning News

A lawyer on the BBC's *World Service* said she logged and charged for every minute she spent on a client's case. 'If I spend ten minutes in the shower thinking of how I am going to present a case in court – that goes on the bill.'

Magistrates in Cornwall abandoned a motoring case when the policeman due to give evidence said he had to go home to baby-sit.

Daily Express

An ambulance service manager in the West Country spends one day a week dealing with speed camera tickets involving ambulances on emergency calls.

Daily Express

Times writer Mary Ann Sieghart had her handbag stolen and wrote about police inaction over the matter. 'The day my column appeared,' she wrote, 'I received an e-mail from the office of the Commissioner of the Met offering apologies, lunch and a promise of swift action... My precious diary and address book were found in a crack house and restored to me.' The strapline on her report said: 'To get good police service, just write an article in *The Times*.'

Birmingham police flushed out a conman who was claiming that his mobile phone had been stolen. They dialled his mobile and heard it ringing in his pocket. He fled from the police station with the phone still ringing.

The Times

Scotland Yard's Operation Trident unit, which investigates Yardie gun crime, has been told not to refer to 'black on black' shootings. 'Gun crimes in the black community that we serve' is preferred.

Daily Mail

A father complained to police that his son had been bumped on the dodgems at a funfair in Staffordshire. Officers spent three hours interviewing witnesses.

Sun/Sunday Telegraph

Britain's most profitable speed camera is netting up to £25,000 a week in fines in Reading, catching speeding drivers at the rate of one every 95 seconds.

Sun

Suspicious staff in a Portsmouth store checked on a man when he went into one of their changing rooms. They found he was wearing a bra and knickers he had stolen for his wife.

Sun/Sunday Telegraph

Prisoners in London are being transferred between jails in chauffeur-driven Mercedes limos because of a shortage of armoured vans. A prison service spokesman said it was cheaper.

Independent

An asylum seeker who used two names to claim benefits of £16,000 was jailed in East Sussex. The court heard that officials still did not know his real name, his nationality or how and when he entered Britain.

The Times/Sunday Telegraph

A warrant has been issued for the arrest of a National Lottery winner after he allegedly continued to claim benefits for three years after winning £1.5m.

Daily Telegraph

A man who stole a car was left better off after Blackburn magistrates gave him a conditional discharge and told him to pay £30 costs and wrote off £200 he owed in back fines. The owner of the car – which was written off – was £300 out of pocket.

The Times

A woman who pinched a policeman's bottom during a demo was charged with indecent assault. An ex-Flying Squad commander told the *Sun*: 'Not so long ago a cop would have been honoured.'

Re the report of a woman charged with pinching a policeman's bottom. Some years ago a woman made an even more personal attack on an officer and was told: 'You must not take the law into your own hands.'

B D Clark, Newcastle, Staffordshire.
Daily Telegraph

Chief Inspector Peter Mills is making house calls on prolific offenders in Eastbourne, telling them to go straight or face jail. He has earned himself the nickname 'Expector Visit'.

The Times

A thief stole a briefcase from a synagogue in Stamford Hill, North London. All it contained was a set of circumcision tools.

Sun

A man went into a tobacconist's shop in Ayr, Scotland, put a £10 note on the counter and asked for cigarettes. When the shopkeeper opened the till his customer produced a hammer and demanded the contents. He then ran from the shop leaving his tenner and his cigarettes on the counter. The robber escaped with the contents of the till – a measly £5.

Independent on Sunday

Andrew Weir, 55, returned from holiday to find that a burglar had stolen the fitted kitchen from his home. Exeter Crown Court heard that everything had gone: the doors, the electric fire, all of the contents and the fittings – including the kitchen sink. The burglar had reinstalled the kitchen into his own home – a mile away.

Daily Telegraph

The Times reviewed a book called Cops and Robbers compiled by two policemen (John Blake Publishing, £6.99). Here are three of the book's many hilarious stories:

- A Kent policeman made a frantic call reporting a mass punch-up outside a local church. Extra patrols arrived to find that the 'fracas' was just worshippers enthusiastically hugging each other after a late-night Christmas service.
- Thieves stole a pot marked 'Charlie' from a mantelpiece. The pot contained some fine white powder and the robbers thought they had found a stash of cocaine. Only after snorting some of the powder did they discover that the pot was an urn containing the ashes of the owner's pet dog.
- A thief charged with stealing a charity box on Christmas Eve told police: 'Well, there's got to be some give and take at Christmas, hasn't there?'

A South Staffordshire woman has been threatened with court action because she breaks wind too loudly and too often. She has been served with an harassment notice ordering her to curb the noise. A next-door neighbour complained: 'Friends won't come round to see me.'

Sun

Because the suspect in a West Midlands identity parade had a shock of dyed hair and pierced ears every member of the line-up wore hats and had their ears covered with sticky tape. None of the witnesses managed to pick out the alleged bag snatcher – prompting the exasperated judge to lament: 'You might as well have a row of people with bags over their heads.'

Daily Mail

Stephen Smith got a message saying a burglar had been seen breaking into his house in Blackburn, Lancashire. He rang the police and they searched the ransacked house but did not find a burglar. Later Mr Smith found the burglar hiding under a bed. He and his neighbours managed to detain the intruder and the police came back to make an arrest.

Daily Mail

A traffic policeman caught a record 329 speeding drivers in a five-hour stint with a mobile camera – one booking every 58 seconds. If every motorist opted to pay the fixed £60 penalty the fines total adds up to £19,740. PC Stephen Thomas's success came on Halifax Road in Grenoside, near Sheffield, and he said: 'It does produce very good figures every time you go there.'

Sunday Times

The walls at Preston prison are being raised to curb people from throwing tennis balls filled with drugs into the jail.

Daily Mirror/Sunday Telegraph

Police in Sussex called in their chaplain after being spooked by a ghost at Lewes police station. They dubbed the apparition The Chief Inspectre.

News of the World

In Scotland, it is illegal to be drunk in charge of a cow.

Observer

Two thieves who stole £200 from a taxi driver in Kent returned the money – plus a 'tip' of £50 – and apologised for 'behaving like drunken prats'.

Daily Telegraph

Shopkeeper Lorraine Avery drenched a thief with the contents of a catering-sized bottle of salad cream. Police had no difficulty in following the salad cream trail out of the shop in Burton-upon-Trent, Staffordshire, into the street where the thief was trying to clean himself up. Said Mrs Avery, 48: 'I bet he feels a bit of a plonker now.'

Daily Telegraph

Police in Sutton, south London, sent Valentine cards to burglars warning them of a property-marking scheme that emits a chemical spray. The unromantic Valentines carried the message:

> **Roses are red**
> **Violets are blue**
> **And when it sprinkles**
> **It's all over you.**

The Times

Newspapers often run stories about poor police response to 999 calls. So burglar victim Trevor Francis got a surprise when two police officers turned up at his bungalow in Lowestoft, Suffolk, within 15 minutes. One of them was Chief Constable Alastair McWhirter. The 71-year-old pensioner said: 'He told me he was new to the job.'

Sun

The trial of four people charged with running a London brothel ground to a halt after an allegation that one of the jurors was a client.

The Economist

An electoral registration form was addressed to a barn belonging to Brenda Gould, of Newmarket. Her cows live there so Brenda jokingly put their names on the form. She was fined £100 with £110 costs by Ely magistrates.

The Times/Guardian/Sun

Dubbed Britain's most dangerous convict, Charles Bronson has written a *Good Prison Guide*. The 51-year-old armed robber has spent 29 years in different prisons. Parkhurst on the Isle of Wight gets 10 out of 10 for its 'parties, hooch, escape plots and violence'. Pentonville scores only 4 along with the comment: 'Mattress was old and lumpy.' Albany, also on the Isle of Wight, has 'lovely' fish and chips and Bristol has the best porridge.

Sun

The snores of Mrs Florence Phillips earned her a place in legal history when magistrates ruled that they contravened the Control of Pollution Act. Neighbours living in the flat above at Alwoodley, Leeds, complained that the 87-year-old widower's snores prevented them getting a good night's sleep.

The Times

'Dorset Chainsaw Massacre' was the headline over a story about police on the lookout for someone hacking down trees and shrubs in the sedate resort of Poole. They suspect the perpetrator is a local who wants an uninterrupted view of Poole harbour.

The Times

A 24-hour police station in Nottingham, guarded by CCTV, was burgled twice in two weeks. Among items stolen were blank interview tapes, a police-issue jumper – and a truncheon.

Sun

In Liverpool a tax officer named John Fiddler got a jail sentence for paying £250,000 in false rebates to his friends.

Sunday Telegraph/Sun

A 63-year-old former bus driver took more than 100 driving tests on behalf of learner drivers too hopeless to pass themselves. He managed to pose as men half his age by donning disguises, sometimes sporting a moustache and changing his hairstyle. He raked in £50,000, but ended up with a nine-month jail sentence from Kingston Crown Court.

Guardian

Mark Sables has been taken to Doncaster magistrates court 60 times in three years over parking offences for a car he doesn't own – even though the DVLA admit the man they are after is called Sadles.

Sun

A man who volunteered to take part in a police identity parade was arrested and charged with theft after he ate a policeman's cheese sandwich. Bournemouth magistrates gave unemployed actor Alan Hunt, 36, a six-month conditional discharge and ordered him to pay £25 costs. Mr Hunt said: 'That was an expensive sandwich. It wasn't even a good one.'

The Times

Britain's smallest police station is a 6ft by 12ft cupboard in the community centre in Leadgate, a former mining village in County Durham. PC Kevin Kilkenny, a 19 stone former rugby player, manages to squeeze himself in along with filing cabinets, a desk lamp – and his helmet.

The Times

Guardian diarist Matthew Norman chose as 'Splash of the Week' a story in the *Ipswich Evening Star* saying that a man faced a possible jail sentence after almost 37,500 child porn images were found on his computer. 'That,' the story goes on, 'is just 500 less than the average attendance at Highbury to see Arsenal play in the Premiership.'

Port Talbot magistrates told jobless 19-year-old Mark Jones that they would quash his fines for motoring offences if he would sit quietly until the court rose for lunch. Mark stayed silent for just over half an hour and escaped having to pay £417.

Western Mail

A prisoner who escaped from Hollesley Bay jail was recaptured after dialling 999 from a phone box in Suffolk and calling an ambulance complaining of chest pains. Paramedics thought there was something suspicious about their caller – because he was wearing prison uniform.

Guardian

Chapter 5

Britishness:
Quintessentially British

It is every true-born Englishman's right to strap jingle bells round his knees and make a hanky-waving wally of himself ...

In the middle of the July 2003 heatwave Roy Strong asked in the *Daily Mail*: 'What is it about the British – normally a reticent island race – and the sun that turns them into raving lunatics?' He chastises Britons for exposing swathes of repellent blubber and looks forward to the return of 'our usual abysmal British summer with its heart-warming, chilly, damp days'.

The quintessentially British preoccupation of enjoying a biscuit with a nice cup of tea has now got its own

website called 'nicecupofteaandasitdown.com'. It is a surprise hit on the Internet, having attracted 250,000 followers. Stuart Payne, 40, an information technology consultant in Cambridge, started the website 'as a bit of joke' and discovered that 'there is a kind of reverence for biscuits because they are part of British life'.

Daily Telegraph

Mr Payne's website reviews packets of biscuits as though they were fine wines or rare malt whiskies. Among biscuit nibblers, the great dilemma is whether to dunk or not to dunk and he says Rich Tea are the best for dunking. But he admits that there are those who regard dunking as being in bad taste.

The Times

Anthony Richards won the *Daily Telegraph's* competition to provide the best 50-word definition of Englishness. His poetic entry included the lines:

He views the Channel as a trench
Laughs at the Germans, hates the French
Though docile on his starchy diet
He'll rush around to quell a riot
He hates a fuss, seldom complains
Accepts poor service and late trains.

Daily Telegraph

Among the best qualities of the British, according to Gerard Errera, the French Ambassador to the United Kingdom: 'Their gift for understatement and the capacity to display strength through self-deprecation.' He also asks: 'Does anyone still think that when there's fog in the Channel it is the Continent that is isolated?'

Independent

The British Lifestyle Survey pulled the rug from those of us who whine about being so busy we never have any spare time. Joe Joseph wrote in *The Times* that the survey revealed that four-fifths of us 'privately admit that we have more than enough spare time to go around... Remember what James Thurber said, that it's better to have loafed and lost than never to have loafed at all. At least I think that's what he said. I would double check it, only I'm too busy right now.'

The British may well express pride in the nation's heritage, but lots of them are ignorant about it. A survey found:

- 1 in 10 adults thought Hitler was not a real person and almost half were convinced that Robin Hood was.
- More than half thought Horatio Nelson commanded British troops at the battle of Waterloo.

- 30 per cent of 11 to 18 year olds thought that Oliver Cromwell fought at the Battle of Hastings.

'In a way,' sighed an expert, 'there is just too much history.'

Sunday Telegraph

Britons spend 1.3 billion hours a year in queues reports a Norwich Union survey. The most stressful waits are for the lavatory.

The Times

After photographer Spencer Tunick got lots of ordinary folk to turn up nude at the Saatchi gallery and at Selfridges in London, Max Davidson wrote in the *Daily Mail*: 'It is the sheer un-Britishness of the new trend which is so unsettling. Showing off in any form goes against the grain of our national character, which is why naturism has never caught on.'

Madonna says she is delighted to be living in Britain – partly because Britons '... are not as rude and obnoxious as Americans'. She also thinks English swear words are 'more charming and more colourful'.

Daily Mail

Desert Island Discs presenter Sue Lawley reveals her favourite island is England and says: 'The truth is you'd have to be a patriotic numbskull not to wince at this country's faults. But if you're English you belong here and nowhere else will do.'

Daily Telegraph

Most people browsing the Web are looking for gossip on soap stars, pop singers and footballers. But some also seek information on zebra racing, walking-stick making, the rules of toe wrestling, naked petanque and black-pudding throwing. MSN Search, used by 12 million people every month, say: 'It provides a fascinating sneak peak into people's weird and wacky interests and proves we really are a nation of eccentrics.'

Independent

For many, the hat-wearing festival of Ladies' Day at Ascot represents all that is worst about Britain. Paul Haigh, chief columnist of the *Racing Post*, attacks Royal Ascot for being an absurdity and a pantomime. It is exactly because it is both of those things that we should hope it long continues.

Neil Clark, in *The Times*

'Cricket and croquet are quintessentially English. They involve wearing white, ambling around on lovely manicured grass and having tea and sandwiches.'

Daily Telegraph

An Englishman's home is his castle – and it seems his hedges are equally revered. The *Sun* revealed that 100,000 hedge wars are being waged in Britain. The campaign group Hedgeline said the nation's gardens are plagued by bitter feuds – after a man involved in such a dispute was shot dead in Lincoln.

The British tip waiters even when the service has been poor. A survey suggests that they 'do not like to make a fuss' and don't like 'to look mean'.

The Times

A poll in July 2003 found high percentages of Britons who think the following are on their way out: Sunday roast lunches with the family, listening to the Queen's speech, giving up seats for women and the elderly, saving for a rainy day, family days at the seaside, going to church and cooked breakfasts. But drinking tea and talking about the weather are here to stay.

Teletext

One in five Britons feels stressed every day says a Samaritans survey. But they are just as likely to make a cup of tea as they are to take alcohol when they feel down.

The Times

Scientists have been pondering on a subject sacred to the British – how to make a perfect cup of tea. *The Daily Telegraph* printed their findings, which ended with: 'Drink at 60–65ºC to avoid vulgar slurping from trying to drink tea that's too hot.'

The *Telegraph's* leader writer argued that the perfect cup of tea 'is something for philosophers and poets to argue about. Let the scientists get on with more trivial matters, like discovering the origins of the universe.'

Anyone who imagines that modesty, civility and good humour are no longer respected in Britain should attend a garden party at Buckingham Palace. Andrew Gimson of the *Daily Telegraph* joined 'the extremely polite queues' and found 400 waiters and waitresses along with 27,000 cups of tea, 10,000 glasses of iced coffee and 20,000 glasses of fruit squash. He reflected that, 'As long as we stood well back, there was little danger of being introduced to a member of the Royal Family.'

'One of Britain's few distinctive contributions to world culture may be doomed,' was how the *Guardian* greeted the news of a survey which suggested that holiday postcards are being e-mailed and texted into extinction.

The Guardian's coverage of the story said that postcard collecting, or deltiology, is third only to coins and stamps in Britain's tradition of collecting things. Collecting boring postcards is now a deltiological sub-group of its own and treasured samples include 'Traffic on the A40' and 'The Forte Excelsior Motor Lodge near Pontefract'.

Britain is a nation of scroungers with about a quarter of adults owing money to their mates to the tune of £29bn. The online bank Egg says Brits also take books, clothes and other goods from friends rather than buy their own – and admit they scrounge simply because they can get away with it.

Sun

The *Daily Telegraph* records a threat to 'an essential part of British life' – train spotting. Concerns over security and an obsession with health and safety may force harmless hobbyists – some 100,000 of them – to hang up their anoraks.

Weather prediction isn't an exact science and how terrible it would be if it were. The surprise of a hot spell or the hope of a break in miserable weather would be gone for ever. And then what would the British find to talk about?

Daily Telegraph leader

Rumpole author John Mortimer gave both barrels to American psychologist Dr Aric Sigman, who said that the British were becoming more like Californians. 'Utter nonsense,' he wrote. 'Such authorities as Dr Sigman fail to notice our extreme contentment with life outside California ... We British remain proud of our past and addicted to villages and small shops ... At heart we are non-conformists, often indulging in private fantasies, cultivating small gardens and becoming, as the years go by, harmless eccentrics ... If we had a fault, as any European would tell you, it was our eccentric consistent belief that it was the finest thing in the world to have been born British.'

Daily Mail

A traditional breakfast is the thing most Britons working or living abroad miss most. They pine for toast, Marmite, bacon sandwiches, beer and marmalade.

The Times

American writer Bill Bryson has been appointed a commissioner of English Heritage. *The Times* reported: 'Although a Bryson travelogue is more about eccentric people than ancient buildings, he is widely regarded as having cracked the British code: a naturally deprecating nation which will allow you to be quite rude about it provided you display a deep underlying affection.'

In his best-selling travel book on Britain *Notes from a Small Island*, Bryson ended his pilgrimage as helplessly affectionate as when he began it. He then spent eight years in the States pining for Radio 4, the English sense of humour and Branston pickle.

Guardian

Britons are often less familiar with their own country than abroad. Four out of five have never visited Oxford or Liverpool, the European City of Culture for 2008.

The Times

Only four people attended a meeting to discuss public apathy in Dorchester, Dorset.

Sunday Times

When a power failure crippled London's Underground it was time for Brits to once again show true grit and a bit of the old spirit-of-the-Blitz. After being rescued from the dark Underground tunnels many found succour in nearby pubs.

The *Guardian* reported: 'The landlady of the Barrow Boy and Banker, 100 yards from London Bridge, saw her pub filled with commuters drowning their sorrows. One of them said: 'It's gridlock on the streets so I may as well stay in the pub.'

'The English section of the guests' information notice in a third-floor hotel room in Copenhagen read: "In the event of fire, open a window and announce your presence in a seemly manner."'

R A Morley, Southport, *The Times*

In a *Reader's Digest* survey Britons emerged as some of the most dishonest people in Europe. Nearly half would happily cheat the taxman, 25 percent would snitch a hotel towel, 60 percent were prepared to travel on a train without paying, 36 percent would use a disabled parking space. The survey gave Britain an 'honesty rating' of 58 percent compared with 70 percent in Italy and 66 percent in France. But did it all mean that Brits answered the researchers' questions more honestly than the foreigners who took part in the survey?

Sun

Tradition-bound Brits don't like folk messing around with the fairy tales they learned at their mother's knee. A shocked correspondence began October 2003 with this letter in *The Times*:

'My recollection of Humpty Dumpty was that it ended in the failure of the royal cavalry and infantry to resurrect him. My two-year-old daughter's tape of the nursery rhyme ends with:

Humpty Dumpty opened his eyes
Falling down was such a surprise

81

Humpty Dumpty counted to ten
Then Humpty Dumpty got back up again.

'Are today's children too sensitive to cope with the demise of an egg?'

Kit Grace, Taunton, *The Times*

It was quickly followed with:

'The basic error was to let the horses have the first try.'

Ken Parton, Broughton Hackett, Worcestershire

'My daughter's grandfather gave her a book of "kind" nursery rhymes. Not only was Humpty put together again, but Jack and Jill sustained no injury and Polly Flinders and Little Miss Muffet et al came up all smiles. My daughter read the book once and put it aside. I think children like a bit of violence.'

Eileen Hocking, Falmouth, Cornwall, *The Times*

Having a gnome in your garden can knock £500 off the value of your home according to research conducted for the BBC.

Sunday Telegraph

'I do not believe it,' writes Roy Hattersley in the *Daily Mail*. 'A gnome is the guardian at the gate of the Englishman's castle ... We know for certain that Prince Charles possesses a gnome ... John Major's father

earned his living from making them ... I possess two figures in the great tradition. One represents Neil Kinnock, the other Tony Blair. They occupy a place of honour ... in my lavatory.'

Lynda Lee-Potter wrote of gnomes: 'They would certainly be a turn-off for me ... ditto French marigolds, chiming door bells, an owner wearing bedroom slippers, a tiled fireplace, orange carpets, a white leather three-piece suite, frilly net curtains, green lavatory paper, an indoor bar.'

Daily Mail

Bonfire night is, so far as I know, the only surviving celebration in the English calendar that commemorates an actual event out of our own history. The fact that the said event was a damp squib makes it even more worthy of an English celebration.

Keith Waterhouse in the *Daily Mail*

Every year Brits take on holiday 250 million items of clothing that remain unworn.

Reader's Digest

A competition has been launched to find Britain's most conventional family. Alongside this story *The Times* printed a 'fact list' on the average family. It has married parents and 1.6 children. The wife speaks 7,000 words a day. The husband 2,000.

In a move which shocked old-time Boy Scout traditionalists it was revealed that the movement is to sell some of its outdoor, under-canvas camp sites – in favour of fully heated accommodation with all mod-cons.

'It sounds like molly coddling,' they snapped. 'Betraying the very principles of the movement. Where is the fun in sleeping in a purpose-built dormitory?'

Daily Mail

'There is hardly anything more disliked in this country than a bad sport and hardly any figure more beloved than the good loser. Who are our national heroes, our emblematic myths? They are Captain Scott, Eddie the Eagle Edwards and the Sinclair C5.'

Boris Johnson in the *Daily Telegraph*

A meteorologist has analysed the weather in 12,000 paintings and discovered that the weather in British paintings is worst of all. Records of real weather show that we have cloudy or overcast skies for 68 percent of the time. But a full 84 percent of British paintings depict bad weather skies. It seems the British like to think that they feel perfectly at home with dreadful weather, but in fact the weather isn't as dreadful as we pretend it is. There is nothing quite as pleasing to us as a disaster.

Daily Telegraph

The winter of 2004 was marked by letters from readers who were thrilled by the early appearance of snowdrops and swallows. But some really English English people got upset. *Daily Telegraph* **columnist Sarah Sands wrote: 'The dramatic changes in our weather are troubling. It cannot be right to have swallows in February. I don't want England to look like Southern Italy; I want it to look like England.'**

It was a very British occasion. Sixteen new Britons attended the nation's first citizenship ceremony at Brent Town Hall in north London. Under a headline saying 'Welcome to the Odd Country', Alan Hamilton, in *The Times*, reported that officials spent the morning wondering whether the Union Jack was the right way up. A brass band provided a pot-pourri of our national music culture, including the theme music from *Four Weddings and a Funeral* and a song from *The Lion King*. The new Britons were welcomed to 'the British family' and were reminded that one of their obligations was tolerance. Prince Charles told them that despite the British talent for self-deprecation there were many ways in which the UK was still Shakespeare's stone set in a silver sea. The paper reminded them that it is not done to price-haggle in supermarkets.

Alice Thomson, in the *Daily Telegraph*, said the ceremony was strangely moving – at different times dignified, profound, funny, amateurish and very British.

Quentin Letts, in the *Daily Mail*, witnessed an unremittingly good day, with some judiciously English reserve and a dusting of farce – a day for pumped chests, glamorous saris and the occasional teary eye. The floors had been scrubbed and flowers placed in the loos.

Gordon Ridgewall of Hertford, Herts, 'was taken aback' to note that at a travel show at Earls Court 'England's national dance was represented by a bevy of lady Morris dancers.'

Mr Ridgewell insisted that 'the English Morris is a ceremonial dance for men sworn to manhood, fiery ecstasy, ale, magic and fertility ... For women to perform it is a contradiction in terms.'

Daily Telegraph

A search on the Net, however, will produce lots of evidence of women Morris dancers, although this reference does not mention them: A House of Commons motion praising Morris dancers prompted the *Daily Telegraph* to defend '... every true-born Englishman's right to strap jingle bells round his knees and make a hanky-waving wally of himself in public.'

Scotland's only troupe of English Morris Dancers is facing a recruitment crisis because 'There's a limit as to how far most Scotsmen are willing to go to make fools of themselves.'

Independent

The garden shed was chosen as one of the top symbols of Britishness to be exhibited in the Millennium Dome. *The Times*, reporting on the launch of the 2004 Shed of the Year competition, reminded its readers that George Bernard Shaw, Rudyard Kipling, Dylan Thomas and Roald Dahl were among distinguished authors who penned their works in garden sheds. Queen Victoria read State papers in a garden shed which revolved to follow the sun. A man called David Alligan converted his shed into a state-of-the-art cinema with an 8ft screen and ten seats.

The Times

Residents of the tiny Scottish village of Lost are so fed up with tourists pinching their welcome sign that they are going to change the name of the village.

The Times sympathised and, in a leader on the charm of distinctive British place names, dug up a list of others: Pity Me, near Durham. Swine in East Yorkshire. Noah's Ark, Thong, and Pratts Bottom in Kent. Looe and Brown Willy in Cornwall. Bottom Flash in Cheshire. Great Cockup and Little Cockup in

Cumbria. Booze in North Yorkshire, Beer in Devon and Once Brewed and Twice Boozed in Northumberland.

The Scots are the most generous people in Britain. A poll for the British Heart Foundation found only 2 percent of Scots admitted never giving charity compared with 8 percent in London and the North-West of England.

Guardian

Leading sociologist Professor Christie Davies laments that political correctness is destroying the jokes that are the essence of Britain's liberty. He has written a report called *The Right to Joke*, published by the Social Affairs Unit. In the *Daily Mail* he repeated jokes he considered 'to be in the robust tradition of British humour, but it's impossible to imagine that they could be broadcast today.' They included:

- How do you conduct a census in Scotland? Drop a £5 note in the street and count the crowd.
- How do you get a Welshman on to your roof? Tell him the drinks are on the house.
- There is no way, says Professor Davies, that a British TV comedy today could use this line, which appeared on TV in the 1970s: 'Finally, a message for our Malaysian viewers. A dog is not just for Christmas. With a bit of care there'll be enough left over to last into the New Year.'

Chapter 6

Eccentric:
Where British is still Best

The Naked Male – a true British hero ...

A baked bean fanatic who calls himself Capt Beany and paints himself orange has been declared an official tourist attraction in Port Talbot, South Wales.

South Wales Evening Post

Telephone callers hoping to speak to God found themselves connected to Andy Green, of Irlam in Lancashire. Andy's number is the same as that given as God's direct line in the film Bruce Almighty, starring Jim Carrey. 'Most people ring off. They don't expect God to have a Lancashire accent,' says Andy.

Sunday Times

A house-hunting Aberdeenshire couple are willing to live in a tent in a field so that their pet cow can be with them.

Aberdeen Press and Journal

Thirteen scruffy notebooks found at a Sussex antiques fair turned out to be Spike Milligan's *Goon Show* scribblings. One of them is inscribed: 'This book belongs to a wandering idiot of no fixed abode known on most police charge sheets as Terence Milligan, also Spike, also Eccles, also Minnie Bannister.'

Daily Telegraph

Derek Atkins, 48, from York, visits an Odeon cinema eight times a week and has done so since 1988. 'I rarely watch the films,' he says. 'I just like to scrutinise the interiors. I can tell instantly if there is a chip out of the paint.' He has visited all 97 Odeon sites in the country and plans to write a book on their architecture, says the *York Evening Press.*

There are plenty of eccentrics in this strange country. It is a place of warm beer, cricket and people who take the monarchy dreadfully seriously. They don't care very much what foreigners think of them. It is also a place where the showers don't work properly. The views of German foreign correspondent Christian Schubert in his book Great Britain – Island Between the Worlds.

Guardian

Eccentricity abounds in the family of the late Lord Longford. His daughter, novelist Rachel Billington, writes in the *Spectator*: 'The unwelcome ubiquity of badgers in country gardens has inspired a fashionable weekend entertainment called Badger Patrol or Marking Your Territory. Males urinate along designated boundaries to repel the badgers. It is recommended that patrols take place after dark.'

Independent

People interested in fairies have formed a group that has a website to record sightings. It has 1,000 members.

Scarborough Evening News

While waiting for passengers to board a train on what was then the Great Western Railway, a director of the GWR demanded impatiently of the guard why he did not blow his whistle to hurry them along. 'Sir,' the guard replied, 'one does not blow whistles at people from Newbury.'

Benedict Le Vay, author of *Eccentric Britain*,
Daily Telegraph

Steve Gough, a campaigner for 'personal freedom', set off from Land's End to walk naked to John o' Groats. After covering some 15 miles, he was arrested, wrapped in an overcoat, and charged with breaching the peace by Devon and Cornwall police.

Independent

Sandy Easton of Hassall, Cheshire, wrote to *The Times* saying that he asked a lady who had seen Steve Gough if she agreed with the banner he was carrying. 'She said that she had not been looking at his banner.'

'It took Steve Gough seven months to walk naked from Land's End to John o' Groats. En route he was arrested 15 times. He did it without sponsorship or a back-up crew. He is a true English hero.'

A A Gill in *The Sunday Times*

To deter motorists from speeding a resident of Seend in Wiltshire parades through the village in a luminous yellow jacket emblazoned with '30MPH'.

Wiltshire Times

Karen Buckley, chosen as 'Mum of the Year' in Rochdale, revealed, after winning the title, that she had had a sex change operation and was, in fact, the father of 'her' three children.

Daily Express

After 64 days, 478 miles and temperatures of -45ºC, Old Harrovian Pen Hadow, 41, from Devon, made history by walking solo to the North Pole. He rang *The Times* and broke the news with the words: 'Erm ... I've done it.'

The Times

In return for a grant from English Heritage, Sir Michael Leighton, 68, must open his home, Loton Park, near Shrewsbury, to the public for 28 days a year. With brutal honesty, this genuine eccentric cheerfully admits he would love to lock his gates to the great unwashed, boot out his tenant farmers and find a shapely fourth wife. 'I don't want the bloody public here,' he says.

Daily Mail

Joseph Leek of Hull wore second-hand clothes, lived in a dilapidated house and watched his neighbour's TV to save money on electricity. When he died at the age of 90 he left £1.1m to the Guide Dogs for the Blind Association – a charity in which he had never shown any interest. He left his two daughters nothing.

The Times

John Williams of Essex collects mugs and wants to beat the world record of 4,500. When he reached nearly 3,000 (stored in the attic) a structural engineer warned that they were in danger of bringing the ceiling down. John's record attempt is still on – but his mugs have been downloaded to the garden shed.

Daily Mail

Tickets for the Cliff Richard concerts in April 2004 went on sale in September 2003. His fans camped outside for three weeks to make sure they got tickets. They lived in tents, heated baked beans on Primus stoves and washed in cloakrooms at Victoria Station.

Lynda Lee-Potter in the *Daily Mail*

John Evans, 28, set a world record by balancing 325 cans of lager on his head in Northampton.

Sun

Soccer fan Steve Adams, 33, has achieved a rare goal at West Ham – by sitting on all 35,056 seats in the ground. The charity sit-in took him 50 hours and Steve said: 'I'm absolutely knackered but it was worth it.'

Sun

Retired toilet attendant Oliver Ellis, 65, now gets paid £200 a time for his after-dinner speeches on 20 years in Warminster's loos in Wiltshire.

Sun

The 141st annual World Black Pudding Throwing Championship in 2003 was held at the Royal Oak in the village of Ramsbottom, Lancashire. It was won by Nick Connor, who dislodged six Yorkshire puddings from a shelf – throwing black puddings wrapped in ladies' tights.

The Times

In an interview with *Hello!* magazine, Sir Elton John says he's ditched most of his Versace wardrobe. 'I'm 57. You can't look like a 30-year-old ... there comes a point when you have to give in gracefully.' For his interview Elton wore a tuxedo-cloth morning coat with silk-satin lapels, a red silk wing-collared shirt and jabot, fluorescent socks and red and black patent leather boots.

Daily Mail

Guy Smith, of Clunton, Scunthorpe, beat 30 other contestants in the British Pipe Smoking Championships at Knowle, West Midlands, by producing smoke from three grams of tobacco for one hour, 38 minutes and 31 seconds.

Guardian

Multi-talented Peter Ustinov died on 28 March 2004 aged 82, and every newspaper carried lengthy obituaries: They quoted him on:

- The English sense of humour: 'I don't think the English take anybody seriously if they can help it. They have tried to colonise humour. *Daily Telegraph*
- 'They have put a Union Jack on humour and said "Keep orff, that belongs to us."' *The Times*
- On grunting tennis star Monica Seles: 'I'd hate to be next door to her on her wedding night.' *Sun*

- The headmaster's report from his preparatory school in Chelsea: 'He shows great originality – which must be curbed at all costs.'
- Later, when asked to choose between the two London public schools St Paul's and Westminster, he chose the latter because the boys wore top hats 'like Fred Astaire'. *Daily Mail*
- Ustinov failed an Army officer selection board after telling them that he had a preference for tanks 'because you can go into battle sitting down'. *Independent*
- His officer selection board report commented: 'At no time should this man be put in charge of others.' *The Times*

Chapter 7

Over Fifties:

Golden Oldies

**Lorry takes away portable toilet –
with 74-year-old woman inside ...**

An 84-year-old Weymouth man stepped out of the
shower and water dripped from him on to his new
bed. He tried to dry it with a hair dryer, but the
mattress caught fire. He dragged the mattress into
the porch, where it ignited a plastic gas pipe. This
started a fire which burned down half of his roof
and caused the evacuation of four nearby houses.

Guardian

**Information on an Over-75 TV licence includes: 'Your
licence does not guarantee a good picture.'**

Sunday Telegraph

Elderly *Daily Telegraph* readers commented that they had never seen an MP in person. Ron Dawes, of Tunbridge Wells, Kent, wrote: 'I have just passed 80 and have also never seen a Member of Parliament in person. Long may such good fortune continue.'

So many elderly people meet to reminisce on a village bench in Darite, Cornwall, that the local council has been asked to provide a longer seat.

Western Morning News

A 90-year-old North Yorkshire man is the oldest active member of York Gliding Centre.

York Evening Press

Just before Christmas 2003 Jo Halliday got married in a Cornish church to Joyce Hake, after getting down on one knee to propose. Jo was 94. Joyce was 71. Joyce's former husband used to do Jo's gardening and used to say to her: 'If I pop my clogs you will look after Jo won't you.'

Western Morning News

Scientists at Bradford University have received a £90,000 grant to study the cause of greying hair.

Sunday Telegraph

At the age of 92, George Barnes is still driving the £570 green Ford Popular car he bought 43 years ago. The retired chauffeur from Kimberworth, South Yorkshire, has an unblemished record – after 73 years of driving.

Sun

Twenty-one years ago a stripper gave Gordon Fielding of Wilton, Wiltshire, her G-string. He still keeps it next to his shaving mirror to make him smile each day. Gordon is 91.

Sun

When Doris How, 82, hurt her leg in a Tesco supermarket in Hertford, a bag of frozen peas was used to ease the pain. Afterwards she discovered that the store had charged her 78p for the peas. Afterwards Tesco apologised and sent her a basket of fruit and a potted plant.

Daily Telegraph/Daily Mail

Christine and Warren Newcombe, 54, had stayed at the same Blackpool B&B twice every year since 1987. Finally, they bought it from landlady Catherine Peters.

Sun

Mary Quant was 70 in 2004. When she invented the mini-skirt in the 1960s angry bowler-hatted men with rolled umbrellas beat on her shop window in Chelsea.

Daily Mail

A 74-year-old woman running in a half-marathon at Reading came last because she went to use a portable lavatory. While she was still in there it was lifted on to a lorry.

The Times

The campaign aimed at banning smoking in all public places has dismayed the indomitable ex-Tory minister Baroness Trumpington. 'At the age of 80,' said the former 40-a-day girl, 'there are very few pleasures left to me, but one of them is passive smoking.'

The Times

Chapter 8

Language:
My Word

A language kit for long-distance lorry drivers enables them to order chips in six languages ...

Call centre employees in India are trained to understand almost any regional UK dialect and to become familiar with British slang and obscenities. A special dictionary explains that: 'Rogering is an act of sexual intercourse', but 'I'll be buggered' is merely an exclamation of surprise.

'Ronking' means to smell badly, as in: 'Blimey, it ronks in here. Who farted?'

The Times

Lynne Truss's book on the importance of punctuation (*Eats, Shoots and Leaves*) became a surprise

bestseller. To help make her point she tells this joke in the *Daily Mail*:

A man sent a telegram to his girlfriend from his sick bed: 'Not getting any better come at once.' What he meant to say was: 'Not Getting Any. Better come at once.'

'As a child in Kent, the lack of punctuation on the church collection box filled me with wonder and awe: "Thanks Be To God This Box Is Emptied Daily."'

Gillian Bailey, SW4, London, *Independent*

'I saw a young woman wearing a T-shirt bearing the slogan: "Practice safe sex – go fcuk yourself." We deserve to be protected from language like this. When the word practise is used as a verb, it is spelled with an "s".'

Andrew Taylor, Knowl Hill, Berkshire, *Independent*

High on a list of most-hated TV ads was the one for the Nissan Micra that invented the word 'Spafe' by merging 'spacious and safe'. Ad industry magazine *Campaign* said it had a word for the Nissan effort: 'Shollocks'.

Sun

Everyday conversation is now so foul-mouthed that only a handful of words can be considered truly taboo. 'Bollocks' and 'gangbang' used to be taboo, but in the 2003 Collins English Dictionary, they have been reclassified as 'slang'. The f-word and the c-word are still taboo.

Daily Telegraph

The *Daily Telegraph* followed this with a leader saying: 'We shall continue to render most of the reclassified words by dashes – if we use them at all. We suspect that the ———- ——- at Collins are simply trying to flog their ——— —— dictionary.'

Tory leader Iain Duncan Smith used the word 'bullshit' in a speech, giving it the final seal of approval according to language experts. (It has been in the Oxford English Dictionary for more than 30 years.)

Sun

The foul language on modern TV pales when compared with the sexual insults traded publicly on the streets of Britain for three centuries, according to a book called *When Gossips Meet* by Professor Bernard Capp, of Warwick University. They included 'jade, quean, baggage, harlot, drab, filth, trull, dirtyheels, draggletail, flap, slut, squirt and strumpet' – all of them synonyms for 'whore'.

Guardian

The National Canine Defence League changed its name to 'Dogs Trust' because too few people understood the word 'canine'.

Daily Mail

Andrew Marr had some fun in his *Daily Telegraph* column over a play produced in London in which a leading lady makes a speech about obedience to husbands. 'It is about as politically incorrect as anything seen on the London stage in modern times. It's shocking.'

The play in question:
Shakespeare's The Taming of the Shrew.

Political correctness and modern business language were challenged in a *Daily Telegraph* letter on the same day. It tells of a new salesman ringing his boss to say he has a problem.

'We don't have problems here – only opportunities,' the boss pontificates.

'Well,' replies the rep, 'you've got the opportunity to buy me a new car. I've just written off the one you gave me yesterday.'

Adrian Perry, Sheffield, *Daily Telegraph*

One hundred and two languages are spoken in east London.

Guardian

Historian Paul Johnson wrote that nobody can be truly English until he can say 'really' in 17 different ways.

Daily Mail

In the row over whether the government had 'sexed up' an intelligence report on Iraq, Foreign Secretary Jack Straw said it was a 'complete Horlicks'. A *Daily Mirror* commentator said: 'Few of us had ever heard this expression before.'

In the *Daily Telegraph*, reader Colin Price, of Barking, Essex, came to the rescue with: 'It originated in the 1980s as a Sloane Ranger euphemism for "bollocks".'

Next day, H S Blagg of Car Colston, Norfolk, wrote: 'Never mind Sloanes in the 80s. In the infantry of the 70s we used "complete Horlicks" to mean "complete balls-up" of exercises, map-readings and parades.'

Doctors recruited from overseas to work in Barnsley, Yorkshire, are to get lessons in the local dialect. A sample of the South Yorkshire vernacular causing problems: 'Av gor eedsake and feel badly', meaning 'I have a headache and feel unwell.'

Daily Telegraph

'When overseas vets apply for positions in my practice I ask them to translate the sentence: "Ey oop mi duck mi dogs got the trots." They never can.'

Mike Hayes, Keyham, Leicestershire,
Daily Telegraph

Liverpool was named European Capital of Culture for 2008 and comedian Ken Dodd said: 'Everybody is taking elocution lessons so they can understand us.'

Sun

The last person to speak only Cornish was Dolly Pentreath, who died in 1777. Her last words were: 'I will not speak English, you ugly black toad.'

Daily Telegraph

Sheltered housing residents in Elgin, Scotland – mostly in their eighties and nineties – have been told off by the manager for too much swearing.

The Herald (Glasgow)

J D Wetherspoon, one of Britain's biggest pub chains, announced it was considering a ban on swearing. *The Daily Telegraph* sent a writer to the Man in the Moon, a Wetherspoon pub in Camden Town, north London.

Drinkers there told him:

'Londoners swear all the time. My mum and dad used to swear at me.'

'Swearing's a part of life, like drinking, smoking and having a laugh.'

'It would be impossible to tell a f*****g joke.'

Brits planning to attend the 2008 Beijing Olympic Games might benefit from a phrase book called *Olympic Security English*, published by China's Public Security Bureau to help policemen deal with foreigners. Samples include:

- **If a policeman catches someone for highway robbery he would remind them of their right to remain silent and then say: 'Are you ready to confess?'**
- **A British woman called Helen is stopped driving a stolen car and protests: 'You are violating my human rights.' Response: 'What lousy luck.'**

A language kit designed to help British long-distance lorry drivers criss-crossing the linguistic frontiers of Europe enables them to order chips in six languages.

The Times

There wasn't much fuss when former Sex Pistol John Lydon used the 'c' word on TV's *I'm a Celebrity, Get Me Out of Here!* in February 2004. The Sun pointed out how times have changed:

- In 1939, cinema audience members walked out when Clark Gable used the famous phrase: 'Frankly, my dear, I don't give a damn' in *Gone With the Wind*. Producer David Selznick was fined £3,000.
- In 1958, Sir Gerald Kelly, 73-year-old president of the Royal Academy, shocked TV audiences by using the words 'bloody', 'damned' and 'confounded'. 'Confounded' counted as naughty in those days.
- In 1965 Kenneth Tynan was banned from appearing on TV after saying the word 'f**k'.
- In 1968 a woman wrote to BBC chairman Lord Hill: 'My bloody husband and I counted the bloody number of times the bloody word "bloody" was used in bloody *Till Death Us Do Part*.
- In 1993 Prime Minister John Major, on ITN, called Cabinet rebels 'b******s'. This was turned into a bootleg tape.

The comments about the c**t word being used on live TV reminded Walter Cairns of Manchester of the 'immortal comment' made on the name of a New Zealand bowler in the mid-1960s: 'Cunis – a strange name that. It's neither one thing or the other.'

Guardian

Bristol University has a website listing molecules with silly names. It includes Parasite (a mineral), Moronic acid, Traumatic acid, Erotic acid, Dickite and Arsole. There are, it seems, 'Studies of the Chemistry of Arsoles' in the *Journal of Organometallic Chemistry*.

Independent on Sunday

Newcastle police plan to clamp down on bad language. The *Sun* pointed out that this will not be welcome on the terraces of Newcastle United and said: 'Chants will have to be cleaned up.' It suggested some alternatives, such as: 'The referee is a nitwit' and 'Who is that blighter in black?'

Sunday Times

'There is a story in my family about Great-Great-Great-Uncle William muttering: "I wandered lonely as a cow."

'"Not a cow," he was told. "A cloud."

'So even he didn't remember the first line. And he wrote the poem ... Well, most of it.'

Rev. Jeremy Wordsworth, Bath, *The Times*

When the Plain English Campaign published a list of the most irritating phrases in the English language, *The Times* asked on page one: 'Is this the most irritating paragraph you will ever read?' It read, in part: 'Basically, I hear what you are saying, but at the end of the day, going forward, let's touch base and apply some blue sky thinking to this language thingy.'

Chapter 9

Drinking:
Drink to me Only

**Spending more time in the pub could be
good for the brain ...**

A 41-year-old man who is fond of a drink wears a
T-shirt carrying directions to his home to help cab
drivers in Barry, South Wales.

Sun

When builder Neil Irwin, 40, goes out drinking he wears
a T-shirt bearing his address and a photograph of his
house so folk can see him home in Herne Bay, Kent.

Sun

'25 bottles of beer, two large brandies and I'm ready to throw darts.'

> *Sun* headline on its report of 30-stone
> Kent publican Andy Fordham winning the
> 2004 World Darts Championship

The highest pub in England is on Tan Hill in Yorkshire. There is a sign behind the bar reading: 'The landlord smokes, his wife smokes, all the staff smoke, most of the locals smoke, those who have made it up the hill need a smoke, if the wind is in the east the pub smokes. If you want a smoke-free zone, go outside.'

> **David Richards, Houghton Regis, Bedfordshire,**
> ***Daily Mail***

Sir Denis Thatcher used an amazing array of words to describe alcoholic drinks, including: an opener, a brightener, a lifter, a tincture, a large gin and tonic without the tonic, a snifter, a snort, a snorter and a snortorino. A snortorino 'more or less empties the bottle in one go'.

> *Sun*

Customers at the Potsdown pub in Portchester, Hampshire, have to pay a £5 deposit for a lavatory seat because ten have already been stolen.

> *Sun*

A woman won £50 in a local pub draw in Wombwell, Yorkshire. But the landlord paid her only £2.50 because her late husband owed the rest.

Yorkshire Evening Press

A pub in Worthing, Sussex, has a misery hour on Sunday lunchtimes for drinkers with Saturday-night hangovers.

Brighton Evening Argus

Peter Ackroyd was 23 when he walked into the office of the *Spectator* magazine in 1973 to ask if he might do a review. The then editor, George Gale, asked if there was anything which might affect Ackroyd's suitability. 'A bit of a drinking problem,' said Ackroyd. He was hired on the spot as literary editor.

Daily Telegraph

Researchers from University College London have declared that spending more time in the pub could be good for your brain. *The Times* rejoiced in this news by putting the story on page one and having a leader on the subject that said: 'When times get tough, the tough go down the pub.'

A team of engineers have designed a beer mat with butterfly wings to improve aerodynamic performance when used in the old pub game of flipping the mat up from the table edge and catching it in mid-air. They had to take into account stability, flippability, repeatability, vorticity, height, distance and touch-down.

The Times

'I don't have a beer belly. It's a burgundy belly and it cost me a lot of money.'
Charles Clarke, Education Secretary.
The Sunday Times

Pimms – one of Britain's quintessential summer accessories – have begun advertising their long, cooling drink being served in pouring rain. A spokesman said: 'Traditionally our adverts focused on Pimms being drunk on a hot sunny day. The reality was something else.'

The Times

The late Jeff Howlett, 73, was a regular at his local pub – and will be buried with his darts and two pints of his favourite real ale in Fletton, Cambridgeshire.

Sun

Sheep farmer Dick Gannon, who lives alone on a remote island off the Mull of Kintyre, has built himself a one-man pub where he can enjoy a quiet drink. He has created the cosy Byron Darnton Tavern from the shell of an old cottage, and says the advantages of being barman and customer include: 'No TV, no drunken brawls, no problems getting served and no chance of being barred.'

The Times

A beer pump which can pour a pint of Guinness in 25 seconds has been scrapped after trials. Drinkers rejected it and said they preferred to wait the usual 119 seconds.

Sun

A timetable of bus services in Somerset lists pubs along the way that sell real ale. It is published by the county council and the Campaign for Real Ale.

Western Morning News

A man has been banned from 1,800 pubs after appearing in court for the 34th time in two years on drink-related charges. He had made obscene gestures to police officers who caught him urinating in a hedge. After being told he would be arrested if he set foot in any licensed premises in Norfolk or Suffolk, the 57-year-old drinker said: 'I like a drink. I will have to move somewhere else now.'

Sun

So many bras have been discarded at a popular pub in Romford, Essex, that it has set up a property phoneline to reunite them with their owners. There are more than 120 to dispose of.

Romford Recorder

A Scottish football fan was thrown out of a pub in Oslo when he began playing the bagpipes.

Sunday Times

Bagpipes have been described as a wind instrument nobody blows good. The *Daily Telegraph* covered a study in the *Pipe and Drummer* magazine saying that, as well as inducing earache, the pipes could be linked to hearing loss, repetitive strain injury, alcoholism and the breakdown of marriages. A former world champion was quoted as saying: 'Piping can take over your life. It tends to revolve around hard drinking and can really take its toll.'

Bagpipers entertaining tourists during the Edinburgh Festival don't always get a good reception. One 12-year-old piper who played outside the Scottish Parliament was deemed so bad that staff opened a window and doused him with water.

Independent

Portsmouth Crown Court was told how a motorist caused £300,000 of damage when he drove into the Lord Arthur Lee pub in Fareham, Hampshire – in revenge for being barred.

Sun

A three-day real-ale festival in Knaresborough, Yorkshire, closed after two days. The beer ran out.

Sunday Telegraph

A host on a TV chat show asked author John Mortimer if he had any addictions. 'I said no,' writes Mr Mortimer, 'but I did drink my first glass of champagne at six in the morning when I started work.' The host looked profoundly shocked and asked: 'Are you getting counselling for this?'

Independent on Sunday

This is stuff we all need to know. Michael Winner, lover of expensive wines, says: 'If you buy a Chateau Latour 1961 in a restaurant, probably for £8,000 a bottle, it is opened and poured immediately. So, allowing for three hours' breathing, your Latour would be just about ready to drink as you get up to leave. I get round this problem when I take my own wines by pouring them out at home into a decanter and let them breathe away to their hearts' content in my living room.

Sometimes I pour my wine from the decanter into a milk bottle and take this to the restaurant. Amazingly, the lady accompanying me refuses to carry the milk bottles. She thinks it looks terrible. But what do I care if I'm saving a couple of thousand pounds on restaurant prices?'

Daily Mail

Kenneth Clarke, reminiscing on BBC radio about Ronnie Scott's jazz club, said the club would start livening up some time after 11 p.m. Under the old licensing laws you could get a drink at this hour only if you were having food. What you did was order sandwiches which you didn't eat. You could then drink until you were drunk and eventually the sandwiches were taken away. 'No doubt some other grateful customer would have the same sandwich the next night ... the same sandwiches did for the week.'

Independent

Britain comes fifth in the world beer-drinking table. They have dropped a place to come in below the Czechs, Irish, Germans and Austrians.

Sun

An employment tribunal was told that wine left by diners in private rooms at the Ritz in Piccadilly was resold by the glass to unsuspecting guests in

120

the main restaurant. The tribunal heard that one of the nation's ritziest venues 'abhorred waste and was fully conversant with the environmentally sound practice of recycling'.

The Times

Sally Burchell wrote a letter of complaint after she was refused a free glass of tap water at the Atlantic Hotel in Newquay. The hotel's managing director replied: 'I buy water from the South West Water Company. I buy the glasses that the water is served in. I buy the ice that goes in the water and I buy the labour to serve the water. I provide the luxury surroundings for the water to be drunk in and again pay for the labour and washing materials to wash the glass after you have used it, and you think I should provide all this free of charge.'

Said Mrs Burchell: 'This is like a letter from Basil Fawlty.'

Daily Telegraph

Della Cannings, Chief Constable of North Yorkshire, was in uniform when she went to buy wine at Tesco in Northallerton. The cashier told her it was against the law to sell alcohol to on-duty police. The Chief then took off her hat, her uniform jacket and epaulettes and told the girl: 'Technically I am now off duty.' She got the wine.

TheTimes/Sun

The landlord of the Otter Inn at Thorpe Marriott, Norfolk, was discouraged from seeking to open late on St George's Day. A phone call from the licensing court advised him that the magistrates were unlikely to regard the day as special. Previously the Otter had been granted late licences for Chinese New Year, American Independence Day and St Patrick's Day.

Norwich Evening News/The Times

Eventually the magistrates backed off to the extent that they allowed the Otter to stay open an extra hour on April 23 ... after landlord Tony Bennett went to court dressed as England's patron saint. But the court still insisted that he drop St George from his application and make a charity donation from his profits.

Sun

Chapter 10

Royalty:
Royal Flush

Two footmen found in the same bath said they were helping the Queen's economy drive ...

Bottles of 'British air hand filled outside Buckingham Palace' are on sale at the e-Bay Internet auction site. Price £9.99.

Sun

A teenage streaker dropped his trousers in front of the Queen at a Buckingham Palace garden party. HE slapped his bottom and yelled: 'Wa-hey' SHE kept her customary composure and said: 'Oh dear. How silly.'

Daily Mail

The *Sun*, commenting on this in its leader column, said: 'She is unflappable. Truly, she is the Queen of cool. The paper also quoted one witness: 'I saw his bottom. It was white and quite spotty. His pants looked horrible. I would have thought that if you were to do something like that you'd wear nice ones.'

Artist Stuart Pearson Wright painted a portrait of Prince Philip with a long, scrawny neck. He asked the Prince if he had caught a likeness. Prince Philip glowered at the painting and snapped: 'I bloody well hope not.'

Guardian

Still at it at the age of 90, Lambeth's Town Crier Alfie Howard told the *Observer Magazine*: 'The Queen Mother invited me to tea at Clarence House. She wanted me to teach her Cockney rhyming slang and asked me about "the Berk" – one she had heard used by the stablemen. Well, it comes from Berkeley Hunt – but how do you explain that to the Queen Mum?'

It is said that Prince Charles once chided Ronnie Scott, the jazz club man, for not paying his musicians enough. Ronnie asked the prince what made him think that. 'Because they're all smoking the same cigarette,' replied Charles.

Daily Mail

On the day Prince Charles launched a campaign 'to shed his image as pampered and extravagant' the *Daily Mail* carried this splash headline: 'Charles: I Don't Live in Luxury (Honestly, it's tough getting by on £2 million a year, 17 personal servants and no house of one's own.')

Keeping the monarchy costs every man, woman and child in Britain the equivalent of one loaf of bread a year.
The Times

The Royal Household is said to sometimes have a cavalier approach to gifts, with some being sold, exchanged or destroyed. But superstitious Prince Charles has taken to wearing a good-luck bracelet worth about 10p, given to him in Bulgaria. According to Bulgarian tradition, the woven string bracelet is a talisman put on in March and must not be taken off until the wearer has seen the first swallow or stork of summer.

Daily Telegraph

As part of a news story claiming that people with an optimistic, happy-go-lucky approach to life tend to be healthier than those who are always miserable, *The Times* reported: 'The Queen Mother, who lived to be 101 … was sustained by her love of art and horse racing. She also believed in the value of exercise and the restorative qualities of a dry martini.'

The late Queen Mother's Castle of Mey, near John o'Groats, opened to the public in May 2003. Among things to see are a surprising number of stuffed animals – including Humpty Dumpty, two bright yellow corgis and the Loch Ness monster wearing a green hat.

Daily Mail

After a *Daily Mirror* reporter got a job as a Buckingham Palace footman and wrote about what he saw there, a high-ranking member of the Queen's staff was reported as saying: 'It's such a shame, he was a damn good footman. Of course, he's blown his chance of working here in the future.'

Daily Mail

Prince Charles's early morning routine is set in stone. The china cup and saucer on his breakfast tray must be placed on the right, with a silver teaspoon pointing outwards at an angle of 5 o'clock. If the teaspoon is placed incorrectly, he has a nasty tantrum.

Lynda Lee-Potter in the *Daily Mail*

The Queen owns more than 500 hats – all designed to help her stand out and ensure that they do not obscure her face and do not disarrange her hair.

The Times

Harry Taylor, 13, of Chipping Camden, Gloucestershire, wrote to the Queen telling her he was taking up pigeon racing. Her Majesty (who is patron of the Royal Pigeon Racing Association) immediately sent him one of hers. The royal racing bird's ring is stamped ER and has been named Prince Harry.

The Times

Ninety-eight of the Queen's hats went on public display at Kensington Palace in May 2003 and the *Guardian* reported that they included a silver-gilt coronet resembling something out of a Shakespearean pageant and a feathery item resembling a dead pigeon (worn at her mother's 80th birthday party in 1980).

Guardian

In her will, Queen Victoria made characteristically forthright demands of her maker: 'I hope to meet those who have so devotedly served me, especially good John Brown.'

Sunday Telegraph

The Coronation of Queen Elizabeth II in 1953 was a solemn occasion, but behind the scenes of pomp and ceremony there were noblemen who split their breeches, maids of honour armed with concealed smelling salts and earls and viscounts producing miniature bottles from inside their coronets. As senior peers kneeled in homage, 'tittering and scowls broke

out in equal measure as one of them knelt down to a clatter of mothballs tumbling from his ancient lordly robes.'

Daily Mail

As Prince William celebrated his 21st birthday, Michael Jacobs, the general secretary of the Fabian Society – a Labour think-tank – wrote: 'The monarchy remains what it always has been – defined by class (aristocratic), religion (Church of England), race (white), territoriality (English, specifically southern English) and culture (corgis and horses).'

Independent on Sunday

George V – who became Prince of Wales at 36 in 1892 – spent his 21st birthday serving with the Royal Navy and thereafter devoted himself to collecting stamps and shooting on the royal estates. He bagged a million birds during his lifetime.

Independent

Evidence emerges of the antediluvian nature of the Prince of Wales' court – the man who would be King does not do e-mail. He employs minions to send and download e-mails for him. Staff are apparently charged with printing out e-mails and typing in the Prince's handwritten replies.

The Times

On the future of the monarchy, the Fabian Commission reported: 'The office of Head of State should operate to the highest standards of professionalism, in keeping with the accepted norms of public office.'

'Oh, for heaven's sake,' responded Simon Hoggart in the *Guardian*, 'The duties of the royal family have nothing to do with keeping to the accepted norms ... and everything to do with drinking too much gin, having affairs with unsuitable people, making rude remarks to foreigners, falling asleep during native dances, talking to plants ... and generally adding to the gaiety, not just of our nation but the whole world.

'The Duke of Edinburgh ... is a perfect paragon of growing old disgracefully. To replace him with some wind-up automaton clinging to the accepted norms of public office would be to lose one of our great national treasures.'

The Princess Royal's husband Timothy Laurence is to be promoted to the same military rank as Anne – rear admiral.

Much to Anne's delight he will still be expected to salute her on the occasions that the two rear admirals find themselves in uniform.

Sunday Telegraph

Kitchen journals from the household of George II reveal epic royal gourmandising.

Christmas dinner in 1737 was a 27-course banquet, which included plum broth with capon, oysters, asparagus, partridges with savoury sausages, potage, sirloin of beef, mince pies, chine of beef, turkey, woodcock, pheasant, stag's tongue, snipe and brawn. The last full meal eaten by Queen Caroline before she died in 1737 involved 33 dishes including oysters, eels and 'peepers' (birds) with noodles and gravy.

The Times

To celebrate the Queen's 1953 Coronation the *Independent on Sunday* unearthed '53 Things You Never Knew About 1953'. They included:

- McDonald's insisted that the design for their restaurants would have golden arches. Architects scoffed and predicted that the chain would not last.
- Disney's *Peter Pan* was released, with Tinkerbell modelled on Marilyn Monroe.

In the Coronation procession there was 'the open landau of the huge Queen Salote of Tonga with "her lunch", as Noël Coward dubbed the tiny Sultan of Kelantan.'

Daily Telegraph

In 1996, when he was director of the National Theatre, Richard Eyre had lunch at Buckingham Palace and the conversation turned to the proposed selling of the royal yacht *Britannia*. Her Majesty said to him: 'I feel rather miffed. They're selling it with the contents, and it's my stuff.'

Daily Telegraph extract from Richard Eyre's book
National Service: Diary of a Decade

Queen Victoria gobbled her meals down within minutes and protocol dictated that the plates for each course be cleared as soon as Her Majesty's palate was sated. Because Prime Minister Gladstone chewed each mouthful 32 times he often left the royal table famished.

Daily Telegraph

A letter written by the Queen Mother shortly after the birth of Princess Margaret said: 'Daughter number two is really very nice and I'm glad to say she has got large blue eyes and a will of iron which is all the equipment a lady needs! As long as she can disguise her will and use her eyes then all will be well.'

Sunday Times

The Queen's sharp eye for economy is well known in royal circles. Two footmen who were found together in a bath in the Royal Mews explained that they were helping Her Majesty's drive to reduce gas bills.

Observer

After 14 years of being the BBC's royal reporter, Jennie Bond said at the Cheltenham Festival of Literature that the royals were 'distant', 'aloof' and 'unapproachable'. 'The Duke of Edinburgh has perfected the art of saying hello and goodbye in the same handshake.'

Daily Telegraph

The BBC's former royal correspondent Jennie Bond has declared that she never wanted the job. 'If you're a political correspondent you can take people out to lunch. I couldn't ring the palace and say: "Can Betty come out for lunch? Does Charles fancy a drink?"'

Independent

For George W Bush's stay at Buckingham Palace, the Queen was not willing to countenance 'bomb and airborne assault proofing' of her London home.

'Her Majesty's view was that since there are going to be 5,000 British policemen involved in the security operation it is not unreasonable to expect guests to have some faith in their abilities.'

Sunday Telegraph

'My evening paper says that the royals like ice in their drinks, but are irritated by the clinking of the cubes. So a machine was installed at Buckingham Palace to make ice into little balls, which make less racket.'

Jane Shilling, *The Times*

Cilla Black recalled meeting the Queen after giving a high-kicking performance at a Royal Command show. 'She came in and said: "I wouldn't have recognised you with your clothes on."'

The Sunday Times

The Royal Family's 2003 Christmas celebrations were somewhat soured when one of the Queen's corgis had to be put down after being savaged by Princess Anne's bull terrier. *The Sunday Times* produced a lengthy profile on the royal corgis and revealed:

- The status of the corgis can transcend that of the Queen's most elevated guests. A visiting bishop realised he had committed lese-majesty by helping himself from a footman's tray. The tray contained dog biscuits.
- Princess Michael has said she sometimes feels like shooting the corgis. (The Queen is said to have remarked: 'They are better behaved than she is.')
- The death of the royal corgi was all the more poignant because the Queen had made up a Christmas stocking for 'the venerable mutt'.
- Doggie presents are ordered from Armitage in Nottingham and include doughnuts, chocolate drops, toys, a cracker and a cake. In 2001 the Queen asked for no more squeaky toys and her dogs got plastic penguins that make hardly any sound.

William G Stewart, presenter of the quiz show *Fifteen To One*, tells how Prince Philip asked him what he did for a living.

'I present a quiz show on Channel 4.'

'Oh, there's nothing but filth on Channel 4,' was the Prince's response.

Daily Mail

When the Queen threw a lunchtime bash for 200 high-achieving women the Duke of Edinburgh slipped out of a side door at Buckingham Palace and scarpered to a Naval Club reception to meet the boys. Back at the Palace the girls found drink was copious, with stiff gin and tonics outnumbering glasses of water, orange juice and wine. Smoking was allowed and they queued up, school-dinner style, for plates of salmon and monkfish casserole and loin of lamb. Lady McCartney told Lady Thatcher how Denis Thatcher had once told her that Margaret 'may be the boss in the boardroom, but I'm the boss in the bedroom'.

The Times/Telegraph

Janet Street Porter wrote in the *Independent on Sunday*: 'The first problem was getting a drink. A couple of surly footmen tried to palm me off with orange or apple juice. Sod that.' A 'mini JSP strop' soon ensured that she was downing bubbly and marvelling at the 'ancient one-bar electric heaters in the fireplaces under the Rembrandts. These gadgets screamed "economy" and seemed more suitable for a council house in Peterlee, circa 1955, than a gallery packed with Old Masters.'

When the Queen and Prince Philip unveiled a plaque in Harrow, celebrating the area's 50 years as a London borough, the band struck up a rousing chorus of 'What Shall We Do With A Drunken Sailor?'

Guardian

As the Queen visited France to celebrate 100 years of the Entente Cordiale, Michael Winner wrote in the *Daily Mail*: 'Why we are bothering to celebrate is quite beyond me. There is no Entente Cordiale ... A cross-channel poll shows that only 15 per cent of us trust the French – and only 4 per cent of them trust us.'

But the French press hailed the Queen's visit as a big success and the venerable *Le Monde* said: 'The Queen doesn't serve any purpose, but she does it well.'

The Times

Chapter 11

Animal Magic

**Man jumps into shark tank and shark
dies from fright ...**

Three puppies dumped in a box in front of an
animal rescue shelter have been named Iain,
Duncan and Smith. Staff at the Dogs Trust
explained: 'They were unwanted, unloved – and
feeling blue.'

The Times

**Environmental health officers in Barbegh, Suffolk,
received a complaint from a woman that a neighbour's
horse was urinating too loudly. The complaint was
among the top ten of their most unusual calls.**

The Sunday Times

Scientists in Canada and Scotland report that schools of herring communicate by farting. Researchers suspect that herrings hear the bubbles as they are expelled and the noise helps them to form protective shoals at night.

National Geographic News

Tash, the pub cat at the Salerie Inn in St Peter Port, Guernsey, bears an unfortunate resemblance to Adolf Hitler. Tash has a striking Führer-type black moustache, which causes customers to advise: 'Don't mention the paw.'

Daily Mail

A survey of American tourists in Scotland revealed that one in four of them believed that haggis was an animal they could hunt.

Evening Standard

Firefighters responded to an urgent call which said that a horse was sinking in mud at Redbridge, Hampshire. They found a perfectly happy Shetland pony which the caller had mistaken for a full-grown horse.

Sun

The Queen was quick to squash reports that she would not be meeting Sunny, the Navy's No. 1 parrot, when she and Prince Philip visited the frigate HMS Lancaster at Portsmouth. The Navy

had planned to put the foul-mouthed African Grey ashore during the royal couple's visit because its repertoire includes 'F*** off', 'Show us your t**s' and 'Bollocks'.

After the *Daily Telegraph* and the *Sun* (which gave Sunny to the *Lancaster*) reported that the bird was to be banished, Her Majesty immediately let it be known that she had no problem with meeting the profane polly.

A lost pet tortoise was found safe and well on a motorway having crawled one-and-a-half miles in three weeks. Freddy, owned by Wendy Passell of Otterbourne, near Winchester, was seen plodding south on the M3 having managed an average speed of 0.0034mph. Proud Mrs Passell said: 'People don't realise how hyperactive Freddie is.'

Evening Standard

Postmen in the quiet Hampshire town of New Milton put a boycott on delivering mail to the house where Purrdey, an 11-year-old cat, lives. Purrdey has drawn blood from seven postmen and -women. A Royal Mail spokesman said: 'This cat leaps in the air as if it believes it is a tiger and lands on people, digging its claws in.'

Other Royal Mail boycotts have been caused by geese, seagulls and, in Gloucestershire, a pheasant.

Guardian

Rice fish have been implanted with fluorescence genes from jellyfish so that aquarium keepers can see their pets in the dark.

Independent on Sunday

A survey in *Our Dogs* magazine found a bull terrier that swallowed a bottle cap, a toy car and some wire and some cling film. It was operated on, the objects were removed and the dog was put on a drip. It ate the drip.

Sunday Times

Eight stolen cockatiels were recovered in Salisbury after a member of the public heard them whistling Laurel and Hardy's theme tune. Police had urged people to listen out for the melody.

The Times

During the 2003 Edinburgh Festival a goldfish was granted a performer's licence to comply with the city's by-laws banning performing animals, however small, unless they got permits in triplicate.

Daily Telegraph

'Townies' often have difficulties when holidaying in the countryside. *Times* reader Bryn Frank, publisher of the *Good Holiday Cottage Guide*, told of a lady who had stayed in an upmarket cottage in Worcestershire. She

reported back: 'The property was fine, but we had to leave. I hated the way the sheep kept staring at me, and I thought the lavatorial habits of the cattle were disgusting.'

The Times

The theory that if a group of monkeys was provided with typewriters they would eventually produce the works of Shakespeare has been put to the test by lecturers and students from Plymouth University. The month-long experiment was abandoned after six primates from Paignton Zoo failed to write one recognisable word. But they did partially destroy the machine, using it as a lavatory.

The Times

A feral ferret got on a train at Leicester station and frightened passengers by running through the carriages before getting into the driver's cab and eating his cheese sandwiches.

The Times

A pet-shop owner in Manchester left a rabbit in a hutch outside his shop. It ended up with a parking ticket.

Daily Mail

An advert for a pets underskin microchipping service, seen in a local paper in Droitwich, Worcestershire: '£9.50 per animal. Pensioners free.'

Daily Mail

Buster, a golden retriever, dived into the River Avon at Durrington, Wiltshire, and came out with a 6lb rainbow trout in its mouth. Owners Helen and Tony Peacock said: 'He's never done anything like this before.'

The Times

'All my cats have loved Marmite. I let them lick the jars before washing and recycling. I had a large ginger tom who not only adored Marmite and fighting, but also crisps and Mars bars.'

Jane Sutherland, Berkshire, *Guardian*

'Our 17-year-old Burmese, Pywackett, has just discovered a taste for Marmite (also Kettle crisps with sea salt). I have not yet let her lick the jar.'

Rowena Dawson, Leicestershire, *Guardian*

It was a frightening experience when a naked comedian jumped into a shark tank. So frightening that the shark died. It was not exactly a Jaws-type specimen – just a 3-foot-long smooth hound and, said an official of Brighton Sea Life Centre, 'very susceptible to stress'.

Daily Telegraph

In the *Independent*'s series *My Greatest Mistake*, Roy Hattersley said: 'I have three – not resigning over the Commonwealth Immigration Act of 1968, not starting serious writing until I was 40, and spending 20 years without a dog.'

Independent

Down Rover! British dog lovers are increasingly giving their pets human names. A survey (in June 2003) revealed the top ten names as Ben, Sam, Max, Toby, Holly, Charlie, Lucy, Barney, Bonnie and Sophie.

Top cat names were Charlie, Tigger, Oscar, Lucy, Soot, Thomas, Poppy, Sophie, Smudge and Molly.

The Times

The Queen's corgis are named Pharos, Emma, Linnet, Rush, Minnie and Monty. Her dorgis are called Brandy, Cider and Berry. A dorgi is a breed invented by the Queen when she crossed her corgi with Princess Margaret's dachshund.

Daily Telegraph

John Wayne called his dog 'Dog'.

The Times

'One of the hottest topics at our parish church council is mice and mousetraps. Our vicar – following a tip from a church warden – caught 3 mice in 24 hours, using a single humane trap and one Rolo.'

Teresa Wills, Isle of Man, *Daily Telegraph*

'In our case the bait was Extra-Strong Mints, which the mice adored. Over a period we caught 66. We used a humane trap and released them at the end of our very long field. My mother always maintained that it was just the original five or six mice returning for more mints.'

June Tucker, Cheltenham, *Daily Telegraph*

'The mice and other rodents here in the old vicarage have a predilection for Snickers. It never fails.'

Keith Cameron, Routenbeck, Cumbria,
Daily Telegraph

'I use a humane trap and have found that a fruit pastille is the most effective.'

Dr John Zorab, Bristol, *Daily Telegraph*

Tory MP Ian Liddel-Grainger brought the attention of the House of Commons to a farmer accused of kidnapping a pair of geese. It is alleged the farmer took the birds from a river in Bridgwater, Somerset, and is fattening them up for Christmas. The RSPCA says the geese seem happy on the farm.

Sun

Britain's reputation for being a nation of pet lovers takes a knock after the RSPCA reports that around 100,000 pets are abandoned every year. One cat owner got rid of her moggy 'because it keeps sitting on my lap'. Other reasons included: 'My dog hurts my legs when wagging its tail.' 'Our puppy hides our shoes.' Three rabbits had to find a new home because 'they don't come out to greet us'.

Sun

Jake, an Alsatian, was disqualified from a dog show for biting a judge during an obedience contest in Tiverton, Devon.

Sun

A £7,000 aquatic garden, built to attract wildlife to a pond in Edinburgh, has been devoured by ducks.

Herald and Post

Pet-loving Britons were delighted to read in the *Daily Telegraph* that the Passports for Pets scheme was being extended to cover gerbils, hamsters, rats, mice, canaries, budgies, tropical fish, terrapins – and worms.

Millionaire theatre impresario Sir Peter Saunders – who earned £11m from Agatha Christie's record-breaking, long-running play *The Mousetrap* – left £100 of it in his will 'to buy for my dogs the world's best hamburger steaks from Beoty's Restaurant in St Martin's Lane, London'.

Mail on Sunday

Farmer Ray Collier soothes his pigs by playing classical music to them at night – causing his neighbours at Locks Heath, Hampshire, to complain about the noise.

Sun

An elephant called Tooth picked up a rock with its trunk and hurled it through the window of a car at the West Midlands Safari Park. The family inside the car – including four-year-old twins – were terrified, but were invited to return to the park 'to make friends' with the ten-year-old African bull elephant.

Daily Telegraph

A £525,000 house for sale in Edinburgh comes with a sitting tenant – Tortie, a 60-year-old tortoise who lives in a compost heap. The owners, Monica Gibb, an actress, and her husband David Grearson, a businessman, thought moving their pet would be too much of a shock for him.

The Times

Mickey, a tortoise that survived the Blitz and is more than 100 years old, now has a hole in its shell after being repeatedly attacked by seagulls in the back garden of its owner, Alan Coleman, of Bristol.

The Times

Jodie King, keeper of a giant octopus called Titan at the Blue Reef Aquarium in Newquay, has trained the 24lb monster to open jam jars to entertain the public.

Daily Mail

Obsessive bird lover Lee Gardiner, 32, of Hever, Kent, was jailed for stealing £2m and spending much of it on rare parrots. Gardiner plundered the accounts of clients at the bank where he worked and ended up with the largest private collection of exotic birds in Britain. He was jailed for nine years.

Sun

Railway staff at Leamington Spa collected £70 for a retirement present for Central, the station cat – more than double the amount usually collected for human colleagues. Central, who caught mice at Leamington for 13 years before developing arthritis, got an engraved collar and lots of cat treats.

News of the World

Scientific experiments at Salford University have exploded the myth that a duck's quack does not echo. Trevor Cox, Professor of Acoustics, took a duck called Daisy into his laboratory and proved beyond doubt that not only do quacks echo, but that 'They are reminiscent of a dropped dustbin lid.'

The Times

A Jack Russell terrier called Part-X is being trained by its owner to water-ski after learning how to ride a surfboard.

Sun

The Royal Family's beloved corgi dogs have been known to nip the odd ankle, but there was regal dismay when the *Daily Telegraph* reported that Italy has added them to its list of dangerous dogs. Minors, delinquents and criminals who have caused harm to people or animals will be barred from owning them.

'A couple we know are owned by two cats. These animals will eat only good steaks and fine fish from china plates, never from plastic. Recently their slaves bought a microwave. This has not gone unnoticed and the cats reject all offerings thus fast-cooked.'

L Lane, Woking, Surrey, *The Times*

Black Prince, a Clydesdale colt, won prizes across Scotland as a top-class stallion-in-the-making. But Prince was stripped of his awards after he was found to be missing essential equipment. He had been castrated at an early age and an official of the Clydesdale Horse Society said: 'Put simply, the necessary ammunition wasn't there – and no balls means no awards.'

The Times

Journalists covering the Hutton inquiry into the death of Dr Kelly were fond of lunching in the Seven Stars pub behind the Law Courts. Simon Hoggart reported that: 'This is close to being the perfect pub... There is no music, but there is a cat, who may not be moved from its bench even when the pub is crowded.'

Guardian

A lager-loving weasel called Carlsberg was buried in a coffin made from beer mats by Nigel Brookes, 59, in Salisbury, Wiltshire.

Sun

Farmer Graham Bailey of Loddington, Northants, has four llamas – Milo, Bertie, Horatio and Felix – to protect his sheep from dogs and foxes. When he fell and broke a hip the llamas protected him – by chasing away paramedics called in to help. An ambulance helicopter had to be used to defeat the over-conscientious llama guards.

Daily Mirror

A stray cat called Tinker, adopted by a widow, has been left a £350,000 detached house in Harrow, north London – plus a £100,000 trust fund to keep him in comfort for the rest of his life. The trustees are neighbours who deliver milk and food to Tinker every day. Their own cat, Lucy, has moved in with Tinker.

Daily Telegraph

A couple suspected of kidnapping a neighbour's cat had to put their Cornish house up for sale after living there for 18 years. Villagers refused to talk to them.

Daily Express

The programme for the International Show Jumping Championships at Olympia in 2003 included displays by the Royal Horse Artillery, a dressage competition, the Shetland Pony Grand National and a warning to asthma sufferers that: 'Horses will be taking part in the performances.'

John Burscough, Brigg, North Lincolnshire,
The Times

A fashion designer has created men's shoes from the skins of the stingray, one of nature's toughest hides. Price: £750 a pair.

The Times

A Norwegian robin – a rare visitor to Britain – took 15 hours to fly 400 miles from Stavanger to Manchester. It landed exhausted – and was eaten by a bird watcher's cat. Said a mournful member of the British Trust of Ornithology: 'It made a gruelling trip only to end up as a cat's lunch.'

Sun

'Some years ago, as a baritone soloist with Berwick Male Voice Choir, I used to walk along Berwick's lengthy pier to practise my songs. Almost invariably, there were seals in the water waiting for salmon. They would turn their heads towards me and listen to my singing. Was it my imagination or were they more interested in songs about the sea than in love songs such as "Come into the Garden Maud"?'

W L A McCreath, Eyemouth, Berwickshire,
Daily Telegraph

'A schoolfriend and I used to sit on a fence singing to cows in a field near Kirkintilloch. The cows would always stop grazing and gradually move towards us, fascinated. "Loch Lomond" was their favourite.'

Dorothy Richardson, Northumberland,
Daily Telegraph

'Pigeons hatched chicks in February at my local Tube station. They have been helped not only by global warming, but also by plastic spikes designed to deter pigeons. The spikes have provided an ideal foundation for their nests.'

Mary Bowden, Harrow, Middlesex, *Guardian*

A survey which indicated that many busy modern couples prefer having a pet to having children produced this comment from Terence Blacker in the *Independent*: 'Like proper middle-class parents they can solve discipline problems by sending their charge away to be knocked into shape by strangers at an expensive boarding establishment. If that fails, they can give it away, lock it up in a kennel, trade it in for a more attractive and amenable replacement or even take it on a one-way trip to the vet. How many parents of children would not, at times of stress, welcome some or all of these options?'

Question: 'How do you stop a neighbour's cat scratching up your garden?'
Answer: 'Concrete one or the other.'
From the *Guardian's* 'Notes and Queries' information exchange

'Neuter your cat at a cut price.' Ad in the *Derby Evening Telegraph*.
Jack Phillips, Derby, *Daily Mail*

Four police cars, sirens screaming, raced to a Devon beach after a dog warden caught Camilla Sharpe's Jack Russell leaving a small souvenir on the sand. Police said they had responded to a report of 'disorder with persons on the beach'. The warden had called the police after Camilla had refused to pay a £50 fine. North Devon District Council's environmental health manager said: 'I am satisfied that policy was followed in this case.'
The Times

A developer is having to spend £120,000 to provide luxury quarters for a colony of horseshoe and natterers bats living in a country house in Wales which is being converted. 'We are building a five-star hotel for humans and five-star hotel for bats,' they say.
Guardian/Daily Mirror

A llama called Laurence became Britain's first full-time municipal long-necked nanny to newborn lambs – at the Ty Mawr park run by Wrexham county borough council. Llamas have established a reputation for seeing off predators. One of their most effective deterrents is that they smell.

Guardian

Crufts dog show was marred in 2004 by unproven claims that a top dog was given doped meat just before it was due to go into the judging ring.

The nobbling of rival contestants is nothing new in the bitterly competitive world of dog shows. In recent years there have been reports of dogs having been fed poisoned beef, sprayed with acid, given valium and having their coats dyed. There are tales of illegal facelifts and of owners sleeping with judges. Other owners have allegedly received death threats and had the wheels of their vehicles tampered with.

Beverley Cuddy, editor of *Dogs Today*, said: 'Some people will wear tight trousers and pretend to be gay if there's a gay judge.'

Independent/Daily Mail/
Sunday Telegraph

Robert Sinclair, 55, fell ill in a deserted farmhouse near Falkirk. He had nothing to eat or drink for seven days. In desperation he scribbled a note on a piece of cardboard, put it in a plastic bottle and dropped it out of the window. It was found by Ben, a border collie, who took it to his farmer owner, three miles away. Mr Sinclair was rescued and made a full recovery in hospital.

Independent

Chapter 12

Media Madness

Police to run down jaywalkers ...

'I am reminded of our report of the elevation of Douglas Daft to chief executive of Coca Cola: "Daft choice for Coke head".'

  Neil Collins, City Editor, in the *Daily Telegraph*

Headline on a story about the 1957 Trans-Antarctic expedition: 'Vivian Fuchs off to the Antarctic.'

  Ken Battersby, Millom, Cumbria, *Daily Telegraph*

When Crystal Palace footballer Gerry Queen was sent off for fighting during a match, the *Sunday Mirror* headline was: 'Queen in Brawl at Palace.'

  J R Wainwright, Wakefield, W Yorkshire,

  Daily Telegraph

'Virgin sleepers. Never been laid. £18 each plus VAT.'
Advertisement in the Farmers' Guardian. *Daily Mail*

Asked if he had ever considered going into politics, *Daily Mirror* editor Piers Morgan replied: 'I would rather tether myself to a barrel of honey in a mile-wide pit of enraged killer bees.'

'I watched a BBC TV weather forecast presented by a beautiful blonde wearing a red dress over her slender shoulders. She had a dazzling smile, perfect diction and a bewitching Scottish accent. When I switched off I could not recall a word she had said.'
Bernard Harper, Felixstowe, Suffolk, *The Times*

On ITV's *This Morning* programme the quizmaster asked a contestant: 'On which river is Newcastle situated?'
Contestant: 'The Thames.'
Quizmaster: 'Yes, well done!'
Daily Mail, selecting extracts from *Mediaballs*, edited by Marcus Berkmann

When *The Times* began publishing a tabloid version in November 2003, there followed a lively debate on the pros and cons, with readers advising: 'The broadsheet is better for lining drawers and stuffing wet boots, but the compact edition makes better paper caps and water bombs.'

Reader Peter Cuming wrote: 'At the end of breakfast, not only is your compact edition marmalade free, but it fits perfectly the food tray of our house rabbit.'

The Times

Nigel Stapley, of Brymbo, Wrexham, recalls his favourite newspaper correction: 'Due to a mishearing on the telephone we reported that Mr and Mrs [name withheld] would be living with the bride's father. They will in fact be living at the Old Manse.'

Guardian

Inflatable single mattress, complete with pump. Ideal for those unwanted guests. (*Advert in Basildon Evening Echo*.)

Sunday Times

From the *Slough and South Bucks Express*: 'In last week's *Express* we wrongly stated that staff who had served five years with Legoland were rewarded with a five-figure sum. The story should have stated they were rewarded with a figure of five made out of Lego bricks.'

Guardian

The *Guardian* recalled some of its classic 2003 corrections:

- 'In our interview with Sir Jack Hayward, chairman of Wolverhampton Wanderers, we mistakenly attributed to him the comment: 'Our team was the worst in the First Division and I'm sure it will be the worst in the Premier League.' What he actually said was: 'Our tea was the worst.'
- 'We omitted a decimal point when quoting a doctor on the optimum temperature of testicles. They should be 2.2 degrees Celsius below core body temperature, not 22 degrees lower.'

Quotes of 2003 from the *Sunday Telegraph*:

- 'It's so bad being homeless in the winter. They should go somewhere hot like the Caribbean, where they can eat free fish all day.' Lady Victoria Hervey
- 'What makes me cross is that he has let down butlering worldwide.' Lady Apsley on Princess Diana's telltale former butler Paul Burrell
- 'It was brilliant. You die of a heart attack, but so what? You die thin.' Sir Bob Geldof on the Atkins diet
- 'If I see something sagging, dragging or bagging, I get it sucked, tucked or plucked.' Singer Dolly Parton

- 'A naked woman seen dangling from a bridge across the A66 could need help, police reported.' *Darlington Times*
- 'A recent survey revealed that many people admitted to "secret disappointment" with their funeral service.' *Crosby Herald*

John Humphrys, the combative interrogator politicians fear to face on Radio 4's *Today* programme, is to present the BBC's quiz show *Mastermind*. This puts him in a doubly unusual position, reports the *Daily Telegraph*: 'Not only will people be keen to answer his questions, but he will also have to give them time to finish.'

Most of the TV watched by children is intended for adults. They prefer *EastEnders* to *Blue Peter*. Among 4 to 15 year olds, one in five is still watching after the 9 p.m. watershed and many could not imagine life without TV.

Daily Telegraph, reporting a study by industry regulators

Nevertheless, adults still watch more TV than their children. Mums and dads are glued to the box for 3 hours 34 minutes daily. The average kid watches two-and-a-half hours a day.

Sun

'Children lack conversational skills, but TV is not the only factor. Have you noticed that nearly all prams and pushchairs face forward – robbing a child of any interaction with the adult.'

Letter from a head teacher, *Sunday Telegraph*

BBC director-general Greg Dyke threatened to send staff who intimidated their juniors on anger management courses. The staff responded with a different solution for Dyke – they bought him a punchbag.

Daily Mail

A few years ago the *New Statesman* asked readers for the ultimate tabloid headline. The winner was: 'Sex change Bishop in mercy dash to Palace' – combining prurience, charity, the Church and the House of Windsor in one glorious and peculiarly English cocktail.

Observer Magazine

The Advertising Standards Authority criticised a dance company for not featuring naked dancers as advertised. A man complained that, after seeing a leaflet showing naked dancers, he was furious to find all the dancers fully clothed.

Sunday Times

Some recent headlines:

- Police Begin Campaign to Run Down Jaywalkers.
- Miners Refuse to Work After Death.
- School Drop-Outs Cut in Half.
- Red Tape Holds Up New Bridges.

Timothy Haas, *Reader's Digest*

Playwright J B Priestley was so enamoured of newsreader Jan Leeming that when she appeared on TV he planted a kiss on the screen.

Daily Mail

Nigel Dempster ran the *Daily Mail*'s gossip column for over 30 years. When the news broke in September 2003 that he was going to retire, the *Sunday Telegraph* recalled that when he was once asked about a libel action Nigel replied: 'Writs are the Oscars of my profession.'

In October 2003, Nigel, 'the greatest gossip in the world', was described in the *Sunday Times* as 'witty, squiffy, charming, urbane and debonair, with a touch of poison. When a poisonous snake was born at London Zoo, they called him Nigel.'

Daily Mail

163

The *Sunday Times* reviewed the *Sun*'s coverage of 'the gawky, adolescent version of *Big Brother*' – broadcast as part of Channel 4's education remit. The *Sun* pictured 'two contestants bonking on camera'. The *Sunday Times* reported that: 'viewers later saw the girl asking the *Big Brother* doctor for a morning after pill. So, children, pay attention and do not try this at home.'

Some branches of the British Legion sold Remembrance Day poppies without their pins because they feared wearers would sue if they were injured by the pins. 'Poppycock!' was the *Sun*'s headline.

The *Daily Mirror* claimed an exclusive when it published a front-page story saying that Paul McCartney's wife had given birth to a boy to be called Joseph. Other newspapers picked up the story and international news agencies flashed the glad tidings around the world. It later emerged that the baby was a girl and would be called Beatrice. *Mirror* editor Piers Morgan said: 'It's a tiny blip in a great scoop,' but added that there was 'a lot of egg on a lot of faces'.

The Times

'Psychopaths, drug addicts, male rape ... and that's just the police.'

>*Daily Mail* headline on a feature about
>Thames TV's police drama *The Bill*

Thousands turned up to watch the last Heathrow landings of three Concordes. The *Sun*'s TV critic asked his readers if they could confirm or deny that ITN's commentator had said: 'There's only one Concorde. And here come three of them.'

The BBC's daily TV news became 50 years old in 2003. Richard Baker introduced it with the words: 'Here is an illustrated summary of the news.' Unseen newsreaders read a script while viewers gazed at stills of maps and diagrams.

>*Independent on Sunday*

Boris Johnson, Tory MP for Henley, editor of the *Spectator* and columnist on the *Daily Telegraph* says in his column that being a leader writer on the *Telegraph* 'was the most boon-doggling job I have ever had. The college of leader writers used to sit around, dozens of us, like a gently bickering senior common room, or pilots killing time at Biggin Hill, knowing that with only three leaders to be produced per day, our chances of seeing action were agreeably small. So there we were ... lolling on our sofas, with – unless my memory is playing tricks on me – a brace of buttered crumpets apiece, and perhaps the odd bottle of port ...'

A *Brighton Argus* reader sent the paper a photograph of an exquisite rainbow over the seafront. They printed it in black and white.

Guardian

The Ephraim Hardcastle column in the *Daily Mail* counted 11 women's nipples – plus a full frontal nude in the March 2004 edition of *Tatler*, the society magazine.

Daily Mail

The Hutton inquiry into the Kelly suicide sparked a heated debate about journalists' anonymous sources. Former *Daily Mirror* editor Roy Greenslade produced an amusing guide to identifying anonymous sources, which included:

- A senior source – someone who really knows what's happening.
- A source – someone who wishes he knew what was happening.
- An insider – someone who hopes to know enough, one day, to be a source.
- A senior backbencher – an MP you may have heard of.

- A backbencher – an MP no one has ever heard of.
Guardian

The *Guardian*'s political editor Michael White was quoted as saying: 'Funny how no one ever quotes a junior backbencher.'

As newspapers filled columns with reports of Britons sinking deeper and deeper into debt, Lloyds TSB revealed some of the reasons its clients gave for wanting a bank loan:

- To buy a tiger.
- To make an online bid to date a footballer.
- To buy a dress that once belonged to a Spice Girl.
- To put a down payment on cyrogenic freezing (the deep freezing of bodies of people who have died of an incurable disease, in the hope of a future cure).
Independent on Sunday

'Talgarth CCTV Takeaway Slapper Hit Garden Urinator'. Classic local paper headline after magistrates in the Black Mountain area of Wales heard the case of a woman who walked into a Chinese takeaway and was caught on CCTV slapping a man in the face. The man had urinated in her garden.

Brecon and Radnor Express and
Powys County Times

'A Pig's Guts' – another headline on the same page from the same busy Brecon magistrates' court. It referred to the case of a Talgarth man 'who has been locked up three times for non-existent crimes'. Defence counsel told the court: 'The technical term for this is a pig's guts.'

Brecon and Radnor Express and
Powys County Times

There was a demonstration of marital arts on the village green.

Byfleet and Addlestone Review, spotted by
Bob Lee of Byfleet, Surrey, *Daily Mail*

The *Independent on Sunday* pointed out a vintage *Guardian* apology for calling Sir Edward Heath 'spritely' rather than 'sprightly'. Sprightly means 'full of vitality, lively', while dictionaries define spritely as 'elflike, dainty'. In other words, Sir Edward is not a fairy, commented the *Independent on Sunday*.

The *Daily Mail* sifted through the 2004 edition of the *Guinness Book of Records* and discovered:

- The longest tongue belongs to Stephen Taylor, of Coventry – measuring 3.7 inches from the tip to the centre of his closed top lip.
- The most successful toe wrestler is Alan 'Nasty' Nash, who scooped five titles at the

toe wrestling championships in Derbyshire from 1994 to 2002.

- The dog with the longest ears is a Bassett hound called Mr Jeffries from Southwick, West Sussex. They measure eleven-and-a-half inches and are insured for £30,000.

Sun columnist Richard Littlejohn is always on the look out for items that qualify for his 'You Couldn't Make It Up' collection. On 10 October 2003 he wrote: 'Handicap International are looking for stewards for a landmine awareness rally. Their advert reads: "Stamp Out Landmines".'

Chapter 13

Religious:
Let us Pray

Thou shalt not worship false pop idols ...

'We shall be meeting on Wednesday when the subject will be: "Heaven. How do we get there?" Transport is available at 7.55 p.m. from the bus stop opposite the Harewood Arms.'

*The magazine of the parish of
Collingham-with-Harewood*

'Would the congregation please note that the bowl at the back of the church labelled "for the sick" is for monetary donations only.'

Churchtown Parish Magazine

An ongoing debate comparing the Bible with the Ikea catalogue produced this letter from John O'Byrne, of Harold's Cross, Dublin: 'Nowhere in the Old Testament is there a mention of God creating the world in six days and on the seventh finding a whole solar system left over.'

The Times

The Bishop of Horsham urged Sussex vicars to take horse dung into their services to make the Nativity more realistic.

Daily Mirror

'My four-year-old son's Sunday school asked children what you had to do to go to Heaven. They suggested things like being good, kind and helpful. My boy said: "You have to die."'

G Brennan, London SW16, *Daily Mail*

The Church of England's Synod announced that it now wants to allow for the possibility that the three travellers who followed the star to the manger at Bethlehem might not have been very wise – and might not, in fact, have been men.

Paul Griffin, of West Malling, Kent, wrote to the *Daily Telegraph* saying that his wife thinks the magi were definitely men. Women would have brought practical gifts such as nappies, gripe water and a changing mat.

Daily Telegraph

The Telegraph's cartoonist Matt had a wife telling her husband: 'They must have been men – they followed a star rather than stop and ask directions.'

Daily Telegraph

The Methodist Church launched a competition to find an 11th Commandment. Among suggestions were: 'Never give out your password.' Political philosopher Roger Scruton came up with: 'Thou shalt not think of any more Commandments.' The *Sunday Telegraph*'s report ended with: 'For many modern sinners the traditional 11th Commandment "Thou shalt not get found out" will take some beating.'

The winner of the competition was: 'Thou shall not be negative'. Runners-up included: 'Thou shall not worship false pop idols' and 'Thou shalt not consume thine own bodyweight in fudge.'

The Times

Norman Sanders from Ipswich asked: 'Was it not Bertrand Russell who said that the Commandments should be treated like an examination – only six need be attempted?'

The Times

The Catholic journal *The Tablet* is looking for a new editor. Suggestions that candidates will be expected to have near-saintly private lives are greeted with dismay: 'Then no one will apply!'

Independent

'The Bishop of Willesden has dyed his hair purple in an effort to make people see that church leaders are human. He says: "People think there is an oddness about them."

'Perish the thought.'

John J Carney, Tankerton, Kent, *The Times*

A team of vicars on *University Challenge* were asked to complete a verse of the Red Flag. All four of them sang it – in tune and word-perfect.

Mail on Sunday

Workers at a church in Portsmouth complained that their purses and handbags were being stolen when they closed their eyes to pray. Stewards have been appointed to guard the pews.

Daily Express

A Church of Scotland minister in Fife did a striptease down to his underwear – in front of teachers and pupils – to mark his retirement as chaplain of a local school.

Aberdeen Press and Journal

Guardian headline about the Church of England's schism over homosexual priests: 'Church in need of a saviour.'

Frank Johnson's column in the *Daily Telegraph*

'Sir, How can the Archbishop of York, dressed as he is on the front page of today's edition, have the gall to request more humility from Tony Blair?'

Ken Tabram, Kent, *The Times*

David Hunt, of Ringmer, Lewes, Sussex, came across a handsomely bound presentation bible in a well-known bookshop but pointed out that the print was too small. The assistant told him that the Bible 'was not designed to be read'. He wrote to *The Times* saying: 'Evidently, in our secular society, there is still a market for "ornamental" bibles.'

The vicar of St Mary's Church in Dorchester, Dorset, has bolted his new church organ to the floor after thieves stole the last one.

Sunday Telegraph

Chapter 14

Sport:

This Unsporting Life

**'Cupid Stunt' not suitable for racehorse name.
But 'Noble Locks' gets the OK ...**

The Jockey Club tries to prevent racehorses being given saucy names, but one called Big Tits seems to have slipped through after being cleared by the French. 'And it's Big Tits way out in front,' was the *Sun*'s headline. Saucy names blocked in the past include Cupid Stunt and Fog Ducker. But a gelding called Noble Locks made the grade, as did Amazing Bust.

'Authorities are reluctant to ban bungee jumping in case they drive it underground.'
        Radio 4, reported in a letter to the *Guardian*

Mrs J Norton of Exeter tells the *Daily Mail* how thrilled her ten-year-old daughter Natasha was when the boys at school let her play football. When asked what position she played Natasha replied: 'I was a goal post.'

When the idea of an all-women team was mooted at the Kendal Rugby Club in Cumbria one man said women were more than welcome to join the club 'if they clean the toilets and tidy up outside'.

Guardian

In Somerset, a footballer in the Morland Challenge Cup Final put a crucial penalty over the bar after a female fan of the opposing team flashed her breasts at him from behind the goal.

Sunday Independent (Plymouth)

Falcon Rovers striker Gary Davenport, aged 27, of West Sussex, was banned from the penalty box after heading 14 own goals.

Sun

'Plant was rooted to the spot.'

Football match report in the
Littlehampton Gazette

A new keep-fit product is being marketed as a portable gym in a travel case (price £19.95). It's a skipping rope 'complete with two handgrips'.

Independent

A rise in the birth rate in England and Wales last year was attributed in part to England's achievement in reaching the quarter-finals of the football World Cup.

Daily Telegraph

There was more evidence of the cheering effect of football triumph – the World Cup also saw a drop in the demand for anti-impotence drugs.

Sunday Times

A 'rough and ready' guide to fly fishing in the *Daily Telegraph* states:

- 'The number of flies attached to a hat is in inverse proportion to the skill of the fisherman.'
- 'It is considered bad form to cut the fly off the cast of the day's best fisherman and use it yourself.'

Great Sporting Moments:
Leeds manager Eddie Gray: 'It was always an uphill task for us and after they scored it was downhill all the way. It left us with a mountain to climb.'

Ally Ross, *Sun*

Great Sporting Moments:
'At Grimsby in 1876 Dr W G Grace was given not out when the superstar cricketer was palpably lbw. According to my father, who was playing in that match, after three confident appeals for lbw against the great man, the umpire turned angrily on the bowler and cried: "The crowd has come to see the doctor bat, not you bowl!"'

Alexander Greenwood, British Columbia,
Financial Times

Dedicated golfer Reg Salisbury, 77, wanted to go out with a bang – so his ashes were packed into 36 rockets and exploded over the Batchwood course at St Albans. After the £1,200 display the retired civil servant's widow said: 'It suited Reg's character.'

Daily Telegraph

In a speech to the Police Federation, Home Secretary David Blunkett attacked 'out-of-touch' judges and said that former High Court judge Sir Oliver Popplewell had confessed in his memoirs that he was surprised that soccer fans swear while watching games. In reporting this, the *Daily Mail* recalled Sir Oliver's question from the bench: 'What is Linford Christie's lunch box?'

A *Sunday Telegraph* reader wrote that he had no objection, per se, to Phil Tufnell selling his racy story to a tabloid newspaper after winning *I'm a Celebrity, Get Me Out of Here!* 'What I do object to,' he said, ' is a cricketer behaving like a footballer.'

Not everybody is pleased that Wimbledon is to drop the tradition of having players bowing to the royals. Britain's No. 1, Tim Henman, said: 'It was one of those traditions which set Wimbledon apart. It also gave us British players a real advantage. The foreign players would sometimes be more worried about getting the bowing right than about playing.'

Daily Mail

On the same day, *Daily Telegraph* reader Tom Walters of Middlesex, wrote in saying: Henmania '... symbolises all that is wrong with the British character, which tends to support the underdog rather than the winner.'

How things have changed. The 1929 Wimbledon programme gave these hints to spectators: 'Please do not applaud a double fault. Please do not confine your applause to one competitor.' Today, cheering double faults, grunting and squealing like pigs to put off one's opponent, spitting, line-call rage, idiot Mexican waves and umpire-abuse are par for the course.

The Times

'A true Englishman may shed a manly tear in a moment of triumph, there is nothing wrong with that, but he never blubs in defeat. Never.' Michael Henderson in the *Daily Mail* after Greg Rusedski's reaction to his sensational defeat at Wimbledon 2003.

'Surely it is time to take Greg Rusedski to our hearts after he used that most British of words, "wanker", which no self-respecting North American would ever use. Greg is now one of us. Good on you son.'
Niall Duffy, Worthing, West Sussex, *Guardian*

The greatest ever Wimbledon champion is British. He is 81-year-old Professor Bernard Neal, who has won Wimbledon's other sporting championship – croquet – 37 times. Croquet was once the principal sport at Wimbledon, which started life as the All England Croquet Club.

The Times

Newspapers competed to provide lists of reasons why the number 23 was a good choice for David Beckham's Real Madrid shirt. The *Daily Mail* filled a whole page, which included 23 celebrities born on the 23rd and reported how an Arab sheikh once offered 23 camels to Dennis Hamilton in exchange for his wife, actress Diana Dors.

In 1744 the Gentleman Golfers of Leith determined 13 rules of golf on a single sheet of paper. The Royal and Ancient Golf Club's rules now run to 176 pages and a companion volume interpreting these rules runs to a staggering 550 pages.

Letter to *The Times*

Henry Longhurst used to say that golf needed only three rules: the player who won the last hole tees off first. The player furthest from the flag putts first. The player who wins stands the first round of drinks.

Letter to *the Times*

The World Peashooting Championships at Witcham, Cambridgeshire, has had to create a new category for competitors who have shooters using laser sights.

Sunday Mercury

A woman's claim for compensation – after being hit by a cricket ball hit out of the Cheetham Cricket Club ground – was referred to the House of Lords and rejected on the grounds that: 'The club were carrying on a lawful and socially useful activity.'

Sunday Telegraph

After eight years, angler Clive White, 35, admitted lying when he claimed to have caught a record 36lb 4oz rainbow trout. He had found it dead in a water near his home in Andover, Hampshire. He said: 'It has destroyed me, my marriage and everything I ever wanted. But I do feel a lot better now it is out in the open.'

Guardian

The end of the football season can bring on feelings of abject misery among fans. Psychologist John Castleton has christened the syndrome 'End of Season Affective Disorder' (ESAD) and says the illness could lead to lethargy, an inability to converse and feelings of hopelessness. Some fans will feel a void, an emptiness on a Saturday afternoon.

Daily Telegraph

ESAD sufferers can ring a helpline that plays football crowd noises including: 'Man just behind you shouting in your ear.'

Sunday Times

Members of the Penn Golf Club near Wolverhampton are trying to stop a local farmer grazing his cows on their course. Farmer Frank Joynson not only claims that his cattle are within their rights, but complains that the golf club is cutting its grass too short for good grazing.

The Times

Cardiff City fan Neil MacNamara was banned from attending matches for five years after setting off a hotel fire alarm to disturb the sleep of opposition players the night before a vital game. Abergavenny Magistrates' Court heard that the intention was to disrupt Queens Park Rangers in the early hours. QPR lost 1-0.

The Times

'English tiddlywink players lead the world. If you want your children to be sporting champions, get them a sick note to get off rugby and buy them a squidger and some winks and tell them to get potting.'

Matt Fayers, Magdalene College, Cambridge,
Daily Telegraph

'Fourteen people in Edinburgh claiming a world record for cramming into a phone box is perhaps indicative of the increasing bulk of the average person. In 1959 students at Hatfield Technical College packed 19 into a standard phone kiosk. It was jolly uncomfortable, but as compensation I was cheek by thigh with one of the girls.'

Roger de Mercado, Stockport, *The Times*

'Shame on Lord MacLaurin, who ran English cricket for six years, for suggesting that cricket risks becoming "a former sport of the summer – like croquet". Over the past 50 years croquet has flourished. This success isn't surprising in such a thrilling, ruthless and adaptable sport ... Even Lord MacLaurin might be charmed by Evelyn Waugh's Croquet-Bowls: the hoops are replaced with champagne bottles, and play proceeds only once they have been emptied into the players.'

Daily Telegraph leader

Boldon Ladies football club from Durham has been carpeted by the FA after four of their players were sent off for swearing at the referee. The match between the Boldon Ladies and Middlesbrough's Marton Ladies had to be abandoned in the 84th minute when Marton were ahead 5-0.

Sun

Women now make up to a fifth of all fans attending Premiership football matches – and they enjoy abusing the ref as much as men. They seem to enjoy the singing and the tribalism – and swearing is just as prevalent as it has always been.

Independent on Sunday

A Cornish family of five sold their house and went to live in Spain to be nearer to David Beckham.

Independent on Sunday

But not all attempts to attract women to the beautiful game have been a roaring success. Fulham fan Christine Wardle, 34, said the club's attempt to woo women with a ladies' bag was dreadful – 'They gave us sanitary towels.'

Independent on Sunday

After being on sale for months, the six works nominated for the Man Booker prize have achieved a combined sale of only 65,000 copies. David Beckham's book sold more than that in its first two days and he expects to sell 1.5 million.

Independent

Football's 'Big Ron' Atkinson is famous for the clear, unambiguous way in which he explains the game to viewers. On one occasion he summed up the spirit of a match with: 'Well, either side could win. Or it could be a draw.'

Sunday Times

A rugby scrum is 'essentially a boxing match for 16 people without the Queensbury rules. It is home to punching, gouging and testicle twisting. Not pretty.'

Guardian

Amid national weeping and wailing over the last flight of the Concorde in October 2003, the Madness singer Suggs boasted that he made the world's longest putt while travelling at twice the speed of sound aboard the airliner. He hit the ball down the aisle and reckons it travelled five miles in 12 seconds.

Daily Mirror

From the *West Highland Free Press*, previewing Stornoway Rugby Club's weekend visit to Aboyne, Aberdeenshire: 'The club will be keen to repeat their first-half performance against Caithness, which enabled them to dominate superior opposition before losing 52-3.

Press Gazette

Plans to stage Britain's first frozen-turkey bowling championships at a Manchester ice rink were abandoned after objections from animal-rights campaigners. Plastic birds were used instead. Frozen-turkey bowling is big in America.

Independent on Sunday

Four international rally drivers were banned from driving after being caught in speed traps during the British leg of the 2002 World Championships. They were among 17 rally drivers caught by the roadside cameras, apparently set up to trap spectators following the rally cars.

Daily Telegraph

Manchester United supporter Martin Warburton, 50, agreed to a life-saving transplant for his brother Paul, 59 – but only after Paul agreed to renounce his support for Manchester City.

> *Daily Telegraph* (*Telegraph* headline:
> 'Better Red Than Dead')

Edward Wynn and James Cullingham created a record when they flipped a tiddlywink one mile in 52 minutes 10 seconds at Stradbroke, Suffolk in 2002.

> *Sun* (reviewing the 2004 edition of the
> *Guinness Book of Records*)

'As Wembley is synonymous with tennis, so snooker is synonymous with Sheffield.'

> Sports Minister Richard Caborn,
> *Observer Magazine*

Frome Town football club has called in white witch Titania Hardie to help improve their goal scoring at home matches in Somerset. They have scored 31 goals in away games, but only three at home. Titania thinks Frome's Badger's Hill ground might be cursed and wants to 'surround the players with huge positive energy'.

> *The Times*

Manchester United employ a team of odd-job men who are on call 24 hours a day, seven days a week to pamper the glamour club's millionaire-style players. They had to sort out the player whose car got a flat tyre. He wanted them to swap it for a new one – not the tyre, the car. Other distressed footie players called for men to cut their lawns and feed their pets – and once to catch a crow stuck in a chimney. 'We had one player who called up to say his vacuum cleaner wasn't working. We sent a man round and found the dust bag was full.'

News of the World

'By far the best treatment for securing a champion conker is to immerse in it cow dung overnight.'

Wyn Thomas, Swansea, Guardian

'A one-hour soaking in vinegar, followed by 12 hours in the airing cupboard would guarantee victory over Wyn Thomas.'

Dr Robert Boon, *Manchester, Guardian*

A smallholder in Appledore, North Devon, is to be sued by a soccer team. He is refusing to return 18 balls kicked on to his land until the end of the football season.

Sun

Scarborough's amateur goalie Leigh Walker played a heroic game keeping mighty Chelsea's FA Cup victory score down to 1-0. He treasured the Chelsea goalie's shirt – given to him bearing the signatures of the Premiership club's team. Leigh planned to frame the shirt, but, immediately after the game, his mum washed it. All the priceless signatures disappeared – but the amateur star knew how to respond like a true professional. He was reported to be as sick as a parrot and said: 'I'm gutted.'

Daily Telegraph/Daily Mail

'The Ashes were originally presented to the losing side as a humiliating reminder. Logic suggests they should remain at Lord's for the foreseeable future.'

Dan Howison, Oakham, Rutland, *Guardian*

Henry VIII was the country's first monarch to play football. In 1525 he paid four shillings (equivalent to £96 in today's money) for a pair of boots. Henry's attachment to football was as transient as that to some of his wives. In 1548 he banned the sport because it incited riots.

The Times

The Cheltenham Festival race meeting is an English ritual sacred to many – particularly to those who strive in the City. It came as a blow, therefore, when Budget Day 2004 was scheduled bang in the middle of the festival. Jeff Randall, the BBC's business editor, lamented: 'This has put back relations between the Treasury and the City by years. I shall have to traipse back to London in a fit enough state to be able to broadcast.'

Sunday Telegraph (for which Mr Randall also writes)

The bookcases of horseracing fan the late Queen Mother contain – among hundreds of other volumes – 13 novels by ex-jockey Dick Francis.

The Times

Sheffield and District Football League banned its clubs from giving match results to the local paper unless the editor agreed not to publish any results in which the score exceeded 14 goals. This follows one of their Under-9 teams being trounced 29-0. The League said that the use of words such as 'trouncing' was liable to humiliate children.

The Times

"The headmaster of Munro College in Jamaica (Eton is the Munro College of Britain) once caned all his First XI players for winning 8-0. He said: "The purpose of the game is to win – not to humiliate the opposition. Four-nil is quite enough. I expect my boys to know that!""

David Shepherd, Woodstock, Oxfordshire, *The Times*

Undignified behaviour is reported from a football game between the Royal Household FC, a team of Buckingham Palace footmen and chefs, and Jeff's Chippy FC. One Household player snobbishly boasted that they could never lose to a chip shop. In a heated game, the Chippy goalie was sent off for handling the ball outside his area – and the royal team won 5-3.

Daily Mail

Chapter 15

Class:

A Touch of Class

A gentleman uses separate knives for butter and marmalade – even when dining alone ...

'Your TV reviewer jokingly suggested that what distinguishes aristocrats from the hoi polloi is that they have multiple names but prefer to use none of them. On the same day, your obituary of a frighteningly upper-class lady reports that her only daughter, Marie-Anna Berta Felicie Johanna Ghislaine Theodora Huberta Georgina Helene Genoveva, is generally known as "Bunny".'

Reg Fort, Tewkesbury, *The Times*

When asked if being an MP and having an MP's salary made one middle class, Deputy Prime Minister John Prescott said: 'I have changed. I no longer keep the coal in the bath. I keep it in the bidet.'

From *Punchlines*: *A Crash Course in English With John Prescott*, by Simon Hoggart, *Daily Mail*

A true gentleman is never rude unintentionally.

The Times

The Garrick Club's colours are salmon and cucumber. A member writes in the club's newsletter: 'I own a pair of Garrick pyjamas. The lady with whom I sometimes share a bed is envious and wants a nightdress in the same livery. In vain, I point out to her that, not being a member, she is not entitled to wear the colours. The disagreement is placing a strain on our relationship.'

Independent

Speaking about men-only clubs, a spokesman for White's said: 'Wives feel happier knowing their husbands are here, not being chatted up by some girl. Members are free to burp, swear and fart in peace.'

Observer

The 83-year-old Duke of Devonshire recalls being beaten three times by fellow students at Eton. 'I deserved the punishment and it did me a great deal of good. One of those who beat me became a distinguished diplomat.'

Daily Mail

Julian Fellowes, actor and Oscar-winning scriptwriter behind *Gosford Park*, exposes the ins and outs of modern snobbery in a new novel called *Snobs*. He told the Oxford Literary Festival: 'Everybody is still excited if a duke walks into the room and they'll all laugh at his jokes, even if they are not normally keen on dukes ... or jokes.'

Daily Telegraph

Super-athlete Tanya Streeter seized the world record for free diving (to a depth of 400ft) – a sport which requires divers to hold their breath for several minutes. She is a former pupil of Roedean, the smart girl's school in Brighton, and one old girl from there responded: 'Anyone brought up on the smell of girls' lacrosse kit at Roedean knows all about holding her nose.'

Daily Mail

The editor of *Debrett's Peerage*, Zoe Gullen, says that the point about etiquette is that it should reflect good manners and is not inflexible. She cites the occasion when the Queen saw a guest drinking from his finger bowl – and followed suit.

Daily Mail

The upper-class way to eat toast was to put butter and marmalade on only part of the slice and then bite off that part. The middle class, being more refined, would cut the toast prior to eating it. The lower class would butter and marmalade the whole slice and eat it uncut.

Canon Simon Pettitt, Newmarket, *The Times*

Bernard Wynick, of Hove, East Sussex, remembers being told that gentlemen, even when eating alone, use separate knives for the butter and the marmalade.

The Times

Lady Helen Windsor complained that a private hospital charged £50 for a baby's dummy. The price of dummies in Boots is £2.99 – for two.

Daily Mail

An exclusive Edinburgh golf club chastised one of its members for breaching etiquette – including the wearing of ordinary shoes on the first tee. Mike Griffin, of Ightham, Kent, remembers playing at a public course near Birmingham airport which had a sign reading: 'Shirts must be worn on the course. No Wellingtons.'

'That's what I call a dress code,' says Mr Griffin.

The Times

Laura Benjamin owns a Knightsbridge boutique where smart society women go to find outfits suitable for

Ladies' Day at Ascot. Her PA bustles around making tea saying that she thinks it helps put clients at ease if the person serving them isn't thinner than they are.

One of Laura's clients tells how they take two cars to Ladies' Day. 'We go down in the Rolls and somebody else comes in the Range Rover' – packed with tables, chairs, cases of champagne and silver ice buckets to put the flowers in. She thinks Ascot is 'England at its finest. There's nowhere else in the world that does it quite like that, with so much tradition.'

Sunday Telegraph Magazine

It was depressing to discover that there are few ladies at Royal Ascot's Ladies' Day. Drugs and alcohol abuse is nothing new and I saw three brunettes make an early start by cracking open a bottle of Tesco's Spanish Cava – to the annoyance of a top-hatted gentleman trying to ignore them. 'Who cares about the 3.45,' giggled one woman as she stumbled out of a toilet cubicle, drink in hand. 'I thought we were here to get drunk – not watch the races.'

Daily Mail

Tattooing has become socially acceptable. Body adornment is catching on among middle-class customers and Selfridge's temporary tattoo parlour is to be kept open indefinitely. Prices range from £60 to £600.

The Times

In a leading article on the same day *The Times* said: 'Logos are popular, with Gucci, Louis Vuitton and Chanel splayed across the choicest backsides.'

At the memorial service in July 2003 for the Queen's couturier Sir Hardy Amies, a 'particularly jaunty' Duchess of Devonshire told an anecdote about herself wearing a new dress to a staff party, but a 25-year-old one for her own ball. 'That', Sir Hardy had said, 'is English style at its best.'

The Times

The Duchess elicited a chorus of chuckles recalling an interviewer asking Sir Hardy: 'Have you ever fallen madly in love?' His answer was: 'Oh, yes, every week, mostly with the milkman.'

Daily Telegraph

The Duchess of Devonshire is publishing a cookery book, despite not having cooked for 60 years. It includes a recipe for seafood bombe to serve 50. The Duchess suggests that you need a cow to make cream. Your gamekeeper must collect gulls eggs and give them to the cook.

Richard Kay in his first gossip column after taking over from veteran Nigel Dempster, *Daily Mail*

The magazine *Harpers & Queen* is to drop Jennifer's Diary, the column in which the slightest doings of the upper classes have been chronicled with slavish sycophancy for 60 years. The decline of deference ... has reduced the public's fascination for the old upper classes ... Also the inclination to call a duke 'your Grace', as the Duke of Westminster likes to be addressed.

Independent on Sunday

Aristocratic girls are brought up to tolerate endless boredom without so much as a murmur. The *Daily Mail*, imagining Prince Philip's reaction to Cherie Blair being caught on camera yawning at the Balmoral Highland Games.

'Hunting in Yorkshire is bred in the bone, and the Bedale has a splendid reputation for good hounds, fine horseflesh and formidable women – all true.'
Fat and formidable Clarissa Dickson Wright in the
Daily Telegraph

To develop a really profound capacity for concealing one's true thoughts and emotions on any given subject, it helps to have belonged for several generations to the English middle class.
Andrew Gibson's Notebook in the Daily Telegraph

Some timely advice for class-conscious Britons who worry whether it is terribly Northern working class to tuck your napkin into your shirt at the top.

Simon Hoggart in the *Guardian* writes: 'It is truly *petit bourgeois* to leave your napkin on your lap. At the Garrick Club they have recently arranged to sew buttonholes into all the napkins so that members can tether them just under the knot in their ties.'

When Lancashire businesswoman Trish Morris was interviewed as a prospective candidate for the Kensington and Chelsea parliamentary seat one of the panel said that it was nice to see she already lived in The Boltons – a 'highly posh millionaires' ghetto in Chelsea'. When Morris pointed out she actually came from the former mill town of Bolton in Lancashire, 'it was downhill all the way'. Michael Portillo bagged the seat.

Observer

It is reported that Prince William wants to join White's, the elite club which was founded in 1693 and is full of dukes and earls – many of whom can trace their pedigrees back far beyond the Windsors. Its members are not overawed by titles ... and the Royal Family is not held in the highest social esteem there. To many members they are simply 'the Krauts'.

Daily Mail

Following the revelation that, down the years, some 300 people had turned down a chance to appear on the Honours List, the *Independent on Sunday* asked a bunch of celebs if they would accept an honour. Art critic Brian Sewell replied: 'I would accept a life peerage for the sole reason that we are a country of bloody snobs and if I had "Lord" in front of my name I would be able to get all the answers I want.'

Eight years ago public schoolgirl Emily Edmondstone complained to the Archbishop of Canterbury and the Equal Opportunities Commission about being barred from an all-boys choir. Now, aged 20, she is a lap dancer in London clubs wearing a PVC French maid's outfit.

Daily Mail

Chapter 16

Nine to Five:
It's off to Work we Go

The Navy has more admirals than ships ...

You Couldn't Make It Up? Some can and do. The *Guardian* reported: 'One in five workers admits to fiddling expenses according to a survey.'

'I always like to get to know people so I ask them where they were born and then ask them why... One interviewee came back with the great reply: 'Because my parents had sex.'

Simon Bradshaw, editor of the
Brighton Argus on interviewing job seekers.
Press Gazette training supplement

A factory worker – annoyed by delays in getting tax credit payments from the Inland Revenue – glued himself to the enquiries desk at his local tax office in Bridgwater, Somerset.

The Times

After 30 years of photographing bare-breasted Page Three girls for the Sun, Beverley Goodway retired in July 2003 and is reported to have said: 'It's a tough job – but somebody had to do it.'

Sun

'I once told my staff that there were no such things as problems, only opportunities.

'It all ended when one retorted: "Well, in that case what we have here is an insurmountable opportunity."'

Simon Baseley, Christchurch, Dorset, *Daily Telegraph*

The Department of Trade and Industry has produced a 6-page, 2,000-word masterpiece of bureaucracy that turns the seemingly simple task of choosing and positioning office plants into a 'DTI foliage strategy'. Some staff are allowed one 5ft–6ft plant every 3 to 4 seats. Others are entitled to one display per 120 sq m of usable floor space. Arrangements will be inspected and may be changed by health and safety officials.

The Times

Twenty-three per cent of photocopier faults are caused by people who sit on them to photocopy their buttocks.

Daily Star

A housewife waited two months before the repair men turned up to fix her washing machine in Tuffley, Gloucestershire. When they did she locked them in and refused to let them out until it was mended.

The Times

Plumbers can earn £70,000 a year said recent reports. A course for plumbing wannabes in Bristol attracted 2,000 applicants for the 36 places available.

Daily Express

A survey reveals that a third of British workers think it is all right to 'pull a sickie'.
Top reason for taking a day off is a hangover. More than 50 per cent said they would be less likely to skive if their pay got docked.

Guardian

Postman Martin Calcutt, 31, of South Shields, had to take sick leave after being bitten by his pet piranha.

The Times

The Confederation of British Industry says bogus absences cost firms £11bn a year.

Sun

A Newcastle firm aiming to help people in debt went into voluntary liquidation owing £3m.

Daily Mirror

'I was always delighted when a minute from my boss ended with TINHAT – meaning There Is No Hurry About This.'

Robert Sanders, Crieff, Perthshire, The Times

A third of workers have come close to leaving their jobs because of the irritating habits of their colleagues. High on the irritation list are those who swear at their computers, those who send e-mails to colleagues who are close by – and those who refuse turns making the tea.

Guardian/Ceefax

The Adam Smith Institute think-tank has named some of the daftest, taxpayer-funded jobs in the country. Jobs cited as contenders for the silliest title include Real Nappy Officers, hired to promote the use of 'real' rather than disposable nappies and Walking Officers hired to promote walking. East Kent Coastal Primary Care Trust has a Smoking Cessation Specialist.

Dr Eamonn Butler, Adam Smith Institute director, also

pointed out that the NHS now has more administrators than beds and the Navy has more admirals than ships.

Daily Mail

The Sunday Times runs a weekly column called the Shock Exchange, reporting on reports in the tabloids. It quoted a *Sun* story saying that eight out of every ten people are useless at their jobs – and added: 'How do we know that this story was written accurately by one of the two out of the ten workers who know what they are doing?'

Times reader David Williams, of Leigh on Sea, Essex, spotted a Safeways' job vacancy ad for 'Ambient Replenishment'.

'I checked with a member of the staff. In plain English it means shelf stacking.'

A friend who has an evening shelf-stacking job at a supermarket tells me that, according to her contract, she is a 'Twilight Merchandiser'.

John Welford, Nuneaton, Warwickshire, *The Times*

Seventy-one per cent of the 10,052 workers who took part in an AOL Internet poll claimed to have had an affair with a colleague. One in ten said they had slept with the boss to further their careers – and one in three said they would do so if the opportunity arose.

Daily Mail

An unemployed man pasted his CV on a sandwich board. He paraded it through Lincoln – and got a job with a firm of recruitment consultants.

Shropshire Star

A 19 stone teenager from Manchester was told he was too fat when he tried to join the Army. Keen to be a soldier, he went on an 18-month-long strict diet and exercise regime, almost halving his weight. He was then rejected having been weakened by his dramatic weight loss. He became a postman while trying to decide to try again.

Daily Mail

Postman Adrian Birch has retired after 34 years. On his round of villages near Kirkham, Lancashire, he helped elderly residents to bring the coal in and light fires in the dead of winter, visited the unwell and was 'always ready to lend a hand, stop for a chat and even help cook breakfast'.

Grateful villagers writing to the *Daily Mail*

The staff of a Manchester primary care trust were told to dunk their arms in cold water rather than use fans during a heatwave.

Manchester Evening News

Answers given on CVs by jobseekers about their hobbies and other interests have included: 'circus knife throwing, pleasing my boyfriend between the sheets, walking my five poodles, stalking celebrities, ferret racing, playing with my cat and tattoos' (from a survey by recruitment website reed.co.uk). Recruiters say applicants whose interests are judged wacky are more likely to fail.

Daily Mail

'Workers at a garden centre in Plymouth found trespassers there – and ended up being accused of forcing them to do one-and-a-half-hours' hard work, including building a perimeter fence to keep out such people as themselves.'

Peter Simple's column, *Daily Telegraph*

There are 150,000 people employed in the UK rail industry. There are at least 200,000 registered train spotters – made up mainly of men over 40.

The Times

Seen in the *Sunday Times* Appointments section: an advertisement for a chairman for the (Rail) Delays Attribution Board.

Warwickshire's trading standards officers have received a complaint from a local firm which booked 'a slim, attractive' strippogram girl – and got a 20 stone, tattooed roly-poly stripper instead. 'You've got the short straw today, love,' she is reported to have said.

Sun/Independent on Sunday

A slimming instructor in Hawick, Scotland, adjusted his scales to trick his clients into thinking they had lost weight. He was suspended after many were found to be up to a stone heavier.

Daily Express

Everybody remembers the Bob Hoskins catchphrase 'It's Good to Talk' in his BT adverts. Bob must – it is claimed he earned enough from the ads 'never to need to work again'.

Independent on Sunday

A *Daily Telegraph* feature on the problems of giving references for unsatisfactory employees produced this possible solution from Richard Weller of Sheffield: 'An employer wrote to my brother-in-law: "You will be very fortunate if you can get this man to work for you."'
This was followed by:

- **My favourite is: 'I am sure he will join your company as he leaves ours – fired with enthusiasm.' Graham Hoyle, Shipley, West Yorkshire, *Daily Telegraph***
- **A reference for a nurse said: 'She has shown**

herself capable of anything and we will be glad to see her back.' Dr Mark Cave, Abergavenny, Wales. *Daily Telegraph*

- A surgeon I worked for in North Wales preferred: 'This man informs me that he has been my house surgeon for six months. He has carried out all his duties to his entire satisfaction.' Dr John Griffiths, Anglesey. *Daily Telegraph*
- A ship's captain was once told: 'This man deserves a berth. Make sure you give him a wide one.' Brian Clifton, Wilmslow, Cheshire, *Daily Telegraph*

Dentist Steven Homewood, 50, commutes 560 miles from his home in the Scottish isle of Bute to his practice in Brighton, East Sussex. It involves him using a ferry, a bus, a plane, a train and a bike.
News of the World

Seen in the back window of a van: 'I owe, I owe, so off to work I go.'
Susan Morris, Chalfont St Peter, *Reader's Digest*

Musicians attended auditions in May 2003 to become London Underground's first licensed, official buskers. They included a jazz trumpeter and a classical violinist and they ranged from professional buskers to hard-up supply teachers. Buskers can earn up to £40 a day, but the figure is usually closer to £10.
The Times

Criticising the licensed busker scheme as misguided, James Delingpole wrote in *The Times*: 'The great joy of busking in its current, unlicensed form is that all musical life is there – the good, the bad and the very, very ugly. And you never know which option you are going to get.'

London Underground's plan to license buskers came in for fierce criticism. The *Independent* had a leader saying: 'Busking is about freedom of choice. It is a powerful and uplifting daily example of the unshakeable power of human optimism.'

Veteran columnist Keith Waterhouse wrote: 'I find the idea infinitely depressing. It is the notion of a tidy mind, and buskers are not tidy people. They are a secretive sub-section of the musical world, with their own rules, their own conventions, their own code and their own network. They do not need regulating.'

Daily Mail

Britons work the longest hours in Europe – and put in more than £23bn of unpaid overtime a year.

Daily Telegraph

One in five British workers has admitted nodding off while at work. More than two in three told a survey that they believe they are too tired to do their job efficiently.

The Times

David Barrington makes swords in Southend-on-Sea. When the Yellow Pages directory advised him that it was no longer going to have a separate section for swordmakers he said: 'I suppose it's being coming for years ... We've been going downhill since the 19th century when duelling was made illegal.'

The Times

A Felixstowe, Suffolk, firm – Seawing International – got an order from Dubai for 3,000 tonnes of sand.

The Times

Trading standard officers hid a camera in the loft of a house in Surrey – and caught a plumber peeing into a vase and then emptying the vase into the hot water tank.

Another workman was filmed searching for a gas leak with a naked flame.

Sun

Don Snyder tells how he tackled the problem of employees abusing their allotted break time. He posted a notice saying: 'Starting immediately, your 15-minute breaks are being cut from a half-hour to 20 minutes.'

Reader's Digest

When companies merge, employees worry about lay-offs. Dianne Stevens' fears appeared justified when her company was bought out. A photograph of the newly merged staff appeared on the firm's website carrying the message: 'Updated Daily'.

Reader's Digest

A circus performer walked the tightrope wearing a hard hat in Folkestone, Kent, to comply with new EU safety rules. 'Ridiculous,' said the assistant manager of the Moscow State Circus. 'Britain is the only country implementing the new regulations.'

The Times

Woolworth executives were baffled by a new Japanese game that was forecast to be a bestseller. They got a boy of nine to explain it to them.

Daily Mirror

Britons now spend 50 million hours a year on hold to call centres says the Consumers' Association.

The Times

Molecular biologist Karl Gensburg, of Streetly, Walsall, is to abandon his academic career for a better-paid job as a gas fitter.

Daily Telegraph

People with large blue eyes, blonde hair, full fleshy lips and childlike features are more likely to get jobs and win court cases according to a study by research company ICM. It also helps if you dress smartly, have well-polished shoes and, for women, well-applied make-up.

Daily Telegraph

One of the troubles about recycled paper, according to Dr George Scott, of Chislehurst, Kent, is that:'You don't know where it's been.'

The Times

Chapter 17

Education, Education, Education ...

Fifty per cent of the population doesn't know what 50% is ...

Answer given in a school music exam: 'Music sung by two people at the same time is called a duel.'
Brian McDowell, Tiverton, *Daily Telegraph*

Childminder Kim Munro, of Whiteparish, Wiltshire, has been warned by Ofsted inspectors because her nursery does not have any black or disabled dolls.

Sun

A London primary school sought to recruit classroom assistants with an advertisement that had 17 grammar and spelling mistakes – without counting missing full stops and rogue capital letters.

Daily Mail

Consultants were paid £5,000 to find a name for a new university at Bradford. They came up with: 'Bradford University, University of Bradford and The University of Bradford.'

Telegraph and Argus

School exam chiefs are to remove all risk of failure by replacing F for 'fail' to N for 'nearly'.

Sunday Telegraph

Mrs Gill Baron, of Kirby Muxloe, Leicestershire, has been helping her son with an IT project for school. 'I know that many parents help their children with their homework,' she writes, 'but my son is 30, and he is the teacher.'

The Times

During his search for a suitable school for his son Sheridan, the actor Robert Morley asked a man from the Midlands why he had bought a school in Oxfordshire: 'Well,' he replied. 'I have always had a bit of thing about whipping very small boys in short trousers.'

Henley Standard

Oxbridge has become famous for throwing oddball questions into interviews with students (such as: 'Tell me about a banana'). But gone are the days of the Cambridge tutor who was said to hurl a rugby ball at interviewees. If they dropped it they were out. If they caught it they were in. If they drop-kicked it through the window they got a scholarship.

Daily Telegraph

The dreaming dons of Oxford create a daily traffic menace on their rusty bicycles and are being offered free places on a cycle safety course. Gillian Evans, a professor of medieval history who lives and teaches in Oxford, agreed with complaining pedestrians that all dons 'ride like complete maniacs. We are absolutely terrifying.'

The Times

'Fifty per cent of the population do not know what 50% is.'

Trade and Industry Secretary
Patricia Hewitt, *Observer*

The 'Instructions and Guidance for Students' booklet for my AS-level history course essay deemed it necessary to print on the front:

'Instructions.
'You must read these instructions carefully.

'You must then carry out the tasks in accordance with these instructions.'

Catherine Negus, Solihull, *The Times*

Times reader Oliver Bellamy wrote in to say that at school he was told how to take drugs, when to have sex and what his rights were. But at no time was he informed about the electoral process.

The Times

Disruptive pupils on school buses on the Isle of Wight are to be punished by being made to travel on an old and unheated bus painted bright pink. It is claimed that the Pink Peril Service shames pupils into behaving.

Independent

In summer 2002, a London primary school banned daisy chains in case children picked up germs from the ground. An Aberdeen primary school curtailed playground football, claiming children were becoming too hot, bothered and muddy. Handstands, conkers, tree climbing, marbles, hide and seek, tag and skipping have also fallen foul of some schools and local councils.

Daily Mail

In addition to the ban on daisy chains, the *Independent on Sunday* records a spate of traditional children's activities being restricted or banned. They include:

- Musical chairs being condemned for encouraging violence.
- School sports called off because children might slip on wet grass.
- Children required to wear hard hats when riding donkeys on the beach.
- Swings removed because they faced the sun and could harm children's eyes.
- Bans on skipping, three-legged races, marbles, hide-and-seek and yo-yos.

Parents were banned from videoing their children taking part in school sports in Wiltshire 'to protect the privacy of the pupils'.

Daily Mail

'My four-year-old daughter came home from school very upset after being told in assembly that conkers were banned "in case the string flies up into your face and the conker hurts you".'

Letter from Norfolk parent in the *Guardian*

Some schools have banned conkers because it is played exclusively by boys 'and therefore sexist'.

Daily Mail

Police held an amnesty so that students at St Andrew's University could hand back items stolen during term time. Nine thousand pounds' worth of goods were returned.

Dundee Evening Telegraph

A new school bus driver got lost while driving the two miles from Bury to Tottington High School. Mischievous pupils then deliberately misdirected him on a 20-mile round trip that kept them away from their studies for two hours.

Daily Telegraph

To be selected as a Rhodes scholar at Oxford it is important to show leadership potential ... Bob Hawke [former Australian Prime Minister], who was at University College in 1953, entered the *Guinness Book of Records* for drinking a yard of ale in 12 seconds.

Daily Telegraph

'When I arrived at Bryanston as headmaster in 1959 the sign on the approach to my house read: "Headmaster, dead slow." I had it removed.'

Robin Fisher, Devon, *The Times*

The number of students applying to the Open University for its course in 'Spanish for Beginners' has more than trebled since David Beckham joined Real Madrid. One theory is that many football fans are switching to European satellite TV channels for Real Madrid's games and they cannot understand the commentary.

Independent

A teenage pupil had to have hospital treatment after being attacked during a lesson on how to combat bullies at a school in Paignton, Devon.

Manchester Evening News

'When teaching [Bertrand] Russell's Paradox I often suggested beer mats with, on one side: "The statement on the other side is false," and on the other side: "The statement on the other side is true."'

Dennis Orton, Weston, Hampshire. *The Times*

Anne Jones, 51, a former teacher from Leicestershire, won the title of the world's fastest reader for the sixth time – 2,284 words a minute. Average reading speed is 250 words a minute.

The Times

Brits came 11th in a list tabling average national IQs. They scored 100 points against the United States' 98 – but were beaten by Hong Kong (107), South Korea (106), Japan (105) and Singapore (103). Researchers said they were not surprised at the high scores from the Far East – 'They are known to be better at mathematics,' they said.

Sunday Times

A typical question from Mensa is: 'Which three-letter word can be attached to the end of the given words to form four longer words? Doctor, alien, fabric, consider. Answer: ate

Sunday Times

An infant school in Basildon, Essex, asked parents to donate loo rolls because it cannot afford to buy its own.

Sunday Telegraph

The Times had some New Year's Eve fun on 31 December 2003 asking why university personnel continually attract funding for studies with blindingly obvious conclusions. Among its top ten results of silly studies were:

- Only one per cent of children visiting Santa Claus smiled or showed any sign of happiness – but nearly all parents were happy and excited.

- Marriage improves women's health, but only when it is a happy one.
- Gamblers are less successful when they are drunk. Big portions might contribute to obesity.

'So, chaps, just how should we tackle truancy?' Page one headline in *The Times* over a picture showing only a dozen or so of our 659 MPs attending a debate on truancy. The Junior Education Minister told the empty benches that there was no magic wand to compel full attendance. The Schools Minister was absent.

Cheating becomes respectable. Students who download exam coursework from the Internet and pass it off as their own are 'self-teaching' says the head of the exams board council. Dr Ellie Johnson Searle told Radio 4's *Today* programme that students can change the language and grammar and put in their own words. 'If they are going to that effort they are essentially taking part in self-teaching; they are learning the subject anyway.'

Sunday Telegraph

Chapter 18

Council Daze

Horses to wear nappies to cut cleaning bills ...

Council workers who turned up to mend a broken window at the home of a disabled woman in the West Midlands replaced every window in the house except the broken one.

Guardian

Lancashire County Council has urged gardeners to wee on their compost heaps to rot them more quickly and add vital nitrogen.

Sun

Robert Marshall, a member of the South Staffordshire District Council, spent £2,300 of his official allowance on a speed camera for his ward. He became one of its first victims – caught doing 43mph in a 30mph zone. Mr Marshall said the policeman who flagged him down 'had difficulty in hiding a smile'.

Daily Telegraph

An Aberdeen county councillor has suggested that money could be saved if yellow no-parking lines were painted thinner.

The Herald **(Glasgow)**

A report advising Rotherham council how to be efficient and save money has had to be redrafted 12 times. Total cost £12,000.

Sheffield Star

When the men's public toilets in Seabrook, Kent, were vandalised, the local council closed them temporarily and alerted residents thusly: 'Although the ladies' toilets have not been vandalised, it would be unacceptable under equal opportunities and sex discrimination and council policy for them to remain open.'

Kent Messenger

A controversial makeover of Henley's town square has been finally finished after many delays. A letter in the *Henley Standard* congratulated the town council with the barbed comment: 'One concludes that the job must be an extremely thorough one since my calculations suggest that had the M6 been constructed at the same rate it would have taken 3,009 years and seven months to complete.'

A traffic warden in Manchester issued 101 parking tickets that had to be cancelled because he forgot he was working on a Bank Holiday when most parking restrictions do not apply.

Daily Mail

A London traffic warden put a ticket on a marked police riot squad van parked in a police bay outside Charing Cross police station.

Sun

Blackburn Council, Lancashire, has sent 38 dustmen on a 'Customer Care' course to learn how to be polite – at a cost of £400 per day, per head.

Daily Mail

Under a spreading chestnut tree in the Hampshire village of Street children have enjoyed a swing which has been there for as long as the locals can remember. (The tree was planted 106 years ago to mark Queen Victoria's Diamond Jubilee.) Now Petersfield Town council say the swing must come down under new health and safety regulations.

Daily Mail

Two motorists parked in a road in Islington, London N1, where yellow no-parking lines had been erased by roadworks. Later yellow lines were painted underneath the vehicles and ten minutes later they were clamped. A council spokesman said: 'It was a daft mistake. We apologise.'

Sun

York council has threatened to make the city's horses wear nappies in a bid to save an annual £6,000 spent cleaning up the animals' dung from the city streets.

Sunday Telegraph

Council chiefs have told donkey ride operators to keep beaches clean at Mablethorpe, Lincolnshire, by putting nappies on their donkeys.

Sun

A 'smash the crockery' stall at a country fair in Crediton, Devon, was closed down after complaints that it could encourage domestic violence.

Sun

A resident of Westonzoyland in Somerset – suspected of being a former 'townie' – complained about the drumming noise coming from the garden of Liz Twose. Sedgemoor District Council warned that she could face a £5,000 fine – but then accepted her explanation

232

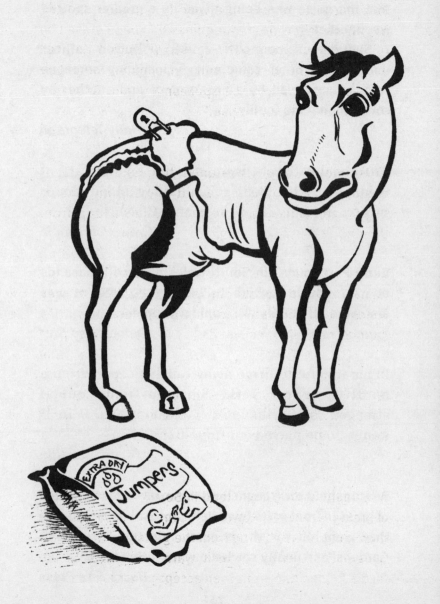

that the noise was being made by a greater spotted woodpecker.

Sedgemoor council's noise pollution officer remembered other complaints – including someone who was annoyed by a creaky door and another by cows mooing too loudly.

Daily Telegraph

£20 penalty tickets were slapped on the cars of volunteers who went to a Sunday blood donor session in Nantwich civic centre, Cheshire.

Crewe Chronicle

Burry Port council in South Wales ordered thousands of its roadside flowers to be dug up after it was discovered that they were opium poppies.

Express and Star

In an attempt to drive away rough sleepers from a multi-storey car park, Stoke-on-Trent council arranged for Beethoven's 'Symphony No. 9 in D minor' to be played continuously.

Guardian

Beaconsfield town council wanted a name for the patch of grass in front of its town hall. A consultation process that went on for three years rejected 'Town Hall Gardens' and finally settled on 'Town Hall Green'.

Bucks Free Press

Following extensive public consultations, dozens of suggestions and months of deliberations, the new name for the Drill Hall has been announced by Lincoln City Council. Suggestions included Razzamatazz Hall and The Big Roof, but the council settled for … Lincoln Drill Hall.

Daily Mail

A traffic warden infuriated firemen when he ticketed three of their vehicles while they were tackling a blaze in a Westminster office block. They accused the warden of being overzealous and the tickets were cancelled.

Daily Mail

Bristol City Council has told its staff to call people 'Sir' or 'Madam' – not 'Love' or 'Dear'. But the city's cherished informality is likely to continue in shops, banks, taxis and doctors' surgeries whether you are old, young, male, female, pretty or ugly.

Daily Mirror/The Times

Three weeks after being elected to Maidstone Borough Council, Annabelle Blackmore went to live in Bermuda – 3,450 miles away. But she insists she will carry on serving, saying she can be contacted by e-mail, fax and phone. Council leader Eric Hodson said the situation was not ideal, 'but she is young and a woman and we don't have enough women'.

Sunday Times

Cambridgeshire County Council say youngsters should be protected from possible injury by restricting sports such as football, rugby and hockey – because playing fields have hardened in the summer sun. The crackdown follows bans elsewhere on sack races and three-legged races because they are considered dangerous.

Daily Mail

'It was hilarious,' said an onlooker when Sir Paul McCartney tried to persuade a London traffic warden to tear up a parking ticket. 'One of the richest men in the world trying to worm out of a parking fine.' It was clearly a matter of principle reported the *Daily Mail* – but the traffic warden was unimpressed by Sir Paul's argument that his Mercedes estate car carried disabled stickers because of his wife's prosthetic leg.

Newcastle council built a £5m library – but forgot to order the books and the shelves to put them on.

Sun

Road safety signs were erected by Sheffield council workmen warning motorists of a school ahead in Bradfield village, South Yorkshire. The school closed down 18 years ago.

The Times

Emma Wood faced a fine of £150 for having her pay-and-display ticket upside down in Balham.

News of the World

Carmarthenshire banned its taxi drivers from wearing Santa Claus outfits 'because they must always resemble their identity-card pictures'.

Guardian

Matthew Eglise, from Croydon, reports that when his windscreen was shattered outside his home the repair van was given a ticket and he was fined because his resident's permit was attached to broken glass on the seat, rather than on the windscreen.

Daily Telegraph

It can cost £50 and involve five people working in three different buildings to get a Hull council light bulb changed. The *Daily Mail* outlined the procedure:

- Step 1: Report broken light to superintendent's office.
- Step 2: Superintendent faxes Property Services.
- Step 3: Property Services issues order for new bulb to Works Department.
- Step 4: Works Department issues job sheet to electrician.
- Step 5: Electrician fits bulb.

The procedure can take up to five weeks.

Light-bulb changing is less complex elsewhere, but can still be a formidable task. Doncaster council's community care staff are alerted to health and safety rules and electrical safety legislation. These regulations require a second person to hold any ladder being used by the person changing the bulb. A third person is needed to switch off the electricity at the mains and stay by the switch until the bulb is changed. Where the client is frail or anxious there may be the need of a fourth person to comfort them while the operation is completed. Many home care workers are not allowed to change light bulbs.

Guardian

Soft toilet rolls are to be issued to all Sheffield council employees after blue-collar workers complained of discrimination because they were getting a coarser wipe.

Financial Times

Lynette Vickers of Crewe, Cheshire, is challenging a council's decision to fine her £50 for putting her rubbish out in the wrong kind of bin bags – ones not issued by the council. The *Sun* ran this story along with a catalogue of other 'daft new penalty laws':

- Crewe and Nantwich council fined a woman for littering when she was feeding birds.

- Traffic wardens can now fine motorists £60 for parking more than 50cm away from the kerb.
- An empty windscreen wash bottle can set you back £60.
- Litter wardens are fining smokers for dropping fag ends.
- There are plans to fine parents £100 for taking their children on holiday during school terms.

In the same edition of the *Sun*, Richard Littlejohn highlighted the case of a man who was put in a cell for four hours for displaying an 'offensive' poster in the window of his mobile phone shop in Northampton. The poster was aimed at encouraging drivers to use only hands-free mobiles and advised them not to be a:

Tango
Whisky
Alpha
Tango

If you clear snow from the pavement outside your home you could be liable if someone slips on it. If you leave the snow alone the council would be liable.

The Times

Dozens of drivers in Birmingham were hit with £60 fines after they were forced to abandon their cars stuck in the snow. One penalty notice was placed on a wrecked motorbike after its driver was carried into an ambulance. The city council said: 'We will consider refunds.'

Mail on Sunday

Hanging baskets have been banned from lamp posts in Bury St Edmunds, Suffolk, because they might fall on people.

Sun

'The Royal Horticultural Society has records going back 40 years covering 1,400 places where hanging baskets are suspended from lamp posts. There has not been a single incident involving a killer hanging basket.'

Richard Littlejohn, *Sun*

Fort Knox, Air Force One and Saddam Hussein's bunker in Baghdad are on a list of ten of the most secure places in the world. So is the multi-storey car park in Bold Lane, Derby. Derby council has installed CCTV cameras, panic buttons and super-sharp sensors which lockdown the whole site if a car so much as wobbles when the central computer thinks it should be still.

The Times/Focus technology magazine

Neil Lyndon fumed in the *Daily Mail*: 'This has never happened in the 18 years that the baskets have been on show.' He condemned 'namby pamby prissiness and pettifogging interference' and dreamed of a society in which:

- The carol singers of High Wycombe are allowed to advertise their Christmas service instead of being banned, as they were, for fear of upsetting Muslims.
- Party-goers in genteel Bath are not prevented from holding a hog roast on the grounds that it may offend animal-rights activists, as they were.
- The bowlers of Carshalton Beeches Bowling Club are not assumed to be closet perverts and thus prevented from giving lessons to schoolgirls.

Daily Mail

Parking wardens slapped three tickets on an illegally parked car in Edinburgh – despite the fact the vehicle was a burned-out wreck with no tyres or windows. A council spokeswoman said: 'We have the car on our system and it has been taxed, so it is the responsibility of the owner or their insurance company to move it.'

Scotsman

Traffic wardens in Westminster compete for a gleaming trophy – awarded to the wardens who dish out most tickets each month.

Sun

On the same day *The Times* reported that Westminster council had a parking bay too small for just about any car. Motorists parking in the 162cm-wide bay in Berkeley Mews, opposite Marble Arch police station, have been ticketed because their car wheels did not fit between the lines. The bay is too narrow even for a Mini. The council promised to investigate.

The Times

Former boxer Chris Eubank has trouble parking his 32ft-long, 8ft-wide, 10-wheeled American truck in London (registration no: 1 KO). His long-suffering secretary deals with Eubank's parking tickets and says: 'He's had about 200 of the things.'

Daily Mail

A local councillor went to investigate complaints of slippery seaweed on a jetty at Warsash, Hampshire. She slipped on the seaweed, broke her ankle and claimed compensation from the council.

Sun

Residents of St Dennis in Cornwall celebrated in March 2004 when work began to provide a pavement for the main road through their village. It was first promised 71 years ago. Barbara Pascoe welcomed the news. She is 81 and was 9 when the pavement was proposed. Matthew Taylor, the local Liberal Democrat MP said: 'To say this is overdue would be an understatement.'

Daily Telegraph/Sun

A Brighton parking attendant challenged a woman's right to use a disabled car park.

So she pulled down her trousers and displayed to him the scar from her hip replacement operation.

Sun

Ellen Geary, 49, parked her car in her usual spot – on an unrestricted road in Bournemouth. When she returned she found that double-yellow lines had been painted along the road – lines which finished at the back of her car and restarted at the front. Ellen also found a parking ticket stuck to her windscreen.

Sun/The Times

To deter vandals, the local council erected an 8ft-high fence around Bigyn Primary School in Carmarthen-shire. Then 350 people signed a petition complaining that a stunning hilltop view over the Gower Peninsula had been spoiled. The solution favoured by the council: spend £50,000 raising the height of the 200-foot hill by 10 feet.

The Times/Sun

Planning officials in Stockport have insisted that two factory chimneys should be painted grey to blend in with the skyline 'because the sky in Stockport is more often than not pale grey'.

Guardian

Ian Smith's grandmother lived in Stockport and used to say: 'If you can see the hills, it's going to rain. If you can't see the hills it is raining.' Woe betide anyone who left washing on the line. It would be slate grey after rain.

Guardian

A ten-wheel asphalt-layer, hired by Swindon council to resurface roads, got a £60 parking ticket from one of the council's own wardens.

News of the World

For 15 years residents of Sturminster Newton in Dorset have organised an annual spring clean to pick up litter and tidy the village. In 2004 they were told by the local authority that they had to abide by 22 pages of guidelines telling them how to run a 'litter pick'. They were also told to take out insurance costing £150. Angry residents simply cancelled the event.

The Times

The backstroke has been banned in Daisyfield swimming pool because Blackburn council fears being sued by swimmers who crash into each other.

Guardian

Van driver Derek Scott stopped in a road in Westminster to ask a traffic warden for directions. While the warden was giving him the directions – a second warden slapped a ticket on his van. The City of Westminster Council's Parking Regulation Unit said: 'We have a firm but fair parking policy.'

Sun

Birmingham's eternal flame, lit to promote world peace and harmony, was snuffed out after a row over the gas bill. It is to be converted to electricity and relit.

Sunday Times

Derby City Council faced protests about a decision to refuse to reinstate an ancient statue of a wild boar in a local park in case it offended Muslims.

Derby Evening Telegraph

The parish council has arranged for a seat donated to Okeford Fitzpaine to be installed in the village pond.

Bournemouth Echo

Chapter 19

Food for Thought

Frogspawn, boiled baby, cat sick, toenail soup, fly cemetery – they're all school meals ...

Viagra chewing gum has been invented by Wrigleys.
Independent on Sunday

Notice in a London restaurant menu: 'There is a very small possibility of finding nuts in our dishes that do not contain them at all.'
F W Crawley, London N6 *The Times*

Sir Clement Freud tells of a pub near where he lives in East Anglia which advertised: 'Special deal. Food, drink and a kindly word: £4.99.' What optimistic customers got was a piece of meat pie and a glass of red wine. When a customer asked about the kindly word they were told: 'Don't eat the pie ...'

Daily Mail

Stories about the new Scottish delicacy – the 1,000-calorie deep-fried chocolate sandwich – brought a warning from the *Sun*: It would take two hours of sex to work off the calorific effect of the 'Suicide Sarnie'.

Dr Rick Jolly, of Crafthole, Cornwall, recalls how: 'in the Commando world we always carried a cardboard tube filled with curry powder. The Royal Marines' delightful nickname for this absolutely essential and taste-making dietary supplement was "Go-faster dust".'

Daily Telegraph

Following a story about Fijians apologising for the cannibalistic tendencies of their ancestors, George Courtauld of Essex wrote: 'Those with a morbid curiosity may see in Ipswich Museum a fork that was used for eating the Rev. Thomas Baker.'

Daily Telegraph

Daily food budget per person on a submarine: £2. Daily food budget for a guard dog at a naval base: £3.50.

Sam Leith, *Daily Telegraph*

Fish and chips are back on top as the nation's favourite food – but it was the only traditional British dish to make the top ten in a 2003 BBC poll. Pizza came in second, followed by crispy duck, chicken tikka masala, sweet and sour chicken, chow mein, lamb rogan josh, chicken madras, Thai green curry and chicken korma.

Daily Mail

'In my youth a Marmite jar was not truly empty until it had been boiled-up at least once for gravy.'

Jeff Teare, Powys, *Guardian*

Staff on a bus promoting British potatoes were found to be handing out spuds imported from Israel.

Daily Telegraph

Enthusiasts welcome the news that efforts are being made to return some of Britain's rarest old fruits back to the grocers' shelves. This despite the fact that some of them are somewhat unattractively named – including Hen's Turd apples and the Bloody Bastard pear. Kill-Boys is a cider apple so strong it allegedly did just that. Shit Smock is 'an exceptionally tasty green plum, but with dire consequences down below if you overindulge'.

Guardian

Meet Britain's most expensive burger – costing £30 at Harrods. It is made with beef from a special herd of

Wagyu cows from Japan. To ensure they are happy they are fed on a top-notch secret diet and enjoy being massaged and drinking beer from a local pub in Wales. Farmer David Wynne Finch says: 'A happy cow means great beef.'

Daily Mail

'Having breakfast at Heathrow Airport, I asked the waitress whether the orange juice was freshly squeezed and she replied: "It's freshly squeezed out of a carton." English is indeed a wonderfully rich language.'

Matthew Dick, West Sussex, *The Times*

The traditional British solution to crisis – putting on the kettle for a nice cup of tea – is the latest victim of the nation's changing habits, which have seen many switching to fruit and herbal teas.

Guardian, reporting on a Datamonitor survey

The *Daily Telegraph*'s report on the survey reminded us that Boy George reckons a cup of tea is better than sex, and that politician Tony Benn drinks a pint of it every hour.

And an *Independent* leader mourned the days when the choice was simple: 'One lump or two.' The office tea round is now a complex exercise in multiple preference: camomile, organic green, rosehip, bag in, bag out, skimmed, semi-skimmed or full fat.

Tapioca is Britain's most hated school meal according to a survey by the BBC's *Good Food* magazine. Children nickname it 'frogspawn'. Among other pet hates: custard (known as 'cat sick'), peas (bullets) and spotted dick (fly cemetery).

The most popular ways of secretly disposing of uneaten food: squashing it between plates, dumping it on someone else's plate, or stuffing it into a hankie.

The Times/Teletext

'The favourite pudding at my school was jam roly-poly and custard, called "flesh, blood and matter".'

Robert Ornbo, Suffolk, *The Times*

'At my school in the years just after the Second World War jam tart was known as "concrete slab".'

Michael Rutt, Bedfordshire, *The Times*

'Sloppy semolina with a dollop of raspberry jam was "death in the desert". Firing spoonfuls at enemies was optional.'

Janet Cockerill, Durham, *The Times*

'Stewed apples (every Wednesday) was "toenail soup".'

Margaret Leyden, Nottingham, *The Times*

'We called tapioca "fish eyes in glue"; Sago was called "frogspawn". A variant of suet pudding, rolled in a cloth and boiled, was "boiled baby".'

J R T Harris, West Sussex, *The Times*

A gift of carrots – part of a scheme to encourage children to eat more fruit and veg – was accompanied by instructions on how to eat them. An e-mail to junior schools in Salford from the 'Area Fruit Co-ordinator' read: 'Wash the carrots, eat them from the bottom and discard the top.'

Sun/Daily Telegraph

Luigi's Italian restaurant opposite Charing Cross Hospital in London offer a 15 percent discount for customers with 30 stitches or more.

The Times

Delia Smith tells Radio Times about her first BBC TV cookery series in 1973. 'There were no facilities. I either had to wash my saucepans in the ladies loo, or in a bucket under the counter.'

Independent

'I noticed that my "vanilla flavour" yoghurt listed 14 added ingredients – not one of which was vanilla.'

Ian Sykes, *The Times*

A pile of tinned baked beans fell on Jim Sullivan, 72, in a store in Warminster, Wilts. He is being given a free tin of beans for every day of the year.

Sun

A couple who complained about a bar of Dairy Milk chocolate in 1959 were sent a replacement bar and offered a guided tour of Cadbury's factory in Bournville, Birmingham.

Arthur and Sheila Carr, of Birtley, Co. Durham, picked up the tour offer in 2003 and, after waiting 44 years, said: 'We were just so busy. Time flies.'

Daily Telegraph

Bassett's Liquorice Allsorts are back in the top-ten best selling confectionery list. The *Daily Mail* celebrated the news with a full page of allsorts about Allsorts:

- Liquorice is the sweetest substance on earth – more than 50 times as sweet as cane sugar.
- When James Bond villain Jaws gnawed his way through a cable car hawser – the hawser was made from braided strands of liquorice.
- When starving Charlie Chaplin ate his boot laces in *The Gold Rush*, the laces he wrapped around his fork like spaghetti were made of liquorice.
- Napoleon was addicted to it. Tutankhamun was buried with it. The majority of it goes to flavour tobacco in the US.

• A 1998 survey found the most effective female aphrodisiac was the aroma produced by blending liquorice and cucumber.

A Northumberland woman saw a TV tip about putting crabs in the fridge for 20 minutes before cooking them. She followed the advice – and the crabs ate ten choc-ices.

Independent on Sunday

A *Times* recipe for wild boar stew involved 21 ingredients, two days' marination and two hours' cooking. Reader Alan Price-Talbot, of Glamorgan, responded: 'I will await the boil-in-the-bag version before pigging out.'

'Fancy a pea starch sandwich?' Headline on a Daily Mail story revealing that chicken sandwiches labelled '100% meat' can include pea starch, maize starch, milk, lactose and dextrose.

'My mother-in-law has a small appetite. In a restaurant in Hastings she asked for a small portion and was told a small portion could be served to an adult only if they were in a wheelchair.'

G N Matthews, Banbury, Oxfordshire, *Daily Mail*

Scientists at Leeds University say that to make perfect toast the bread must be heated to a minimum of 120ºC. Butter must be spread within two minutes of the bread popping up from the toaster (while the temperature is still between 60ºC and 70ºC). Use an amount of butter at least one-seventeenth the thickness of the bread.

The Times

American writer Bill Bryson has not only returned from the US to live in England again – he has been made a commissioner of English Heritage. Elizabeth Grice, writing in the *Daily Telegraph*, calls him 'the outsider who loves us better than we love ourselves', and he told her: 'I come from a part of the world where the Egg McMuffin would be a heritage object.'

A new guide to transport cafés inspired author Kathryn Hughes to take time off from her biography of Mrs Beeton to write about greasy spoon caffs: 'There is a warm, companionable fug that rises to meet you as you step through the door on a late autumn day ... It is real, it is human and it beats anything I know.'

The Times

Winston Churchill's grandson Nicholas Soames (appointed shadow defence secretary in 2003) is described as a man 'with a large frame' in the *Sunday Telegraph* and as 'the Crawley Food Mountain' by Labour MP Tony Banks.

- Mr Soames said he was not on the Atkins diet, but was 'very much in favour of any diet that involves eating large quantities of meat'.
  And he revealed: 'I only gave up hunting when my poor horse Rocky gave up the effort of carting me around. He was magnificent but he couldn't manage it.'

'Easter eggs have been on sale in Potters Bar since Christmas Eve.'

Annette Liston, *Guardian*

'Our Tesco was selling hot cross buns on Boxing Day.'
Barbara Oxley, Cheadle Hume,
Cheshire, *Guardian*

In February 2004 the Food Standards Agency attacked food labels that mislead shoppers. The Sun illustrated this complaint with a list of 'What Labels Really Mean'.

It said that in products claiming to be 'Traditional' the word 'Should Mean: Uses a recipe that has existed for at least 50 years.

'Does Mean: Packed in a traditional-looking jar with a picture of an old lady stuck on the front.'

'The government chose to announce a White Paper on tackling obesity during National Doughnut Week.'
Philip Blenkinsop, Reed, Hertfordshire, *Guardian*

An inquiry into the food provided by the buffet car on the Plymouth to London express was told by a railway catering manager: 'I thought the bacon rolls were not company issue because there was too much bacon and they looked very fresh.'

Independent on Sunday

Chapter 20

Transport:
Keeping Britain Moving

You wait 30 years for a bus stop – then they cancel the bus.

Virgin Trains announcement: 'The buffet will be closed from 12.30 to 1.30 for the staff lunch break.'

Guardian

A year after Rugby railway station was modernised at a cost of £8m it was decided to knock it down as part of a mainline upgrade.

Guardian

Ruth Spurgin writes from Sleaford, Lincolnshire, about the day she gave up her bus seat to an elderly lady: 'The conductor then counted me as one more than the five allowed to stand and promptly turned me off the bus.'

The Times

A lorry carrying 10 tonnes of cheese produced a giant fondue when it caught fire and its load melted on the A44 near Aberystwyth.

Bournemouth Daily Echo

Network Rail managers are to visit Japan to study how they manage to achieve near-perfect punctuality without a fatal crash in 40 years of running their 'bullet' trains. In Japan 15 seconds late is recorded as a delay. In Britain, ten minutes is allowed.

The Times

'I used to travel regularly by train between Bath and Coventry. I was once offered a lift from Birmingham to Coventry, but found that a ticket for the shorter distance between Bath and Birmingham cost more than one for the full journey to Coventry. I pointed this out and asked for my usual ticket to Coventry but was told I couldn't have it because they knew that I wouldn't be using the Birmingham to Coventry part.'

Helen Bratt, Coventry, *Daily Mail*

The government never tires of telling us to use public transport, but spends more than £4,000 a day on taxis – almost £1.5m a year.

Independent on Sunday

Seminars have been organised to teach commuters how to meditate while travelling on the Underground. But when a reporter asked travellers for their reactions one response was: 'Great. You relax, close your eyes and when you open them again your mobile phone and wallet have gone.'

The Times

During the 'Phew What a Scorcher' heatwave in August 2003 the *Daily Mail* reminded London Underground passengers that temperatures in the carriages could exceed 48.5ºC and pointed out that it is illegal to transport cattle in such conditions – but not humans.

And the *Sun* hired a helicopter and sent its 'Heatwave Correspondent' to the top of Ben Nevis to sit in a patch of snow up there.

A Bournemouth bus drove off carrying a three-year-old boy before his mother had time to get on board. She raised the alarm and was told by another driver to telephone lost property.

Daily Mirror

The 6.55 a.m. King's Lynn to London train was running 20 minutes late when the driver announced that he was going to try to make up for lost time. 'Hold your breath,' he said, according to passengers who complained of being terrified by the speeds that followed.

Guardian/Daily Mail

Repair work on a notorious section of road between North and South Wales has begun – six years after temporary traffic lights were installed.

Western Mail

Jim Warnock is the only passenger to use the tiny, unmanned station at Breich in Scotland – commuting daily to his job in Edinburgh. For four years he fought plans to close the station and finally the Strategic Rail Authority agreed to keep it open as long as he continues to use it.

The Times

Barbara Amiel, wife of newspaper magnate Conrad Black, 'protests that she had not availed herself of both her husband's private jets. She made a sacrifice and used only one.'

Andrew Pierce, *The Times*

Headline on *Daily Mail* story: 'You wait 30 years for a bus stop ... and then they cancel the bus'. A £20,000 bus shelter, built of oak and Cornish slate, was unveiled in Menheniot, near Liskeard, in Cornwall in March 2004. But the local bus service was cancelled just before Christmas 2003. The local council said: 'We've been left with egg on our face.'

Chapter 21

Love and Marriage:
From Miss to Mrs.
Is this what bliss is?

Holiday cottage sleeps three. Ideal for honeymoon ...

Sir John Harvey, former chairman of the mighty ICI, says he would never have survived in business without the support of his wife. 'Every day when I went to work she used to pat me on the head and kiss me goodbye and say: 'Off you go and play with your toys.'

Independent

As a joke a Wrexham man put up his wife for sale on the Internet – and was inundated with offers. Bids opened at £1, but the ad was withdrawn after one bidder offered an £8,000 motorcycle plus his own wife.

Daily Express

'Wedding dress size 16 – £75. Worn once. Big mistake.'

Seen in Kettering local paper *Daily Mail*

'Beautiful ivory wedding dress, size 10, never worn due to pregnancy.'

Rugby Observer

A bride sought compensation after claiming that her wedding dress made her look flat chested. She lost – and the Dundee Sheriff explained: 'She wanted a degree of voluptuousness. Unfortunately, she did not have the basic ingredients.

Daily Mirror

A Yorkshireman asked his wife where she would like to be buried. She replied: 'On top o' thee.'

Bernard Breckon, Beverley, Yorkshire, The Times

Mrs Jeanne Brinton wrote to *The Times* saying that the term 'a couple' no longer means 'two'.

Her letter was quickly followed by a letter from Colin Parsons wondering how often she had told her husband she would be ready to go out 'in a couple of minutes'.

And by another, from Jacqui Butt, who supported Mrs Brinton by reporting: 'My husband often visits our local hostelry for "a couple" of pints.'

It remains an unsolved mystery – why men end up with single socks. *Times* readers rushed to join the debate:

- 'My wife tackles the problem of disappearing socks by making me wear unconventional varieties. Funnily enough my Homer Simpson, South Park and Elvis the King socks never go missing. I have to buy longer trousers to cover my embarrassment.' Robin Kempster, Brighouse, West Yorkshire
- 'My husband wears only canary yellow or bright red knee-length woollen socks. When a pair is reduced to one he simply wears one of each colour. Tourists regard him with fascination.' M J Murray, Fayence, France
- 'For a long time I suspected that my wife was having an affair with a one-legged man.' Brian Brass, London NW11

Britney Spears' whirlwind marriage and divorce in January 2004 inspired Ted Evans, of Worthing, East Sussex, to write in the *Independent*: 'It confirms the rumour that Americans like to marry early in the day. If the marriage doesn't work out the whole of the day isn't wasted.'

Ten days after her wedding, a 20-year-old Arbroath bride found her husband in bed with her 44-year-old mother. Divorce followed and then the husband married the mother – with his first wife acting as bridesmaid. Bride No. 1 said: 'He never apologised, but everyone makes mistakes. I've lost a husband, but gained a father.

Independent on Sunday

A man in Wigan was too shy to propose to his girlfriend – so he tucked a note asking her to marry him underneath her pet dog's collar.

Manchester Evening News

A couple aged 79 and 78 cancelled their wedding when they learned that they would lose £100 in benefits if they married. They still went on their 'honeymoon' to the Isle of Wight.

Guardian

To celebrate Brussels dropping a plan to ban sexist jokes, the *Daily Mail* printed a page of sexist jokes submitted by readers Samples:

- Eve told God she was lonely. God said: 'I'll create a man for you to satisfy your physical needs and hunt and gather for you. He will also be proud and arrogant – so you'll have to let him believe that I made him first. That'll be our secret, just between us two girls.'
- Most men define marriage as an expensive way to get laundry done free.

After the vicar and a wedding photographer got involved in a punch-up on Teeside, the newlyweds complained that their big day was ruined.

Independent on Sunday

Advert for a holiday let in Polperro, Cornwall: 'Fishermen's cottages. Sleeping three. Ideal for honeymoon.'

Daily Telegraph

A young couple fell 20ft off the harbour wall at Saundersfoot, South Wales, and had to be rescued from thick mud. They had been hugging each other after the man had proposed.

The Times

A Manchester husband died from a drug overdose after an argument he had with his wife during the TV quiz Test the Nation. She had scored more points than him.

Daily Express

Psychologists have worked out that men and women can shop together for precisely 72 minutes before they start to fight.

Independent

Over 23 years a woman from Tamworth, Staffordshire, married two brothers and lived with a third. She produced two children from the first, a son from the second and three children from the third. 'I never planned to fall in love with all three of them,' she said. 'There are seven brothers in the family – just think how complicated it would be if it had happened with all of them.'

Daily Mail

After their wedding, Adrian Rose and Lindsay Raller decided to paddle to their reception in a canoe rather than ride in a carriage. They were thrown into the sea by a big wave. The *Aberdeen Evening Express* headlined the story: 'With this ring … I thee wet.'

Trevor Beer writes on 'Countryside Matters' in the *Western Morning News* and reminds us that 18 October is St Luke's Day – a good day to choose a husband or to see who it will be. According to legend what you must do is: 'make a mixture of dried marigold flowers, marjoram, thyme and wormwood. Simmer it in virgin honey and white vinegar and rub it on your stomach, breasts and lips before going to bed. During the night your future husband will appear.'

Spotted by Annie Mills of London in the *Guardian's* Marriage Announcements: a GOTCH marrying a HER.

Guardian

Adam and Melanie Redgrave think they bring a whole new meaning to the concept of childhood sweethearts. They first met the day they were born in a Penzance hospital on 12 August 1982 and were in cots next to each other. They married in September 2003 at St Michael's Church in Helston, Cornwall.

Daily Mail

I sent flowers to my wife, dictating this greeting over the phone: 'To Dearest Anne. All my love Brian.' She received the flowers along with a card reading: 'To Dear Stan. All my love Brian.'

The Times

Jayne Cox, 42, of Exmouth, Devon, lost 6 stone before marrying Terry Hughes – 13 years after telling him that she was too fat at 15 stone.

Sun

Growing numbers of bridegrooms are choosing women to be their 'best man'. A best woman is considered to be less likely to organise a stag night that ends up with a plastered groom being tied to a lamp post minus his trousers. She is less likely to deliver a speech revealing the groom's more outrageous bachelor indiscretions. But she must not try to look more pretty than the bride and must not let the bride see her trying on the wedding ring.

The Times

Men have half an hour more free time each day than women and they are likely to spend it watching TV. Women spend 2 hours 30 minutes a day doing housework and cooking. Men spend an hour. Nine in ten lone parents in the UK are women.

From the Office for National Statistics, *Guardian*

Anthony Sampson, writing in the *Spectator*, says the Prime Minister's wife Cherie Blair asked Ted Heath what it was like not having a wife in Number 10. The bachelor former prime minister said he had coped quite well with a staff of 82.

Daily Mail

When a woman won £2,700 on his Radio City show in Liverpool disc jockey Kev Seed said: 'Well done. What are you going to do with it?' Her reply was: 'I'm going to leave that cheating a***hole husband of mine.'

Daily Mirror

Britain is a nation of Do-It-Yourself fanatics. But DIY accidents cause a quarter of a million accidents each year and the *Daily Mail* asked long-suffering wives for their DIY stories. They included:

- Eleanor Yates, 53, of Mickleover, Derbyshire, said: 'Our daughter is now 29, but her playroom still isn't finished.'
- A Bristol wife said: 'We got divorced because he was so bad at DIY.'
- Debbie Monks, 46, of Lancashire, said: 'Our pine doors have taken so long to fit, they've gone out of fashion.'
- Hilary Grist, 32, of Carshalton, Surrey, said: 'We should camp in the garden – it's nicer than the house.'

Chapter 22

Motoring:

Driven to Distraction

Drivers regard it as unlucky to run over nuns ...

Damien O'Keefe, a customer-service rep with a car rental company, got a call from a customer who was stranded on a motorway and needed a tow. He asked for a more detailed description of the car beyond the driver's vague 'a nice blue four door' and was told: 'It's the one on fire.'

Reader's Digest

Scaled-down rubber models of speed cameras are being made so that frustrated motorists can vent their anger by squeezing, kicking or running over them.

Sun

A North Yorkshire man got fed up of fending off motoring fines imposed on his wife for alleged offences committed after she had died. He stormed to his local council's office carrying his wife's ashes in a casket. 'Now do you believe she's dead?' he said.

Daily Mail

Kettleshulme in the Peak District has a sign welcoming careful drivers: 'Please Drive Slowly – Old People Playing.'

Daily Mail

Fifty per cent of all drivers read, write and send text messages while driving. One in three uses a mobile phone. One in ten sends texts and one in five reads or writes at the wheel, says a survey by the Zurich insurance company.

Guardian

Lord Renton, 94 – a motorist long before the driving test was introduced back in the 1930s – has become one of the oldest people to pass the test, reports the *Daily Telegraph*.

'I thought it would be a good idea to brush up my skills,' he said. 'The motor car is such a marvellous invention.' When his family suggested that he might want to practise for the test he told them: 'Don't be stupid.'

A car hire company in Menorca gave us a pamphlet with the following advice listed under Local Customs: 'If you see a motorcyclist raise his left hand this usually means that he is turning right. But take care as the rider may not be local, in which case he may turn left.'

Hugo Wurzer, Andover, Hampshire, *The Times*

A motorist involved in a three-car pile-up near Blackpool told police that he had lost his concentration because he was telling his cockatiel to shut up.

Sunday Times

A senior police officer started a nose-to-tail convoy by accidentally switching on his car roof sign: 'Police. Follow Me.' Motorists driving through Great Totham, Essex, thought he meant them and patiently followed his every move. He has been nicknamed 'the Pied Piper'.

The Times

Britain's drivers top the league in Europe when it comes to making obscene gestures to other drivers. A study found three out of four British motorists admitting giving abusive signals, and the *Sunday Telegraph* reported: 'The stiff middle finger has replaced the stiff upper lip.'

Drivers speeding through Merrymeet, Cornwall, brake hard when they see a policeman aiming a radar gun at them. Only after they have eased back to the limit do they realise that the officer is a scarecrow – known as PC Worzel Gummidge – wearing a toy policeman's hat.

Devon and Cornwall police said they welcomed any reduction in speeding.

Daily Telegraph

'We have got a new car journey game – "Spot the Speed Camera". Each time a child spots one they get 10p. It is a lot cheaper than a £40 fine and keeps the children amused for the whole journey.'

David Harding, Lincoln, *The Times*

The 2003 August heatwave produced temperatures of over 100ºF – and one case of frostbite. Manchester solicitor Mike Ball was diagnosed with the condition after driving 250 miles with his air-conditioning on maximum and directed at his midge-bitten foot.

Guardian

Owners of pink and yellow cars are twice as likely to be victims of road rage as drivers of vehicles in other colours.

RAC survey, *Sunday Telegraph*

A temporary police speed camera on a country road in Hartlepool, Teeside, chalked up £7,500 in three hours (£42 a minute) – catching 125 drivers out of 1,200 at a rate of one every 86 seconds.

Daily Mail

Motorists paid a record £165m in parking fines in 2002. A survey by Privilege Insurance says the country's 32 million drivers are competing for just 2 million car-park spaces – fuelling rebellious parking-rage behaviour. Parking costs are often so high that fines are the cheaper option. Knightsbridge tops the list, where two hours' parking can cost more than £7.

Ceefax

A *Times* reader from Loughborough advised English visitors to Rome that the only safe way to use a pedestrian crossing there is to mingle with a group of nuns. 'Seemingly, Italian drivers regard it as unlucky to run over a nun.'

When West Yorkshire road safety police checked Richard Jeffery's Vauxhall Cavalier they could not find anything wrong – except that his windscreen fluid reservoir was empty and he had a loose battery connection. To his astonishment they gave him a £60 fixed-penalty fine and a three-point endorsement. His protests led to a recommendation that the punishment be withdrawn and replaced by a written caution.

It remains true that Number 34 of the 1986 Construction and Use Regulations makes it a legal obligation to have wipers capable of cleaning the windscreen.

Daily Mail

A motorist in Ipswich got booked for displaying his parking ticket upside down even though the details on the ticket were easily readable.

Daily Telegraph

Joanna James, 28, of Port Talbot, got a speeding ticket claiming she had been clocked on camera doing 480mph in the old Austin Maestro she bought for £100. Her husband, Kenneth, said: 'I am waiting for NASA to ring asking for the engine details.' The South Wales camera company involved blamed a clerical error and issued a new ticket showing 48mph.

Daily Telegraph

Car insurer Admiral says that using lie detectors has led to a quarter of its clients abandoning theft claims.

Sun

'In the late 1950s I owned an Austin A30. When the cylinder-head gasket blew, I purchased a new one for, I think, 7s 6d and, although possessing only a rudimentary knowledge of car engines, fitted it myself and was back on the road in about two hours.

'Recently my present car, a turbo-charged, diesel-engine modern saloon, blew a gasket. Five days later and £325.30 poorer, I was back on the road. Has anyone an Austin A30 for sale?'

Roy Jenkinson, Exmouth, *The Times*

'In the early 1960s we ran an Austin 12. Not only did we fit new gaskets but we made them. Being home-made they blew fairly frequently.

'We still have the car and a new gasket for it is approximately £30. Mr Jenkinson might like to know that a gasket for a Morris Minor of similar vintage to his A30 costs about £3.50.'

Joe Stalker, Wimborne, Dorset, *The Times*

'I bought a lovingly maintained 1964 Morris Traveller. It always starts, runs like a top, gets 45 miles to the gallon, and any part from a single bolt to a complete body is readily and inexpensively obtainable. It's free of road tax, and a paragon of simplicity and, though everyone else whizzes past me, I carry on at a steady 60mph secure in the knowledge that my car is individual and that we'll still be motoring together when most of those other cars are rusting in salvage yards. The one small problem is dealing with the number of people asking if I'd consider selling it.'

Ruth Hopkins-Green, Baldock, Hertfordshire, *The Times*

'My Austin A35 was registered in 1958. Home maintenance was the norm. However, when it began to "burn oil" after 9 years and 90,000 miles-plus, I purchased a reconditioned engine. The total cost was rather high: more than £85. But that included fitting, of course.'

Anthony Jury, Cheltenham, *The Times*

Times reader Mike Gallagher of Salisbury, Wiltshire, tells how he was in collision with a Parcelforce van. No one was hurt and the van driver gave him a card carrying the number of his depot and also this message: 'Parcelforce – Sorry we missed you.'

The Times

The 27-mile M6 toll road, opened in December 2003 to combat congestion in the West Midlands, was built on two-and-a-half million copies of shredded Mills and Boon romance novels. A spokesman said: 'Ironically, the books are renowned for their slushiness but when pulped they help to make the road solid and hold the tarmac and asphalt in place.'

Daily Telegraph

One motorway camera caught 1,000 speeding motorists in a single day at the M4/M5 junction near Bristol – netting £60,000 in fines.

Daily Mail

Lou Clarke, 72, of Yeovil, Somerset, sold his car for £900 and gave the money to a hedgehog sanctuary to compensate for any that he might have squashed during his years of driving.

Sunday Times

A motorist in Durrington noticed smoke coming from the back of his car. Firefighters from Worthing were called and, before long, the car was engulfed in flames.

Worthing Herald

Chapter 23

Afterlife:

Life's a Bitch and then you Die

Man excused jury service because he had died ...

Award-winning novelist, playwright and columnist Keith Waterhouse — whose first job was with a firm of Leeds undertakers – recalls the days when 'somebody in our street died, the body was brought home to lie in state in the front room with all and sundry trooping through the house to pay their respects. "Doesn't he look well?" was a common observation on these occasions.'

A few days later Mrs Heather Rubin, of Manchester, reminded Waterhouse that the inevitable rejoinder to the 'Doesn't he look well' compliment was: 'No, but he should – he's just had a week in Blackpool.'

Daily Mail

A Post Office travel insurance offer includes: 'We will pay you up to £5,000 if you cut short your trip as a result of your death.'

Daily Mail

Part of a junk-mail funeral plan received by *Times* reader Norman Taylor, of Northallerton, North Yorkshire:

The plan will cover the cost of the funeral after the first two years. Within this period, should you die, we will return the premiums paid plus 20 percent from then on you can rest assured that you'll never need to think of your funeral again.

The Times

'The Cemetery of the Year Awards 2004 is relaunching its search for Britain's best burial ground and stiff competition is guaranteed.'

Press release from the Confederation of Burial Authorities – sent to the *Press Gazette* by Alex Millson, news editor of the *Welwyn & Hatfield Times*

Joanna Booth, the widow of a vintage shotgun expert, had her husband's ashes loaded into cartridges and used by friends for the last shoot of the season in Aberdeenshire. The cartridges were blessed by Church of Scotland minister the Rev.

Alistair Donald and accounted for 70 partridges, 23 pheasants, seven ducks and one fox.

Daily Telegraph

The funeral industry held a two-day event at Morpeth, Northumberland, to show how it is changing to meet modern needs. On show were coffins looking like a cricket bag complete with stumps, a huge wine bottle cork complete with bottle opener and a rubbish skip. Also on show – a motorbike-powered hearse.

Daily Mail

The Rev. Paul Sinclair, who runs Britain's only motorcycle hearse, was stopped by police because the vicar was not wearing a crash helmet. Mr Sinclair, 37, was on his way to a funeral at Yeovil crematorium in Dorset, with the coffin in his sidecar hearse. The funeral director was riding pillion wearing tails – but no helmet.

The Times

A Devon artist offers to paint the portraits of people who have been cremated – using their ashes. The service is described as providing unique memorials.

Basildon Echo

Increasing rates of obesity in Britain are causing crematoria to struggle with the growing problem of outsize coffins. Besides bigger ovens, other improvements are required, such as sturdier trolleys.

The Times

War veteran George O'Key was shocked to find his name on a war memorial in his home town, Middlesbrough. George, 83, said: 'All these years I have been wandering around the town while it listed me as dead.'

Sunday Times

The death of Bob Hope, aged 100, in July 2003, made front-page news around the world.

In Eltham, South London, where he was born, locals were quoted as saying: 'He has done well for an Eltham boy. We don't have a lot of famous residents.'

The Times

In January 2003 a warden in Leith, Scotland, booked a hearse when it was parked on yellow lines while funeral directors went to fetch a coffin.

Daily Mail

In Newent, Gloucestershire, a woman took basket-weaving lessons so that she could make a wicker coffin for herself.

Gloucester Citizen

A Cambridge man had his dying wish fulfilled – by arranging for his coffin to be driven at 70mph on a motorway journey to the cemetery.

Cambridge Weekly News

'After my husband died a summons for him to do jury service arrived. I notified the court of his death and got another letter addressed to him saying: "You have been permanently excused jury duty based on documentation indicating your permanent incapacity to serve."'

Barbara Muskin, *Reader's Digest*

The BBC compiled a list of 50 Things To Do Before You Die – compiled from a survey involving 20,000 Britons. High on the list were: dive with sharks, climb Sydney Harbour Bridge, travel into space, go wing walking, gamble in Las Vegas.

Independent

Edward Box and his brother Andrew are the sixth generation of the funereal Boxes who have run a funeral company in Dewsbury, Yorkshire, for 150 years. He recalls 'a chap with a weird sense of humour who asked us not to tell anybody which tune he had asked to be played at the crematorium. It was "Blaze Away".'

Yorkshire Post

Parking wardens had to flee when 200 mourners emerged from a baby's funeral and found them issuing tickets. A clergyman and the funeral director intervened and the wardens agreed to leave. The Rev. David Foster, of St Andrew's Church, High Wycombe, said: 'Emotions ran high.'

Daily Mail

Undertakers in Southampton got an overtime bill for £185. It was for gravediggers who had been kept waiting because mourners spent too long at the cemetery.

Sun/Sunday Telegraph

Jo Dean, of Cheltenham, wrote to *The Times* that at the age of 90 her mother took out a funeral plan and specified that she wanted cremation. She got a letter of confirmation which also offered her 'a very warm welcome'.

'My mother says she can't wait,' comments Jo.

Regulars at the Church Inn, Uppermill, near Oldham, can make sure they stay close to their local when they die. Landlord Julian Taylor has turned a field at the back of the pub into a cemetery and customers are putting their names down for a plot. One of them has asked fellow drinkers to pop into the cemetery with their pints on Friday nights after he dies.

Daily Telegraph/Daily Mail/Guardian

The local council has told a Solihull couple to remove the headstone from their 11-year-old daughter's grave – because it is an inch above the cemetery regulation of 8 inches.

Daily Express

Above a sign pointing to the mortuary at the Rotherham District General Hospital there is another which reads: 'Dead Slow.'

Lee Price, Brough, East Yorkshire,
Daily Mail

A man who was given out lbw in a cricket match in a Berkshire village died from a heart attack as he left the wicket. His last words were: 'I was never out.'

Daily Mail/Sunday Telegraph

A lifestyle questionnaire that can determine how long people will live has been developed by a university professor. The questionnaire is based on an average life expectancy of 79. Questions include:

- Do you have a sense of humour? If Yes add three years. If No subtract three years.
- Are you always going on and off diets? Subtract five years.
- Do you own a pet? If a dog or a cat, etc. add two years. One year for a passive pet, fish, etc.

- Are you in love? Add seven years.
- Are you a smoker? Subtract seven years.

Daily Telegraph

Having printed the above story straight on its page 9 news page, the Telegraph then says this in its page 27 leader:

'It's all tosh, of course ... Smokers don't have to be great mathematicians to work out that all the ill effects of their vice can be cancelled out by simply falling in love – and then buying a goldfish.'

Chapter 24

Army Life:
Barmy Army

**Dad's Army inspect knickers of female residents
for signs of enemy ...**

Officer cadets at Llandrindod Wells were told:
'You have been sent here to be trained into officers
and gentlemen. There is time only to turn some of
you into officers.'

The Times

**'I remember the wartime headline: "Eighth Army push
bottles up Germans."'**

Jonathan Cheal, Beckington,
Somerset, *Daily Telegraph*

'My favourite wartime newspaper headline: "MacArthur flies back to front."'

Daily Telegraph

During the Dunkirk retreat Major General Lord Burnham encountered his son on the beach. He greeted him with: 'I see you failed to shave this morning.'

W F Deedes in the *Daily Telegraph*

'I still shave every morning using the rear-view mirror of the last Spitfire I flew in World War II.'

Jack Feeney, Plymouth, *Guardian*

Spotted on a website: 'On this day in 1953 Sir Winston Churchill was educated at Harrow and at Sandhurst after which he saw service in India and the Sudan, and acted off-duty as a war correspondent.'

The Sunday Times, under the strapline: 'Busy schedule'

After serving in the Iraq campaign a sailor returned home to Edinburgh to find that a neighbour had started legal proceedings against him for not paying towards the cost of mowing a communal lawn.

Guardian

Some British troops in the Gulf only received their desert boots after the fall of Baghdad.

Daily Telegraph

Trooper Christopher Finney became the youngest soldier ever to be awarded the George Cross (second only to the Victoria Cross). He was 18 and in Iraq when 'he displayed clear-headed courage out of all proportion to his age and experience ... acting with complete disregard for his own safety even when wounded. His bravery was of the highest order throughout.'

After the Queen pinned the medal to his Blues and Royal tunic the lifesaving young hero said: 'I thought all I would get would be a pat on the back and a "Well done, mate."'

Daily Telegraph

To mark his 90th birthday, the *Daily Telegraph* recorded some of the highlights of its legendary former editor W F Deedes (still writing for them in 2003).

During World War II the King's Royal Rifle Corps company he commanded was caught in terrible enemy machine-gun and mortar fire. Brigade ordered them back, but Deedes would not pull out until he got the wounded to safety. He was awarded the Military Cross and said: 'I got the MC for retreating, imagine that.'

Daily Telegraph

Mary Swinger of Nether Row, Thetford, Norfolk, remembers when, during World War II, the Home Guard came around wanting to inspect the knickers of female residents. 'Dad's Army' was doggedly on the track of a man selling underwear made from parachute material and needed to determine whether it had belonged to the enemy.

Independent

Chapter 25

Christmas:

Let Nothing you Dismay

**Christmas mince pies labelled 'Best before
November 17'**

Merry Christmas. Many Britons would rather go to
the dentist than go Christmas shopping.

A Royal Mail survey reveals that Christmas
shopping can induce one or more of the following
symptoms: headaches, sleeplessness, feeling faint,
tears, stomach ache, dizziness, claustrophobia,
irritability or loss of temper. More than 5 million
men do no Christmas shopping at all. Three-fifths
of women spend more than five days at it.

The Times

David McNickle, of St Albans, Hertfordshire, wrote about the frenzy of Christmas and suggested '... a law to stop us going crazy at this time of year. From now on Christmas should come with a Sanity Clause.'

Independent

Five-year-old Lucie told researchers that she knows three wise men brought presents for Jesus because she saw it on a video. Another five-year-old said the presents were gold, frankenstein and bronze. Lucie said: 'I think Jesus would have preferred toys.'

Daily Mail

Suspects wanted on warrant are being sent Christmas cards by West Midlands police saying: 'Give yourselves up or face the festive season in a cell.'

Guardian

Margaret Richey, a former teacher from Tiverton, Devon, has had the same 3ft artificial Christmas tree for 67 years. She even takes it on trips abroad.

Sun

Researchers say that the average Brit tucks into 10,000 calories on Christmas Day.

News of the World

Christmas comes with a government warning. The 2002 festive season put some 8,000 in hospital following accidents involving Christmas trees, fairy lights, hanging decorations, swallowing coins in Christmas puddings, tripping over games consoles' wiring. 'It's a dangerous time of year,' says the DTI.

News of the World

In order to get airborne, Father Christmas's reindeer would need wings 10m (33ft) long according to the calculations of Paolo Viscardi, a flight physiologist at the University of Leeds. He worked out that Rudolph & Co would need a total wing area of at least 9 sq m (97 sq ft).

Guardian

'Festively packaged Christmas Mince Pies in Tesco were marked: "Best Before November 17."'

Ron Dawson, Dorset, *Independent*

Henry Christmas has spent almost 50 years researching his ancestors – and come up with 10,000 people who share his surname. He traced his own roots back more than 400 years to yeoman Thomas Christmas from Hampshire who died in 1589. The family tree he has created is 24ft long.

Sun

Ever heard of Snow White and the FIVE Dwarves?
There were so many Snow White pantos in the
2003–04 season that there was a severe shortage of
dwarf actors. Some productions had to make do
with five.

The Times

The Rev. Peter Ramsden of The Vicarage, Benton,
Newcastle upon Tyne, reported an easy way of getting
round the problem. He wrote to the *Times* to say that St
Bartholomew's Parish Church produced 'Snow White
and the Beanstalk'.

Times reader Jasper Winn, of Cork, had a solution:
'Look for extremely tall Snow Whites rather than seven
times as many very small people.'

Leslie Freitag, of Harpenden, Hertfordshire, came
up with a scheme for escaping Christmas Day
altogether: 'Fly from Heathrow to San Francisco on
Christmas Eve. Plane refuels and goes on to New
Zealand. Just as Christmas Day is bearing down on
you the plane crosses the International Date Line
and you are into Boxing Day.'

Guardian

Forget the turkey. In parts of the Outer Hebrides the
Christmas bird of choice is the guga (or baby gannet).
This unusual festive seabird is a highly prized delicacy
and some are sent around the world to expatriates.

Traditionally eaten with boiled potatoes and no trimmings, preparation involves scrubbing off the salt and soaking overnight. Old hands suggest cooking the guga outdoors 'because of the dreadful smell'. It is said to taste like a cross between duck and mackerel.

Daily Telegraph

Barnsley council banned lollipop lady Pam Bowen, 54, from putting tinsel on her STOP sign – even though she has been doing it at Christmas time for 20 years. The council said: 'The sign carried by School Crossing Patrols is prescribed by an Act of Parliament. To change it in any way makes it illegal.'

Sun

Tony Vaughan, 27, says he was shunned by workmates who made him sit near a window. He is Tesco's chief sprout tester and had to eat five kilos a week of the windy vegetable in the run-up to Christmas.

Sunday Times

'For some people queuing for the post-Christmas sales has become a ritual. They go for the camaraderie, the sheer bravado of sleeping in frost-resistant sleeping bags, heating up soups on a small portable stove and getting up at 6 a.m. to grab a purple jumper reduced from £50 to £30.'

Lucia van der Post, *The Times*

A survey revealed that one of the reasons why pubs are so popular at Christmas is that people go to bars to escape the in-laws.

Sun

Receiving a Christmas card with a robin on it is a sign of something nasty to come according to the *Penguin Guide to the Superstitions of Britain and Ireland*. But wearing a spider in a bag around your neck until it dies will bring good luck.

Daily Mail

Nurses in Plymouth saved £900 in gifts from patients to pay for a Christmas party. Then the Inland Revenue demanded backdated tax on the gifts. They ended up £44 in the red.

Daily Express/Sunday Telegraph

Carol singers in Gosport, Hampshire, sang 'We Wish You a Merry Christmas' to the accompaniment of the tune on their mobile phone.

Sunday Times quoting a letter to *The Times*

The three-year-old daughter of Joan Blackhall, of Sudbury, Suffolk, realised that the Father Christmas who brought her presents was her dad because '... he trod on the electric blanket plug and said "Sod it". Father Christmas would never swear.'

Daily Mail

Traffic police in Kent celebrated Christmas 2003 by sending out advent calendars featuring 24 speed cameras.

News of the World

Chapter 26

Odds and Sods

Battery-driven pepper grinder with a light for grinding in the dark ...

Commenting on a complaint from a Mr Arthur Purdey about a large gas bill, a spokesman for North West Gas said: 'We agree it was rather high for the time of year. It's possible Mr Purdey has been charged for the gas used up during the explosion that destroyed his house.'

Daily Telegraph/BBC News Quiz

Roger Bateman, 69, of Llanelli in Wales, got a gas bill for £0.00 – along with a threat to cut him off if he didn't settle up.

Sun

At the height of a gale, the harbour master radioed a coastguard and asked him to estimate the wind speed. He replied he was sorry, but he didn't have a gauge. However, if it was any help, the wind had just blown his Land Rover off the cliff.

Aberdeen Evening Express/BBC News Quiz

'My friend's four-year-old girl announced very loudly at the ballet: "Look, Mum, that man is hiding his sweeties where I hide mine."'

Mrs S Smith, Uxbridge, *Daily Mail*

George Bernard Shaw cabled Winston Churchill: 'Have reserved two tickets for my first night. Bring a friend if you have one.' Churchill replied: 'Impossible to come first night. Will come second night if you have one.'

Reader's Digest

A woman trying to dry her bra in the microwave caused a kitchen fire in Morden, south London.

Wimbledon Guardian

A Tesco survey found that 72 percent of men rated their shopping trolley pushing skills as excellent while only 60 percent of women awarded themselves high marks.

The Times

When he was at his Shakespearean best the late Richard Harris received a letter saying: 'My wife and I go to the theatre about once a year and this year we decided to see you in *Henry IV*. We very much looked forward to it, but the evening was completely ruined for us when you broke wind just before your first entrance.'

Daily Express

In a Mother's Union survey 23.2 percent chose Marge from the dysfunctional Simpson family as a good role model for mothers. She came in well ahead of Prime Minister's wife Cherie Blair.

The Times

Whenever I feel I am being ripped off – I buy shares in the company involved. My investment in Nokia has more than paid for all my mobile phones and bills.

Christopher Robinson, London W1,
Daily Telegraph

'Our younger daughter spent £60 on text messages in one month – mainly to a girl in the next bedroom at school asking if she was ready to go to breakfast.'

Amanda Douglas, Kelso, *The Times*

The Markou family of London use their mobiles to communicate with each other inside their own house. Jill Markou says that when her son's friends visit she rings him 'to say they're here. Often they ring him themselves and he rings me to let them in. It's a big house and he's right at the top.' Mobiles, she says, are 'just so much a part of life you wonder how you ever managed without them'.

Daily Telegraph

'Returning from a holiday in Morocco, where I had bargained for a carpet, I declared it at Customs. They told me I had overpaid so much they did not feel able to charge me tax on top. I have hated the carpet ever since.'

Sarah-Jane Kitching, London SW, *Daily Telegraph*

Former Liberal MP Sir Clement Freud used to amuse friends by showing them a valuable-looking fob watch and saying: 'It belonged to my grandfather [Sigmund Freud]. He sold it to me on his deathbed.'

Daily Mail

An index of the world's most expensive signatures revealed the following prices:
The Beatles £12,500, Adolf Hitler £6,000, Winston Churchill and Marilyn Monroe £4,950.

The Times

A journalist asked British astronomer Sir Arthur Eddington if it was true that he was one of only three people who could understand Einstein's theory. Sir

Arthur concentrated for a long while before replying: 'I am trying to think who the third person is.'

The *Mail on Sunday* review of Bill Bryson's book
A Short History of Nearly Everything

Some of Britain's laziest people have been prodded into action in a search for the worst place to live in the UK. Hull was an early leader in the contest, organised by a magazine for the lazy called *The Idler*.

The Times

Action Man dolls that can BURP are to go on sale.

Sun

Mrs Joan Webb of Stowmarket, Suffolk, remembers that when her brother was a little boy he was told that Auntie Gertie's name was really Gertrude. The little chap then asked: 'So is Auntie Beattie's name really Beetroot?'

Daily Mail

Villages competing in the 2003 Britain in Bloom contest admitted shipping in hundreds of plants for the day of the judging – then shipping them out next day.

The Times

It is possible that an asteroid will strike Earth on 21 March 2014 with a force 8 million times more powerful than the Hiroshima atom bomb – but the odds against it are 909,000 to 1.

Independent

The odds against being killed in a road accident are one in 8,000 and against being injured in a game of tennis, water-skiing or surfboarding are one in 500.

The Times

Nudists have complained that they were sprayed with weedkiller while sunbathing on a Dorset beach.

Dorset Evening Echo

Caravan fans Mike and Josie Chapman, both 49, travelled to their favourite site for their holidays – only a few hundred yards from their home in Wimblington, Cambridgeshire.

Sun

Excavations for the Channel Tunnel rail link at Stratford East reveal that the East End of London was once a sub-tropical oyster bed bathed in warm seawater in an area dotted with palms. There were also 6ft sharks – 55.5 million years ago,

The Times/Daily Telegraph

It is one of the more bizarre events in Britain's horticultural calendar – the Giant Vegetables Championship at Shepton Mallet, Somerset. The 2003 show was stolen by a 590lb pumpkin – equal to the weight of three men. Its grower, Mark Raymont, from St Merryn, Cornwall, needed a forklift truck to get it to the show. King of the cabbages was a 5ft-wide specimen weighing 57lb 12oz.

Daily Mail

Southend Museum looked forward to having an exciting new exhibit after the reported finding of a 20,000-year-old woolly mammoth tusk in a garden at Leigh-on-Sea, Essex. An excavation was planned but the find turned out to be a 120-year-old clay drainpipe.

The Times

More than £3.2bn has been spent on gadgets that have no better use than taking up cupboard space according to research published by the home insurance group Esure.

Top of the unused gadgets list is the sandwich maker, followed closely by the electric knife, the foot spa, the fondue set, the ice-cream maker, pasta makers and bread machines.

Daily Telegraph

Meanwhile, that bible of the gadget-obsessed, the *Innovations Catalogue*, has been scrapped after its publishers said it was no longer a viable concern. Now, 'the nation mourns the passing of the means to buy things like the electric tie rack, the motorised spider catcher and the potato-powered clock.' But website surfers can still find a battery-driven pepper mill with a handy light for when you need pepper in the dark.

Independent

Cherie Blair's latest hostess, Italian socialite Carla Powell, has a battery-driven pepper mill with electric lights for use in the dark. It was a gift from Ronald Reagan and bears the seal of the President of the United States.

Daily Mail

Sir Michael Caine is quoted as saying that he refuses to open any mail that is not addressed to him as 'Sir Michael'. 'I just feel that if they don't put "Sir" on the envelope, they don't know anything about me, so why should I open the letter?'

Independent

'A switchboard operator had difficulty catching my name when I wanted to leave a message for a colleague. Eventually, I said: "Noah, as in ark." When

my colleague called back he gleefully noted that the message read: "Dr Noah Asinarc rang."'

Professor Norman Noah, *The Times*

A Swiss doctor of philosophy who hopes to find the laughter capital of Europe chose Aberdeen – a city famed for its dour dispositions – for the first leg of his tour.

'Aberdeen has been a difficult case,' he said after a morning of parading in the city with his wife, dressed in red and orange wigs and exotic glasses.

The Times

In reporting the academic's admission that 90 percent of the people he met in the granite city had shown no inclination to laugh, *The Times* could not resist retelling a celebrated tale from the 1920s:

A party on a motoring holiday in Scotland asked a local urchin:
'What town is this?'
'I'll tell ye if ye give me saxpence.'
'Move on driver, we're in Aberdeen.'

Noël Coward wrote to one of his critics: 'Sir, I am seated in the smallest room in the house. Your review is in front of me. In a moment it will be behind me.'

Independent

Halfway through David Blaine's attempt to starve for 44 days the *News of the World* got a sample of his urine. Tests on the sample proved that Blaine really was going without food and the newspaper claimed it had settled 'the question which was gripping the nation'. It ran a leader saying: 'It just goes to show that all the best stories are leaked to the *News of the World*.'

The hair of P&O cruise passengers turned bright green when they swam in the liner's pool. They were given free hairdos.

Daily Express

A study by Lloyds TSB Private Banking reported that the rich make every penny count when it comes to loyalty cards and haggling. Rich people are much more likely to haggle over purchases while just a third of the general population dare to barter.

Daily Telegraph

A Liverpool museum is planning to put on a display of six guns owned by hip-swiveller Elvis Presley. Museum director Jerry Goldman says: 'We've heard of Elvis watching television and shooting the screen out if he didn't like the programme. But he also used to shoot at his cars if they failed to start and to shoot squirrels from the comfort of his toilet seat.'

Independent on Sunday

The tiny Scottish village of Lonmay in north-east Scotland is all shook up over claims that it is the ancestral home of Elvis Presley. A Scottish author says the King's great-great-great-great-great-great grandfather was married in the village 300 years ago. Villagers hope fans will flock to their Aberdeenshire hamlet, but the Elvis Presley Fan Club of Great Britain points out that: 'There have been claims that Elvis was Welsh, Scottish, half-Indian, Nordic, Icelandic and even African.'

Times/Independent

A young couple searching for a house in the country paid £7 for a 100-year-old postcard showing a delightful thatched cottage. The same day they accidentally came across the cottage pictured on the postcard in Charminster, Dorset. It was up for sale. They sold their Islington flat and bought their dream cottage for £250,000.

Daily Mail

The Sultan of Oman, who has no known Scottish blood, has ordered his own tartan. Oman has a long-standing love affair with things Scottish and boasts one of the world's more military musical ensembles – the Royal Omani Mounted Police Camel Pipe Band.

The Times

Sixteen suspected illegal immigrants were arrested when they climbed off the back of a lorry in Basingstoke. They were held at the police station – and then given maps showing them the way to the offices of the Immigration and Nationality Directorate – 40 miles away in Croydon. The Home Office refused to say whether any of them ever turned up.

Daily Telegraph

A row developed over America sending allegedly polluted old ships to Hartlepool to be dismantled. It prompted Alan Spicker of Durham to write to the *Daily Telegraph*: 'I should have thought that the ships are in such a bad state that they are unlikely to suffer any extra pollution from being berthed on Teeside.'

Angry Scots have forced European bureaucrats to back down over a decision to classify the kilt as 'women's wear'. Scottish manufacturers reacted strongly to an EU questionnaire that asked them to fill in how many kilts they had sold in the space provided for women's skirts. The dispute flared on to the front page of the Glasgow based *Daily Record*, bringing condemnation from the likes of Sean Connery.

Independent

Margaret Ezell's baby was born at 1.57 a.m. Her twin Emily had her baby 28 minutes later.

But, it is being argued, Emily's baby is older than Margaret's. The babies were born on the Sunday that clocks were put back an hour at 2 a.m. – making Emily's birth time 1.25 a.m – 32 minutes before her sister's.

Independent on Sunday

Barclaycard makes £450m a year from those who borrow on their Barclay credit cards.

Matt Barrett, chief executive of Barclays, admitted that he would never borrow on a credit card because it was too expensive. He has advised his children to follow his example.

The Times

Following reports that high interest rates on retail store cards were to be investigated by the Competition Commission, the *Sun* revealed that it would take ten years to repay £500 borrowed on a store card if you make only the minimum monthly payment.

Visitors to the giant Ferris wheel erected in November 2003 in central Birmingham found that the accompanying commentary was in French. It told them they were looking out over the Arc de Triomphe and the Eiffel Tower when in fact they were gazing down on Smethwick.

The 197ft wheel had been brought over from

France – but technical difficulties got in the way of replacing the commentary on Paris with one on the mighty Midlands city.

Daily Telegraph

Barnsley factory worker Mick Henry, 60, discovered that he had a brother and sister called Sitting Eagle and Thunder Woman. He visited them on their Red Indian reservation in Canada and learned that his dad had been chief of the Ojibwy people. The chief had died – making Mick the head of the tribe.

Sun

Ronnie Scott's jazz club had its drawbacks in the early years. George Melly remembers how the club was run: 'without airs or graces or even basic amenities like a toilet ... most of us used the washbasin in the dressing room.'

George said on a BBC Radio 3 programme: 'I once told the audience everybody used the washbasin ... with the possible exception of Ella Fitzgerald.'

The Times

The statue of Brunel has been moved from the main concourse of Paddington Station, which he designed. *Guardian* reader Kay Hyman points out that the concourse is now presided over by the station's other genius loci, Paddington Bear.

Wacky Wagers for 2004. William Hill opened a book on intelligent aliens being found in space (100/1) and the Second Coming of Christ (1,000/1).

Sun

The sale of garden gnomes is in decline, but manufacturers hope to make them popular again by replacing their fishing rods with mobiles and laptops.

Daily Mail

Scientists researching the best way to ventilate office buildings have come up with a radical solution – open the windows.

Financial Times

A woman reader wrote to *The Times* about the way that, as a child, she had to wear those 'wretched ringlets' made popular by Shirley Temple. Letters of sympathy followed, particularly one on 5 January 2004 which read: 'I wore them from 1936 to 1939. Photographs of me, aged five, still amuse my children and horrify my grandchildren. I remain, Sir, now happily bald.'

A Times reader was told that smoke bombs used for clearing gardens of moles cannot be bought in the UK because of EU rules. But some friends brought some over from France and they did the job. The reader signs off: 'Could we please join the French EU? I'm sick of the British one.'

The Times

This was followed by another saying: 'I have found that eviscerating musical Christmas and birthday cards and inserting the active ingredient into the mole run is effective ... I do wonder, though, whether exposure to Postman Pat is more or less humane than mothballs.'

The Times

American actress Alyson Hannigan, on visiting London: 'It's like a history book. You have all these buildings that were built before 1980.'

Sunday Times

Gerry Ranger, 68, of Stratton, Gloucestershire, saved all his junk mail for a year and ended up with a pile of 701 unwanted brochures and letters – 3ft high and weighing 70lb.

News of the World

Commenting on a report that John Major's autobiography ranks only 53,609th on the Amazon bestseller list, Professor David Stevenson writes that the former prime minister should be congratulated. 'A book edited by my wife and me (*Scottish Texts and Calendars*) ranks 1,170,808th. We take a perverse pride in this.'

The Times

A total of 131 million copies of the Ikea catalogue were printed in 45 editions and 23 languages in 2003. Its circulation is bigger than that of the Bible.

In the early 1990s one in ten Europeans was conceived on an Ikea bed.

Linda Dagless, of Norwich, named her baby Ikea.

The Times

A Swansea woman was banned from her local supermarket for approaching the checkout with the trolley the 'wrong' way round.

Independent on Sunday

People who live under the Gatwick Airport flight path are angry about the Emirates airline treating passengers to live film shows of the countryside below. Said one of them: 'I sunbathe and don't like being shown to strangers.'

Daily Express

Traditionalists will be cheered that the old-fashioned English rose still reigns supreme in the affections of gardeners. It topped a *Country Life* survey. But non-traditional roses – hybrid tea and floribunda – were voted second least liked.

Guardian

All the men are either bastards or wimps. The women are heroically struggling to tolerate the men. Any ethnic character is a model of rectitude and beautiful or handsome. No white character may criticise a black or Asian character. No one may make sustained criticism of any gay character. Welcome to 'The Archers – An Everyday Story of Country Folk' as described by Ian Philip (a Londoner).

Sunday Telegraph

Sir Anthony Hopkins tells the story of Alec Guinness, Laurence Olivier and John Gielgud being photographed together outside the BBC. A child spectator said: 'Look – there's that geezer from *Star Wars*.' Sir Alec said: 'So much for professionalism and great acting.'

Independent

Bonnybridge in Stirlingshire has been named UFO capital of the UK. There have been 60,000 sightings of flying saucers reported there.

The Times

The publishers would like to acknowledge the following organisations and publications

Aberdeen Evening Express, Aberdeen Press and Journal, Avon and Somerset Police website, Basildon Echo, Bournemouth Echo, Brecon and Radnor Express and Powys County Times, Brighton Evening Argus, Bucks Free Press, Cambridge Weekly News, Ceefax, Churchtown Parish Magazine, County Times, Crewe Chronicle, Cumberland News, Daily Express, Daily Mail, Daily Telegraph, Derby Evening Telegraph, Dorset Echo, Dundee Evening Telegraph, Evening Standard, Exeter Express and Echo, Express and Star, Financial Times, Focus technology magazine, Gloucester Citizen, Guardian, Halifax Evening Courier, Hartlepool Mail, Hastings Observer, Henley Standard, Herald and Post, Independent, Independent on Sunday, Kent Messenger, Lincolnshire Free Press, Littlehampton Gazette, Manchester Evening News, Manchester Metro News, National Geographic News, News of the World, North West Evening Mail, Norwich Evening News, Observer, Press Gazette, Reader's Digest, Romford Recorder, Rugby Observer, Scarborough Evening News, Scotsman, Sheffield Star, Shropshire Star, Soldier Magazine, South Wales Evening Post, Sun, Sunday Express, Sunday Independent (Plymouth), Sunday Mercury, Sunday

Telegraph, Sunday Times, Sussex Express, Telegraph and Argus, Teletext, the BBC, The Economist, The Herald (Glasgow), the magazine of the parish of Collingham-with-Harwood, The Times, Warrington Guardian, Western Mail, Western Morning News, West Highland Free Press, Wiltshire Times, Wimbledon Guardian, Worthing Herald, York Evening Press, York Star, Yorkshire Evening Post

ALL
THE
LONELY
PEOPLE

David Owen

ATOM

First published in Great Britain in 2019 by Atom

1 3 5 7 9 10 8 6 4 2

Copyright © 2019 by David Owen

The moral right of the author has been asserted.

A CIP catalogue record for this book
is available from the British Library.

ISBN 978-0-349-00320-7

Printed and bound in Great Britain by Clays Ltd, Elcograf S.p.A.

Papers used by Atom are from well-managed forests
and other responsible sources.

Atom
An imprint of
Little, Brown Book Group
Carmelite House
50 Victoria Embankment
London EC4Y 0DZ

An Hachette UK Company
www.hachette.co.uk

www.atombooks.co.uk

David Owen resents the fact that he was not raised by wolves and was therefore robbed of a good story to tell at parties. He turned to fiction to compensate for his unremarkable existence. He studied creative writing at The University of Winchester, where he went on to teach for three years. David is the author of two novels: *Panther* (2015), which was longlisted for the Carnegie Medal, and *The Fallen Children* (2017). David works in the travel industry, and mostly thinks about biscuits.

ALSO BY DAVID OWEN

Panther

The Fallen Children

For Hannah,
who is verr good.

I woke up and I had a big idea,
to buy a new soul at the start of every year.
I paid up, and it cost me pretty dear.
Here's a hymn to those that disappear.

— 'Buying New Soul', Porcupine Tree

I think this is why loneliness is a darker thing
than just being alone. It's a stillness that gives you
a preview of death; it's seeing the world carry on
just fine without you in it.

— Hayley Campbell

You're ridiculous, and men's rights is nothing.

— Leslie Knope

1

A Cure for Empathy

The photos transferred in a handful of seconds, morsels of naked flesh flickering across the progress bar as the three boys shielded the screen with their bodies. Every tab open in the browser was a weapon, armed, the images their ammunition. Target locked.

It seemed funny, that exposure could wipe somebody out of existence.

Wesley Graham couldn't stop jiggling his legs – nerves, excitement, he didn't know – as he glanced around at the half-empty study room, squinting against the early autumn sunshine that glowed in the scratches and finger-smears on the windows. Most of the school PCs were occupied, screens of half-finished essays or YouTube videos. Others in their class, apparently taking the final year of school seriously, had ranged their burden of early coursework across the tables in the centre of the room. Mr Buttercliff, charged with supervising, was much more invested in *Clash of Clans* on his phone.

'Can you *please* stop that?' said Luke, punching Wesley's leg.

The dull pain did little to help him hold it still. Although Wesley had been around during the last trolling campaign, one undoubtedly larger than this, he had been little more than a spectator. This time he was on the front line. They had somebody to impress, so this had to go off without a hitch. He willed his restless leg to stop betraying his gut full of nerves.

In the far corner of the room, hunched over her MacBook, was Kat Waldgrave. It was the first time they'd seen her in school for a few days, and her usual ponytail had gained a strand of plasticky pink that curled into the light brown skin of her neck. The sunlight conspired to hide her screen from Wesley's gaze, but he was sure her website would be open in a tab somewhere, just as it was on their screen.

'Imagine if she actually looked like this,' said Justin, sandwiched between them in front of the computer.

Luke plucked a USB stick from the PC and grinned. 'We'll always have Photoshop.'

Scrolling through the images, Justin sighed under his breath. 'I wish any actual girl looked like this.'

'Sounds like somebody's struggling with NoFap,' said Wesley.

The joke was a risk. They hadn't been friends for long, and sometimes it took a while to earn the right to take the piss.

'No way!' said Justin, apparently not offended despite his protest. 'It's been three weeks and I swear my mind is clearer than it's—'

'*Please* don't start with that again.' Luke brought up the login window for Kat's site and typed in the password that had been stolen for them.

'How long's it going to take?' said Wesley, pressing his fists into his knees to keep them from bouncing. The Photoshopped pornography had been his idea, and he had felt elated when it was accepted. That had been tempered a little since by the reality of doing it, the fear of getting caught, but he still couldn't wait to deal this final blow. People like Kat deserved everything they got – that's what TrumourPixel said.

'Not long,' said Luke, clicking to edit the home page. 'Let's give our snowflake something worth crying about.'

Kat Waldgrave was only at school because of the email she'd received complaining that she rarely went to school. It was an injustice, as far as she was concerned, that a mandatory attendance meeting should be allowed to upset her regular schedule of pretending to revise while actually watching Tinker videos and *Doctor Backwash* bloopers on YouTube. As if she hadn't seen them all a million times before.

She tabbed to one of her favourites, putting in her earphones and angling the screen away from the window glare. Tinker showing off her new hairstyle, a neat bob dyed electric pink, dusky eye shadow applied to match. God damn, she was beautiful. Kat fiddled with the pink extension she had added to her own hair yesterday. It was supposed to be a tribute to Tinker, borrowing a little of her boldness, but now it just felt pathetic.

The meeting had not gone well. Despite her being head of sixth form, Miss Jalloh's office was the size of a bus shelter, and smelled even worse. Kat would gladly have not attended her attendance meeting, except the email had threatened to get in touch with her dad. A phone call from school would certainly contravene their unspoken accord to keep their lives as separate as possible.

'Your attendance is nowhere near acceptable,' had been Miss Jalloh's opening line, peering over her half-moon glasses.

The word *attendance* had begun to lose all meaning. 'I still did fine in my exams,' Kat pointed out. It was true too – nothing below a B grade in her mocks.

'That's hardly the point!' The bangles on Miss Jalloh's wrists rattled as she slapped her hands on the desk, living up to her reputation for being *expressive*. 'Everybody knows you're a bright girl.'

That was funny; as far as Kat could tell everybody hardly knew she existed.

Tinker had started out recording make-up tutorials – perfectly shaped eyebrows were her trademark – before moving on to discuss topics such as sexuality and feminism. She identified as pansexual, and was so open about everything it meant for her, posting regular videos on the impact it had on her dating and sex life. These were all mysteries to Kat, abstract ideas, and it was easy enough to pretend Tinker's life was her own. Pretend these regular updates fleshed her out with experience. In between those personal videos she still posted about make-up, *Doctor Backwash*, books . . . a video almost every day made it feel like having a one-way conversation with a best friend. The friend Kat had always wanted, had always missed despite never having nor losing them.

4

'If anything is going on to keep you away from school, I want to know about it,' Miss Jalloh had said.

Kat had kept her gaze on the dusty desk surface, wondering if there was any way the teacher would understand: the threatening emails, attacks on social media, blurry photos of her sitting alone in the canteen or going into the toilets at break, even walking up the path to her house, always taken around corners or zoomed in from a distance. It was all part of a world the teachers couldn't comprehend. Reporting it would be futile, and only risked making it worse.

Instead, she'd set about deleting her online presence. If she wasn't there, they couldn't attack her.

She reached out to type a comment on the video, before remembering that she had deleted her profile a week ago. It shouldn't have made her feel so disconnected – it's not like Tinker had ever replied.

'It's nothing,' Kat had said, finally lifting her head. She had left the teacher's office having barely heard the threats of phone calls home or possible suspension. It would never come to that.

It was pretty obvious who was responsible for this campaign against her. Luke and Justin sat across the room from her now. Everybody knew they had played a big part in what happened to Selena Jensen last year, and they had never been caught. The problem was proving it; if it was them, they were good at hiding it.

On her desktop was an unsent letter she had written to them, titled *Please Stop*. Into it she had poured everything she really felt about these attacks against her, everything she had nobody in her life to tell. She was so *angry*. Every blow they struck made her want to scream. But who would listen? Even if there was someone, she would have to convince them of the truth, prove she wasn't overreacting. The thought of it made anxiety wring her chest like a wet washcloth. It was better not to bother anybody else and handle it herself.

She let the cursor hover over the letter and wondered if she had ever really intended to send it, or if simply typing it had convinced her she wielded some kind of power.

The video finished. Kat set the next one playing and turned the volume up.

Wesley had to admire the fact that it had taken over a month for them to force Kat into closing down her Twitter profile, suspending her Facebook, deleting her YouTube channel and abandoning Instagram. At first she had fought back, retweeting and mocking them to try and get some support. All it really did was attract more trolls, enough to shut down anybody who came to her defence.

The hardest part had been getting her banned from the official *Doctor Backwash* fan forums. Wesley had never seen the web series, but all of his favourite YouTubers considered it worse than cancer. In the end, they had targeted a few major players on the forum until they identified Kat as the common denominator and cut her loose.

The only part of her online presence left standing was her personal website, and they'd made the photographs so that they could nuke this last outpost from orbit.

'Almost ready,' said Luke, dragging an image into place.

She brought it on herself. Wesley couldn't let himself forget it. Before the summer, Kat had given a presentation in media studies about misogyny on YouTube and toxic masculinity, calling out a local YouTuber named TrumourPixel who ran a gaming and pranks channel. *Everybody* at school watched and loved him – she was just too sensitive about his non-PC style of humour.

Wesley had sent TrumourPixel an email about it as soon as the class was over, and couldn't believe it when he got a response. It turned out Luke and Justin had done the same thing. Did they want to team up to take her down? Wesley had jumped at the chance. While Tru talked about it on his livestreams and made an attack video against her, they had begun to plot together.

This was an opportunity to prove himself. He had to take it.

'Is that the best picture to use?' said Justin.

'It doesn't matter, blue balls.'

Her website was mainly used for updates on the video game Kat was making. The home page hosted a sort of biography and a video of her, chatting self-consciously into the lens. Luke deleted it all, dropped his chosen image into place, and attached the rest to an email.

He leaned back in his chair. 'We're ready to go.'

As soon as the video shuffled to the next in the playlist Kat tabbed to Twitter. Muscle memory. *Oops . . . That person doesn't exist!* She could still lurk on her favourite feeds if she wanted, but the well was poisoned now. When the harassment aimed at her had splashed onto innocent people, she knew she had lost.

Innocent people. As if *she* deserved it.

After the summer, she thought it had all blown over. The video attacking her had stopped being shared. Everybody had gone back to ignoring her.

Now anonymous threats and faceless trolls meant she never felt safe, not even at home. She felt responsible, as if she was at fault for daring to exist in those online spaces in the first place.

Tinker constantly experienced the same kind of abuse, but on a much larger scale. This video was all about why she was supporting the forthcoming women's march in London, an event Kat wholeheartedly agreed with but was too scared to attend. Story of her life. The topics Tinker spoke about painted a target on her back, but she never let the trolls win. Tinker was kind of a hero.

They would totally probably be BFFs if they ever met.

A chronic loner. That's what Kat's sister Suzy always used to call her, flippantly, apparently unaware it was her fault Kat had slowly but surely faded into the background of their lives.

The fan forums and online communities had been there for her then. At first she'd believed what Suzy said, that it was all a substitute for real life, that online personas were inherently fake, an idealised facsimile of the truth – who you are online is who you *want* to be. Online Kat was confident, comfortable expressing her opinions and talking openly about the things she loved. She reached out into the void desperate to make friends and actually succeeded. Friends that loved Tinker and *Doctor Backwash* as much as she did, who always understood her references and appreciated her gif game. Online, Kat had been everything she wasn't in 'real life'.

After a while, she began to think that her online self *was* the real Kat. The Internet provided a proxy in which she was able to thrive.

Shutting those channels down felt like cutting pieces of herself away. She missed tweeting work-in-progress screenshots of her game and seeking development advice, debating what the *heck* was up with Esme's hair in the *Backwash* Christmas special, playing games online with friends. When she had a bad day it was her only way to purge the negativity from her body, the bracing catharsis of casting a gloomy selfie or grumpy tweet into the social media abyss. Nobody ever replied, but at least it had left her brain.

Last night, with every outlet gone, she'd caught herself leaning into the balmy glow of her blank screen, hoping it might nourish her in some small way like a hothouse plant.

Maybe none of it had ever been real.

Maybe it was pathetic to miss it so much.

Kat had never felt so lonely.

When the email was finished – third-party account, nothing to do with the school system – and they had double-checked their handiwork on her website, Luke and Justin turned to Wesley. 'Want to do the honours?'

This was an audition, and Wesley was determined to pass. He scooted his chair across, almost dizzy with pride and fear and excitement.

The first click saved all changes to the website.

He hesitated, just for a moment, before his second click sent the email.

They all spun their chairs around to watch the fallout.

An email notification popped, and Kat expected it to be from Miss Jalloh, sending through her 'improvement expectations'. Instead it was from a sender she didn't recognise, so it had to be the trolls. Usually she deleted without reading, but it was impossible to ignore the subject line: *THE WALDGRAVE WANK BANK IS OPEN FOR BUSINESS*. The panic in her chest, the corrosive demon of anxiety she always had to fight to suppress, began to stir awake.

It was different to any email they had sent her before. All it contained was a link to the home page of her website. And instead of being addressed only to her, it had been sent to the entire school directory.

With shaking hands, she clicked the link.

For a moment, Kat could not quite comprehend what she was seeing. The trolls had somehow hacked her website and replaced the welcome video with pornography. A photograph of a dark-skinned woman, naked but for long white socks, her hand between her legs.

And Kat's face, deftly superimposed over the woman's own so you could hardly see the join.

Around the room, people began to gasp and laugh.

Wesley couldn't keep his legs from dancing as they waited for her to react. She stared at her screen, body rigid, before she lowered it from view and spun to look around the room.

All three of them turned away just in time, Luke stifling a laugh in his thick palm. Wesley stared hard at the assortment of paper spread over his desk.

'She's going to lose it,' whispered Luke.

It seemed that everybody had opened the email now, those at the centre tables gravitating to the nearest screen to see what the fuss was about. Most looked shocked, glancing uncertainly at Kat, while others laughed and whistled.

'Wahey, Waldgrave!' cheered one of the boys.

Mr Buttercliff looked up from his phone. 'What's all this noise about?'

Wesley risked glancing back. Kat was staring at her screen, paralysed, as the noise around her continued to grow. He felt a stab of panic that she might have figured it out, that she would point the finger at him and this would all come crashing down on his head.

It was only when she finally moved to log in to her website that he wilted with relief.

They had won.

Kat's whole body seemed to vibrate and her skin felt white hot. The images were doctored, fakes designed to mess with her head. Still, seeing herself like that, *everybody* seeing her like that, made her body feel as

11

if it might disintegrate, and she would let it so that everybody would stop *looking*.

Behind her, Buttercliff heaved himself up from the desk and began walking towards the nearest PC. There was only one thing she could do to stop it. If the trolls were willing to do this, there was no way she could beat them.

Kat took a final look at the website she had built herself: her name in custom pixel art for the banner, animated sprites of *Backwash* characters dancing underneath, the developer diaries and blog posts, random videos and memes she had shared. It was supposed to be a sanctuary for her personality, her true self squeezed into a glass bottle and entrusted to the departing tide.

She wanted to scream, stand tall in front of them all and demand to know who had done this. Instead, she opened her website options and navigated to the delete menu.

Here, at the end, was nothing but defeat.

Are you sure? it asked.

There was no other choice. She pressed the button.

Luke refreshed the tab. Her website was gone.

'Fucking *yes*, mate!' he hissed.

Across the room, Kat had closed her MacBook and pressed her forehead into the edge of the desk. The adrenaline that had surged through Wesley moments before was quickly ebbing, his triumph eaten away by a growing nausea.

Buttercliff was leaning into a screen, demanding to be

shown what had caused the commotion, but the girls there refused to relent.

'I'll show you, sir!' shouted one of the boys.

Looking back, Wesley saw Kat grip the edge of her desk as if trying to tear chunks of it loose. Her whole body shook, too violently to be caused only by tears.

Melodrama, Wesley told himself. TrumourPixel had warned them about this; girls like her always played the victim, even when they got exactly what they deserved.

Luke and Justin were already collecting their things. Ten minutes remained of the period but there was no obligation to stay. Buttercliff wouldn't stop them. They had their victory, and now they were fleeing the scene of the crime.

'Where you guys heading now?' asked Wesley.

'We'll report this to Tru and catch you later,' said Luke, shouldering his bag. 'Drop us a message when you're finished at your new job or whatever.'

'We could—'

They turned their backs on him and left, as if Wesley had ceased to exist.

At the back of the room, Kat's convulsions had turned violent, her breathing sharpened into high-pitched rasps. Other people in the room could no longer pretend they didn't notice, tearing their eyes away from the photograph preserved on their screens to watch the real thing.

'Live demonstration!' crowed one of the boys.

Buttercliff saw what was on their screen and gasped, fumbling for the mouse to close it.

Finally, Kat's head jerked up, and she stared at her

13

hands gripping the desk, like she didn't recognise them. Her knuckles had bleached so white it was almost as if Wesley could see right through them.

A lump caught in his throat, and he made to stand up. It was different, seeing a victim in real life and not inside a computer screen. Before he could move, Kat swept everything off the desk into her bag and stood up sharply enough for her chair to clatter over.

'Who is responsible for this?' shouted Buttercliff.

Kat ignored him, everyone, and rushed for the door. As she passed Wesley, something about her changed that sent goosebumps skittering across his skin. The light from the windows seemed to consume her entirely, shining through her body as if it was made of glass. By the time he had blinked, trying to blot the illusion, she was out of the door and out of sight.

The room fell quiet around him. Buttercliff glanced around in bewilderment, and then returned to his seat at the front of the class to resume his game. Everybody at a computer closed the website, the email, and returned to whatever they had been doing before as if nothing had happened at all.

2

Nothing and Nobody

The world spun around Kat's head as she fell to her knees in the toilets. Every atom in her body seemed to be in open rebellion, trying to shake loose its bonds. The smell of bleach scorched her nose, stinging eyes already raw with tears. The contents of her bag had spilled across the grimy tiles.

'Stop crying,' she whispered, forcing herself back onto her feet.

Before she could catch sight of herself in the mirror above the sinks she clenched her eyes shut. For a bizarre moment back in the classroom she had thought herself to be disappearing. She was sure she had seen through her hands, through skin and flesh and bone, and had gripped the desk in a last-ditch attempt to anchor herself to the world. A trick of the light, surely, caused by tears blurring her vision.

So why was she so frightened to face herself now?

Kat wiped her face with trembling fingers, and she could feel them, solid matter against her skin. It gave her the courage she needed to open her eyes.

A ghost looked back. Her reflection was exactly where it should be, but it was spectral; a sunblind afterimage. Her body had faded, just a little. Haltingly, she turned her head side-to-side, and the reflection mimicked her as it should. Through herself she could see the toilet stalls behind and the crinkled cleaning notices fixed on their doors, but she retained enough substance to render their words indecipherable.

The panic caged inside her chest was a feral creature, and now it threw its body against the bars. Whenever it tried to claw its way out Kat tried to imagine her breathing as a moustachioed tamer jabbing at it with a kitchen chair. Now the beast caught it in its jaws and splintered the wood into matchsticks.

Irrationally, she spun around, expecting to find her body splayed on the tiles. She had died and become a wayward spirit. It was the only rational – *ha!* – explanation. But there was nothing there.

'That was *Backwash* season one, episode five,' she told herself, trying to keep calm. '"Zenon's Temporary Demise".'

A sob split her open. Despair and horror poured out in a scream, long and dreadful, resounding around the toilet walls.

It only stopped when a boy pushed through the door.

Wesley tried to stay in his seat. If something was wrong, if she was upset, he wasn't supposed to care. Everybody else in the room had seen it too. Let them play the white knight.

Except they continued with their work, Buttercliff his game, the session continuing as if it had all been the most natural thing in the world. They had seen the picture. They had looked *right at her* as she turned transparent, like a chameleon excusing itself from a threat. The period would be over in minutes, but he couldn't wait. He needed to debunk what his eyes had told him – that was the only reason he was going. It wasn't because he cared. He swore under his breath and hurried out.

Wesley followed the corridor, peering into classrooms, sure she would have looked for somewhere to hide. Every vacant room on the floor was dark and empty. It was only when he reached the stairs that he heard the scream from the girls' toilet. He rushed to the door, hesitating to cross the boundary. The agonising cry, its seemingly endless keening, pulled him inside.

'Is everything o—?'

He cut himself off mid-sentence.

Nobody was there.

At the sight of him, Kat tried to tear herself into three: one to gather up her laptop and bag, one to stand straight, wipe the snot from her face and smile as if everything was okay, and one to hide, hide, hide.

She held her breath as the boy stared in bafflement. Kat searched her mind for an excuse, a reasonable answer to his unfinished question.

'I don't know what's happened,' she said, the only truth she knew.

The boy didn't answer, instead peering around the room as if there might be somebody else hiding there.

The parts of Kat's mind scattered by panic began to draw back together. She knew this boy – Wesley, from her year. They had met before, seen each other around school. He must have seen the photo along with everybody else. She swallowed her shame. Regardless of why he was here now, she needed help.

'I have to get home,' she said.

Wesley stepped closer and she flinched away, only for him to move past her and check the stalls. Why didn't he say anything? She reached for his arm, craving its fixedness and desperate despite everything for his attention. The sight of her translucent hand, like paper held to light, made her snatch it away before she could make contact.

When he finally turned back they were close enough to waltz, but no sooner had his eyes found Kat than they grew large and unfocused, sliding away to look somewhere else. Anywhere else.

Although her reflection showed she had faded but a little, he was unable to see her at all.

The scream had come from inside the toilets. There was nowhere else. It had cut off sharply as if disturbed when Wesley opened the door. And there was her bag, discarded, MacBook and make-up scattered.

It felt like a trick, as if somebody was watching and recording his reaction. Twice when he turned his head he thought somebody stood at the edges of his vision, only to vanish if he tried to focus. He was sure he could *feel* another person in the room. Something like vertigo, a sense that the rules of the universe were unravelling, lurched inside him.

Quickly, before anybody could catch him there, Wesley scooped the contents of her bag back inside and gathered it up. It was a lifeline, an excuse to find her again. A chance, perhaps, to sate the guilt that was beginning to gnaw at his heart.

Kat followed a few paces behind as he returned to the corridor, only dimly aware that he had taken her bag. Keeping up with Wesley as he hurried down the stairs offered a linear future, one she didn't need to decide for herself, if only for a few minutes. Long enough to get out of there.

At the bottom floor, Wesley turned a corner and came to a halt. Kat huddled against the wall as a familiar imperious voice rang along the corridor.

'If I didn't know better, I'd say you were heading for the exit.'

Kat peeked around the corner. The way out was blocked by Miss Jalloh, hands on her abundant hips, hunkered low in a way that suggested she was perfectly willing to tackle him bodily if necessary.

'I was, uh . . .' Wesley stammered, and Kat saw him push her bag out of sight behind his back.

'Mr Graham, you realise there's no excuse I'll accept from you right now?'

'I do now, miss.'

'You know that *I* know you don't have final period free today, so there's no reason in the world you should be heading outside right now.'

'I know, miss, but I was just looking for—'

Miss Jalloh held up a hand to silence him, fingers splayed, before counting them off one by one. Kat had seen her perform this trick before: the moment she folded her little finger into her palm the bell rang, electronic pips repeating throughout the building.

'How do you do that?' said Wesley.

Miss Jalloh smiled sweetly and answered by pointing him back along the corridor. 'To final period, if you please.'

The school had stirred to life, chairs scraping and voices tumbling over each other, the shouts of teachers' final instructions competing with the excited babble of their students. Kat fought the urge to run. Stepping out from the wall, Miss Jalloh's all-seeing eyes flicked to her, and Kat braced herself for punishment or fright. Neither came – almost at once the teacher's attention reverted to Wesley.

'Sorry, miss,' he said, and turned around to pass Kat without so much as a glance.

The classrooms behind her boiled over into the corridor. Kat waited for somebody to notice. She would almost have welcomed a gasp or scream, anything but the vacant tide that broke around her, as if she were a boulder in the flow of a river, unworthy of attention. Smothering her rising panic, she hurried past the unseeing Miss Jalloh and out of the building.

Then she ran across the car park to swipe her pass at the gate. Ran towards home until her lungs burned and a sharp pain in her side pulled her up short. Doubled over, she tried not to see the pavement through her ankles, the thread of her jeans embroidered in her hands.

A breeze made something rustle on her back. Kat reached under her arm to find a piece of paper stuck to her blouse with chewing gum. It was folded in half once, and inside was a scrawled, smudged message.

I see you.
contact@thelonelypeople.com

Kat clutched the message to her chest. Somebody had seen what had happened.

Somebody had seen *her*.

3

The Peak of Human Ingenuity

Wesley had known for a while that there was little hope for his future, but he would have thought he was at least qualified to wash cars. The one-hour tutorial before he was even allowed to hold a sponge suggested otherwise.

'The second coat of wax is where it really counts,' said Dave zealously, Mum's latest boyfriend. 'It might seem like overkill, but a good shine can really make up a customer's mind.'

Although he was there to work, Wesley had known in advance that the whole endeavour would be set up like a bonding experience. Still, Dave seemed more interested in romancing the electric lime Ford Focus at his fingertips than playing dad-in-waiting. Even though he owned the used car dealership, he'd stripped down to a T-shirt as soon as Wesley arrived and started filling buckets with water ('power hoses damage the paintwork!').

While Dave dabbed on the second helping of wax, Wesley watched him closely. He was better looking than the last couple of boyfriends: head shaved to fuzz, tattoos so dark on his black skin they could have been etched there at birth. This was the first time Mum had dated anyone since they finally got away to their own place. Two months together and counting. Long enough that Wesley needed to worry.

'How long have you had this one?' he asked. The oil-stained forecourt was only big enough to hold seven or eight cars, parked in two tight rows.

'A few months,' said Dave. 'I think the colour might put people off.'

Usually, Wesley would refuse to do anything like this with one of Mum's boyfriends. They always got on better without them. It had been an unspoken rule with his older brother Jordan that they would never relinquish any of their power to some new bloke on the scene. Except Jordan had betrayed all that when he left.

If only Mum hadn't looked so hopeful when she asked. Plus, the extra money would finally give him the chance to contribute.

'All right, grab the chamois,' said Dave.

'You sure you two don't want some alone time?'

Dave whipped the cloth at him playfully, and they spent the next few minutes quietly buffing the wax like it might magically transform the car's fortunes.

'That's the ticket.' Dave beamed, showing off his wheeler-dealer silver tooth.

The repetitive work did little to take Wesley's mind off Kat Waldgrave. He had expected to feel in some way different when the attack was over. It should have proved that he wasn't soft, that he could act like Tru said men were supposed to. The trolling campaign had been a success, but instead of basking in triumph alongside Luke and Justin he was still stuck here washing cars. He was still himself. Hopefully they had reported their success to TrumourPixel by now. He wasn't sure exactly what might come next, but it had to be better than this.

Thinking of Kat made his stomach drop, like an airlock opening. He couldn't shake the thought that the effects of their attack had been worse than intended.

Behind him, hanging on a hook in the dealership office, was Kat's bag and MacBook. It would offer some answers. The more Wesley tried not to think about it, the more he needed to uncover the truth.

Kat woke inside the sweaty cavern of the duvet pulled over her head. Somebody was knocking on her bedroom door.

'Are you coming down for dinner?' said Dad.

The door was locked, and she knew giving no response would quickly make him give up. She couldn't risk him seeing what had happened. Against all reason she felt embarrassed, as if she was to blame. On the way home she had kept her head down and walked quickly, determinedly not noticing if anybody was noticing.

If there was something wrong. She was still hoping the whole affair was some kind of hallucinatory panic attack. She couldn't bring herself to check. She had fallen asleep while watching Tinker videos to comfort herself.

'You need to eat,' said Dad.

This was how he went through the motions: meals cooked, clothes washed, schoolwork checked. If he did what was expected of him, and she played along, they could both avoid ever acknowledging that the last year had reduced them to little more than strangers.

'I'll put it in the oven so it stays warm,' said Dad.

Kat listened to his feet padding down the stairs and drew the duvet tighter to her skin, willing herself to sleep again so that waking afresh would chase the nightmare away.

There was no denying the iridescent shine of the paint-work after the second coat of wax. Wesley stood back while Dave circled the car, checking for any spots they'd missed. There was an ember inside him, smouldering guiltily in the dark. It felt dangerously like pride. Wesley quickly stamped it out.

'Real boy racer car, this. You thinking of learning any time soon?'

'I can't even think about affording it.'

Dave nodded, leaving Wesley to wonder if he knew how tough they'd had it during the last couple of years. Mum's zero hours contract, which meant they could never know how much money they'd have, was no secret. It seemed less likely Dave knew about having to outstay their welcome with friends and boyfriends because they had nowhere else to go, or the queues at the Salvation Army food bank, or shopping for his half-sister Evie's clothes in charity shops so they could afford nursery a few days a week. If he knew all of that, Wesley wasn't so sure he'd have stuck around.

'What else needs cleaning?' said Wesley, looking around

at the assortment of cars on show. They all looked clean enough already. Mum had insisted Dave was shorthanded, but Wesley suspected otherwise.

'I see what you're thinking,' said Dave. 'That you're only here cos your mum bullied me into it. It's not true. Yeah, I'm happy to help you out. But it takes a lot of work keeping every car presentable. I don't care about horsepower and nought-to-sixty or any of that. The real magic is in a properly clean motor, like you're paying proper homage to the peak of human ingenuity.'

Wesley looked at him like he was mad, but he kept the smile off his face; Dave clearly believed every word.

Dave grinned back. 'Come on, look around and tell me it's not a glorious sight worth maintaining.'

Near the office door, tucked back in the second row, was a silver BMW that had caught Wesley's eye as soon as he arrived. He knew nothing about cars except that *this* was the sort of thing he should be driving one day.

Dave followed his gaze, and his grin turned mischievous. 'Wait here a tick.'

He slipped into the office and opened the wall-mounted lock box where all the keys were kept, returning with a fresh set. A button press made the BMW's lights flash and doors click open. Dave tossed the keys to Wesley, and he caught them, bemused.

'Am I cleaning inside?'

'Just get behind the wheel.'

The plush synthetic leather exhaled a breath of cigarettes and sweat under Wesley's weight. Dave dropped into the passenger seat and pointed to the ignition.

'I thought we'd established I can't drive.'

'It's clamped, so you can't go nowhere,' said Dave, knocking the gear stick so that it wobbled loosely. 'All right, it's in neutral. Start her up.'

The engine grumbled awake as Wesley turned the key. He gripped the steering wheel reflexively, as if the car might jolt forward and he'd have to wrestle it into submission.

'It's all right, you can put your foot down.'

They were parked two feet behind an old Peugeot, and Wesley peered through the windscreen uncertainly.

'Hey,' said Dave, making Wesley turn to him. 'I wouldn't let you behind the wheel if it wasn't safe.'

What was supposed to be reassuring sounded to Wesley like condescension, and all at once he felt like a child playing at being a man. He gripped the wheel tighter and looked down at the pedals. There were three, almost identical. The shame of having to ask burnt hot inside his chest. 'Which one is it?'

'On the right – just apply a little pressure.'

Jordan would have laughed at him, but that didn't matter now. He eased the pedal down, the car raising its hackles and growling in reply.

Beside him Dave was grinning. 'A little more.'

Wesley pushed harder and the engine roared, thundering in his ears, quaking through the car and into his bones. He felt as if he were bullying it, and feathered the accelerator so the engine seemed to pulse.

'Yeah!' shouted Dave.

When he let it go the power ebbed, but the sensation of it seemed to linger in his muscles, itch at his fingertips.

'How about that?' said Dave.

27

Wesley couldn't keep himself from beaming in response.

'I'll give you some lessons some time. It's not fair your brother got them and you didn't.'

Wesley's stomach clenched. 'How do you know about that?'

Dave looked puzzled. 'He turned up in his car last week and I wondered when he learned.'

Any power Wesley still felt evaporated instantly. 'Jordan's home?'

Dave winced. 'I thought your mum'd told you. Me and my big mouth.'

It had been almost two years since any of them had heard from Jordan. After everything they had been through together since, Wesley couldn't believe Mum wouldn't tell him his brother was back. 'What did he want?'

'Maybe your mum should—' His phone rang in his pocket and he couldn't hide his relief at the interruption. 'Speak of the devil. Hey, love,' he said, answering the call.

Wesley wrung the steering wheel between his hands. Jordan being back had to be bad news, and if Wesley had known he'd have . . . what? He was powerless against his brother and always had been.

'It's no bother, I'll send him home now,' said Dave, and ended the call.

'Let me guess,' said Wesley, his voice tight. 'Last-minute shift.'

He nodded. 'Needs you to watch Evie.'

'I've still got two hours here, not babysitting my little sister.'

'Don't worry about it.' Dave produced a twenty-pound note and offered it. 'You can make it up another time.'

It was more money than Wesley had had for a long time. Even if he gave half to Mum he could make the rest last a while. That didn't stop him throwing open the door and leaving it behind, grabbing his stuff to head home without another word.

Kat woke again, convinced it was all fragments of a dream caught in her mind so that they leaked into the waking world. It wouldn't have been the first time: once she'd stayed home from school after dreaming somebody died in the canteen (plausible given the food they served). A few months ago she thought she had dreamed the pass code to the staff toilets; Miss Jalloh caught her repeatedly entering '1337 80085' into the keypad.

'Okay, grow a pair,' she told herself.

Grudgingly, she cracked open her eyes and looked at her hands.

The room was too dark to see for sure, so she fumbled to open the blinds. Thin LED street light cut through her fingers. That's all it was! There was nothing *wrong*, just unnecessary panic and fantastical hypochondria!

A car outside passed behind her hand, and Kat saw it move through her skin, like the hull of a ship in murky water.

'The best thing you can do is stay calm,' she told herself.

She practically fell backwards off the bed, holding her hand aloft like a live grenade, losing her balance and catching herself against a *Doctor Backwash* poster on the wall. The logo showed through like a paling tattoo.

'I'm a leaf on the wind,' she whispered, urging herself to be calm.

Automatically she reached for her phone, and then pulled away as if it would scald her.

It hit her like a blow to the chest; the reason this had happened. For so long, Kat had only been her real self online – or as close to her real self as it seemed possible for her to get – where she could escape the indefinable stress of everyday life. Now those proxies into which she had poured herself were gone, and hardly anything of her was left behind. The posters on her walls, the figurines and the merch lining her shelves, were mere covers for her lack of substance.

It almost made her laugh. It was *pathetic*.

She grabbed her phone and opened the self-facing camera, averting her eyes as she snapped a selfie. There was no mirror in the room – looking at her face wasn't Kat's favourite pastime – but she had always taken a selfie once a week to post online. It felt like a way to keep in touch with herself, every photo throwing down the gauntlet to her continuing existence, fortifying her online life.

This selfie was different. Every inch of her was affected. Her body, her physical self, had become . . . what? Less corporeal; less present; simply *less*.

Kat focused on a single point on the far wall, a dent from a rogue yo-yo years before. The beast of panic was awakening, clawing. At the end of a long exhale she threw a fist sideways into the wall.

'Ow!'

Pain throbbing in her knuckles was proof enough that she still existed, in one form or another. She had faded, like a chalk drawing in rain, but she was still there – just a little less there than before.

4

Building a Snowman

The block of flats Wesley called home was longer than it was tall, two storeys of brown brick that ran the length of a car park before dog-legging away to pull up short at a railway bridge. The top floor doors lined a sheltered walkway, almost like a shared balcony, so he could see his front door as he crossed the tarmac and came around the grubby metal bins.

His anger had only spiralled on the walk home, every hard step stoking the fire hotter, so he was fuming by the time he reached the main entrance. He fumbled in his pocket for his keys. Before he had it open he heard a soft *mew* behind him, and a scrawny, tawny cat appeared at his heels.

'Hey, Buttnugget,' Wesley cooed in reply.

Buttnugget was probably not its real name. The cat belonged to one of the old ladies on the ground floor, and was mostly allowed to roam freely. It had taken a liking to Wesley as soon as they moved in, possibly because he was always keen to offer prolonged head scritchings. Lately it had been spending some nights curled up with him in his room. The cat wound around his ankles now, mewing insistently, and Wesley scratched its ears and sank his fingers into the animal's warm fur. It always seemed like a small marvel, to have his touch so welcomed.

It was enough, at least, to calm him down a little, and by the time he made it upstairs and picked his way along the walkway's obstacle course of flowerpots and chained bicycles, he knew he wouldn't shout. Like he'd promised Evie he never would.

The door opened straight into the sitting room, and he shut it too hard behind him, sending his little sister scurrying away from her usual position in front of the TV. Mum was through in the kitchen, wrapping a sad-looking sandwich in tin foil.

'Do you want me to work there or not?' Wesley said.

Mum dropped the sandwich into her bag. 'Shady Acres care home needs an extra assistant for the night shift, and we need the money. I'm sure Dave doesn't mind.'

'*I* mind,' Wesley said, following her back to the front door. 'It's embarrassing.'

'What do you want me to do?' Mum turned on him, voice officially raised. 'I have to work.'

Wesley shrunk back, knowing there was no arguing with that. Even after all this time it surprised him how powerless she could make him feel.

'I've tried to get a job,' he said, quieter now.

'You know that doesn't matter. I want you to focus on your exams.'

Wesley had let her down there too – he had failed almost all of them so far.

33

'What kind of mother am I if the only way we can pay bills is for my son to work?'

'Jordan did.'

Mum stiffened. 'That was different.'

It was clear then that if he didn't ask she would try and hide it from him for as long as she could.

'When were you going to tell me he was back?'

Mum sighed, like she'd been caught stealing. 'Dave and his big bloody mouth.'

'After two years I think I have a right to know.'

'You're right. I just . . .' Mum unhooked her keys from behind the door and squeezed them in her fist. 'It was last week, and I still need some time to think about it. Don't let him inside if he turns up.'

'What did he—?'

'I'm going to be late, we can talk about this later,' she said, pocketing the keys. 'Evie needs dinner, there's stuff in the freezer. Love you.'

She reached out to ruffle his hair, but Wesley ducked away. 'Fuck!' he growled, as soon as she was gone.

'Wezzer?' Evie was marooned in the doorway to their bedroom.

'It's okay, Eves. Sorry about the shouting.' Wesley's promise to himself that he'd always keep his temper around his four-year-old half-sister had been harder to keep than expected.

She was spattered with paint, the result of this month's hobby that had covered her wall of the bedroom they shared in bright, messy finger-paintings. She marched over to him, one strap of her dungarees broken and flapping, and he opened his arms for a hug.

Instead she presented him with her copy of *Frozen* on DVD.

'You know what would be fun?' Wesley said, making his voice light. 'Watching any other movie ever made.'

Evie pouted; it was a losing argument. As soon as he set the film playing for the millionth time she began to run miniature laps of the cramped sitting room, burbling vaguely about building a snowman.

Mum having work meant food in the cupboards and money on the electricity key, so Wesley knew he shouldn't complain about babysitting duty. It was being stuck in the flat that really bothered him: the smell of the bins drifting up from downstairs, the rattle of commuter trains passing on the bridge, the peeling wallpaper by the TV and the wall behind it bruised yellow by previous tenants' cigarette smoke. The patch of damp in their bedroom had blackened and spread over summer, and he was getting worried it would soon gain sentience and eat them in the night.

It was a shithole. It was also the first place they had lived where they didn't have to worry about somebody kicking them out in the night. Home, no matter how grim. Wesley was proud of that.

Still, it was lonely. As much as he loved her, a four-year-old wasn't the kind of company he wanted. Hours could feel unending if he didn't find something to fill them. He took out his phone and opened YouTube. There were some new TrumourPixel let's play videos, showing off his shooter skills.

'What's up, guys?' the first video began. 'Once again we're on the hunt for a delicious chicken dinner.'

TrumourPixel wasn't the best YouTuber out there. It was mainly video game let's plays, with a few prank videos thrown in. He didn't have the best equipment, which meant his face in the bottom corner of the screen was always a little blurred. What Wesley liked was that Tru was local, had grown up in all the same places he had, so he understood what it was like. It made him easier to trust.

'The latest patch has slightly nerfed the fire rate of the SCAR assault rifle, but I can still kick ass with it.' TrumourPixel gunned down three advancing enemies in succession and whooped with delight. 'You see that? A whole squad of women! That's why they shouldn't be allowed to play. Fucking bitches.' He moved his character to stand over their bodies and teabagged them, crouching and standing repeatedly until somebody else started shooting at him.

Watching these videos was almost like having someone to sit and play with himself. Half an hour bursts of company. Sometimes Wesley imagined them being friends. Maybe they would be, when Tru learned what they had done to Kat.

The video finished, TrumourPixel giving his trademark sign-off: 'The fight never stops.' Wesley's stomach rumbled. The smell of damp seemed to grow stronger again. No matter how many videos he watched, sometimes he just needed to escape.

'Eves,' he called. 'Fancy a McDonald's?'

After Suzy went to university, Kat had spent countless nights lying awake wondering what she'd do if she came home to find Dad collapsed at the foot of the stairs, or some kind of radioactive spillage in the kitchen that had transformed the tea towels into bloodthirsty goblins. The last thing she considered herself was a responsible adult, and she'd never needed to call 999 before. This was probably the right time to start, but people didn't just randomly *fade* – it had to be against some law of physics she probably wouldn't understand.

'Research time,' she said to herself.

The phone was pleasingly heavy in her hand, ballast she hoped might keep her from floating away. First, Kat opened her contacts and found her sister's number. Kat's thumb hovered over the call button. They hadn't spoken in months – Suzy hadn't even come home from university over the summer break – and even if they had she wasn't sure her sister would believe her about everything that had happened.

She opened their dormant chat log and tapped out a message instead. *Hey, can we catch up soon? Call me. x*

The rest of her contacts was populated by acquaintances at best. There was never any need to exchange numbers with her so-called online friends, and anyway, they'd all been scared off by the trolls. Kat remembered all too well the final conversation with her regular gaming group.

Sorry, we can't let you play with us any more, they had said over headsets.

What do you mean?

The long silence was ripe with social awkwardness, but Kat had been determined that one of them be brave enough to strike the final blow.

They said they'd come for us too. We do this to escape that kind of crap, you know? We're sorry.

Kat almost asked where *she* was supposed to go to escape it. It had been so humiliating, like not getting picked for a team in PE, and she'd deleted the game immediately. Another piece of her gone.

With a hollow pang, she realised she had nobody to tell about what had happened. At least with social media it felt like there were people in the world who cared about what you were doing, who were invested in your existence. In some small way they were always beside you – even if it was just an illusion. She couldn't go downstairs and talk to Dad, couldn't face that yet.

Kat moved to the window and watched cars pass for a while, pedestrians hurrying home, and wondered who was waiting for them there.

She needed to focus. Searching on her phone was a pain, but without her laptop she had no choice. First she checked her website: it hadn't been revived in her absence, and there was no sign of the photograph. It could have been saved by somebody else, but she couldn't worry about that now.

Google was safe, but she opened an incognito tab just in case. Flexing her thumbs over the keypad, letters nudging through her nails, she tried to think of any search term that wasn't completely ridiculous.

Fading . . . disappearing . . . becoming a ghost . . .

This line of questioning mostly turned up obscure films, rainforest charities, cleaning services, paranormal conspiracies, fetishes. She decided not to check the images.

Kat tried a different tack: *detached from life.*

Half way down the results she found a website that compiled suicide notes posted to social media, nobody able to save their authors in time – if anybody had even tried. Another website focused on Japanese teenagers who withdrew from society so completely they spent their entire lives online, literally never leaving their bedrooms. They were called *hikikomori*, literally 'pulling inward, being confined'.

'I wasn't that bad,' Kat muttered, then realised she was saying it to herself, alone in her bedroom.

If any of the *hikikomori* had experienced what was happening to her, there was no evidence of it here.

She checked the chat log, a double-tick confirming the message had been delivered. As she was locking the phone, the ticks turned blue. Suzy had read the message. Swiping the screen awake again, she waited to see *typing* . . .

Ten minutes passed without her sister even attempting a reply.

That left Kat only one place left to go.

She had been strangely afraid of the note crumpled in her pocket. It was dangerously close to confirmation that this wasn't all in her head. Plus it could have been written by anybody, Luke and Justin or whoever caused all this in the first place. It could easily be another trick.

She ran her fingers over the note, its scrawled letters unwinding under her skin. *I see you.* She wouldn't blindly write to the email address included, that was asking for trouble. Instead she typed the domain name – *The Lonely People* – into the search bar, and clicked.

5

Nesting Dolls

It was a delicate operation, boring a hole through the centre of a burger and threading it onto the drinking straw so that the base of the bun rested evenly on the lid of the cup. Thankfully Evie was a veteran, and was soon slurping milkshake through its meaty centre with a minimum of fuss or waste.

'That's disgusting,' said Wesley.

'*You're* disgusting,' she shot back, before leaning forward to nibble at the edges of the burger.

The dinner rush was over and McDonald's was quiet, a few lone diners exiled to the fringe seats by a raucous group of lads at the long centre table. Wesley had taken his usual spot by the window, where he had a view of the car park. He kept his eyes fixed outside, watching closely any vehicle that turned off the road.

'Can I save some for Jeff?' said Evie.

Her invisible dog. They couldn't afford a real one. Nobody had yet worked out why she had decided to call it Jeff.

'I don't think he's hungry, Eves.'

There wasn't enough money for them both to eat, let alone an invisible dog. Thankfully the MacBook on the table in front of him had already killed his appetite.

'Who's that?' asked Evie, pointing with a greasy chip.

'I got it from a friend,' he said, and opened the lid.

Twitter, Facebook, YouTube, Tumblr . . . he checked each of her accounts in turn and found them all still gone.

Again, he waited for the triumph of victory, but there was nothing but sickness. That didn't seem fair; Luke and Justin had been treated like heroes after the *#SelloutSelena* campaign last year, even after the police got involved and they went to ground.

Headlights passed across the window, and Wesley craned his head to peer through the darkness. In almost two years of sitting there every week, the car he wanted to see had never turned into the restaurant.

Dad had always brought them to this McDonald's when they were kids. That ended when he was arrested for burglary and Mum had finally left him. He avoided prison, but they didn't see him after that. Until Wesley discovered that Jordan had been meeting him in secret at this same McDonald's. Six months of visits – of meals and pocket money and driving lessons – before Mum found out and flipped her lid. The resulting argument made all that had come before it seem like little more than spirited debate. When Wesley had tried to break them up, Jordan's wrath had turned on him.

Dad didn't want to see you because he's embarrassed you're his son!

Jordan didn't come home after that. Last they'd heard he was backpacking around Australia. Until now, anyway.

There was more to the McDonald's visits than that, of course. It was cheap, and Evie always enjoyed inventing new ways to push the boundaries of culinary decency. It felt good to be around people too, rather than sitting alone at home, even if they were strangers (emphasis often on the strange).

Still, he always sat by the window in case Dad pulled into the car park. Wesley had so many questions he wanted to ask.

The website was called *All the Lonely People*.

It was sparingly laid out, title stencilled in black Gothic lettering on a white background, like words wrought in an iron graveyard gate.

Are you disappearing and don't know what to do?

Below this opening line was a strange symbol, seemingly hand-drawn; a Russian nesting doll with the hazy outline of a person standing inside it, the smaller dolls queued up behind and fading into the distance.

You know that feeling, the post continued, *of living in a house with no door and no windows, and knowing the world is rolling along outside but it doesn't matter because it will never come calling for you? You are just too irrevocably separate.*

It read like a bad copypasta, destined to be pasted onto memes for eternity. Yet Kat *did* know that feeling, better than she had ever wanted to admit.

The fade is loneliness made material, for a time. You have detached, a hot air balloon lifting steadily upward, and soon you'll be out of sight.

Kat skimmed the rest of the text, most of it further

cryptic hints and poetic nothings dancing on the edge of the truths she really needed to know.

The loneliness isn't death, the page ended. *Have you ever wanted to become somebody else? This is your opportunity. This is your second chance.*

A few days ago, she'd have dismissed the website as crazy. Now it seemed her best – her *only* – chance of finding answers. Whoever pinned the note had seen her when nobody else would.

Kat opened her email, copied the handwritten address, and began to type.

Quickly, before Evie could finish her meal and ask for a dessert he couldn't afford, Wesley scrolled through Kat's search history. Mostly searches for coding tutorials and word definitions, but also questions: *collective noun platypus? weird stomach pain dying?* Tinker's videos on YouTube. She had also looked at the website for a women's march in central London that Sunday. Next he went through the MacBook's files. Nothing unexpected: folders of Tinker and *Doctor Backwash* clips, photos, gifs, artwork and more. There were films and games and music, backing up everything he already knew about her.

Now that the campaign was over – now that he'd won – he *missed* her. That was the sick truth of it. She had become a part of his life, far more integral than he could ever have realised. Everything she had had online was so complete. So *full*. If only dismantling all of it had turned that fullness over to him.

A single document on the desktop caught his eye, titled simply *Please Stop*. Somehow he knew it was written for him, and he opened it to find a letter.

> To whoever is doing this, I'm asking you to stop. I don't know why you decided to come after me, and if I ever did anything to you I'm truly sorry. You're scaring me. We all know what happened to Selena. You're ruining my life, taking away everything I love. I just wanted to find my place, find the people who would accept me for who I am. I ask you, from the bottom of my heart, to show some kindness and please stop. This is all I have left. Without it I have nothing. I am nothing.

Wesley had expected the letter to be angry, to rail against him for the things he had done and demand they stop. She had never sent it, and he knew it wouldn't have worked. Luke and Justin would have laughed and distributed it around the school. Would it have been enough to make Wesley stop? He wanted to believe it would, but he knew better than to think so highly of himself.

He could feel the words breaching his defences, resonating with something inside himself; a lengthening shadow of desolation he had long thought to deny. He knew what it felt like to have an empty life despite

44

wanting so much. Friends. Purpose. Wesley had never been good at finding either. There were times when the weight of his loneliness was almost too much to bear.

The reply dropped into Kat's inbox ten minutes later. *Re: Who are the Lonely People?* read the subject line. She took a moment to steel herself before thumbing it open.

```
We're a group of people who know
exactly what you're going through.
Meet us tomorrow in the drama re-
hearsal room after school, 3.45pm.
```

School was possibly the last place on the planet she wanted to go. A small part of her still insisted this was an elaborate prank. Smoke and mirrors. One way or another, she needed to find out.

The email gave her the option to automatically enter the appointment into her calendar. *The Lonely People*, it auto-populated, as well as the time and location. Kat added a note: *Consider this an official record so if I get murdered I hope somebody finds it and avenges my death.*

Not that there was anybody to find it. Entering it into the calendar allowed Kat to pretend she had a plan, that she was in control, rather than clinging to the edge of a precipice by her fingernails.

Wesley needed to know that Kat was okay. He tabbed to her email, just to check. It signed in automatically, and he quickly scanned her inbox. The counter claimed there was one unread email, but he couldn't see it. A glitch? He refreshed the page and the counter didn't change.

There was no new information here. No indication of her wellbeing, no explanation for what he thought he had seen.

The screen shifted slightly, and the unread counter cleared to zero. Wesley stared at the screen for a long moment, sure something was being hidden from him, and then closed the tab. It was probably just the restaurant's crappy Wi-Fi.

Whatever was going on, he needed to return her MacBook. Tomorrow, he would use it as an excuse to track her down.

He would see her for himself.

6

Hashtags and Heartbreaks

They caught up to Wesley as he made his way onto the playground at lunch. Luke flanked left and shouldered him sideways for Justin to catch in a headlock, squeezing tight enough that Wesley thought his head might pop off. When they let him go he laughed and straightened his tie. He couldn't let them think he wasn't a good sport.

'No sign of Kat Waldgrave,' said Justin.

It was like they could read his mind. Wesley had spent the morning trying to find her, looking into classrooms and waiting in the corridor between lessons (Miss Jalloh had caught him twice, ushering him away as she would a beggar).

Luke stretched to lean against the wall in a way that blocked Wesley from escaping. A dark sweat stain had blossomed in his armpit. 'Tru likes how that went.'

'Even if she was an easy target,' added Justin.

Wesley tried to push any thoughts of the unsent letter on her MacBook desktop out of his mind. 'You spoke to him?'

'Online, yeah,' said Luke, before jabbing him in the

chest. 'Don't worry, we told him everything *you* did to make it happen.'

'Yeah?' Wesley couldn't keep the smile from his face.

Luke glanced around slyly before he spoke again. 'He's got something else going on, something we've been part of for a few weeks. Something bigger.'

Wesley's smile faltered. A few weeks? Easily long enough that they had kept it a secret while they worked together on Kat. He swallowed, refusing to let them see how much it bothered him. 'Bigger?'

Justin grinned. 'Bigger than Selena.'

The name made his heart beat faster. Selena Jensen had been in the year above them, and dated a guy called Gabriel Clark. She had done some modelling work, and almost every boy (and a lot of the girls) in school were obsessed with her. When she broke up with Gabriel, he didn't take it well.

First he wrote a blog post detailing how Selena had cheated on him, taken his money to support her career, and strung him along. Whether any of it was true or not, he sent the post to the whole school and enough people chose to believe him. It struck a spark. Every guy who wanted Selena so badly they had come to resent her was mobilised. The blog post confirmed all their worst fears: that girls like Selena only slept with guys they could use; that boys like them could unfairly be painted as the bad guy.

It became a crusade, and Luke and Justin led it online, coining #*SelloutSelena*. It immediately caught on across social media, hundreds of (mostly anonymous) accounts bombarding her – and anybody who spoke up in her defence – with abuse, as well as spreading rumours and ideas for action, using it to promote videos about the evils of modern women and feminism. Even TrumourPixel joined the hunt, talking about it on his streams and making videos in support of the cause.

It all ended with the attack. One day after school this guy, egged on by everything he had seen on the hashtag, waited in the car park and hit Selena with his car. Apparently he'd been at school two years before and she had rejected him.

She survived, though she never came back to school. The hashtag died, but despite how it ended Luke and Justin became legends in certain circles. Wesley couldn't help but envy them that.

'We think you proved yourself,' said Luke, watching him closely. 'Tru's looking for more help, and he thinks you'd be perfect for the job. I'll tell him you're up for it?'

The thought of being part of anything bigger than #SelloutSelena terrified him, but he couldn't let them see. They were inviting him to be part of the next campaign. *TrumourPixel* was inviting him. It was exactly what he had wanted.

So why could he not stop thinking about Kat Waldgrave?

'What's it about?' he said, trying to sound casual.

Justin lowered his voice to a dramatic whisper. 'We can't tell you yet.'

'We just need to know if you're up for it,' said Luke, leaning closer. 'And I can ask to bring you along to meet him.'

Wesley's stomach seemed to backflip. He was almost

overwhelmed by the urge to retreat, to surrender to his fear because doing so would confirm the simplest truth he knew about himself: that he wasn't up to this, and never had been.

Now Kat's letter gave him strength – *he* had done that. For better or worse, it propelled him forward.

'Yeah,' Wesley said. 'I'm up for it.'

If this strange fade was caused by withdrawal from the real world, maybe all Kat needed to do was re-engage. Maybe she just needed to go outside. Suzy had always told her to get out more.

There were a few hours before she was due to meet the Lonely People, and sitting at home was driving her crazy. Going to school would at least give her the chance to test the limits of the fade – it wasn't like she had anywhere else to go, and she might feel better knowing what she was up against. Right?

Alongside her usual school clothes, Kat added tights and a blazer in an attempt to make herself as solid as possible. She was almost dressed when Dad knocked on her door. 'Are you okay in there?'

Dinner had still been waiting forlornly in the oven when Kat snuck downstairs in the middle of the night. She'd thrown it away and helped herself to a selection of luminous orange snacks instead, although once she'd brought them up to her room her appetite had abandoned her.

'I'm going to work now,' said Dad. 'Let's catch up later, okay?'

Kat had always joked – to herself – that she learned most of what she knew about video game mechanics from studiously avoiding her dad. Over time, she'd realised it might be true. In the evenings Dad would pour a glass of wine and spread his marking across the living room carpet while Kat stayed upstairs, making toilet runs when she was certain he wasn't nearby.

Excluding the weirdness of the fade, there was no actual reason for it be so difficult to talk to Dad. Generally speaking, they got along fine. The word that always came to mind was *estrangement*. It had only become apparent after Suzy went to university.

Before Mum left, Dad and Suzy had always got on. They watched films and went shopping together. They even looked more alike, Suzy's skin a similar dark brown where Kat's was lighter, closer to Mum's.

There was a vacuum to be filled after Mum was gone. Suzy's already BIG personality expanded further to fill the space. It was always unclear why, but she began to clash with Dad, and after a while it seemed like they never stopped fighting. Kat was left no territory but the sidelines. Even though Suzy was gone, and had barely been in touch since, Kat hadn't found a way back. She thought if they kept to themselves, their relationship couldn't sour like it had with her mum and sister. So they became like former best friends who had moved on, obliging them to be cordial and nothing more whenever they ran into each other. Awkward, when you live together.

Now, as she listened to Dad's feet shift uncertainly on the carpet outside her bedroom door, she wondered if trying so hard to find herself online had made her neglect the scraps of life she still had here.

She wanted to show Dad what had happened. She wanted him to see and tell her that she would be okay. There had to be a not-crazy way to do it. Maybe she could wrap herself in a hooded cape, hurl a smoke bomb into the room, and then unveil herself – *ta da!* She had the cape (for cosplay reasons) but she was fresh out of smoke bombs.

'Have a good day,' said Dad, before he headed downstairs.

Kat knew the real reason she couldn't show him. It was one thing to be invisible to the world. Her dad not seeing her would be to lose a fundamental part of her existence.

Once he had left, she went downstairs and stood behind the front door, trying to psyche herself up.

In the *Doctor Backwash* episode 'The QWOP Factory', Vladimir is stung by an escaped genetically modified hornet and his hands swell to three times their normal size. The only way to fix it is to get back to his lab, except he can't drive and his wallet is stuck in the hornet hive (long story). So he faces up to the ridicule he knows he's going to face, and sets off across campus.

'For science,' Kat said, and opened the door.

There was no sign of her in the canteen or the playground, in any of the classrooms where they sometimes played lunchtime games. The last place Wesley checked was the library, poking his head into all the nooks and crannies created by the shelves arranged around the computer tables. The MacBook was burning a hole in his bag, making him feel more like a thief with every passing second.

He found Mutya, a girl from their year, in the corner reading a book with sperm on the cover.

'Do you have any idea where Kat Waldgrave hangs out?' Wesley asked, probably the first time he had ever spoken to her.

Her face went blank. 'No idea who you're talking about.'

Wesley found a quiet corner and opened the MacBook to watch a TrumourPixel video, a tirade about the evils of loot boxes in video games. It almost felt like Kat had disappeared from the face of the planet.

A calendar notification popped in the corner of the screen. He fumbled the touchpad and opened it. *The Lonely People. Drama rehearsal room. 3.45pm.* There was no way of seeing when the entry was made, but it was the closest he had to a lead. Maybe Kat was planning to show up at the bell. If he went to the meeting himself she would know he had used her MacBook, but he couldn't see any other choice.

Wesley squinted at the calendar appointment. Whenever he turned his head he was sure he saw additional text there, filling up the *Notes* field, but whenever he looked square on it was gone.

He needed to get to the bottom of this once and for all.

Kat arrived at school just as the bell signalled the end of lunch. By the time she made it inside the corridors were quiet, most people already in registration. As Kat reached the second floor a couple of younger girls scurried past, and she found herself shrinking away, ashamed. The photos everybody had seen of her weren't real, but she still felt – ironically – as if she had been exposed.

Anxiety tightened inside her chest. If she was going to face this down she needed to be brave. She forced herself to keep moving, because she knew stopping meant she would turn back.

Her registration room had two rows of desks, and everybody was already seated by the time Kat pushed open the door. A few glanced up at the movement, and then returned to staring into space. Mr Delaney insisted on five minutes of torturous silence before he took the register. Kat inhaled, determined to draw any loose pieces of herself back to the whole, and began the walk to her seat towards the rear of the room.

Usually Mr Delaney made a show of chastising anybody for being late. Today he stayed focused on whatever he was reading, and nobody looked up at her as she passed. She had expected to find them all still talking about the photograph that had been sent around on her website the day before – the fallout of anything like that usually lasted for days – but it was as if it had never happened.

It was fairly normal for people to ignore her at school, so she needed to push a little to test the boundaries of the fade. Before she reached her seat, Kat stopped at the desk of a boy engaged in drawing a painstakingly detailed penis in the margins of his homework, and knocked the exercise book to the floor.

'Hey!' he said, glaring up at her. Before they could settle his eyes grew unfocused and his gaze slipped away. He bent to retrieve his artwork without giving her a second glance.

Some of the desks were old, their surfaces scratched and scrawled with graffiti, and when Kat reached her place she didn't sit, instead laying her hands flat on the tabletop to read the tags and love notes through her skin. Mutya, her desk-mate, was engrossed in her phone hidden behind a stack of books.

'Hey,' said Kat, emboldened by desperation.

Mutya didn't look up. 'Hmm?'

'I said hey.'

It was like being teased by so-called friends – *Do you hear something? I could swear I heard something but it must have been the wind.*

Kat had become the wind. She had always longed for the security of invisibility at school, but now she had it she felt only empty.

Mr Delaney stood wearily to call the register. 'Let's do this so we can get the afternoon over with, shall we?' he said, scanning the room. If he saw Kat still standing at the back of the room he didn't show it.

Her surname placed her near the foot of the register. Mr Delaney reeled off the names in a near-continuous drawl, punctuated by tired acknowledgements and the beeps of the electronic register.

Finally, he called, 'Kat Waldgrave.'

'Here, sir,' she said.

Mr Delaney waited a beat, and then flicked his eyes up to the class. 'Kat Waldgrave?'

He spoke the name like it offended him. Kat took a steadying breath and walked towards him, but he aimed his frown right past her.

'I'm sure I saw her earlier,' he muttered to himself, and marked her as present.

She might never need another mandatory attendance meeting if she was automatically considered here. It should be a blessing, a superpower she could twist to her advantage. Yet when the bell rang and everybody carefully avoided her while simultaneously not seeing her on their way out, she begged for somebody to concede to her presence.

The usual crowd was heading to English, and she tagged along behind. While the rest of the class took their seats, Kat remained standing at the front of the room. The lesson began regardless, Miss Ellis enthusiastically reciting Shakespeare as if she was on stage. Every time Kat blocked her path the teacher threw her an irritated glance, and then stepped aside to find herself more space.

It wasn't that she was invisible, Kat was learning. Not quite. Everybody could see her, they just forgot her as soon as they looked. She had become an absence, a void that nobody could tolerate to stare into for even the most fleeting moment.

'Come on!' she shouted. 'I'm right here!'

The Shakespeare didn't stop. It felt like Kat's lungs had faded too, the air escaping before she could breathe it, and she ran out into the empty corridor, rushing back to the toilets where this had all started. She slammed into a cubicle and locked the door.

She had thought that being outside and forcing people to see her would snap the fade like an over-stretched elastic band, leave it no choice but to loosen its grip and return her to the world. Seeing its power, its stubborn totality, felt like receiving a death sentence, or worse, being doomed to walk in limbo for the rest of her days.

Home. She wanted to go home, and she knew nobody would stop her. Anxiety begged her to run for it. It was only the thought of meeting the Lonely People that kept her there. One of them had seen her. They might have answers. They might be able to stop this fade.

The door to the toilets creaked open, and Kat listened to a single set of footsteps pace deliberately to her stall.

'Occupied,' she said timidly, knowing they wouldn't hear.

'My dude, I know you're in there.' A girl's voice Kat didn't recognise. 'Open up.'

It was such a wonder to have somebody speaking directly to her that she didn't think twice, and pulled the door open.

The doorway framed a smaller girl with wavy brown hair and unruly eyebrows, grinning like they shared a secret. Unlike Kat, she wore a skirt with no leggings and shirt sleeves rolled proudly to the elbow. Every inch of her bare, pale skin looked cut from paper, pasted onto reality with too much glue so that the room shone through her.

This girl was fading too.

7

Eurydice

The girl reached out and took Kat's hand even though it hadn't been offered. Her touch felt electric, like it had always been missing from Kat's life. Before she could stop herself she lurched forward and pulled the girl into a hug.

'You can see me.'

Laughing into Kat's shoulder, the girl squeezed her tight. 'And I can feel you.'

Kat numbly pulled away. Witnessing the fade in somebody else gave her a sense of vertigo, as if the world was spinning off its axis. She wasn't alone, and she had never felt so relieved.

'I hope you washed your hands after whatever you did in there.' The girl was shorter than Kat, but she held herself like she was much larger, hands on hips and elbows wide. It was like she thought there was too much space in the universe and wanted to claim as much of it for herself as she could. 'I'm Safa.'

'Kat.'

'*That* I already knew. I still can't believe it's actually

happened to somebody else at the same time. It's true what they say about buses.'

'I still don't really know what's happened to me,' Kat said shyly.

'You must have some idea. A fade like that,' said Safa, arching a bushy eyebrow, 'is brought on by something.'

Kat forced herself to remember that she hadn't done anything wrong, that she wasn't being accused of anything. 'You left me that note.'

'I'm the only person who can see you now, remember? I spotted you sneaking past Miss Jalloh. Figured I might be able to help. Tell me how it happened.'

It was still humiliating to tell the story of being chased off the Internet, that it could cause something like this, but Safa listened with rapt attention, nodding along seriously like it was a story she'd heard before.

'I still thought it could all be in my head,' Kat finished. 'Until I saw you.'

'Don't get me wrong, when I first heard about the fade I thought it was a stupid rumour, or an urban legend,' said Safa. 'It had always happened to a friend's boyfriend's sister's wet nurse or whatever. Too good to be true, you know? Then I found the blog, and that's how I met somebody who swore down it happened to her ex-girlfriend after they broke up. I looked into it – nobody else remembered this girl at all, even people I *know* were her friends, unless I showed them pictures and *made* them remember. Even then, they just accepted that she was gone, no body or goodbye note, like it was the most normal thing in the world.'

Kat shivered, and decided to change the subject. 'You don't run the blog?'

'I do now,' said Safa. 'It gets passed on to somebody new every time.'

'If it's happened to so many people, you must know what causes it.'

Safa moved away to lean against the sinks and Kat followed, worrying for a second that somebody could walk in before remembering it apparently wouldn't matter. They could never have anything but total privacy.

'It's not like catching a cold,' said Safa. 'The nature of it means it's difficult to pass along any concrete info. Best we know is that it seems to happen when somebody feels completely alienated by life. When they lose any tangible connection to themselves and the world. When they absolutely, positively don't want to be here any more, at least as themselves. They just . . . break free. But not all at once. It's like gravity stops applying to them, except instead of floating away they begin to fade.'

'So the fade's going to get worse?' said Kat, voicing a fear she had before now tried to suppress. 'Until I'm just *gone*?'

'There's more to it than that.'

Safa turned to study her reflection in the mirror. She looked at herself with relish, like she'd had a makeover and was admiring the results. It was enough to make Kat realise the truth.

'You wanted this to happen. You've been *trying* to fade.'

'I've been in the year below you for as long as I've been at this school. Safa Hargreaves. Did you know that?'

Kat wracked her brain, but she couldn't ever remember noticing her. 'I'm sorry.'

'It doesn't matter, I'm just proving my point. Fading into the background is what the Lonely People is all about.' When Safa turned around, she was holding a tiny nesting doll locket that hung around her neck, rolling it gently between finger and thumb. 'Let's get out of here, it stinks.'

'But—'

She took Kat's hand again, and the ecstasy of being touched was too powerful to resist. 'For the first time in your life you don't need to hide.'

The corridor was quiet midway through final period, the only sound the muffled voices of orating teachers and unruly classes. As they passed a classroom Safa pushed open the door, hard enough for it to bash against the wall. Inside, the teacher frowned across but kept the rhythm of his ongoing lecture. Safa stuck her middle finger up at him and then laughed.

'See?'

The school belonged to them, an alternative reality laid close over the one Kat thought she had known. It should have terrified her, but as Safa threw open another classroom door she felt – almost – in control. Almost safe.

Wesley was sure the equation in front of him was unsolvable, a jumble of numbers and letters selected specifically to make him feel like an idiot. He tried for a glimpse of his neighbour's answers but found them similarly incomprehensible. Maths almost made him pine for that sad little candle flame of self worth that had flickered to life after waxing the car at the dealership, standing back to admire its shine.

His mind turned to Luke and Justin, no doubt sitting together in the upper-set classroom thanks to expensive tutoring and unexpected maths genius respectively. Whatever Tru was planning couldn't be bigger than *#SelloutSelena*. They had to be exaggerating to impress him. If they weren't—

The classroom door flew open and thudded into the wall loudly enough to make him jump. Nobody else did the same, or even looked up from their work. Peering across, there was nobody outside. A gust of wind, maybe.

The equation refused to give up its secret. Wesley growled in frustration under his breath. Most important now was finding Kat Waldgrave and proving that she hadn't mysteriously disappeared. He could worry about Luke and Justin later.

'How did you feel, when it happened?' asked Safa as they strolled away from the maths classrooms.

'Scared,' said Kat, as if that did it justice. 'Like I was coming apart.'

'After everything that happened I thought you might be relieved.'

'It's hard to explain. It's not like it's the first time I've had abuse online – I was a girl in geek communities, for god's sake.' Kat didn't quite manage to smile. 'It's always awful, but you only see *how* awful when you're the target. You can't ignore it when people are saying they want to punch you, kill you, rape you, even when it's mostly coming from anonymous accounts you *know* don't really mean it.'

'That's disgusting.'

'I thought it would be bad for a while and then just fade—' She pulled herself up at the poor choice of language. 'Instead it followed me everywhere, even onto the *Doctor Backwash* forums. I guess my mistake was talking back, expecting other people to defend me. Like, some did, but these communities really just want to pretend everything is okay, that nothing like this happens on their platform. As soon as anything kicks off the good people go quiet so they won't become targets too, while all the trolls are trying to one-up each other by getting nastier and nastier.'

They had reached the stairs now, their leisurely pace slowly taking them down towards the ground floor.

'You're not exactly selling the online experience,' said Safa.

'That's the thing: a lot of the time it was *brilliant*,' said Kat, finding it strange to talk in the past tense when only a day had passed since giving up her last online account. So much had changed. 'I made real friends there, found people in these communities who were like me – who *liked* me – and I could actually be myself without worrying I was being judged for it. Well, I thought so, anyway. Now I'm not so sure any of it was real.'

'It sounds like a lot to worry about,' said Safa. 'You can see why I asked if you were relieved when the fade started.'

'Like *this* isn't something to worry about,' said Kat, holding up her hazy hands.

'It doesn't have to be.' Safa had the mischievous grin of somebody used to causing trouble and getting away with it. They had reached the ground floor now, and Kat realised they had stopped outside Miss Jalloh's office. Safa raised a fist to the door, ready to knock.

Kat froze. 'You're about to make a poor life decision.'

'That's never stopped me before.' Safa rapped her knuckles against the foggy glass. From inside they heard Miss Jalloh grunt as she got to her feet. As the teacher's silhouette filled the window, Kat tried to duck away. Safa caught her sleeve and bundled her into the room as the door opened. Behind them, Miss Jalloh peered blankly into the corridor, before cursing under her breath and shutting them all inside. As she returned to her desk she glowered at them both, and then went back to her paperwork.

'Keep absolutely still,' whispered Kat. 'Her vision is based on movement.'

'It's okay, she can't hear us,' Safa said significantly louder than was necessary. 'Can you, Miss Jalloh?'

The teacher pushed her glasses up her nose and began to hum, as if she was trying to drown them out.

'Two years ago she gave me detention for talking in class when it wasn't me,' said Safa. 'I swore I would have my revenge.'

Kat swallowed hard, remembering she hardly knew this girl or what she was capable of. 'What are you going to do?'

'Something petty yet satisfying, of course.'

64

She snatched up a thick set of keys from the desk and threw them to the floor beside Miss Jalloh's chair. The teacher eyed them accusingly before she bent to retrieve them, coming back up just in time to watch her pen roll off the desk where Safa had batted it like an impish cat.

'This whole damn place is haunted,' Miss Jalloh murmured darkly, bowing to pick it up.

That gave Safa the opportunity to scoop the paperwork from the desk, causing Miss Jalloh to cry out in alarm when she resurfaced and found it missing.

Kat couldn't help but smile. 'You weren't joking when you said petty.'

'Now you know never to cross me,' said Safa, riffling through the papers.

'We could take her glasses.' The way the teacher haughtily looked over them had always rubbed Kat the wrong way.

'That's the spirit! But actually, we can't.'

'Not petty enough?'

'Oh, it's totally petty,' said Safa, then nodded her chin towards Miss Jalloh. 'See if you can touch her.'

Emboldened by watching Safa, Kat moved around the desk until she was beside the teacher. The glasses were loose on her nose, but secured by a metallic chain that hung behind her neck. Kat reached for it as gently as she could.

Before her fingers could touch Miss Jalloh's skin, there was a spark. A sharp burst of energy that made her hand bounce away. The teacher slapped her neck, like a mosquito had bitten her.

Safa grinned at Kat's outraged surprise. 'Hate to say I told you so.'

'What the hell was that?' Kat rubbed her tingling fingers.

'A symptom of the fade. There's a sort of force field around us now. Means we can't touch anybody who isn't fading. So nobody, basically.'

Years of being held at arm's length from other people should have prepared her for this. Seeing it become real was different. It left no possibility to ever break that barrier down.

'Don't sweat it, we can still have fun.' Safa threw the papers she was holding into the air, lifted her arms as they fluttered to the carpet. Miss Jalloh immediately went after them. There was inarguable satisfaction in messing with the teacher who prided herself on being all-seeing, but it lacked the gratification of a fair fight.

'Now for the *coup de grâce*,' said Safa, pronouncing it as literally as possible. She moved around the desk and behind the unattended computer, rapidly clicking the mouse. Kat joined her, but she didn't recognise the program onscreen.

'I saw her checking it once,' said Safa. 'It controls the bell. There's ten minutes left of final period, right?'

'You can't mess with the bell, you'll give her an aneurysm.'

Safa clicked. The electronic pips started up. 'Too late.'

Miss Jalloh shot upright and cried out as if the world was ending, before rushing out into the hallway. They followed, and doubled over with laughter as the teacher went haring towards the main office.

The end of the day always saw classroom doors thrown open immediately, the first wave of kids racing for the exits like rats from a fire, and the early reprieve only made them move faster. Miss Jalloh's voice came over the loudspeakers, ordering everybody back to their rooms, but nobody was paying attention now.

Despite everything Kat had learned about the fade, or maybe because of it, the rapidly filling corridor made the panic inside her rattle the bars of its cage.

'Hey,' said Safa, seeing the expression on her face and taking both her hands. 'You know the words to "Mr Pretzel's Patriotic Pastry"?'

It was a song from the musical episode of *Doctor Backwash*, a rousing march renowned for its earworm chorus. Kat nodded as the crowd began to flow past them.

Safa met her eyes and smiled. 'Sing it with me.'

'Wha—?'

'*The US Army loves his pretzels,*' Safa sang at the top of her voice.

'*The working man he loves his pretzels,*' Kat responded without quite the same gusto.

'*The Illuminati loves his pretzels.*'

They finished the verse together. '*Now bow down and eat, eat, eat!*'

The corridor was packed, a murmuration of people opening and closing around their invisible force. Kat's confidence was growing, and as they reached the chorus they sang it together as loudly as they could.

'*Mr Pretzel, he makes lots of nice pretzels,*
'*Mr Pretzel, they're delicious, yum, yum, yum.*

'*Mr Pretzel, surrender to his pretzels,*

'*Mr Pretzel, you'll soon be under his thumb.*'

By the time the song was finished (neither quite feeling bold enough to a cappella the keyboard solo) the corridor was emptying out. They stood at its centre, clasping each other's hands between them.

'You didn't tell me you were a *Backwash* fan,' said Kat breathlessly.

Safa shrugged like a movie mobster, lip curled and shoulders rising to her ears. 'That song always helps me stay calm when I'm having a little panic.'

More than that, it had been the first time since the fade took hold that Kat hadn't been terrified of it, a perfect moment that couldn't have happened *without* it.

'Okay,' said Safa, finally pulling her hands away. 'So when I invited you to the Lonely People meeting today I kind of forgot they might not be able to see us any more. But we should totally go. There's still loads you don't know.'

Kat nodded. Right then she probably would have followed Safa anywhere.

8

The Lonely People
(Are Getting Lonelier)

It was easy enough for Wesley to hang back in the classroom and wait for everybody else to leave before he made for the stairs that would take him into the bowels of the building. The door to the drama rehearsal room was ajar, and no sound came from inside. Wesley hesitated, unable to shake the feeling that he was an intruder about to stumble onto some secret world where he didn't belong, and then pushed the door open.

It was little more than a cellar, windowless and painted black, a rack of mostly burnt-out lights screwed into the ceiling. A half-moon of plastic chairs faced the door, occupied by three kids spaced apart from each other as if they were strangers. They watched him wide-eyed as if this was some kind of raid.

'Hey,' said Wesley. 'Is this the, uh, Lonely People?'

He felt so stupid using that name – it was like calling a group the Lone Wolves. Still, it seemed to make them all relax a little.

'That's us,' said a frizzy-haired younger girl Wesley didn't know.

Two seats to her right was a Korean boy he recognised from the year below, wearing a black beanie hat with his school uniform, rashes of spots across his cheeks. To her left was a smaller boy, maybe year seven or eight, wearing an oversized blazer, milk-white skin now flushing red as he scowled at the floor.

Wesley wondered if he should have stayed outside, tried to catch Kat before she made it into the room. Too late now. 'I saw an email about your meeting . . .'

'A new member,' said the smaller boy. 'Nice of Safa to let us know.'

'Who's Safa?' Wesley said to the girl.

She narrowed her eyes at that. 'I'm Aoife.'

The boy in the hat introduced himself as Jae, while the other refused to even look at him.

'He's Robbie,' said Aoife, earning herself a scowl. 'Safa's sort of our leader, I guess.'

'Leader in what?'

Robbie glared at him like it was a stupid question. 'In trying to achieve the fade.' Then he turned to the others. 'We should get started.'

'Do we have to, if Safa's not here?' said Jae.

Aoife glanced self-consciously at Wesley. 'And with him here.'

'If Safa has succeeded it shows we're doing something right!' Robbie waved them to their feet, and then flashed challenging eyes at Wesley. 'You're here to learn, aren't you?

Wesley nodded, while making sure nothing was blocking his way to the door if they tried anything weird.

'Stay there and watch.'

They each moved into a separate corner of the room and pressed their faces to the wall, let their arms hang limp at their sides. 'Repeat after me,' said Robbie, voice shaking. Undoubtedly he was taking up the absent Safa's usual role. 'We do not belong.'

From their separate corners, the others echoed, *'We do not belong.'*

'We are not safe as we are.'

'We are not safe.'

Robbie was growing in confidence now, his voice bounding around the room. 'We will walk in somebody else's skin.'

'We will walk in somebody else's skin.'

'We must escape ourselves.'

'We must escape.'

They chanted this line together three times over. Wesley had to fight his own urge to escape. They had crossed the line from weirdness into cult-like fervour.

Robbie's voice reached a crescendo. 'We are nothing!'

'WE ARE NOTHING.'

There was a long silence, the atmosphere in the room growing thick, before they each turned away from the wall and took a breath.

'Very good,' said Aoife, smiling shyly. 'Now we can have some snacks.'

Kat had arrived in time to see the end of the ritual, and if Safa hadn't been blocking the doorway she probably would have turned straight around and left.

'The prayer was my idea,' said Safa. 'I thought it might get them in the right mindset.'

'The mindset of deranged cultists?'

'Would cultists put on such a marvellous spread?'

The members of the Lonely People pulled half-packets of biscuits and flattened bags of crisps from their pockets. Jae even contributed some cold chicken nuggets.

'They've been in my bag all day but they're probably fine,' he said.

Occupying a seat at the centre of the feast was Wesley, and it had to be more than the prospect of food poisoning that made him so pale.

'What's he doing here?' said Kat.

Safa shrugged. 'I didn't invite him.'

Yesterday, when he had come looking for her in the toilets, he had taken her laptop. He could only know about this meeting if he had read her email. When the whole school – when *everybody* – had forgotten her existence, he was suddenly interested when he had never been before. Something wasn't right, and it was more than the invasion of her privacy.

'I thought if anybody might be able to see us it would be these guys,' said Safa, waving her arms in front of the group as they tucked in to the snacks. 'But I guess not.'

'They don't seem to miss you.'

'Yeah, I taught them well.' Safa pinched a Bourbon biscuit and shoved the whole thing into her mouth, spraying crumbs when she spoke again. 'In hindsight it's a bit counter-intuitive to run a support group to help people disappear.'

Kat moved to stand right in front of them, but the

group just kept eating and talking about nothing in particular. Watching Wesley closely, she could see him growing tense with frustration, hands curling into fists pressed on top of his bouncing knees.

Safa began jumping up and down on the spot. 'If I could just show them it's actually possible, it might be the push they need. Then we could have a whole crew of faders.'

'Do you think Safa has actually done it?' said Aoife, lowering her voice as if spilling the latest scandalous gossip.

'MY DUDES, I HAVE DEFINITELY ACTUALLY DONE IT.'

'She was always the most serious about it,' said Jae.

Robbie scowled at him. '*I'm* serious about it.'

'You know what I mean though.'

'At least they haven't forgotten me yet.' Safa gave up her jumping and grinned at Kat. 'I'm a role model to these kids, like an athlete, or a YouTuber.'

'*What* has she done?' said Wesley, finally losing patience. 'You said you want to achieve the fade – what does that mean?'

They all looked to each other before fixing their eyes on him. It was Aoife who spoke. 'Do you remember Aaron Musley?'

Wesley shook his head.

Reluctantly, as if she was revealing a government secret, Aoife said, 'He was in the year above you, tall with . . . short hair, I think? Even we have to make a real effort to remember him sometimes.'

There had never been anybody in the year above called

Aaron, she was sure of it. Kat may not have been friends with anybody at school, but she paid enough attention to know most people from a distance. The look on his face suggested Wesley was drawing a similar blank.

'Aaron used to be one of us, sort of our leader for a while,' said Aoife. 'He believed in the fade so much, but he couldn't make it happen. Until one day he just stopped showing up to school, and he never came to a meeting again.'

'So he might have just run away?' said Wesley.

Dread was walking its fingers across Kat's chest, like she was listening to a horror story over a campfire. Aoife seemed exhausted by what she'd said, and Robbie was busy blowing up an empty crisp packet with his mouth, so Jae took over.

'He was never declared missing, no police looking for him or anything. Almost nobody at school remembers him unless we really work hard to jog their memory, and even then they don't think there's anything strange about it. He's just gone, and everybody accepts it. We even went to his house once, just to see . . .'

Wesley was leaning forward in his chair. 'And?'

Smashing it between his hands, Robbie burst the crisp packet, making all of them jump. 'His family didn't care. We saw them just going about their day like Aaron never existed.'

Kat kept her eyes fixed on Wesley's face. Any normal person would refuse to believe them, call them freaks and storm off. Instead she saw his jaw squeeze, the colour drain from his skin. He believed every word of it was true.

Somehow, he was tied up in everything that had happened. She just needed to work out how.

It was his fault.

Wesley really *had* seen through her after she'd deleted her website and rushed from the room. He hadn't seen her since, despite finding her bag on the toilet floor. A shiver went down his spine; had she been there the whole time? It wasn't possible – it *couldn't* be.

'Why do you remember Aaron if nobody else does?'

'We think it's because we knew what he was trying to do. We were too involved to forget him completely,' said Aoife. 'But we don't remember him as well as we should. He's slipping away from us too.'

'And how long does it take to fade completely?'

Aoife looked to the others for support. 'We don't know for sure. Maybe around a week? Anyway, it's not like he's completely gone.'

'You just said—'

'You think we'd all be here if it was as simple as disappearing?' said Robbie. 'If that was the case we could just kill ourselves.'

Aoife put a hand on his leg to calm him down, but Robbie pushed it away

'Before the end of the fade, it allows you to hitch a ride on somebody else's life,' she said. 'Just before you disappear completely you can sort of transfer yourself to another person and become a part of them.'

'You mean take over their body?'

Aoife shook her head, struggling for the right words.

'What would be the point of just being yourself in another body? No, the host would still be in control. We don't even know if they'd be aware you're inside. We call them a Cradle, and you're hidden inside them like a passenger. It means you can experience everything they do – every emotion, every life moment – almost as if you *were* them. But you wouldn't be responsible for making any of it happen.'

Wesley's mind seemed to reject the idea outright, a headache flaring up almost instantly. It was *wrong*. Nobody could escape who they were, nobody could be forgotten just like that. He hadn't forgotten Kat, and he promised he wouldn't.

Maybe that would give him the power to bring her back.

'This can't be real,' said Kat, turning away from the group and pressing her fingers into her temples. If they had punctured her skin and sunk through her skull she wouldn't have been surprised.

'Twenty-four hours ago you would have thought this whole thing was a *Backwash* plotline,' said Safa. 'Imagine not having to be yourself any more. I haven't been trying to make this happen for so long just so I can disappear – I want a second chance. I want to be somebody who *fits*.'

'But becoming somebody else? That's . . .' Kat didn't know what it was, only that it frightened her to her core. Not just because the idea was so alien. No . . . some part of her yearned for it to be true. 'You can't just give up on yourself.'

'Why not? Imagine the pleasure of experiencing everything like somebody who actually knows how to get along in the world. A *normal* person.'

'Why can't you?'

Safa tilted her head disparagingly. 'Come on. Tell me you haven't tried that already.'

She had, and for a while she'd thought she had found a way to belong. The last month – even the last few days – had shown her otherwise.

'Even if you inhabit another person, it's not like they'll be happy all the time.'

'Obviously I've chosen carefully—'

'You've already picked somebody?'

Safa waved her away. 'Even when they're not happy, none of it will be your fault. You still get to feel it all, but you won't hate yourself for it.' Her lip curled into a cynical smile. 'Don't think of it like dying – it's more like finding a way to live.'

The dark walls of the room seemed to be closing in on Kat, edging tighter every time she blinked. It would be so much easier to become somebody else already adept at living. To shrug off the loneliness and doubt and assume a ready-made identity already accepted by the world. But it would also be acceptance that she herself was broken beyond repair.

'You've been trying to fade for so long,' said Kat, turning on Safa. 'What happened to you to finally trigger it?'

Safa's hand went to the locket at her neck. 'What do you mean?'

'My final straw was deleting my website,' said Kat, stepping closer. 'So what broke your camel's back?'

Safa turned away, but before Kat could keep pressing there was a noise from the group behind them. Wesley had stood up sharply, tipping his chair over with a clatter.

'What's so bad about all of your lives?' Wesley shouted. 'Why do you want to leave them behind so badly?'

His hands were shaking, and the ferocity of his anger shocked even him. He looked at each of them in turn, daring them to respond.

It was Robbie who spoke. 'We don't owe you answers. You have no right to any part of us.'

Anger burning hotter, Wesley strode to the door and threw it open so that it slammed into the wall. Then he turned, clenching his trembling hands into fists.

'If you knew what my life has been like . . . you don't see me looking for an easy way out.'

Robbie stood sharply, and despite his size he looked ready to tear somebody apart. 'You know your biggest problem? You don't know how to care about other people. Why don't you stop feeling sorry for yourself and think about what somebody else might be feeling?'

The rest of the group watched him solemnly. The room felt full of eyes, silently observing and judging. All at once his anger collapsed.

'They can't have forgotten him,' he said. 'They can't.'

Aoife stood and approached him slowly, like he was a wild animal to be calmed. 'Take my number, in case you have more questions or anything.'

Her kindness seemed to scald him, but he handed

over his phone and let her enter her number before he fled the room without another word.

The group packed away their snacks and stacked the chairs into a leaning tower. Safa nabbed a quarter-packet of biscuits – as if anybody could stop her. Kat turned to the door, wanting to go after Wesley.

'Watch this,' said Safa, turning her attention back to the room.

The floor cleared, the three remaining members of the Lonely People gathered in a tight circle and dropped to their knees.

'Closing ceremony. My idea,' said Safa.

'Make us lonely,' the group said together, bowing their heads to a central point in the carpet. 'Make us lonely so we can be loved.' They repeated the words again and again, heads almost touching, like a prayer.

Kat struggled to find her voice. 'What do they mean?'

'For some people, love means butterflies in the stomach and magic carpet rides,' said Safa. 'For people like us, it means not being isolated from the world. It means loving yourself enough to be glad you exist.'

Make us lonely so we can be loved.

It made Kat hurt in a way she could not name. She ran from the room and up the stairs, gasping in the cool evening air as she made it outside. It felt like she had escaped something dangerous, like she might not have made it out of that room whole if she'd stayed a moment longer.

Was she still whole? Maybe things were worse than she had ever realised.

'Hey!' Safa emerged from the building behind her, chewing a biscuit as she ran. 'Meet me tomorrow night?'

'Are we going to sacrifice a goat?'

'You're a funny guy,' said Safa, pretending to pinch her cheek before her expression turned serious. 'You don't want to be alone in this, do you?'

Through a mouthful of biscuit it almost sounded casual, but Kat caught the longing there, the same fear she recognised in herself. So she nodded.

Safa smiled. 'I've pinned my number to your blazer.'

Kat looked down to find a scrap of paper hanging from a buttonhole. 'How do you keep doing that?'

'My secret life as a street urchin. I'm going to head back inside and mess with them a little before they leave. Call me, my dude.'

As Kat approached the school gate, she saw Wesley. He had been cornered by Luke and Justin, the two guys she thought had to be responsible for the campaign against her. What was he doing with them? She crept closer, even though she knew creeping was unnecessary.

'I had detention,' Wesley was saying, apparently explaining why he was leaving school so late.

'You need to get better at not being caught,' said Luke. 'Learn a thing or two from Mr NoFap here.'

Justin punched his arm. 'Shut up!'

'He keeps getting *excited* during lessons, but to be fair he's good at hiding it under the table.'

'It's just while my body adjusts,' mumbled Justin.

Kat grimaced at the mental image. She watched Wesley shift uncomfortably on his feet.

'Anyway, we told Tru you're interested,' said Luke,

grabbing Wesley's shoulder and squeezing tighter than seemed necessary. 'We'll send you an email later. Are you around tonight to chat?'

A range of expressions tried to settle on Wesley's face at the same time, leaving him hovering somewhere between happy and nauseous. 'Yeah,' he said weakly.

'Come on, you can do better than that,' said Luke, still gripping his shoulder. 'You know Tinker? He's been planning a way to shut her up for a while.'

That seemed to be as much as they were willing to say now, but it was enough to let Kat know she had stumbled onto something important. If they were going after Tinker, there was no way she could just ignore it.

Kat looked again at Wesley, squirming in the other boy's grip. Had he been a part of the campaign against her? They hardly knew each other, might never even have spoken. She had given him no reason to come after her so fiercely.

'Sorry, yeah, it's cool,' said Wesley. 'I'll look out for the email.'

They let him go, laughing, children playing at being bad guys. Kat watched them go their separate ways, and knew with a startling certainty that she had to stop whatever they were up to.

9

Us and Them

The nursery was only five minutes from home, and Wesley hoped they wouldn't have called Mum because he was late. It sat behind a doctor's surgery, a short driveway leading around to a low-fenced playground and a colourful bestiary of animal-shaped climbing frames. The walls of the nursery building itself were a chaos of finger paintings. It was a *good* place, and no matter how much it stretched their budget Wesley was proud they could send Evie there a few times a week.

A woman spattered in a miscellany of stains came out to meet him, leading Evie – dressed as Princess Elsa – by the hand.

'Sorry I'm late,' said Wesley.

The woman – he had forgotten her name again – frowned. 'She fell and tore her dress today.'

'I didn't fall over,' said Evie, taking Wesley's hand. 'I was using ice powers and slipped on the ice.'

'I bet you didn't cry, either,' said Wesley.

Her face scrunched up in disgust at the very idea, and Wesley ruffled her hair until she burst out laughing.

On the walk home she detailed the mixed results of her ice power summoning, and insisted she'd have to watch *Frozen* again to perfect her technique.

The day had taken a couple of unexpected turns, and Wesley could practically hear his brain turning it all over. He had expected to find Kat, return her MacBook, and confirm that she was okay. Instead he had discovered that in all likelihood the things he had done against her had caused her to literally fade from existence. Craziest of all was that he *believed* it.

And there would be an email arriving from Luke and Justin. Nerves seemed to be boring a hole through his stomach.

A train was rattling over the bridge when they reached home. Parked underneath their flat was a long, silver Jaguar. Several neighbours hung out of their windows for a better look.

'He's such a flash git,' Wesley muttered under his breath.

'Git!' mimicked Evie.

'Don't tell him I said that.'

'Git! Git!'

They had a practised routine of going up the stairs together, Wesley swinging her around the turns on the end of his arm. He was already talking when he opened the front door.

'You've got about three more minutes before that car gets . . .'

The words died in his throat. Mum was by the front window, Dave holding her around the shoulders like she would fall without his support. Beyond them, standing inside the kitchen door, was Jordan.

'All right, bro?' he said.

Behind him, Wesley felt Evie shelter against his legs.

'Git?' she said quietly.

It was habit for Kat to avoid the second and eighth stairs, the ones that creaked like seaside piers in the wind, and she wasn't going to stop now. She could hear Dad setting up for the night in the front room. After everything she had heard that afternoon she still didn't have the courage to see if the fade had removed her from his life for good.

She bolted her bedroom door and leaned against it, looking around the walls at her posters and books and collectibles.

'I love this stuff,' she said.

Crossing to the ceiling-high shelves behind her bed, she plucked a knitted Totoro from the middle shelf and cuddled it into her chest. With her free hand she ran her fingers along the spines of her DVDs, books and games, arranged in colour order to form a makeshift rainbow from left to right.

'I don't think I want to become somebody else,' she told Totoro.

It had taken years to collect it all, and she had always felt proud at every new addition, like she was adding bricks to a podium on which she could proudly stand tall. She had never been ashamed of any of it, even though she knew it had kept her separate from everybody at school. Even when Suzy had called her Queen of the Nerds and told her to enjoy dying a virgin. This was who she was.

'So why am I definitely-one-hundred-and-one-per-cent going to meet Safa tomorrow night?' she asked Totoro.

She caught sight of her reflection in the window, the fade making it faint, like an apparition breathing fog onto the glass.

'I don't want to be nothing,' she told herself.

It was the only truth she knew.

'It's been a while,' said Jordan, pushing off the kitchen doorframe and stepping closer.

Wesley wasn't sure if he was surprised or not how little his brother had changed. He was a bit leaner, and his tanned skin looked as if it had been baked brown in an oven, but everything else, from his perpetual bed hair to his swaggering steps, was the same.

'What are you doing here?' said Wesley, fighting to hold his voice firm.

'I thought it was time to come home.' Jordan glanced around the room, flicked a loose thread trailing from the sofa arm. 'Though I guess you can't call a place you've never been "home".'

Mum crossed her arms. 'I let you know where we were every time we moved. You never replied.'

'I didn't mean to leave it so long before I got in touch,' said Jordan. 'I wasn't sure how welcome I'd be after . . . how we left it.'

Another moment of quiet descended, and nobody moved, as if each were carefully planning their next move. A stand-off, everybody looking for a way to draw their gun.

Mum broke the deadlock. 'You can't expect us to forget the things you said.'

Us. Gratitude at being recognised swelled in Wesley's chest.

Jordan nodded slowly. 'I know that, and—'

'And you can't just walk back in here like nothing happened.'

Quiet again, apart from Jordan blowing a sharp, frustrated breath from his nose. They both knew how stubborn Mum could be, and Wesley was glad she had decided to play it like this: cautious, but proving she wasn't a pushover. If they let him come back he would walk all over them. He would try and force them back into their previous shape, where there was barely room for Wesley. Perhaps a couple of years apart had finally lent her the courage to stand up to him.

Small hands gripped the seat of Wesley's trousers, and he reached back to place a reassuring hand in Evie's soft hair.

'What would you like me to do?' said Jordan, clearly choosing his words carefully.

'Tonight, nothing,' said Mum. 'Dave's borrowed a nice car and he's taking me out.'

At the sound of his name, Dave took her hand and squeezed it gently. Jordan fixed him with a long look, his expression unreadable.

'Can I have a word with Wes before I go?' he said.

Wesley's nerves jangled, but he managed to keep himself from reeling backwards.

'Hey,' said Dave, catching his eye. 'You'll be all right?'

'Yeah,' said Wesley, pulling himself taller. If he was

going to keep his new place in the family, it was up to him to sort this out. He had kept them safe for the last two years and he would do it now. 'We should probably talk.'

Mum kissed him on the forehead as she passed, and Dave gave his shoulder a squeeze, before they both said goodbye to Evie and left them alone.

Immediately the atmosphere seemed to shift, a subtle change in the air pressure that made Wesley's chest ache. He had to stand his ground. He took a step into the room, and Jordan took two.

'Christ, you've grown,' he said.

Wesley was still shorter, and they both knew it. 'Well, it's been two years.'

'Too long.'

The feigned sentimentality was a disarming tactic. He had to ignore it. 'I need to get Evie's dinner ready.'

Jordan took out his phone. 'I could order pizza?'

'Pizza,' said Evie firmly, and that settled it. A series of well-practised taps on the screen sent the order in seconds. Wesley couldn't help but feel he'd lost the first exchange.

'You got big too,' said Jordan, squatting down and holding a hand out to Evie, like he was summoning a pet. She shrank away behind the armchair, wedging as many fingers as she could into her mouth.

'Evie, why don't you go and paint in the bedroom?' said Wesley. And then once she was gone, 'She doesn't remember you.'

When Jordan had left, their half-sister was little more than a toddler. It had always seemed a blessing that she

87

wouldn't remember anything of what had brought them there, and would only have memories from when things were, if not good, at least settled.

'I thought I should see where you're living now,' said Jordan, again casting his eyes around the room. 'I didn't think you could do worse than the last place.'

'You never saw our last place, or the place before that.' Wesley felt his cheeks growing hot. 'We had to take whatever we could afford after you left.'

No matter where they had been or what they had been through, Wesley had done everything he could to care for his family. He wasn't worth much, but he was proud of that. It was the only worthwhile thing he had ever done. He wouldn't let Jordan walk back in and take that away from him.

'Do you have any idea how hard it was?' he said. 'How hard it's been to look after everyone?'

Jordan snorted. 'Yeah, you're clearly doing such a good job.' He changed then, holding himself taller and moving a little too close. Wesley recognised the brother he used to know.

'We needed you,' he said, refusing to back down. 'And you abandoned us.'

Jordan waved his words away. 'I didn't *abandon* you. It's not that simple.'

'It looked that simple from where I was standing.'

Jordan took a breath, ready to retaliate, before biting the words off. He turned away, cramming his hands into his pockets.

The words rose in Wesley's throat unbidden, and he knew he shouldn't let them out, knew he was winning and this would make him look weak. But these words had been waiting two years to be spoken and they wouldn't be stopped now.

'Why didn't you tell me you were seeing Dad?'

'This *again?*' Jordan turned back, face clouding with anger. 'Why can't you let it go?'

'What you told me, after I found out,' said Wesley. 'Is that really why he didn't want to see me?'

'It doesn't matter. I want to be part of the family again. Speak to Mum for me, you were always her favourite.'

If that was another way of saying he was soft, Wesley didn't care. He squared his shoulders and pointed to the door. 'You should go.'

'It doesn't have to be like this, Wes.'

'Go.'

Jordan nodded, finally looking defeated, until he brushed past to reach the door and stopped in the threshold.

'No wonder Dad didn't want anything to do with you.'

Wesley wore his blank expression like a shield. He waited until Jordan banged the door shut behind him before collapsing onto the couch, gasping for air like he had come up from underwater. If he had won that battle, the war was going to be hell.

10

Virtue Signalling

The pizzas arrived just as Wesley had convinced his whole body to stop shaking. He'd forgotten it had been ordered, and it felt like winning the lottery.

'Reckon you can eat a whole pizza, Eves?'

She nodded enthusiastically, and after she had climbed into the armchair Wesley put the box on her lap, knowing full well she would only manage a couple of slices. That meant there would be plenty left for breakfast.

Before he could sit down with his own pizza a message came through on his phone.

check your email mate.

While *Frozen* kicked off on the TV, Wesley retrieved the MacBook, setting it beside him on the sofa while he munched a slice of pizza.

He couldn't bring himself to check his email right away. First he put in earphones to block out the film and started a TrumourPixel video playing.

Next, he opened Facebook and typed 'Aaron Musley' into the search bar. He came up immediately. *Friends.* Wesley almost choked on his pizza. Facebook friends were not the real thing – plenty of people he had never spoken to at school had accepted his friend requests. Still . . . how could he be friends with Aaron here and not remember him at all?

The profile had been inactive for months. No updates, nobody tagging him in anything. Wesley stared at his profile picture. Blonde and blue-eyed, round jaw, grinning like he was the happiest person alive. If they had been at school together, Wesley would remember.

So why didn't he?

The email subject line read #SJWSlaughter Operations. He recognised the hashtag – it was the rallying cry for a growing online movement that railed against what it called PC culture, as well as decrying feminism and any other social movement calling for progress. A lot of critics called them a hate group, accusing them of spreading fascist propaganda and leading online mobs to attack outspoken women and people of colour.

The movement's leader was Niko Denton, a young right-wing journalist with a massive online following. His supporters were always desperate to impress him. He always knew what buttons to push to get them riled up, and could set them on a target without ever explicitly inciting attack. If you ever met him in the street, you'd probably think he was a nice young man.

While people like TrumourPixel had eagerly embraced #SJWSlaughter, Wesley had skirted carefully around it. He didn't care about most of what it stood for. It just seemed like a group that might accept him.

He opened the email.

all right mate click this and use the password NiK0sEl337ArMy.

The link brought up a login window, and he followed the instructions. It led to an encrypted chat channel, three other usernames already listed as present. Wesley recognised Luke and Justin's tags, but the third made his heart leap into his throat – *TrumourPixel.*

this is him, wrote Luke.

Wesley didn't know if he should say hello or introduce himself. He felt star-struck. in the end he stayed quiet. Across the room Evie laughed at something in the film, spitting a piece of pepperoni onto the carpet in the process.

'Jeff!' she shouted to her imaginary dog, clicking her fingers for him to clear it up.

After a few seconds TrumourPixel posted a link, and Wesley clicked. It opened a document hundreds of pages long. *#SJWSLAUGHTER CENTRAL ARCHIVE,* it began, above a royal coat of arms customised with an anime cartoon of a guy at his computer. That was followed by links to numerous 'operations' forums and chat rooms, and the Twitter handles of the document authors. Wesley didn't recognise the names.

Calling all agents of #SJWSlaughter! it continued. *We have victory on numerous fronts, thanks in no small part to fearless leader Niko Denton.*

As far as Wesley was aware Niko had never actually used the hashtag, though he referred to it often enough.

What exactly is Operation #SJWSlaughter? read a sub-header. *New tactics and strategic timing. Our enemies are moving against us. We must rise to meet the threat, and all of us must fight the cause.*

Another anime image, this time a guy wielding an oversized sword with #SJWSlaughter etched onto the blade. Wesley scrolled through the document. Every page was the same: a bizarre mixture of militaristic fervour and anime memes.

Evie began singing along with the film, and Wesley moved the MacBook screen away as if she might be able to read it, judge him for what she saw.

Back at the top, Wesley clicked through to one of the forums and scanned the topics. It was the usual sort of stuff:

Beta cucks taking over my school.

MRA gamer tag list.

Pick-up artistry Snapchat techniques?

Anybody on these forums would celebrate what he had done to Kat. She was an obvious target, a typical victim, the kind of girl who needed bringing down a peg or two. Nobody here would keep worrying about what had happened to her afterwards.

The chat pinged, and Wesley minimised the document.

Do you want to show them all what this fight really looks like? TrumourPixel had typed.

YES! replied Luke.

Bring it, wrote Justin.

Wesley's hands hovered over the keyboard, shaking just as badly as they had after facing Jordan, and he couldn't bring himself to type a reply.

Here's our target.

TrumourPixel added a picture of a girl with short curls of pink hair and bright red lipstick, smiling widely at the camera. Tinker, the YouTuber that attracted trolls like flies thanks to videos about feminism and sex and stuff. A thick black crosshair had been plastered across the image, aimed right between her eyes.

It's time they know we mean business, wrote Trumour-Pixel. *No more games, no more fucking about on the Internet.*

Wesley read the words three times over, trying to glimpse the truth behind them. Luke and Justin had said this was something bigger than *#SelloutSelena*, but that had to be because Tinker was a higher profile target. It would still be an online campaign. He had never considered that it might be *real*.

After a few seconds TrumourPixel posted an address for somewhere the other side of town.

2pm tomorrow, he wrote, and left the chat.

you in? wrote Luke.

Wesley needed to respond, so he told them what they wanted to hear, for now at least.

Yeah.

meet us tomorrow my house

The chat emptied out, and Wesley closed the MacBook quickly. Immediately he felt stupid – what had he really just agreed to? There was something about all of this that felt much more sinister than anything he'd been part of before.

Still, they had asked him to meet them, and he couldn't deny the flush of pleasure that gave him. He was actually going to meet TrumourPixel!

It didn't stop him thinking about Kat – he still needed to return her MacBook.

He opened the screen again and stared at Aaron's picture, trying to force himself to remember. Surely people couldn't be forgotten so easily? He picked up his phone and sent a message to Aoife.

You said you remember where Aaron lived?

The reply came a minute later. *Wesley? Yes, we remember.*

Can you meet me at school tonight? With everybody? he typed. *I need to see for myself.*

Okay, I'll try.

Wesley pocketed the phone. 'Finished, Eves?'

She groaned, having managed two and a half slices. Wesley's pizza sat forgotten beside him, his appetite gone.

'Get your shoes,' he said. 'You can walk it off.'

11

One of Us is Missing

Wesley arrived at school half an hour later, and was surprised to find not just Aoife waiting outside the gate, but Robbie and Jae too. They were bundled in thick coats, as if expecting an arduous winter to arrive overnight.

'My second Lonely People meeting,' Wesley said as he reached them.

'Unofficial,' added Robbie pointedly.

Nobody moved, perhaps because nobody really knew why they were there. They met every week, as far as Wesley understood it, yet they still seemed like strangers to each other.

'This is my little sister,' he said, trying to keep Evie from hiding behind him. 'Sorry, there was nobody else to look after her.'

'It's okay,' said Aoife, smiling warmly at her.

'Where does Aaron's family live?' asked Wesley.

'Not far,' said Aoife, pointing a direction and getting them moving. 'He used to walk to school. I think.'

They trailed away from the school in silence, heading deeper into the knots of residential streets that contained it. Street lights were beginning to come awake. The unseasonably chilly evening seemed to have kept people indoors, bikes and footballs abandoned in front gardens. A lone car belched steam into the air as it started up on a driveway.

Wesley had asked for this trip, leaving him obligated to try and chip away at the awkward atmosphere between them. 'So . . . you guys ever do stuff like this normally?'

'Stuff like what?' said Jae.

'I don't know. Hang out. Get some food, go to the cinema, whatever,' said Wesley, listing things he himself never did.

Robbie kicked a stone, sending it skittering into the empty road. 'The Lonely People isn't a social club. We're not just messing about.'

Changing the subject would avoid pushing the younger boy over the edge of his temper, but their group dynamic just didn't make sense.

'You shouldn't be lonely. You have each other,' Wesley said. 'Just send each other a message now and again. *How are you doing?* or *Look at my cat.* Whatever.'

'I don't have a cat,' said Aoife.

'I do,' said Jae, holding up his phone. 'She's called Minion.'

They all gathered around to look at a picture – all of them except for Robbie – Evie stroking the screen before she started telling Jae about Jeff. Wesley tore himself away from the cat.

'Why are you all so determined to not actually be friends?'

Robbie scowled. 'You don't understand.'

97

'More than you think,' said Wesley. 'All I know is I'd have killed to have people who understood what I was feeling.'

The silence as they continued walking was different this time, charged with every unspoken word of countless Lonely People meetings. It wasn't their fault, not really. Loneliness could make you reach out for company in all the wrong places, or make it seem an impossibility, even if an outlet was staring you in the face. There was comfort in being alone, unable to disappoint or be disappointed by others. Tell yourself enough, and it's not hard to believe that's the best you're ever likely to get from the world.

'We agreed to take you so we could remind ourselves what we're aiming for,' said Robbie. 'It's good to remember it really can be done.'

The others remained quiet.

The house sat on the corner, weeds poking through the brickwork driveway. The wall running alongside the pavement on one side was daubed with random graffiti. They huddled across the road, an indecisive stakeout.

'How long ago did Aaron disappear?' asked Wesley.

Blank faces. After everything, he believed a boy could fade out of existence. It had happened to Kat, and apparently to this other girl who used to be part of the Lonely People. What he couldn't believe – *wouldn't* believe – was that the boy's family could forget him. As if he'd never existed at all.

'Tell me three things you remember about Aaron.'

Robbie went first. 'He was tall.'

'Short hair,' added Jae.

'He lived there,' said Aoife, pointing to the house. 'And walked to school.'

Week after week sitting with Aaron in their meetings, and now he was a cardboard cut-out in their memories. If any one of them succeeded in fading, would the others here forget them like this?

The boy had been in the year above him. Or so they said. Wesley had forgotten him just as easily.

'When it's over . . .' he said. 'Where is Aaron now?'

They stumbled over each other to talk, Robbie winning out. 'He'll have chosen a Cradle and merged with them. He'll be somebody else now. He'll be happy.'

'That's not fair,' said Wesley, and set off across the road with Evie.

'What are you doing?'

He didn't look back. 'I'm going to knock for Aaron.'

The woman who answered the door was tall with short hair, and Wesley fought the urge to laugh. The other members of the group clustered behind him, and she stared at them all as if they were unwelcome trick-or-treaters.

'Mrs Musley?' Wesley asked. 'I'm looking for Aaron.'

She frowned a little, whether at the name or their presence on her doorstep. 'I'm afraid you must have the wrong house.'

Somebody plucked at his T-shirt, whispered that they should go, but Wesley put out a hand to stop her closing the door.

'He definitely used to live here.'

Mrs Musley shook her head, and for a moment sadness was etched into her face, dislodged from a shipwreck somewhere deep inside. She *hadn't* forgotten her son. Not completely. Wesley would make her remember, conjure Aaron back into existence like a rabbit from a hat.

'Can we come in?' he asked.

An expression of indescribable yearning greeted the request, as if some part of her had been awaiting this moment for a long time. 'Of course,' she said, and opened the door wide so they could shuffle guiltily past.

It was quiet inside, just a clock ticking somewhere unseen and the shush of their feet on the thick carpet as they were led past the stairs and deeper into the house.

'Eves, can you wait out here for just a minute?' Wesley asked, and she nodded, apparently glad not to go further.

They reached a big room flooded with dim light from glass sliding doors that overlooked the garden. Matching sofas edged the room, facing a huge TV. Every other patch of wall was taken up by mounted photographs. Family and individual portraits, candid shots from a wedding, photos of children taken in this very room. Wesley didn't have much description to go on, but in almost every photograph stood a boy who had to be Aaron.

Tall. Short hair. Vanished into thin air.

'Is that him?' he whispered to Robbie, who had to study a photo hard before confirming with a nod.

'Sit down, if you want,' said Mrs Musley. 'I'm sure we can figure out where your friend lived.'

Nobody sat. Wesley pointed to the largest family portrait: mother and father seated with their two boys behind them, one – Aaron – slouching so he wouldn't tower over his little brother. Jordan would never have done that. 'That's a nice photo.'

Mrs Musley answered without looking at it. 'Thank you.'

The others toured the photographs as if trying to commit them to memory. Jae took out his phone and snapped a picture of one where Aaron stood proudly in a sharp new suit.

'I'm sorry to barge in,' said Wesley, unable to keep himself from talking as if she were standing on a high ledge and threatening to jump. 'I just really think my friend – Aaron – used to live here.'

He was sure she flinched at the name, as if failing to pretend it meant nothing to her. 'We've lived here for over ten years,' said Mrs Musley, pointing to the neat garden through the glass as if that proved it. 'My son is home, I'll see if he knows who it might be. Joseph!'

My son. As if she had only one.

Footsteps thudded above their heads, and then a voice shouted from the top of the stairs. 'What?'

'I have some people here who might need your help.'

Wesley knew them only from the photos, but Joseph looked just like his brother. A little stockier, perhaps, but bearing the same bright eyes and rounded jaw. It had to be like having a ghost living in the house. Joseph stopped in the doorway, glancing between them uncertainly.

'They're looking for somebody called Aaron,' said Mrs Musley.

Something like anger bubbled to the surface before the boy could smother it. 'There's no Aaron here.'

There was a weight in Wesley's stomach, and he would only lift it by breaking through to these people and forcing them to admit the truth. He stepped closer to the family portrait and pressed a finger to Aaron.

'Who's this?'

At first, neither mother or son looked at the photograph. It wasn't deliberate denial; that might have been understandable. No, they seemed *incapable* of seeing him. Any memory of the other boy who used to live here was held just out of reach. They were surrounded by his image, and yet they never saw.

'Leave it,' said Robbie. The Lonely People had bunched together again, eyes on the carpet as if ashamed.

Wesley couldn't. 'You had another son. You had a brother. Now he's gone.' He looked between them pleadingly. 'You can't have forgotten him.'

Joseph spoke through gritted teeth. 'Get out of our house.'

'He's right there!' shouted Wesley, ripping the portrait from the wall and holding it out to them. 'Can't you see him?'

'I see him!' Mrs Musley cried, seeming to collapse. 'Aaron is gone!'

'Where? Where has he gone?'

She shook her head, dislodging tears that tracked down her cheeks. 'I don't know. He's just *gone*. Most of the time I don't even remember . . . it's like he was never here at all. And then the absence hits me like a wave . . . oh god!' She stumbled and slumped onto the nearest sofa, covering her face as sobs wracked her body.

Joseph grabbed hold of Wesley's shoulder and wrestled him towards the door. 'Get out of here!'

Still clutching the photograph, he was bundled along the hallway, the others grabbing Evie and following behind.

'Please, I just need to know what happened,' said Wesley. 'It's happening to somebody else and I need to stop it.'

'You're no better than the people who were sniffing around when we first realised he was gone!' shouted Joseph, shoving him through the front door.

'Who?' said Wesley as the rest of the group joined him outside, hurrying quickly back onto the road. 'Who was looking for your brother?'

The boy's expression softened. 'His friend Lukundo. He knew him from church.'

They hurried away and didn't stop until they were well clear of the house. Jae began to cry, and Aoife let him push his face into her shoulder. Robbie shoved his hands into his pockets and kicked his toes hard into the ground, over and over.

The family portrait felt heavy in Wesley's hands. He stared at it for a long moment, a bitter taste in his mouth.

'Do you want that to happen for all of you?' he said.

Not one of them would meet his gaze. They didn't speak again until they had traipsed back to the school.

'I want to know what happened to Aaron,' said Aoife. 'What really happened.'

'Me too,' said Jae.

Robbie watched them for a moment, and then nodded.

Wesley almost smiled, he was so relieved that he wouldn't have to do it alone. 'We'll find this friend his brother mentioned. He might know something.'

They split up to head home, but Wesley wasn't ready to go back to the flat. He had hardly learned anything new about the fade, and nothing that would help him pull Kat from its grasp.

He still remembered her when he shouldn't. There had to be a chance that he could see her, speak to her, when others couldn't. At the least, he still needed to return her MacBook. If he couldn't do it at school, he would just have to try her at home.

12

Confessions to the Void

Kat was supposed to be working on her video game, but concentration was in short supply. A *Backwash* episode – the one where Esme tries to recruit a crooked nuclear physicist through an elite dating website – was playing in the background. No matter how many times she watched the show, she never stopped swooning for Esme. She almost always wore this high-necked, flowing white dress, almost like a Victorian nightie. It would have made her look like she was floating, except she paired it with knee-high biker boots and spiked gauntlets. Her perm would have made the '90s blush.

In short, she was perfect. Kat wanted to be her and be with her. Whenever her boyfriend Roland came on screen she practically growled at him.

The other distraction was her stubbornly silent phone. She checked the chat log with Suzy again.

Hey, can we catch up soon? Call me. x - Seen 23.08

Nearly twenty-four hours ago and no reply.

Before any of this, she had considered inviting her sister to the women's march on Sunday. She felt strongly about its purpose, to stand up to the myriad injustices faced by women every day. It was the kind of event Kat had always wished she could attend if the mere idea didn't crumple up her lungs like an old paper bag. She certainly couldn't go alone, and Suzy had always liked to shout as loud as possible when she deemed anything unfair. It might have been something they could reconnect over. It's not like she could invite her sister to the WonderVerse comic convention that was running throughout next week. Suzy would have died laughing at the idea.

Oh well. Both could be added to the tottering pile of events she had missed because going anywhere there were other people was a terrifying ordeal. If only she could have been more like Tinker . . .

The concept of the game Kat was making was simple enough. The player took control of a barren planet devoid of atmosphere. The planet wants to prove it's as good as *popular bitch* Earth. To do that, the player must work to attract people and aliens, which is a problem when the planet has nothing to offer potential settlers.

So, using the planet's weak gravitational pull, you fish for resources – asteroids, space debris, astronaut corpses – and craft them into essential tools to improve gravitational pull, communication, terraforming, avocado growing etc. This gives the planet a better chance of attracting the lowliest living creatures, who further improve the planet, and so on. The end goal is to make the planet more populous than Earth (and not destroy it in some kind of terrible apocalypse).

It didn't do much of that yet, of course. It was mostly a wireframe rock floating on a field of stars.

Game development had never come naturally to Kat. Growing up she had mostly sucked at video games and always lost to Suzy. It was the *conjuring* of coding that appealed to her – out of nothing she could create little worlds that danced exclusively to her tune (and often to the cacophony of bugs and glitches before she rooted them out).

The deadline for the Spaced Out game jam competition was two months away, plenty of time to get a prototype working.

If she focused on the game, she wouldn't think about Safa and everything she had learned about the fade. She wouldn't think how singing 'Mr Pretzel' in the school corridor had made her feel more like herself than she had for months. She wouldn't think about how *important* it felt to have her hands held, skin-on-skin, irrefutably real.

She jumped when somebody knocked on her door.

'You okay in there?' said Dad.

The door was bolted, as always, but Kat still froze like she might be caught doing something she shouldn't. She paused the TV, leaving Esme frozen in the moment she accidentally seals her preferred physicist inside her secret lab and has to watch her die of radioactivity poisoning.

Usually Dad would give up if he didn't get an immediate response, but this time he kept talking. 'It feels like I haven't seen you in ages. I had this strange sense that I couldn't remember . . .' A strange hesitance laced his words as they trailed off, as if he felt he was breaching the rules of their arrangement. Kat stood, and padded gently to rest her ear against the wood.

On the other side, Dad sighed. 'It was like this with your sister, you know. She was here, and she made sure everybody knew it. Except when it came to me . . . she wasn't really there at all.'

They had each been there enough to argue, to wound each other with their words and make the house feel like a warzone. It had seemed so much, so overwhelming, that Kat had never thought it could be the result of something missing.

'I didn't want it to be the same with you,' said Dad. 'You clearly wanted space, and I thought if I gave it to you, did what I couldn't for Suzy or your mum, you wouldn't come to resent me the way they did.'

Kat pressed her fingers to the door, wishing they could push through to reach him. It was only fear of the fade that kept her from calling out to him, screaming that she didn't resent him at all. They had ended up like this because she had thought it was the best way to preserve what they had.

She had always thought he was going through the motions, but maybe she saw it that way to justify her unwillingness, her incapability to be there for him the way he wanted. Dad had tried, and she had not. She had been looking for connection everywhere else but here, the one place where she might have found it. Where it might have been needed the most.

There was a long pause, but she knew Dad was still there, breathing against the door. Finally he said, 'I miss you.'

Kat pulled back the bolt as quietly as she could and gripped the door handle.

'Go,' she whispered to herself, desperate to hug him, to feel his arms around her.

It was too great a risk. She couldn't face knowing for sure if her own father couldn't see her. If she had let their relationship decay for so long it could no longer be salvaged.

The doorbell rang downstairs, and she listened to Dad's footsteps move away to answer. Nobody ever knocked on the door, especially not at this time of night. Kat darted out onto the landing and leaned over the banister to listen.

'Hi, Mr Waldgrave.' It couldn't be – it was Wesley's voice. 'Is Kat home? I have her MacBook.'

There was a strange pause before Dad answered. 'I think she's upstairs. Go up, if you're quick.'

Feet scraped against the doormat. Kat couldn't believe he had got inside so *easily*. She had expected a hard line of questioning, aspersions cast on Wesley's character, some kind of ancestral background check. As far as Dad knew he was just sending some random *boy* up to her room.

Had he forgotten who she was, even for a moment?

She caught sight of Wesley at the bottom of the stairs, leading a little girl after him. Whirling away from the banister, she slammed her door shut behind her and threw the bolt across. Outside she heard the eighth stair creak as he neared the top.

If the door was locked he would go away, and Kat's heart wouldn't smash its way through her ribcage. Except she wanted to know why he was here. He could have left her laptop downstairs. Maybe there would be a chance to find out more about whatever he was planning against Tinker.

So, as feet moved along the landing towards her door, she slid back the bolt and retreated into a corner to watch.

Wesley knocked, once-twice-three times, counting them out to try and steady his nerves. There was no answer, and he didn't know if he had expected one. Beside him, Evie sneezed, failing as ever to cover her mouth.

'Hello?' he said.

He reached for the handle, and the door opened easily. Warm orange light spilled out from a desk lamp, and the TV was paused, a woman in a lab coat apparently choking to death behind a pane of glass. It seemed like somebody had been here just seconds before, but had evaporated as soon as his hand touched the door.

'Wow!' exclaimed Evie, spotting a shelf full of action figures and soft toys, pulling free of his grip to run for them.

'Careful, they're not yours.'

It was almost twice as big as the room he shared with Evie at home. He recognised the posters taking up every inch of wall, the tall shelving units filled with books, magazines, games and toys. The only strange thing was that he felt as if he was seeing it all from the wrong direction, and then he realised he was used to seeing it through Kat's MacBook set up on the desk. During the campaign against her he had watched every video, seen every photo she had put online, and they almost all came from her webcam. In a way, he had been here countless times before.

Evie gently picked up some kind of overstuffed squirrel and began whispering to it. The long, white desk sat opposite the bed, its surface clean except for a scattering of Post-it notes and the small TV at one end. He placed the MacBook down carefully, as if returning a sacred relic to its rightful place.

A brush of air against his ear, and his skin prickled as he whirled around to find nothing behind him but Evie fastidiously rearranging the shelves into some order only she understood.

'Are you here?' he said quietly.

A flush of embarrassment rose up his neck, but he knew without doubt that he believed it, that Kat had faded from sight. Somehow the room, seemingly frozen in time, proved it.

'If you can hear me, can you make a noise or blink a light or something?' he said.

A car passed outside, headlights grazing the ceiling. Nothing else.

There seemed to be a chasm in the room, hanging invisible in the air, and Wesley's body wanted to turn inside out to fill it. Before he could stop himself, he gave his confession to the empty space.

Kat stayed in the corner, making herself as small she could, and watched him peer around the room. It was an invasion, and she had to fight every urge that told her to fight or run. Invisibility made her safe.

While the little girl explored her stuff, Wesley took her laptop from his bag and placed it carefully on the desk.

The sight of it made her feel oddly bold. She moved behind him and leaned close to his ear.

'You can't hear me, can you?'

His ears pricked. He turned to look right at her, but almost at once his gaze slid away. When he spoke he turned on the spot, as if surrounded by unseen snipers.

'I brought your MacBook back. I'm sorry I took it.'

He leaned on the back of her desk chair and gripped the plastic until it creaked. All at once he seemed to break. 'It was me. I made you delete your website and everything. The last few weeks . . . it was all me.'

Kat was rooted to the spot, the meaning of his words sinking in slowly. She had suspected Luke and Justin, but until earlier that day had never had reason to even think of him.

'I read the letter on your MacBook, the one you didn't send to us,' he said. 'I didn't think it would be this bad. I didn't know something like this could happen.'

He turned on the spot again, looking to the corners of the room, like Kat might be watching him through hidden cameras. She was close enough to try and push him, but before her hands could make contact they bounced away, knocking her off balance. The force field. Anger filled her up, surely hot enough to burn through the fade and let her give him a piece of her mind.

'Am I supposed to feel sorry for you?'

'I'm alone. And I'm *angry*,' he said, oblivious. 'I just want somebody to know.'

Kat wanted to scream. Nobody could actually be this selfish. Could do this to her – to anybody – and consider themselves the victim.

'You can't fix your shitty life by doing shitty things to other people,' she told him. 'Except I bet you think you deserve better for nothing.'

'I can't tell anybody about it,' Wesley was saying. 'I can't look weak. I went online to find somewhere to belong, and this is all there was. Either I joined in, or I had nothing.'

For a long time, Kat was sure her online life had saved her. It hadn't just been a place to watch Tinker videos and trade *Backwash* theories and read fan fiction. It had offered a place to vent about feeling sad or frustrated. To seek advice from people who felt the same. Without it, she didn't know what she would have become. If young men couldn't find those spaces to explore what they were feeling . . .

'I didn't mean for this to happen to you. It was supposed to be fun,' said Wesley. 'I don't believe all that stuff they say in videos and forums. I know there's a lot of bad people there, but maybe it's the only community that will have me.'

'That's how it starts,' said Kat, circling around to face his blank eyes. 'It looks innocent enough, just a bunch of nerds spewing bile into the abyss. Until somebody else decides to capitalise on how detached they all are, makes them feel like they belong to something, and exposes them to more dangerous ideas. It's easier to talk openly about your inadequacies if you believe they're caused by a global conspiracy against you. Young men have nowhere else to deal with their anger, so these people aim it at a target that suits them. They recruit you, and you probably don't even notice it.'

Tinker had spoken about exactly this in one of her videos. It was no surprise they had identified her as a target.

Kat had never done anything to Wesley, and yet he had decided to destroy her life. Kat could hardly fathom the cruelty. Still, something about his confession made her feel for him; that he could only make it in a room that appeared to him to be empty.

'If this is my fault, I won't forget you. I want to fix it,' Wesley said. 'I just don't know how.'

'It's not your job to fix me,' Kat replied. 'That's not why you're really here. You think if I can be forgotten so easily, it could happen to you too. And that terrifies you.'

'They're planning something against Tinker. I know how much you love her,' he said. 'Whatever it is, I have to do it. I have to make them accept me. We're meeting tomorrow. I've left the address on your MacBook.'

Kat edged closer to him. 'Why are you telling me this?'

At the shelves, the little girl had grown bored of arranging her action figures into strange poses, and came back to Wesley, taking his hand.

'Tired now, Wezzer,' she said. 'Home?'

'In a minute, Eves,' he said. And then, to the room, 'I'm sorry.'

Kat couldn't help but sneer at that. 'I hope that makes you feel better about yourself.'

She followed them onto the landing, watched them put on their shoes and leave without Dad appearing to see them off.

Her eyes settled on her laptop. She closed herself back inside her room and opened the lid. There were still tabs open in a browser, and she scrolled through until she found the chat window.

There were so few details, but one thing was clear: TrumourPixel was planning an attack – either online or in the real world – on Tinker.

'This time it's personal,' she muttered to herself.

The trolls had defeated Kat, and she hated that she had let them. This was her chance to fight back – they were targeting Tinker for all the same reasons they had targeted her. This time she wouldn't lose.

Wesley had made it sound as if she needed him, and she couldn't allow that to be true. She retrieved her phone and found Safa's number.

What time tomorrow? she sent. Why keep lying to herself that she might not go? Everything she had seen, had been told by Safa and the Lonely People, screamed !!!DANGER!!! (wanton exclamation marks warranted), but she couldn't resist.

The response came a minute later.

Meat by the font tin about sex.

Kat stared at the message for a long time and wondered if she had forgotten how to read. *I don't know what that means*, she replied.

FUCKING SIRI. I use voice chat to write messages.

Why?

Because it's cool. That first message was meant to say MEET by the FOUNTAIN about SIX.

Kat paused a moment before typing a reply. Why did it feel like she was doing something illicit? *I'll see you there.*

You're the only person who will.

Mum was in bed when Wesley returned, so he retired quietly to the bedroom, breathing in the damp as he put Evie to bed.

The Musley family portrait had been stowed safely in his bag. Digging his fingers into the picture frame, he dismantled it and took out the photograph, turned it over and around as if to check it was real. Aaron beamed out at him, flanked by the family that had forgotten him.

Their own son. Brother.

Gone.

Carefully, he returned the portrait to the frame and reassembled it. A fleck of dust had become trapped under the glass. It pressed against Aaron's cheek like a blemish on his skin.

Wesley pushed the photograph under his pillows, and then tugged the covers up over his head to blot out the world.

13

Drive-in Saturday

Wesley pondered all the ways he would rather be spending his Saturday morning: working at the dealership, running a three-legged race with Jordan, and watching *Frozen* on loop with his eyes fixed open all came above paying a visit to the food bank.

'Thanks for coming with me,' said Mum, squeezing his arm as they neared the community centre.

Wesley nodded – as if he'd let her go by herself – but he knew he didn't deserve any thanks. The Salvation Army food bank was open to anybody who was struggling, which meant they didn't need a referral. It was hard enough for Mum to admit she needed help when she hadn't been able to pick up enough hours, without needing to seek permission for it. They were lucky, really, that they had only needed it a couple of times so far this year. That didn't make Wesley feel any less ashamed. Any less of a failure for not being able to look after his family.

The community centre was only around the corner, an old brown brick building next to a modern glass church of some kind. Nobody from school lived near here, that Wesley knew of, so they would only see him if they were in the same boat.

'You can wait outside if you want,' said Mum.

If he was ashamed, he wouldn't show it. He marched inside ahead of her. The double-door entrance was plastered with notices for Slimming World, only a single lopsided sandwich board to announce the availability of the food bank. Together they walked along a musty corridor, feet echoing on scuffed tiles, and turned in to the hall.

Although it was only mid-morning, it was already busy. A ragged queue trailed from a row of tables. Other people sat on plastic chairs lined against the walls. Before she joined the queue, Mum carefully scanned the room, apparently deciding the coast was clear.

'They're taking Evie to the zoo today,' said Mum as they waited their turn.

'Who's paying?'

She gave him a knowing look. 'They said it was their treat.'

Every other Saturday, Evie spent the day with a friend she had made at nursery. Their family said they were glad to have her, and they usually just played at their house. Sometimes they took them out on more expensive trips, and it was always their treat. Evie would come home raving about it, a new toy clutched in her arms, before settling in for another long two weeks stuck at home. Wesley was glad she could have those experiences, but he wished it was he that could provide them.

'You can't tell Dave about this, okay?' said Mum.

Wesley blinked, taken by surprise. It hadn't even occurred to him. He wasn't in the habit of telling anybody about the food bank. 'He must know we're not rolling in it.'

'That doesn't mean he needs to know we take hand-outs.'

The first time he had come here, Wesley had expected everybody to look homeless. To be queuing in dirty rags and loading their food into stolen shopping trolleys. Instead it was always mothers and fathers with prams, young people in their work uniforms, old men and women with walking sticks and hearing aids.

'If he judges you for this then he's no better than any of the others,' said Wesley.

'He won't *judge* me. It's just easier if . . .' Mum trailed off. 'He really does care about me. About *us*.'

We don't need him to, he thought. 'You said the same thing about the others.'

'And I can admit I was wrong. But I'm not wrong this time. I'm happy with Dave, and I think . . . can you please just do what I ask?'

Behind the tables, the food and supplies were kept in colour-coded plastic boxes loaded into a rack of shelves, a few tins and larger packets stacked separately. Everything was offered in carrier bags, some already made up and others pieced together based on somebody's needs. They usually took just enough to keep them going for a few days, to bolster the few things they already had. Thankfully Evie was the world's number one fan of baked beans on toast.

When it was their turn, Wesley accepted a couple of

119

pre-made bags. The cans clanked against each other as he lifted them. Then he moved across the room so Mum could ask for some personal items in peace. An older lady smiled at him from the next seat, and he returned it, before discouraging any further contact by taking out his phone.

It wasn't long before he was due to meet Luke and Justin. They wouldn't think much of this place, or of him for being there. It made him a failure – as a son and as a man.'Everything okay?' said Mum, joining him with a third bag.

Wesley stood. 'Yeah. Of course.'

'Not just here. With Dave, and everything.'

'I told you, it's fine.' He took the bag from her. 'Let's go.'

Outside, a beaten-up red Nissan Micra was waiting for them on the kerb. Jordan leaned against it, and when he spotted them he hurried over. Wesley gritted his teeth. There was no hiding where they had been. His brother tried to take the bags, but Wesley held tight.

'I saw you going inside,' Jordan said. 'Thought I could give you a lift back?'

'Thanks,' Mum said uncertainly.

Wesley released the bags suddenly. Cans spilled onto the pavement. Both boys dropped for them, racing to collect the most.

'I didn't know things were this bad,' said Jordan as he returned the food to the bag.

Under his mask of concern was an accusation. Two years had passed, and Wesley had failed to keep this from being necessary.

After the bags were loaded in the boot, Mum got into the passenger seat. Wesley lingered on the kerb.

'You coming?' said Jordan.

'I'm going to meet some friends.'

The jokey smile that always meant an insult was coming hadn't changed after two years away. 'Since when did you have friends?'

Wesley smouldered with anger. Without another word he turned away from the car and began the walk towards Luke's house.

Weekends had never really meant anything to Kat. The break between long blocks of duty and stress meant little when a Saturday morning began just as Friday had ended: alone in her room, a tenuous grip on existence. Days bled together.

So it felt strange to be outside, staking out Luke's house across town. Alongside everything else, Wesley had left Google Maps open with its location. It was a big place, on a block where every house was big and had more than one vehicle parked on its lengthy gravel driveway. This whole thing would have been cooler if she'd required an inconspicuous car and binoculars rather than standing across the road in what should have been plain sight, but she'd take what she could get.

That morning's selfie hadn't seemed to show the fade growing any more severe. It was possible that the Lonely People's information was wrong – but if nobody had ever been able to report back after experiencing the fade, that suggested they had never come back at all. Kat couldn't be complacent about it. If nothing else, the fade gave her the ability to investigate where nobody else could.

Shortly before the prearranged time, Wesley came along the road and stopped at the end of the driveway. He hesitated, like an alarm might sound if he put so much as a toe on the grounds. He took out his phone instead of making the trek to the front door. A few minutes later Luke and Justin crunched down to meet him, and after some needlessly aggressive back-slapping they set off.

Kat could have walked beside them unnoticed, but decided to maintain what she assumed was a customary tailing distance ten paces behind. Somehow she knew that whatever they were saying now wouldn't offer any detail on what they were planning. It was clear from Wesley's emails that they enjoyed knowing more than he did, dangling the danger over his head as if it proved something about their ability to handle it. It reminded her of how when they were little Suzy used to listen at doors and pretend to have overheard something salacious from their parents. She would use it to make Kat trail her around for a whole day, begging to be let in on the secret.

Luke and Justin walked tightly at Wesley's sides. Luke lit a cigarette and blew smoke luxuriously up into the air so that it gusted back into Kat's face. Away from the block of big houses the area changed rapidly, independent coffee houses and expensive-looking salons giving way to chicken shops and local cafes, the front line against the area's creeping gentrification. They had walked for around twenty minutes before they reached a row of flats, and cut into a wide track of sandy-coloured gravel to some garages tucked behind. They were old, a few garage doors buckled or missing completely. Weeds grew freely in the cracks between bricks.

As they approached a garage with its door still intact, Wesley glanced over his shoulder as if to check if anybody was following them. It could have been a reflex of nerves, or genuine expectation. Kat crept closer, knowing she might need to run to make it inside. The gravel under her feet sounded like a storm of hailstones, but none of them seemed to notice.

When Luke knocked, she half-expected a secret code and not just a simple thud on the metal. A moment later the door creaked and began to open. As the three boys ducked inside, Kat steadied herself with a breath and ran, slipping under the door just as it rattled down closed behind her.

14

It's Not the Horniness, It's the Loneliness

Most of the space was taken up by a car: an old Ford Mondeo, wheel arch rust stark against grey paint. A white strip light buzzed overhead, and the smell of oil clung to his nose. Wesley dismissed the idea that he was being taken prisoner, even as the garage door shrieking on its tracks and booming shut behind him seemed to reinforce it.

There was no sign of Kat. But that didn't mean she wasn't there.

'We're here,' Luke called into the garage.

A man stood up sharply from behind the car, moving quickly around to meet them. It was strange to see TrumourPixel in the flesh. He was only a couple of years older than them, but he seemed much larger, almost too wide to fit comfortably between the car and the wall. Muscle and fat had combined to lend him a threatening bulk. He held out a hand, and Wesley grinned as he took it. It was like meeting a celebrity.

'Glad you could come,' he said, voice so familiar from his videos.

'This is Wesley,' said Justin.

The man nodded as if he already knew. 'Call me Tru.'

'I watch all your videos,' Wesley blurted, growing hot with embarrassment.

'Thanks, man. These guys told me about you. Good work on that Kat girl. I had to take my video about her down or they were going to suspend my account. Censorship. Glad you guys could keep the torch burning.'

Wesley couldn't help but glow with the praise.

Luke ran his hand lightly along the roof of the car, and then rubbed the dirt between his fingers. 'This is a piece of shit.'

'It's inconspicuous,' said Tru, turning away from Wesley. 'More importantly, it can't be traced back to any of us.'

Luke moved around the car, checking the tyres and the lights. He didn't know anything about cars, but it was a convincing performance. Justin hung back near the door. For all their swagger coming over here, they were both on edge now. Both uncertain how to behave. That meant there had to be something big at stake.

'Relax,' said Tru, patting him on the shoulder. Wesley realised his entire body was rigid. 'Your friends here think you can help us out, so I wanted to meet you.'

'I'm not really good for anything,' said Wesley, automatically. He winced. Two minutes and he had already said the wrong thing.

Tru perched on the edge of the bonnet, and his face changed, softened, as if he had switched to a different persona. 'That's the kind of thinking we need to fight against. Why do you put yourself down like that?'

Wesley had never thought of it like that. He had always just thought there was no point in lying to himself.

'When you think like that you make yourself weak,' continued Tru. 'You can't reach an optimal state if you think you don't deserve it, and that means you can't go out and take what's rightly yours. That's why they make you think that way.'

'Who?' asked Wesley quietly.

The corner of Tru's mouth twitched into a smile. 'Females.'

It was a statement of fact, as if the answer should have been obvious. Wesley nodded, and nothing more. It was safer to stay quiet and let him talk.

'I showed you the target last night,' said Tru.

Wesley glanced into the empty spaces of the garage, wondering if he would see a shadow lurking there. 'Tinker?'

Behind him, Luke thumped the roof of the car. 'Bitch!'

'You seen her videos? Anti-men propaganda. As if we needed more proof that *feminists* are coming for our balls.' Tru's voice rose with every word, and it rang around the garage's walls. 'Look at what happens when you take away a man's rightful place: displaced, depressed, suicidal. You're not useless. They've made you feel that way because they want men like us gone.'

Men like us. He already thought of Wesley as somebody like him.

'We're going to do something to get Niko Denton's attention,' said Tru.

The garage was beginning to grow hot, the air stifling. Sweat prickled around Wesley's collar, and he swallowed hard. Tru must have noticed his reaction, because his eyes narrowed before he spoke again.

'There's this comic convention running near here all next week. Tinker's speaking there,' continued Tru. 'There'll be too much security for us to do anything inside, but there's plenty we can do with a car before she ever makes it into the building.'

The image of the car ploughing through a crowd of people flashed across Wesley's mind. There would be no online campaign. This was something else completely. He turned to the others, wondering if they already knew about this.

Luke smirked. 'Think of it like a prank. No big deal.'

'We're actually going to attack her?'

Tru studied him for a moment. 'If we were . . . would you have a problem with that?'

'I don't know, I mean, uh—' Wesley stammered.

Tru pushed past him and threw open the front passenger door of the car. 'Get inside.'

Wesley tried to pull away, but Luke grabbed his neck and wrestled him down, shoving him into the seat and slamming the door shut. While Tru rounded the car, Wesley tugged on the door release. Luke laughed as he used his weight to hold it shut. The car lurched as Tru dropped into the driver's seat. There was an electronic whir as he locked all the doors. Wesley banged on the glass, sweat now pouring down his face.

'You don't think I'm right?' said Tru, voice eerily calm.

'I don't know!'

'You think it's fair you have to look after your little sister?'

Wesley stopped, and slowly turned to face him. 'You don't know anything about that.'

Tru shrugged. 'Just what your friends told me. You can't *want* to spend all your time babysitting, doing women's work while your life goes nowhere.'

'It's not their fault.'

'I'm just saying, I've seen it before. Females convince a boy like you that he has to accept being a beta. Your mum doesn't respect you the way she should, especially after everything you've done for her. Girls at school won't even look at you, let alone think about going anywhere near your cock. When you finish school you've got no idea what you're going to do next. You can't tell me you think that's right?'

Wesley had never thought there could be anybody as pathetic as him. If he was a specimen in a glass jar, he would be hidden at the back of a museum, too unremarkable for anybody to want to see.

'How can it be their fault?'

'If it's not,' said Tru, smiling like he could see victory three moves ahead in the conversation, 'why did you go after Kat Waldgrave?'

That caught Wesley off-guard, and he stammered, 'I don't know, I—'

'You *do* know.'

He remembered everything he'd poured out into Kat's empty room last night, hoping some remnant of her was there to hear it. There was something wrong with him, and he had hoped that going after Kat might fix it. Nobody else was responsible for the way he was.

Unless . . . it would be so much easier if they were.

'Can't we just make her take her channels down?' Wesley said. 'You know I've done it before, maybe if we—'

Tru cut him off with a cold laugh, and used the driver controls to lower the window, allowing Luke to lean inside. 'You said he was for real.'

Luke eyed them both warily. 'I thought he was.'

Pinned between them, Wesley felt like a prey animal. Toyed with before the killing blow. The garage could have been another world, one where something terrible could happen to him and nobody outside it would ever know. He had no idea if Kat had taken the hint to follow him, but he hoped she would be here to see it.

'I told you,' said Tru. 'It's just going to be a prank video. Something to shake her up a little.'

'What kind of prank?'

'I can't tell you until I know you're with us.'

Wesley looked to Luke for help, but the boy's amusement had turned to something colder as he waited for the answer. All Wesley had wanted was for Luke and Justin to accept him. It would have been so easy to nod his head, tell them what they wanted to hear, just so they would let him be part of their group. All he had to say was . . .

'I want to go.'

Luke leaned into his face. 'What?'

'Whatever you're planning, I just need some time to think about it.'

Tru watched him coldly. 'If you're not with us, you've already seen too much.'

A chill ran down Wesley's spine. He needed to get out of there. The door handle slipped in his sweaty palm.

'I won't tell anybody anything, just let me out!'

The doors whirred again. Wesley shoved it hard, smashing it into Luke's stomach. That gave him the space to wheel away towards the garage door. Justin had turned white as a sheet and seemed to have no intention of stopping him. The door was unlocked, and Wesley threw it open, blinking in the sharp daylight.

'Next time I see you I'll show you what happens to traitors!' shouted Luke.

Wesley didn't look back, kicking up gravel as he ran.

Kat pushed herself against the wall as Luke came around the car to heave the door closed again. She had to fight the urge to escape. She had heard enough to know that these men were dangerous, without learning any real information. If they were planning to attack Tinker, she wanted to have every chance to stop it.

'Bravery is a beggar's death,' she muttered, a line from *Doctor Backwash*.

'Why did you bring him here?' roared Tru, voice booming around the garage. 'Do you think we're just fucking around?'

Now Luke looked like he wished he had run while he had the chance. 'It doesn't matter, right? We're still good to go next week without him.'

Next week. Tinker had talked about it in one of her latest videos. WonderVerse comic convention was at a venue across town, and she was speaking on Tuesday's headline panel about online abuse of women.

'Females like Tinker are trying to *destroy* men,' shouted Tru, thumping the roof of the car. 'And all these little boys think they're alpha because they shitpost on message boards. Nobody is *doing* anything. You think Niko Denton's going to be impressed if we hit her social media with dank memes? Or a stupid prank?'

Luke and Justin shook their head like chastised choir boys.

'We can follow her every move – attention whore makes it too easy.' He waved his phone at them. 'It's our duty to take action.'

Whatever they were planning, it was more than a prank. Kat had heard this kind of rhetoric before, though usually hidden behind anonymous Twitter accounts. If it spilled into the real world, there was no telling the damage it could do.

'I don't need to worry about your mate, do I?' said Tru, locking up the car.

'No, no, definitely not,' said Luke, a little too quickly. 'He's not our mate. And he's too much of a pussy to tell anybody. He doesn't even know anything, anyway!'

Kat watched Tru lean down to hide the car keys inside the front wheel arch. Then he opened the garage door again. 'I'll be in touch tonight,' he said.

Luke and Justin hurried away down the gravel track, while Tru carefully locked up the garage before returning to the road. Kat lingered until he was gone.

The promise of an attack on Tinker felt like another

attack against her. She hadn't fought back before, but she could now.

She laughed. It was almost perverse that the fade was allowing her to be more herself than she ever had been before it. She had always wanted to make a difference, to stand up for what she believed in, but never had the confidence. The fade gave her that.

'I won't let you get away with this,' she said, scooping up a handful of the sand-coloured gravel and dropping it into her pocket. Although she deepened her voice like a wannabe hero, she knew in her heart that it was true.

15

Always Punch Nazis

There was still some time to kill before Kat was due to meet Safa, so she went home to do a little research.

First, she emptied the gravel from her pocket onto the desk, scooping it into a neat heap that would be difficult for anybody to miss. Then she dialled 999.

'Which service do you require?'

'Police,' she said.

Silence, and then again. *'Which service do you require?'*

'They're turning my car into Swiss cheese!' Kat shouted. 'I need back up, now goddammit now!'

The call disconnected. As she had suspected, the automatic operator, like everybody else on this stupid planet, couldn't hear her. She'd have to figure this one out by herself.

Next, she went online and looked up TrumourPixel. His Twitter account came up first, and Kat couldn't help but laugh. His profile picture was him drawn as an anime character, muscles bulging out of a vest, wielding an axe bigger than his body. It was a well-worn tradition in troll accounts: anime avatars, or failing that no image at all. Certainly few of them were brave enough to reveal their true face.

She had seen his profile before, when he released the attack video against her. It had seemed innocent enough, as it did now – mostly links to his videos, screenshots from games, updates on what he was eating. There were only a few telltale signs: retweets from gaming outlets owned by right-wing media; an article about it being hypocritical to punch Nazis; frequent use of the green frog emoji.

'Pepe the fucking Frog,' Kat muttered to herself. It was hard to think of anything she hated more than the cartoon frog appropriated as a meme for Internet trolls and bigots.

She decided to delve deeper and check who he was following. Straight away she found more extreme accounts. Some were the usual suspects: prominent personalities who peddled hate while posing as film reviewers or video game streamers, always studiously avoiding saying anything too inflammatory. Others had blatant fascist imagery as profile pictures.

'Nazis,' Kat muttered. 'I hate those guys.'

She clicked one and read its profile.

Fighting for the #truth against #whitegenocide. #AllLives-Matter #FeminismIsCancer #IslamIsCancer #Brexit #Stand-UpandFight. Finished with raised fist and English flag emojis. The account reposted news from thoroughly disreputable sources about anti-fascist protests turning violent, Muslim terror suspects being released from custody early, feminist critics rallying against a movie about zombie strippers.

Of course, TrumourPixel was also following Niko Denton. She clicked through to his profile and read his latest tweet. It was quoting a question somebody had asked him.

Should we take action against the women's march in London tomorrow?

Niko's response read: *I don't know, what do you think?* It was finished with an emoji of somebody painting their nails.

It was a simple but effective trick: incite hatred and violence, but always in a way that would allow you to wash your hands of it.

This was who TrumourPixel was trying to impress with whatever he was planning. These were the people Kat had always wanted to fight. Maybe the fade meant she could.

Wesley knew he shouldn't feel proud about his ability to wax cars, but he was definitely getting better at it. Every time Dave walked past and offered an impressed nod he couldn't deny the surge of pleasure it gave him.

'You're a loser,' he whispered to himself as he circled away the last smear of wax from his third car of the afternoon. The pleasure always quickly caved into shame.

At least it took his mind off what had happened earlier. The looks on their faces as he had run from the garage. Whether they were going to come after him or not. The fact that he couldn't stop thinking about the reasons Tru had given him for everything in his life going wrong.

'Take a break,' said Dave, emerging from the back office to hand him a mug of tea. They leaned against one of the unwashed cars and sipped their drinks – not half enough sugar for Wesley's taste – in silence for a few moments.

Dave sighed with pleasure and held his mug against his chest. 'You're a natural at this.'

'It's not exactly rocket science.'

'Rocket scientists are too smug to polish their rockets.'

Wesley looked at him sideways. 'I bet you'd never stop polishing your rocket if you had the chance.'

Dave lifted his mug, oblivious. 'You're not wrong.'

They both took a long draught of tea, Wesley using it to stifle his laughter, before exhaling contentedly together.

'Was everything all right with your brother the other night?'

Wesley stiffened, defences automatically coming awake. 'Yeah, nothing to worry about.'

'That's good.' Dave turned to face him in a movement that was meant to be casual, but was clearly anything but. 'I don't need to worry about him, right?'

'What do you mean?'

'Maybe it's not my place to judge because I wasn't around before, but from what your mum's told me . . . I need to know Jordan can be trusted.'

Wesley put his mug on the roof of the car and turned to face him. 'Or you'll do what?'

Dave smiled unconvincingly. 'It's not like that. It's my job to look after you both.'

'It's not your job. We were fine before you showed up.'

'Hey, Wes, I didn't mean—'

Wesley turned away and made for the office, satisfied that his shift was over. All at once he was desperate to be home. If there was any problem with Jordan, he would deal with it himself.

16

People Like Us

The fountain sent three perfect jets of water arcing up and up, where they seemed to hang suspended for a long moment, glistening in the lights of the surrounding bars and restaurants, before they dropped into the pool below where crisp packets floated like lily pads. Specks of water darkened the paving stones at Safa's feet as she spotted Kat's approach, pushing herself up from the edge of the concrete bowl.

Their condition should have made it impossible to be brazen, but Safa had managed it; she wore jean shorts cut off high up her thighs, white frays dancing against her skin as she walked, and a sleeveless top left her arms bare. The nesting doll locket rested on her collar bone. The fade was visible even in the dying light, the balletics of the fountain shimmering through her skin like shooting stars across a night sky. It was oddly mesmerising, and Kat's doubts about the evening seemed to melt away as she sped up to reach her.

'Whoa, careful!' shouted Safa.

There was a screech of wheels. Kat jumped out of the

path of the mobility train, an electronic cart that towed people up and down the slope of the high street. The driver glared at his feet, searching for some technical problem to blame, and then swerved around her to resume his rounds.

'You're invisible, not invincible,' chastised Safa, pulling Kat into a hug that made her tingle from head to toe. The fade seemed to have set her nerve endings alight, like flowers opening to drink the sun, and any physical contact was the sweetest pleasure.

'That explains why the invisible man went extinct,' said Kat. She immediately winced at her own joke.

'You're such a dork.' Safa said it with a grin. 'I'm glad you came.'

Kat smiled, realising just how glad she was too. 'How could I resist a night on the town?'

Safa looked the length of the high street and shrugged with her mouth, lips twisting. 'I remember when you couldn't walk down here at night without being stabbed, or worse.'

It had been rough there, years ago, though not quite as rough as that. There had been empty shops, the occasional drunk man shouting from a doorway. The pervasive smell of urine. Gentrification had stripped most of that away and turned those empty shops into artisan cafes and pop-up restaurants, classy boutiques and shiny estate agencies. The high street had been pedestrianised, the area at the top developed into a wider square with bars and restaurants on all sides, tables and terraces spilling onto the street. It had, in short, lost all its character. The fountain, Kat had always thought, was a touch too far.

'There was a time when the pavements were nothing but broken glass,' said Kat. 'You're probably too young to remember.'

'You'd never know if a sniper would just *pop!* Burst your head like a melon.'

'And of course the flashers, lining the road to salute you with their—'

'Okay, stop you win!' said Safa, skipping away from the fountain and across the square. 'Geez, potty mouth, I think you have a problem.'

Kat laughed, and followed her towards a wide seating area where outdoor heaters were beginning to glow. It was too early to be busy, straggling shoppers not yet giving way to the vanguard of a big night out. Safa led her to Cluckers, a chicken place that was comfortably the least classy choice on the square, which meant it was always crowded. A queue of people waited to be seated, but Safa waltzed past them and promptly found a small table pushed against the far wall.

'Shouldn't we . . .?' said Kat.

Safa dropped into her seat and spread her arms wide. 'Who's going to stop us?'

Before Kat could even sit a waiter weaved through the tables towards them, leading a young couple after him. When he reached their table he frowned like he had forgotten something, glanced at them for the briefest moment, before turning back to his customers apologetically and taking them elsewhere.

Kat took a seat. 'Have you done this before?'

'No, I was worried they might end up sitting in our

laps.' She had surprisingly dark eyes that nevertheless seemed to glow with good humour.

'I still don't understand how you're not scared about this.'

'I am scared.' Safa leaned forwards on her elbows. 'Because I've just realised we're not going to get served, and I am – literally – wasting away.' She peered hungrily at the food on other tables, licking her lips.

'Can you be serious for long enough to give me a straight answer?'

Safa sighed theatrically. 'Fine. What are you scared about?'

'Uh, well, let's start with the fact that I'm *disappearing*,' said Kat. 'As far as the rest of the world is concerned I don't exist any more.'

Safa slammed her palms on the table, cutlery and condiments rattling. 'Of *course* you're scared if you're thinking about it like that! Let me rearrange your world view a little.' She swept a hand across the restaurant. 'What if it was everybody else in the world who had disappeared, and there was nobody else here – just me and you?'

'That doesn't make—'

Safa held up a faded finger to silence her. 'That's how it might as well be. If we don't exist to any of them, they don't have to exist to us.'

Slowly, she scraped back her seat and leaned across to the next table, plucking a limp chip from a plate. The woman it belonged to looked puzzled, almost aware that something was amiss, before the moment passed and she returned to her meal. Safa chomped the chip triumphantly.

'You really shouldn't do that,' said Kat, but she couldn't keep a smile from her lips.

'Gotta steal to eat, gotta eat to live.'

Hesitantly, Kat stood and surveyed what the woman's dining companion had in front of him. His half chicken had already been reduced to greasy bones, but a bowl of mashed potato sat neglected. Before she could lose her nerve, Kat scooped up a glob with her finger and pressed it to her tongue.

'Yes!' said Safa, punching the air. 'Does danger make it taste sweeter?'

Kat grimaced. 'Not really.'

'What do you expect? We're in Cluckers.'

Safa danced away, pirouetting between tables. She plucked a chicken wing as she went, gripping it between her teeth like a rose. Although Kat had little appetite, she grabbed at somebody's plate as she followed towards the door, and ended up liberating almost a full chicken.

'Should we leave a tip?' said Safa, and they burst laughing back onto the square.

The high street was busier than before, people migrating to the pubs and restaurants now night had fallen. Safa was in full flow, discarding the chicken wing and grabbing the cap of a passing student to frisbee it onto the handles of a nearby pram. Its owner fumbled after it, all apologies, while the girls cackled.

'We might as well enjoy ourselves,' said Safa, already scanning the street for more potential mischief. 'Are you telling me you've never thought about what you'd do if you turned invisible?'

She would never admit it, but Kat had a plan of action for

the sudden onset of all garden-variety superpowers (and a few niche ones too). This was different. A superpower could be called upon at will, switched off or disguised. The fade didn't feel like a superpower. It felt like a failing.

Safa had approached a group of schoolboys who were passing a football between them in a ragged circle. As it bobbled over the paving stones she intercepted and rolled it to Kat. One of the boys ran after it, prompting her to panic and punt it away down the street. The schoolboys watched after it helplessly.

There wasn't time to feel bad. They ran along the high street, launching off benches and whooping at the tops of their voices. Nobody paid them any mind unless there was no choice, and even then little more than a cursory glance, a resigned sidestep. It made Kat want to push harder, push as far as she could to find their breaking point and force them to acknowledge her existence.

A middle-aged woman was moving leisurely between shops, watching lights flick off and shutters come down. In full view, Kat reached into her handbag and took her purse. The woman didn't see, even as Kat lifted a twenty-pound note.

'Now you're getting the hang of it!' said Safa, before snatching the money and setting off at a run.

'Hey!' said Kat, smothering her guilt and giving chase.

It might not have been a superpower, but she would never have believed it could be so much fun.

There was wax in his mouth, and Wesley wasn't sure he would ever get it out. His arms ached, and his hands felt wrinkled and tight from all the water. If there was more than £10 from his mum's boyfriend in his pocket, he might have felt proud.

'The men have returned from work,' announced Dave.

'Oh yeah, I wouldn't know anything about that,' Mum called from the kitchen, 'having spent the afternoon cleaning up diarrhoea from a bingo hall.'

'All right, you win.' They met in the kitchen doorway and Dave pulled her into a hug, kissing the top of her head. Despite the diarrhoea, she looked happier than Wesley could remember in a long time. He felt a pang of jealousy, almost like a stitch in his side.

There was no sign of Jordan, which meant he'd decided to stay away for now. Wesley's place here was already slipping. It would go completely if his brother got his way. Wesley took out his phone and sent him a message.

We need to talk.

At almost the same moment a message arrived from Aoife. *We've found Lukundo. He's in the choir at Aaron's old church. Should we go see him?*

Wesley replied immediately. *Do you want to?*

I think we all do. You?

Almost nothing else in his life seemed more important. *Meet tomorrow morning at school.*

He paused in his bedroom doorway to hug Evie, and then went to the bathroom to scrub his hands and wash out his mouth.

The phone vibrated, and as he dried his hands he tried to guess who had replied. He guessed wrong – the message was from Jordan.

Where?

Wesley thought quickly. *Garden Hill in half an hour.*

It was somewhere they had gone together as kids, when things were different. It seemed fitting now he wanted things to change.

A slushie stall was open late, wringing the dregs of summer business, and Safa stepped past the attendant to slap the twenty-pound note on the counter and poured them both tall cups of bright red ice. Before Kat could take a sip the mobility train stopped behind them to pick up an elderly couple and their shopping.

'Come on,' said Safa.

In one smooth motion she leaped onto the luggage platform at the back of the train and deftly kicked herself up onto the roof of the rear cart. Significantly less confident in her climbing ability, especially while clutching a slushie, Kat wedged a foot into the rack. Before she could heave up her weight the train began to move, leaving her skipping one-legged behind it.

'This is an embarrassing moment you'll remember for ever,' called Safa, reaching down a helping hand.

Kat dropped the slushie and hauled herself forward, gripping Safa's fingers and scrabbling awkwardly onto the juddering roof.

'You're freakishly strong,' she breathed.

'Like a mother lifting a car off her child.'

The roof of the mobility train was cold and smooth. They sat cross-legged and facing each other as it moved off down the high street.

Her own beverage lost, Kat accepted the remaining cup of fluorescent slush and took a long sip, before clutching her forehead.

'Jesus Christ, brain freeze.' It felt like being trepanned with an icicle.

'Press your thumb against the roof of your mouth,' said Safa.

'You what?'

Safa huffed frustratedly and shoved her thumb into Kat's mouth. Its incongruous warmth swiftly thawed the painful frost.

'Uh, thanks,' said Kat once her mouth was a thumb-free zone, and then smacked her lips. 'What's that taste?'

'Nobody knows what orifices this humble thumb has plumbed before.'

Kat took a slug of slush to wash out the unsettling flavour, which only gave her brain freeze again. 'Dammit!'

The train eased to the bottom of the high street, where gentrification had been held at bay by a butcher that had been there longer than Kat had been alive, newsagents and phone-unlocking shops. Nobody was waiting for collection, so their ride turned around and began the slow return journey uphill.

'Shouldn't this be enough?' said Kat, as the street glided by.

'We had two before you dropped yours.'

'No, I mean us. We're together and we're having fun.' It came out as a question – what if Safa wasn't having fun at all? – but the other girl nodded for her to continue. 'Shouldn't this reverse the fade? It should count as a connection to the world.'

Safa seemed to consider this for a second, and then turned her head to watch the people they were passing. 'Look at everybody here. It all comes so naturally to them.'

On cue a group of lads clutching pints outside a pub burst into laughter. Couples were strolling hand-in-hand between restaurants, casually checking menus in the window.

'They belong here, the way they are. They always have,' said Safa. 'They have a real place.'

For as long as she could remember Kat had felt separate to these people. To *all* people. She had envied how easily they fit, how the fabric of the world had made space for them.

'And we don't?' she said.

'It's not just us. Some people never manage to find it. You remember Aaron? Well, *of course* you don't remember him, that's kind of the point.' Safa rolled her eyes. 'Anyway, he was secretly dating Selena.'

'Selena *Jensen*?'

'Selena freakin' Jensen. I caught them kissing once. Literally the hottest girl in school, the one *everybody* wanted. And I think he really loved her. But he couldn't make that connection last. Some people just can't.' Safa took her hand, chilled from the drink, and it felt more real than anything. 'Can you honestly tell me you've ever felt like you belong?'

She had, for a time, in the communities she'd found online. That might have unravelled, but it had been real. Losing it wouldn't have affected her so severely had it not. Had it come at the expense of relationships in the real world? She might have been putting her eggs in the wrong basket all along.

The cart rumbled underneath them. In that moment, face-to-face with Safa, Kat felt like she had found a place to belong. They were like an undiscovered deep sea species, strange and translucent, unseen by human eyes.

'I always wanted a friend who would message me out of the blue, even if it was something totally random, a picture or video they thought I'd like,' said Kat. 'It shows somebody out there is thinking of you. I thought when I grew up I would find my people. My lifetime friends, like the *Backwash* crew have. It just . . . never happened. Maybe it doesn't happen for people like me.'

'It can happen now,' said Safa, eyes zealously wide. 'The fade is the only chance we have to make a place for ourselves.'

Kat took a shaky breath. 'You really believe it'll let you become another person?'

'It has to!' Safa said. 'You think I made this happen just so I could steal some chips and mess with people?'

A façade had slipped, though only enough for Kat to know it was there, not to glimpse beneath it. There was so much Safa was hiding, so much she was pretending to be. She tugged at her jean shorts, and Kat saw now how uneven they were. Wildly frayed edges spoke of scissors and spur of the moment.

They jumped down from the mobility train when it stopped to let pass an already bedraggled hen party. When they returned to the square they found the night in full swing, outside seats at capacity with more standing around them. Kat yearned for each person they passed, as if they were tugging at her soul, coaxing it closer to become inextricably bound up with theirs.

She tried to ignore it. 'Being ourselves has to be better than being nothing.'

'The fade doesn't make us nothing,' said Safa.

'So what are we?'

'Whatever the fuck we want! Who do you want to be tonight?'

The answer surged to the surface of Kat's mind, like flotsam on a swell. If the fade was an opportunity to be somebody else, *anybody* else, it would allow her to be who she had never been: herself. The person she had always wanted to be in the real world.

'There's something I want to do,' she said. 'It's dangerous, and a bit stupid.'

Safa seemed to puff herself up, the façade snapping firmly back into place. 'I like the sound of it already.'

17

The Fight Never Stops

Garden Hill was the focal point of the nearest park, a lump of mud and grass rising tall enough to be seen above the houses around it, a ring of trees scratching at the sky from its top. By day it was the domain of dog walkers and joggers, and by night an unearned reputation for being dangerous meant it was studiously avoided.

A lifetime of warnings jangled in Wesley's head as he shut the metal gate behind him and made his way up the concrete path. It was beginning to drizzle, fallen leaves growing slick underfoot. It wasn't the idea of unknown assailants lingering in the dark that worried him. It was facing who he knew would be waiting at the top.

Jordan was silhouetted against the sky, a human shape blotting the town's jumble of lights. When he heard Wesley's approach and turned, it was impossible to see the expression on his face.

'Haven't been up here in a long time,' he said.

'I know,' said Wesley, trying to remember his last visit, sure it must have been together.

'I remember when I first came here – not specifically, you know, but when I was little – it seemed so *huge*. I probably thought I could see the whole country from up here. It's weird, thinking how small my world used to be.'

Wesley gritted his teeth. 'I bet you saw a lot more impressive things in Australia.'

'You don't have to go that far to expand your horizons.'

Being stuck at home, looking after the mess Jordan had left behind, hadn't given him much of a chance.

'Why did you want to meet up here?' said Jordan.

'I thought it would bring back some memories.'

'It does.' The low light caught Jordan's smile. 'Remember when we had that frisbee, and we thought if we threw it from up here it would go all the way to our house?'

'It's probably still in that bush.'

'We must have lost so many things up here, man. Like that random baseball you had from the charity shop.'

Wesley remembered it. 'It was signed by some American player. I really loved it. You dropped it in the mud and rubbed it off.'

'Ah, shit. I don't remember that.'

They stood with an empty space between them, and Wesley kept his eyes on the view. Headlights traced familiar roads and cranes blinked red and white. If his brother had forgotten what used to happen there, Wesley was ready to help him remember.

'What about that time you invited me to come up here with all your friends?'

Jordan frowned. 'You came up here with us a few times, didn't you?'

'Twice,' said Wesley. 'I was so excited the first time because I'd been wanting an invite for ages instead of being stuck at home by myself. They were already up here, and soon as we joined them you ordered them all not to speak to me.'

Beside him, Jordan was silent, though he let out a sharp breath through his nose.

'At first we were all just sitting around, and nobody would even look at me. When we played football, you made sure nobody passed it to me. It was like I didn't exist. Then you went home and left me here by myself.'

'Come on, I was probably just messing—'

'The second time,' said Wesley, knowing he wouldn't be able to stop until he was finished, 'you had to convince me because I didn't want the same thing to happen again. You said you had just been messing around, that it was like a test, and I'd passed. So I went with you again.'

'Look—'

This time Wesley could tell that his brother remembered, and he wanted to make him squirm. He had bottled these memories up for years, and now the cork had popped.

'You put me in a fight against somebody else's little brother. I didn't want to do it, but you said I'd embarrass you if I chickened out. All your mates crowded round and I knew I didn't have a choice. When I lost, you told me I'd let you down and you wished the other boy was your brother.'

'What's your point?' said Jordan, rounding on him, feet scraping in the dirt. 'I did shitty things as a kid. I'm sorry, all right.'

'Why couldn't you have been kind to me?' said Wesley, feeling his throat grow thick. He fixed his eyes on the horizon's lights, tried not to notice how they blurred.

Jordan laughed sharply. 'Kind? What makes you think you deserved it?'

'I needed it,' Wesley said, turning to face his brother, noticing for the first time that they were almost the same height now.

'Nobody was ever kind to me, you don't see me crying about it.'

'What about Dad?' Wesley shouted.

'You wanted to know if it was true, what he said about you? I think you've just proved it,' spat Jordan. 'You really are too soft to be his son.'

The garage seemed ten times more sinister by night, and the gravel underfoot ten times louder. Kat kept admonishing herself for not wearing a balaclava, each time remembering it would have been pointless.

'A balaclava wrecks your peripheral vision, anyway,' said Safa. 'And your hair.'

They reached the flaking garage door, and Kat pushed its top. It rocked on its rail before the latch caught.

'It's locked,' said Safa, who seemed to have a particular passion for stating the obvious.

The door was old. By leaning enough of her weight on it the bottom opened by a couple of inches before the locking mechanism could stop it. She transferred the pressure to Safa, and then dropped to her knees, snaking an arm into the gap. Paint and dust lodged in her fingernails. The mechanism was old, little more than a rusty latch, and a few hard tugs dislodged it.

'Kat burglar,' whispered Safa.

Kat answered with a regal bow.

Inside, everything was as it had been just a few hours before, the old car blocking the shelves at the far end of the space. Kat slipped around it and checked the shelves quickly for anything she might have missed earlier, but there was nothing significant.

'This is the bad guys' lair?' said Safa, swiping dust from the roof of the car.

On the walk over, Kat had told her everything she knew about their plot. Safa hadn't seemed to care too much about foiling Nazi terrorists and saving Tinker, but she was *very* excited about stealing a car.

'All the cars in the world and you want this pile of junk.'

The key was still in the wheel arch, and Kat held it up triumphantly. 'If they don't have the car, they can't hit anybody with it.'

Safa shrugged her lip. 'You don't have to get involved at all.'

'You said you didn't fade so you could just mess around,' said Kat, opening the driver door. 'If it gives me a chance to stop them, I have to take it.'

She slipped in behind the wheel, and Safa dropped into the passenger side. The car smelled of cheap deodorant, the kind little boys were told would attract fantasy women.

'Do you know how to drive?'

'I've had a lesson.'

'That isn't at all the same thing.'

After fumbling the key into the ignition, Kat gripped the steering wheel in both hands. Stealing a car was not something she would usually do, or even *think* about doing. Maybe that was the point; she was either more herself than ever or not herself at all. The boundaries of her body had blurred. It was time to be boundless.

Kat fired up the engine. 'You'd better put on your seatbelt.'

Safa urgently obeyed, and Kat put her foot down hard.

The car juddered forward, and stalled. They sat in confused silence for a moment.

'That wasn't quite as dramatic as I'd hoped,' said Kat.

'It hasn't filled me with confidence about this whole endeavour.'

Again, and this time she did everything a little more gently. The car inched forward and out of the garage, gravel grinding under their wheels.

The hill and everything around it seemed to recede, and Wesley tried to brace himself against the shaking in his legs as he squared up to his brother.

'I want you to apologise.'

Jordan choked out a laugh. 'For what?'

For pretending he didn't exist. For letting his friends beat him up. For making him feel worthless and running out on them when they needed him most.

'For everything,' he said.

Jordan kicked at a chunk of tree branch, sending it tumbling down the slope and into darkness. 'You can't go through life expecting apologies, Wes.'

155

'You left us,' said Wesley. 'Do you know how difficult it was after you were gone?'

'It's not as simple as that.'

'It seems pretty simple to me.'

Jordan lifted a hand, as if trying to dredge up the right words. Then he growled with frustration and wheeled away towards the trees, swinging his arms at the air as if fighting invisible enemies.

'You think it's fair I was expected to support my family when I was still at school?' he said. 'I had to work every night to bring money home, and it still wasn't enough! I wanted to get my exams and see what I could do with myself, but there was no chance. It was too much pressure.'

'But that's how it was, and you still left,' said Wesley, holding his voice steady. 'You knew you were leaving that same pressure on me.'

Jordan turned back towards him, arms now hanging limp at his sides. 'So you should know how it feels.'

'Apologise, or I can't let you come back.'

'What are you going to do to stop me?'

Wesley's punch caught his brother above the eye, a wide swing that landed with a dull thud and sent pain careening up his arm. Hardly flinching, Jordan replied by digging a fist into Wesley's stomach, doubling him over. As he staggered away, gasping for breath, his brother walked him down.

'You want me to say it's all my fault?'

There was no air in his lungs to form the words, but Wesley forced himself to nod. Jordan answered by kicking him in the side, knocking him over into the dirt.

'Just tell me one thing,' said his brother. 'Instead of blaming me, why don't you blame Dad for anything? If it's anybody's fault, it's his.'

'At least he cared about you,' Wesley gasped.

Their eyes met. Jordan lifted a foot to kick him again, and Wesley braced himself. The blow never came, his brother pulling out of it at the last moment.

'If only you knew,' he said. 'Go.'

Wesley climbed to his feet. 'You can't just—'

'Get out of here before I kick the shit out of you!'

Pain throbbed in his stomach and reached tendrils out into his body with every step. Back down the hill and onto the road. It was nothing compared to the shame that came crashing into his mind, like a wave breaking on rocks. He had sworn he would stop Jordan from hurting them again, and instead he had ended up in the dirt.

As he hurried past a row of local shops that were closed for the night, he knew he should head home, work out what his next move would be. Instead his feet led him somewhere else, and before he knew it he saw the McDonald's sign glowing in the night.

Before he could turn into the car park, hands grabbed him from behind and slammed him into a shop's metal shutter.

'I told you he hangs out here.'

'We've been looking for you.'

Blocking any route of escape, Luke and Justin took down their hoods.

18

Collision Course

Kat imagined that some people, caught in the throes of youthful rebellion, would find themselves transformed into a rally driver as soon as they took control of a car, regardless of previous driving experience and the panic gnashing in their chest. They probably wouldn't lose all sense of coordination and be forced to use the kerbs on either side of the road like children's rails at a bowling alley.

'Watch out for that post!' shrieked Safa, and Kat wrenched the steering wheel, bumping up onto the pavement.

'Rock, rock, rock!'

Some kind of malformed decorative stone loomed in the headlights and Kat managed to swerve around it with all the elegance of butter in a hot pan.

If video games had taught her anything (and as much as she loved them she really hoped they hadn't) it was that driving recklessly should summon half the city's police force into her rear-view mirror, send pedestrians swearing and screaming, and ultimately see the car catch fire for no apparent reason. Luckily the streets were largely quiet, the only onlookers a couple of guys safe on the opposite pavement who whipped around at the sound of groaning suspension, but hardly seemed to see the car at all.

Adrenaline surged through her veins, foxtrotted with the panic, a comingling that made her giddy. She could get used to this. Not driving a car – twenty or thirty more lessons were required there – but delivering vigilante justice, using the power of the fade to make the world a better place. Tomorrow, TrumourPixel would arrive at the garage and find it empty. Kat wished she could be there to see his face. Just the thought of it made her—

'Red light!'

Kat snapped out of it in time to see the red traffic light and the rear lights of another car stopped there flare through the windscreen. She stamped on the brakes. Their wheels screeched, and Kat braced herself as the car skidded irrepressibly onward.

BANG.

The impact threw them forwards, seatbelts crushing their chests. Metal crumpled and glass broke, tinkling onto the tarmac.

'Are you okay?' said Kat.

Beside her, Safa was slouched back in her seat, hair plastered to her face. 'I think I shit a lung.'

Ahead of them, the driver door of the other car was flung open.

'Okay, now I *definitely* did.'

An older guy got out, glowering over the top of a heavy beard and rubbing his neck, before stomping to the back of his car.

'Do you think he's going to be angry?' asked Safa.

The guy took one look at the car's crumpled rear and threw his hands in the air.

Kat gulped. 'I think there's a very good chance.'

Finally he turned to them, face set with rage. He took one purposeful step closer, the advance of a one-man army. And all at once he forgot them. His anger softened into confusion, and he stopped short of his next stride, glass scraping under his feet. Their car – and most importantly the two terrified girls sitting inside it – had ceased to exist for him. He took out his phone and began making a call, turning away from them completely.

Safa cleared her throat. 'Will it still go?'

When Kat tried the ignition it stuttered for a long moment, and they both looked up, expecting it to bring the wrath they deserved down upon their heads. The guy didn't hear, and the engine caught, allowing her to reverse away from the crash. 'We should—'

'Get out of here? I couldn't agree more.'

They gave the guy – now swearing explosively into his phone – as wide a berth as possible, and Kat guided them away at a crawl.

'Ha!' Safa slapped the dashboard. 'We can actually do anything.'

Every molecule in her body was shaking, but Kat couldn't keep the smile from her face. Oh, it would be so easy to get carried away, to lose herself to the powerful transience of the fade. And she wanted to, if only for the night.

She put her foot down, and sent them roaring away into town.

Wesley had always felt the simmering threat of violence with Luke and Justin, as if they might decide to turn on him if he made a single wrong move. Until now he'd thought of it as something to overcome, a challenge to be surmounted before they accepted him. Until now, it had never *frightened* him.

They smiled and, cornered against the shop shutter, he saw in their eyes how they wanted to hurt him.

'Leave me alone,' he said, for all the good it would do.

'You made us look like idiots,' said Luke.

'I didn't mean to.'

'You don't understand the risk we were taking to introduce you like that. We were trying to do you a favour.' He looked rattled. 'You don't know what he's capable of.'

Even though they were just a few feet from McDonald's there was nobody else around, and even if there were Wesley knew they probably wouldn't help him anyway.

'I didn't mean anything by it,' he said. Maybe he could flatter them, talk his way out of this. 'It was just such a big step up that I needed to think about it.'

Luke kicked the shutter, sending metallic thunder rolling through Wesley's bones, pain throbbing in his injured ribs. '*Needed to think about it*? This isn't your university application, you do it because you believe it's right.'

'I'm not going to university,' said Wesley. Not enough money. Not good enough grades.

Another kick of the shutter. 'Don't you want anything in your pathetic little life?'

'The fight never stops,' added Justin.

TrumourPixel's words, coming out of his mouth. It was clear now that they believed it. Whether they always had, or whether prolonged exposure had drawn them deeper into the ideology behind the catchphrase than they knew, Wesley couldn't tell.

'He's going to drive that car into a crowd of people just to get to her,' he said.

'You think that's what he's planning? Why would he need us for that?'

'The car is so we can get her away—' Justin was cut short by a sharp look from Luke.

'I don't want to hurt anybody,' Wesley said, trying to get his back off the shutter.

Luke shoved him against it again. 'You already did! It's too late to act like you're too good for us.'

'I'm not, I—'

'You're a cuck,' said Luke, as if the idea had just dawned on him. 'You've been trying to hide it all this time, but you're just like all the others.'

Again, Wesley tried to pull away, and Luke grabbed his arms, swinging him around and throwing him into the empty road. Wesley tripped and sprawled onto his front, pain jangling through his ribs. He curled himself into a protective ball, knowing he couldn't fight, and waited for the blows to rain down.

'Hey!'

Wesley looked up to find somebody striding towards them. It was enough to make Luke and Justin back away a step. He could hardly believe it when he saw his brother, marching across the street, a crust of dried blood on his eyebrow.

'Get the fuck away from him,' said Jordan, shoving Luke hard and sending him staggering backwards. At first they both looked shocked; as far as they knew Jordan had been gone for two years, and when he was angry he was like an avenging demon. Still, Wesley could see Luke weighing up their chances: two of them against Jordan, Wesley still on the ground and too pathetic to factor into the equation. They stood in the middle of the road, facing each other down.

'He had it coming,' said Justin.

Jordan brandished his fists. 'Maybe you've got this coming.'

Somewhere close by, Wesley heard an engine roar, growing louder. It was quickly lost to the sound of scraping feet as Luke lunged and threw a punch. It missed, and Jordan caught him in a headlock. The two of them stumbled towards Justin, who stood paralysed, the reality of a fight apparently wholly less appealing.

Behind them, Wesley heard the engine again, louder than before. He sat up, but couldn't see anything approaching from either direction.

Jordan let the headlock go and tried to throw a punch, but they ended up tangled again, turning circles in the road and spitting insults.

'You stay away from my brother!'

'Or you'll what, run away again?'

The engine sounded like it was practically on top of them now. Wesley scrambled to his feet, wondering how nobody else had heard it. 'Jordan.'

They broke apart, panting, and his brother was saying, 'You'll regret it, trust me on that.'

'Jordan!'

Headlights flared suddenly, right on top of them, as if the car had appeared out of thin air. Jordan whipped around and saw it bearing down on him, too late to move. Wesley was already running. He knocked into Jordan's back, sending them both stumbling out of the path of the car as it came tearing through, wheels screeching out of control. Luke and Justin fell into the gutter on the other side of the road.

Wesley heard the car judder onto the kerb and come to a stop further down the street, but when he had recovered enough to look there was no sign of it at all.

'Where the hell did it go?' he said.

Across the road, Justin cried out and held his leg. 'Call an ambulance!'

'It doesn't matter.' Jordan pulled him to his feet. 'Let's get out of here.'

Kat thought her body might shake itself into pieces. She brought her hands slowly away from the wheel, as if it might explode if she made too sudden a move.

'I almost hit them,' she said.

Safa was wide-eyed, pressed back in her seat. 'I have no more lungs left to shit.'

'What if I'd . . .'

'Hey, you didn't, it's okay,' she said, leaning closer. 'You've gotta admit . . . it was kind of exciting.'

The car was half on the pavement, half off, and Kat could do nothing but stare at her skewed view on the world.

'That wasn't me,' she said. 'I would never be that reckless.'

Safa reached across and put a hand on her arm. 'I told you, the fade is a chance to be somebody new.'

For the first time, Kat didn't relish the touch. She saw how, even laid on top of each other, their hands made an absence. Maybe the fade could make her who she wanted to be, but tonight it had made her foolhardy. It was luring her – daring her – to follow its dark path. Safa might already have gone ahead.

'I just want to get rid of the car and go home,' she said, pulling her arm away. That's what they should have done in the first place. 'Do we need to burn it or something?'

'This isn't *Hollyoaks*,' said Safa. 'Leave it like this and the police will tow it away soon enough.'

It couldn't be traced back to Tru – Kat had heard him say that – but at least they would lose their car for good. They wiped down the steering wheel and dashboard, unsure if anybody would be able to see their fingerprints, and then left the car behind. The people they had almost hit were already gone.

Wesley wasn't usually one to look for silver linings in bad situations, but at least nobody had punched him in the face. It meant he wouldn't have to explain anything to Mum or Evie. Even so, he felt like home was the last place he wanted to go.

'Where are you staying, anyway?'

'With a mate,' said Jordan.

165

They had stopped a few streets from the flat, and neither of them quite seemed able to look at the other.

'You'll be all right, yeah?'

Wesley nodded. 'Thanks for stepping in.'

Jordan nodded back, shuffling his feet. 'I'm sorry.'

There was no indication of how far the apology extended, but Wesley was more grateful for it than his brother would ever know.

They parted ways and, as soon as Jordan was out of sight, Wesley turned away from home. There was somewhere else he needed to be.

Kat's hands shook the entire way home. They walked in silence, until they reached the corner that would send them their separate ways.

'It *was* pretty fun,' ventured Safa, smiling tentatively.

She could put this right. She had caught herself pretending to be somebody she wasn't, playacting at being herself. It was time to remember what really mattered to her. The fade could still be a chance to do the things she had always wanted, but had been too scared. 'There's a march in London tomorrow,' she said. 'A protest for women's rights.'

'Sounds boring.'

'I want to go. But not alone.'

'Oh.' Safa shrugged her lip. 'Okay, I'll go.'

Kat smiled. 'Are you sure?'

'If it's important to you.'

It was, especially since seeing Niko Denton's tweet about it. Before, Kat would never have had the courage to go. If the fade could give her this, she couldn't waste it.

'Text me the deets,' said Safa, starting away down the road.

'I can't believe you just said deets,' Kat called after her.

Safa stuck up her middle finger, and Kat turned towards home.

19

Whatever is Wrong with You, Is So Right For Me

Kat had never had any need to sneak into the house before, and although she should have been grateful she wouldn't need to now, it was disappointing to simply open the door and step inside. She could slam the door and give an a cappella rendition of the *Backwash* theme song and Dad wouldn't hear.

He was in the sitting room, the TV up loud, snoring on the sofa. An empty bottle of wine sat on the table beside him, and sweat patches were spreading wide from his armpits. 'Dad,' she said, standing over him.

He had always slept like it was the last chance he would ever get, and he didn't stir now.

Tonight she had behaved like somebody she didn't recognise. If Dad woke up, Kat wondered if he would see his daughter, another person entirely, or nothing at all. She didn't know which would break her heart most.

'I thought we were better off at a distance,' she said. 'After Mum, and Suzy, I was all you had left, and I couldn't risk us getting driven apart too. But by keeping my distance, I made it happen anyway. And now I need you . . .'

Dad did not stir. Slowly, Kat reached towards him, feeling that same yearning pull that had tempted her on the high street. It might not be too late to reconnect with him, to make amends for turning them into strangers.

'I'm still here,' she said.

No response. Kat took her hand away and moved back to the hallway, sloping up the stairs, alone.

Wesley made his way upstairs and let himself into the quiet flat. A light had been left on for him. Mum was home for the night, magazines and dirty plates scattered across the front room, but she was in bed now. His phone vibrated as he reached his bedroom door. A message from Aoife.

Everybody's up for it. The church has a morning service tomorrow, so we'll probably find him there.

Soft snoring greeted him as he opened the door. Evie was bundled in blankets and drooling into her pillow. He wanted to kiss her on the forehead, something older brothers were supposed to do, but he knew it would wake her up.

Instead he took off his shoes and dirty jeans and climbed into bed. Aaron's family portrait was under his pillow, and he peered at it in the street light that slanted through the window. He wondered if they dreamed of their lost son, if he came to them in their sleep, only to be forgotten all over again by morning.

A shape appeared at the window and blocked the light. Wesley opened it to let Buttnugget inside. The cat immediately found the bed, turned circles, and then collapsed purring against his side. His closeness was enough to lead Wesley quickly into sleep.

It was a crush. It had to be a crush.

Less than an hour after coming home, she received a video from Safa; kittens dressed up in tiny *Backwash* outfits and tottering about miniature replica sets.

This is highly relevant to my interests, she replied.

They spent half the night messaging back and forth, as if they had known each other for ever, and every time Kat saw the words *Safa is typing* her heart skipped a beat.

Definitely a crush. Or was this what it felt like to finally have a friend? She refused to let confusion hinder her enjoyment.

The think about Esme is that she's a melon dramatic but whole.

Thankfully Kat had fast become an expert in translating Siri's interpretations of Safa's dictated messages.

You really should just type your messages like a normal person.

We live in a gilt earring future, replied Safa. *It's people like you that hold human itty back.*

If you insult Esme again, I will find you and I will kill you.

They had spent the entire evening – and would spend most of tomorrow – together, but Kat didn't want the conversation to end. This was something – some*one* – she had always wanted.

Messaging Safa took her mind off the fade. Focusing on the words made it easier to ignore the fingers typing them. Despite what brought them together, Safa made it easy to pretend everything was normal. No supernatural asterisk on their relationship. A crush always makes people feel like the only two in the world; for them it was almost true.

What time we meeting too moz?

Did you actually say '2moz' out loud?

And ''?!

WHAT TIME.

The march starts at midday, so I can come to yours for 9.30?

A minute later a photo arrived of Safa's address on a crumpled ASOS invoice.

You really do hate typing, don't you?

:) *I'm typing this one just for you. C u 2moz my dude xxx*

They might have been a joke, but the kisses made Kat's heart gasp.

20

Good Memories are Bullshit

Google Maps guided Kat to the three residential streets that constituted the 'good' part of town, where the houses were a little bigger, the driveways a little longer, and the crime rate a little lower. Turning the corner, she almost walked into Safa as she leaned against a low garden wall. 'Thought I'd save you the trouble of finding the place,' she said, reaching over the garden wall. 'I made a protest sign.'

It was the inside of a cereal box taped lopsidedly to a splintered bamboo cane. In handwritten block capitals it read: I AM PROTESTING.

'You're not so eloquent without Siri, are you?'

'Nobody's going to see it anyway,' said Safa, leaning the placard against her shoulder. 'But I thought I'd get into the spirit.'

They had enough time before the train for Safa to loudly lament their inability to purchase coffee. When it arrived they sat facing each other diagonally in a four-seater at the end of the carriage. The windows were fogged with cold. It was hard to tell, but she was sure Safa appeared a little more faded than the night before.

'It's getting worse,' Kat said.

'It's progressing, the way it's supposed to,' corrected Safa. 'Yours too.'

Kat examined her hand. There was no scale to judge it by. If she had faded further – and there was no reason to believe she wasn't following Safa – it was subtle enough to be almost undetectable. Maybe that's how it would be; a steady ebb, like the tide receding down a beach, noticed only when you no longer hear the crash of the waves.

'Why are you so bothered about this march, anyway?' asked Safa.

'I believe in it,' said Kat. 'And I know it's exactly the kind of thing that would piss off the guys whose car we stole last night.'

'I definitely support pissing people off.' Safa put her feet up on the seat opposite as if to prove the point. 'But it's not like it makes any difference if you're there or not.'

'If everybody thought that there'd be no march at all.'

'No, I mean *literally* nobody but me will know you're there.'

This had already occurred to Kat, and it was probably why she had the courage to go in the first place. After all, nothing could go wrong if nobody could see her. It was frightening how liberating that could feel.

'I'll know I'm there,' she said.

Safa smiled in return, and Kat wondered if her heart would ever stop tripping over its own feet.

As they drew closer to central London the train steadily filled with fellow protesters chattering excitedly and snapping photos of signs, alongside weary weekend workers and befuddled tourists. Every seat was taken except for those beside the invisible girls. It would have been lonely, if Kat hadn't already been completely happy with who she was with.

'Do you believe in an afterlife?' she asked.

'I keep telling you we're not dying.'

'You can't tell me you haven't thought about it during all this,' said Kat. 'My mum believed that when we die we go back to the time we were happiest and just . . . stay there for ever. That's what heaven would be.' Absentmindedly, she ran a finger through the cold condensation on the window. 'I asked her where she would go, and she said back to when she was a teenager, in her final year of school. I remember thinking it was messed up she picked a time before she met my dad, or had me and my sister. Maybe that was a warning.'

Safa pushed herself higher in her seat. 'I'm not gonna lie, I didn't want to ask about her in case she was dead.'

'Not quite. She left.' No point saying more than that. 'Where do you think you would go?'

Across the aisle a man began hissing into his phone – *you said it would be done by Thursday!* – as if that was quieter than shouting. Safa watched him closely, tilting her head quizzically.

'When I was a kid, I had this friend for one summer. We spent every day together, riding bikes, watching TV, begging money for sweets. It's the last time I can remember not having to worry about anything.' Safa sighed, and it sounded more angry than wistful. 'Good memories are bullshit though, aren't they? I was probably bored, and we probably argued, but you don't remember that stuff. Maybe I wasn't happy at all.'

174

Kat waited a moment before she asked, 'What happened to your friend?'

Straightening up as if she'd been caught slacking on a job, Safa frowned. 'I don't remember.'

'You must—'

'Did you know scientists have been tracking a single whale since the 1980s because it sings at a frequency no other whale in the world can hear?' Safa kept her eyes on the foggy window. 'It swims across the world, singing out to any other whale it meets, but nobody will ever reply. It's been lonely far longer than we have.'

There was an edge to her voice that made Kat wonder if she had pried too far. The thought of scaring Safa away was unbearable. She needed to set them back on course.

'The whale was your friend for a summer?' she said, forcing lightness into her voice.

A weight was lifted when Safa smiled. 'We're off at the next stop,' she said, and nodded to what Kat's drifting fingers had drawn in the condensation.

It was the symbol of the Lonely People, a rogue droplet carving open the nesting doll to free the stick figure trapped inside. Kat shivered, and as they left the train she erased it with a swipe of her hand, the moisture shining through her skin.

The Trinity Church stood around the corner from Aaron's house, a short, broad tower rising into a tiled spire, the nave following the line of the pavement until it broke into a small cemetery. A pathway through the headstones brought them to arched double doors, open and welcoming, soft organ music and choral voices spilling into the morning.

'I don't think I've ever been inside a church,' said Wesley.

'Sshh, don't tell him,' said Aoife, pointing to the sky. 'He'll smite you down.'

Robbie huffed and pushed past them. 'Let's just go.' He had been in a bad mood since they first met up, determined to make it clear that he was against this idea.

They crossed the threshold – Jae hastily pulling off his beanie hat and whispering an apology to the ether – and passed through a small, chilly lobby into the church itself. It was surprisingly bright, late-morning light streaming down from high windows spaced along the entire length to illuminate thick wooden roof beams, rows of sparsely populated pews, and a choir assembled between twin pulpits on a raised chancel at the front, the organ pipes on the wall behind them. The hymn they sang was slow and exultant, their voices rising and falling like the breath of a slumbering giant.

The congregation was spread out in couples and small groups, standing for the hymn, so the four of them shuffled along the central aisle and settled into a space a few pews from the front. A few people eyed them curiously, but weren't put off their song.

'That's him,' said Robbie, pointing to a boy at the back of the choir.

There were around twelve of them arranged into two rows and led by a conductor, a mix of men and women, young and old. Lukundo appeared to be among the youngest, though his smart shirt and straight-creased trousers could have belonged to a much older man. He smiled while he sang, eyes never once flicking to the hymn book in his hands.

'What do we do now?' whispered Wesley.

Robbie pressed a finger to his lips, and they settled into the hard-backed pew to listen. It was peaceful, letting the soft music wash over him. Wesley almost closed his eyes to enjoy it better, but was worried the others might notice.

The hymn wound up with a grand organ crescendo that made the subsequent silence feel like the air had been sucked from the room. The choir took a moment to catch its breath while the congregation settled back into their seats. A minister rose to the left-side pulpit to give the final blessing.

'I've been told I have a nice singing voice,' Jae whispered.

'We'll make sure to ask if you can join the choir,' said Aoife.

The minister finished the blessing and bowed her head. 'Amen.' The congregation around them answered the same, before people began to talk or collect their things to leave. The organ spiralled up to play them out.

A few people moved to the front to speak to the minister. After a moment she broke away from them and stepped down to approach the group of newcomers, smiling kindly.

'I don't think I've seen you here before?'

'No, sorry,' said Wesley, before pointing to Lukundo. 'We actually came to see him.'

'All right, give me a second and I'll get him for you.'

They watched nervously as the minister pointed them out, Lukundo's brow furrowing before he came down and edged into the pew ahead of them. 'You're waiting for me?'

'Yeah,' said Wesley, wishing he had planned what to say. 'We actually came to ask about someone we think you know. Knew. Aaron Musley?'

'Ah,' said Lukundo, his expression brightening as if the name had jogged a pleasant memory. 'Let's go somewhere we can talk privately.'

The march was larger than Kat expected. The square from which it was due to start was already a sea of banners and placards. Chants bounced back and forth, jostling for air time with whistles and loudspeakers. Together they weaved through the bodies, pressing as close as the forcefield would allow. She wouldn't turn back from the noise and the heat. Before, when all these people would have seen her, she couldn't have been here. The beast of panic caged inside her wouldn't have allowed it. Now she could. She would raise her muted voice as if it mattered.

Having pushed ahead, Safa now reached back to grasp Kat's hand. Electricity seemed to leap between them, all the confirmation she needed that it wasn't the touch of just anyone she craved; it was Safa, alone.

Protest signs ranged from the hastily scrawled and barely legible to carefully crafted works of art and catchy slogans destined to become memes. Safa proudly hoisted her own.

'I'M PROTESTING!' she bellowed.

'At least pretend you're taking this seriously,' said Kat.

Safa shrugged, but stayed quiet. Somebody had taken to the makeshift stage at the far end of the square, but their words were lost over the heads of the crowd, chants rising up to swallow them.

'*Hey hey! Ho ho! Patriarchy's got to go!*'

And

'*What do we do when they attack? We fight back!*'

'So many people turned up!' said Kat, breathless with it all.

After a few minutes the crowd shifted, and began to slowly move away across the square. The route of the march was little more than a mile, ending in front of Downing Street, but with this many people it was bound to take hours.

'You okay?' shouted Safa over a woman beside them banging a drum.

Kat beamed back. 'I'm great.'

Here was everything she believed in – tolerance, diversity, equality – being celebrated in public, where trolls couldn't isolate and punish her. For years, Kat had searched for her people close to home and online, and here they were at last.

Beyond the square, the crowds narrowed into a procession as they took to the closed street. The chanting resumed, and Kat lifted her voice to sing along as loud as she could.

'Hey hey! Ho ho! Patriarchy's got to go!'

'Hey hey! Ho ho!' sang Safa. 'Check out that protesting doggo!'

Waddling beside them on the end of a lead was a sausage dog with a *Bitches Got Rights* sign strapped across its back. Safa snatched it up, bouncing it in her arms, while the owner stared in confusion at its apparent levitation.

'Put it down!' hissed Kat, snatching the dog and plopping it back beside its owner. Startled, it sniffed at the air before it was dragged unceremoniously away.

'This is supposed to be fun, isn't it?'

'Not if you don't care about why we're here.'

Safa sagged her shoulders. '*Sor-ry*, it's just hard to care about anything else right now, don't you think? We've got more important things to focus on.'

'What caused this for me in the first place is happening to thousands of women every day,' said Kat. 'Maybe I can do something to stop any of them fading too.'

There were so many different people here: groups of women marching together, parents carrying their children, people on crutches and in wheelchairs. A boy, maybe a few years older than them, was taking photos of the march on his phone and grinning as people posed for him. He wore a bright orange T-shirt and jeans artfully torn at the knees, and when a message arrived on his phone he laughed at it openly, like he wanted to bring the whole crowd into the joke. It baffled Kat, how anybody could be so comfortable in their own skin. She couldn't stop herself moving closer to him, close enough to smell his cologne.

'You're going to have a *very* hard time chatting anybody up,' said Safa behind her.

The boy was attractive, but only in a way that made

Kat envy him. Made her want to *be* him. That strange yearning tugged at her again, made her take another step closer and reach out shaking fingers to touch him.

The organ reverberated as they moved to the back of the church, where crooked stacks of hymn books teetered and children's distractions lay scattered across the floor.

'I haven't seen Aaron in . . . I don't know how long,' said Lukundo, a soft southern-African accent doing little to disguise the tension in his voice, as if he was being confronted with a secret from his past.

'How did you know him?' asked Wesley.

'From here.' Lukundo held up his hands to the building around them. 'We had both attended this church since we were little. We were good friends, until he decided to stop coming.' He spoke tentatively, like he was remembering their history as he went.

'He just stopped?'

'I remember, he told me he had stopped believing. I'm sure we promised to stay friends, but you know what happens.'

Wesley looked to the others for help, but they appeared just as uncertain how to continue. They had all seen how Aaron's family reacted to being confronted with a truth the fade had worked to scour clean. Still, Lukundo seemed different, pleased to be reminded of a friend he had lost.

'You seem to remember him really well,' said Wesley.

Lukundo frowned. 'It's strange. It wasn't that long ago he was my best friend, but until you said his name I don't think I had thought about him in a while.'

Aoife leaned forward. 'Do you know what happened to him?' she said delicately.

'I know *something* happened,' he said, eyes flicking quickly between them. 'I know he's . . . *gone*.'

The fade seemed to erase its victims from the world, do everything it could to omit them from the annals of reality, until even their loved ones learned not to question their uncanny absence unless compelled. The simple act of reminding them felt like bestowing a gift.

'Look, we spoke to his brother and he told us you were hanging around his house around the time Aaron disappeared,' said Robbie. 'We want to know why.'

'I think he visited me,' said Lukundo, unflustered by this sudden frankness.

'You saw him?'

'No, I *felt* him. It's hard to explain. At first I thought he had died and come to say goodbye before he moved on.'

The boy cupped a hand to his chest, as if covering a hole there.

'He was right here. Aaron was inside my body.'

Kat's fingers hovered inches from the boy. What would it take for her to become like him? Surely she was well past the point of no return. Mum gone; Suzy refusing to answer her messages; Dad holding conversations with her bedroom door; her empty online life destroyed. This crowd would never be her people. Somehow, she would always be separate.

There was hardly anything of her left. Why shouldn't she just . . .?

The boy glanced behind him, and Kat lunged. In that moment she was empty, unravelling like thread caught on a nail, and this time no barrier stood in her way. Her hand was on his skin. The yearning beckoned harder, and her hand was inside his body. In one swift movement, she pulled the boy around her like a shroud.

21

Internal Landscapes

The purpose of the fade was to allow somebody to choose a Cradle, a host person to reside in before their own body ceased to exist. That's what the Lonely People had told him. Wesley grabbed Lukundo's broad shoulders and peered into his eyes, trying to see if anybody else lurked behind them.

'What are you doing?' he said, as the others leaned closer and gaped.

'Can you speak to him?' asked Robbie eagerly. 'Can he hear us?'

Lukundo shook himself free and held up his hands. 'You don't understand. It was only for a moment.'

The Lonely People looked at each other, shell-shocked, as they struggled to realise what this might mean.

'I'm sorry if this is a surprise,' said Lukundo. 'I remember feeling strange, and I think by the time I knew what had happened he was already gone. It was like he was inside my mind, trying to talk to me. Asking for help. It felt . . . like he needed to cling onto something. He wanted something to live for.'

Wesley laughed before he could help it. 'Try before you buy.' It made sense, inasmuch as any of this did. If the fade offered the power to slip inside the bodies of others, why shouldn't it allow them to do it temporarily before they had to make a choice that would decide the rest of their life?

'We had no idea,' said Aoife.

It wasn't like anybody who faded was ever able to report back.

'When I realised he wasn't dead, I kept it to myself. I suppose I stopped thinking about it. It didn't seem so strange until now.' Lukundo smiled uncertainly. 'You believe me?'

'It's a bit mind-blowing,' said Jae.

'But we believe you,' finished Wesley.

A jolt, the sensation of being dragged across a great distance. Kat buckled with something like vertigo. She had split in half: one seeing the ongoing march through eyes not her own, moving with feet not her own, participating at a remove in the world as she knew it.

The other was pushing through a rainforest, skin slick in the humid air, nudging aside the rope-like vines that hung from trees filled with flowers of red and yellow and blue. Birds whistled from branches. Unseen creatures stirred amongst the leaves.

When she lifted a hand to clear her path she found her flesh stubbornly whole, the fade repealed. It was a shock, like finding an extra limb.

The forest was inside the boy . . . no, it *was* the boy,

comprised of everything he felt: happiness at being surrounded by people just like him, pride at joining their number, lending him the confidence to strut between them and ask for their photos. She even heard the swirl of his thoughts, most of them centred on a boy he would meet later that day for a second date, who had sent him a gift basket of jams after a shared joke. Whose voice made his heart pirouette and his knees tremble.

Invisible antibodies, a familiar barrier force, were trying to push her out, but she had grip enough to push against it and walk further into the trees. Underneath this lushness, other feelings vied for attention. Whenever she tried to read them the colours of the canopy flashed brighter in distraction.

It made her feel dizzy. She had never felt anything so strongly as this, had never come close to being so happy or confident. Surely she never would.

The repelling force grew stronger, and in moments every step seemed like fighting hurricane winds. Those other feelings were so close. They hid in the underbrush ahead, just out of reach.

There. A box, sealed tight amid the decay of fallen leaves. It *leaked*, but just what was escaping she couldn't identify, never mind how familiar it felt.

All at once the pressure became too much. It ripped her backwards, both the view through his eyes and the forest diminishing as the boy's body rejected the invasion.

The world lurched and she landed hard on her back. The march's cacophony battered her senses. Blinking, she found Safa crouched over her.

'You're back,' she whispered, eyes brimming with tears. 'How did you do that?'

Kat picked herself up and scrambled to the edge of the crowd, like they might realise what she'd done and turn against her. Looking back, she saw the boy had already slipped out of sight.

She lifted a hand, and found she could see through it again. Safa gripped her shoulder tight, as if scared she might try and escape with the secret. 'Tell me.'

'I just . . .' There were hardly words. She felt drunk, the boy's emotions still filling her up, swimming inside her skull. These feelings were everything she had ever wanted, but they didn't belong to her. Soon they would ebb away and leave her, and then . . .

'I thought of everything that's gone wrong, and I reached for something that might fix it.'

Safa nodded as if she had never heard more perfect sense, and pulled away to delve back into the crowd. She stopped in the path of an older woman in a bright blue wig blowing a whistle and swinging a jumper around her head. The woman didn't steer to avoid her. Safa closed her eyes in concentration, no doubt summoning all the things she kept private, all the real things Kat longed for her to share. When the woman almost blundered into her, Safa reached.

It was like a magic trick. The air blurred, and Safa was gone. The woman stopped and blinked, belched wetly, and then resumed her tuneless whistle work.

Kat ran to her. 'Safa?'

The woman turned, almost as if she would answer to the name, and then Safa was beside her again. In that moment the woman saw her and glared, furious at the violation committed. And then forgot her again. Wandered away with the flow of the crowd.

'I did it,' said Safa dreamily.

The march carried them along. Kat felt lighter, as if only the weight of her shoes kept her on the ground.

'I had no idea we could do it before the end!' said Safa, waking from her reverie. 'I was actually her, just for a second. I felt everything – she was so *happy* to be here, and she wished her dead husband could see it, and she had this bad taste in her mouth . . .'

'Was there something else?' asked Kat. 'Something underneath it all?'

'A meadow! Grass swaying in the breeze as far as I could see. Every blade of grass was important, like they made up my soul.'

The box hidden under the trees had felt so familiar, but the feelings were blurring together now as they withdrew, making her hands shake.

They had long been teetering on the brink of something dangerous, and this might finally push them over the edge. If they backed away now, tried to pretend it had never happened, they might still go back to normal. There was a still a chance they could be saved.

'I couldn't hold on for long,' Safa was saying. 'It was like matching poles of magnets pushing each other apart.'

'What did you think about?' said Kat. 'To make it happen?'

Safa's smile faded. 'I thought about all the times in my life I've woken up and felt disappointed to still be me.'

And then she threw up her hands and danced away into the crowd.

Something to live for.

That's what Aaron had been searching for while the fade took hold, and he had come to his old friend to try to find it. Was Kat out there right now looking for the same thing? If he could help her find it, perhaps he could draw her back into the world. It could be his chance to save her.

He realised Robbie was talking again. 'You didn't answer the first question. If you knew Aaron was gone, why did you go to his house?'

'I had to,' said Lukundo. 'For a whole day I missed him more than I have ever missed anything, like he had taken a piece of me and I needed it back to be complete. For a whole day, I couldn't resist it. I kept trying to speak to his brother, but he kept sending me away.'

'Yeah, we know that feeling,' said Jae.

'Did you see anybody else there?' asked Wesley, remembering what Aaron's brother had said. 'Anybody else hanging around like you.'

Lukundo thought for a moment, nodded. 'A girl. I didn't recognise her.'

If being inhabited made the host go to Aaron's house in search of him, it may have happened to this girl too. She might know more about what had really happened to him.

'Any idea who she could be?' he asked the group. They each shook their heads.

'I have to go, we have practice,' said Lukundo, pointing to the front of the church where the choir was gathering again. 'Thank you for helping me to remember my friend. If you find him, tell him I miss him.'

The organ boomed up behind them, echoed in their chests. He missed him now, but it wouldn't be long before he forgot.

Kat chased, her reinstated invisible charge forcing people aside, and grabbed Safa back by the arm.

'We can't do that again.'

Safa arched an eyebrow. 'Why the hell not? It was brilliant.'

'I don't know . . . something about it isn't right.'

'It was everything I've ever wanted!' said Safa. 'And I bet it was for you, too.'

It made a sick kind of sense; she had spent years operating through a proxy online, and now the fade allowed her to do the same in real life. She couldn't deny the exhilaration it made her feel.

Up ahead, the march turned at a corner, a blocked-off adjoining road narrowing the space. They heard shouting, a few people jostling.

'Promise me you won't do it again,' said Kat. 'Not until I've worked out what I felt in there.'

'I don't see why I should—'

The raised voices ahead broke into screams, and a glass bottle shattered on the road. The crowd parted. Men dressed in black with their faces covered were jumping the metal barrier. They swung boards at marchers as they tried to run. There were more behind, hurling bottles and stones.

Half the crowd surged away round the corner, while the rest turned and ran back, panicking, dropping their signs and knocking into others.

'We need to go,' said Kat, panic stirring in her chest to strangle her voice.

A few marchers went to meet the attackers, swinging their placards as improvised weapons, ducking the flying bottles. A man in black connected with a punch and sent another man sprawling, before a woman barrelled into his side and wrestled him to the ground.

There was a stampede now, those seeking escape falling, being trampled underfoot. Kat reached for Safa, but somebody staggered into her first. The forcefield fired them apart and sent Kat tumbling onto the pavement.

'Hey!' Safa's voice.

Kat looked up in time to see her striding towards the nearest attacker, a man twice her size, fist cocked to throw a punch.

'Safa!'

She swung, but instead of landing on his jaw her arm bounced away from the air around him, knocking her off balance. Another marcher kicked him to the ground as sirens spiralled up nearby. Horses' hooves clattered on the road.

Safa grinned as she came back to pull Kat to her feet, and when they set off running she laughed until she ran out of breath.

*

Before they made it through the cemetery, Robbie shoved away from them to move between the headstones. The others called after him and then followed to find him standing in front of a mossy cross-shaped monument.

Robbie kept his eyes on the grave. 'Did you hear what he said?' His voice wobbled on the edge of tears. 'Aaron came looking for help.'

Wesley looked to the others, and found them both stony-faced. 'Of course he did.'

'*Of course*?' Robbie whirled around, jaw jutting out hard. 'If he wanted help, it means he achieved the fade – got exactly what he wanted – and regretted it.'

A hitch in his voice was the sound of faith being shaken. They had all convinced themselves that this was what they wanted, what they *needed* to make their lives right, and here was evidence that even this wouldn't work.

'Isn't it better to know?' said Wesley.

Robbie pushed past him, and when Wesley called after him Aoife shook her head.

'Let him go.'

'I didn't mean to upset him.'

'It's difficult, seeing the reality,' said Jae. 'This morning before I met you guys, I realised I couldn't remember Safa's name. It took me ages to think of it.'

'We knew so little about her. About Aaron,' said Aoife. 'Staying distant made sense at the time, but now I don't know why.' She met Wesley's eye. 'I'm glad we're doing this.'

'Me too,' said Jae.

It was enough to make Wesley sure, for the first time in a long while, that he was doing the right thing.

They were almost back at the square, and leaned against traffic bollards to rest. People who had fled were everywhere, some bleeding from cuts hidden in their hair.

'What the fuck just happened?' said Kat.

Safa planted her hands on her hips and sucked in a deep breath. 'That was nuts.'

'I mean *you*.' Kat shoved her, hard enough to make her stagger.

'What did *I* do?'

'You think it's all a big joke, but it's not! This hatred has been allowed to grow and grow, but because it was online everybody could ignore it, pretend it wasn't serious. Now it's legitimised. It's *here*. It could have killed us. It *wants* to kill people like us.'

An ambulance pulled up to the square, injured people crossing to it as paramedics in high-vis jackets came out to meet them. More police were arriving too, cars edging through the throngs of people.

Safa raised her arms out in a martyr's shrug. 'I'm sorry, but I don't *care*. None of this is my problem any more.'

'It's everybody's problem. They just don't realise until it's too late.'

'I don't need this,' said Safa, oddly calm, as if she got caught in a street brawl every other weekend. 'I'm just . . . killing time before I say goodbye to myself for ever.'

Kat stepped away as if she had been hit, feeling winded as a hole opened up inside her. Is that all she was to her? A pastime?

'It looks to me like you're having the time of your life,' she said, fighting the wobble in her voice. 'Why do you still want to go so much?'

When Safa stepped closer it felt aggressive, and Kat stepped away again.

'I can only be like this *because* of the fade. *Because* nothing matters,' said Safa. 'This isn't the real me.'

Kat wiped at her eyes. 'I don't think that's true.'

'You remember "The Girl Cut Out of the World"?'

Kat nodded. It was the last episode of *Doctor Backwash* season two, where Zenon decides to punish Esme for rejecting him. He manages to rewrite reality so that she never existed, the entire world reshaping itself to gloss over her absence. Nobody else remembers Esme was ever there, not even her boyfriend Roland. The show went on hiatus after that, and two years had passed with no sign of season three. That meant Esme was lost – nobody *ever* remembered, or discovered what Zenon had done.

'*Don't you feel like something is missing?*' quoted Kat, a line from the final scene of the episode. When she saw it for the first time she'd sat on the edge of her bed, tears streaming down her face, begging them to remember.

'*Yeah*,' said Safa, quoting Roland's response. '*There's an emptiness inside, but who doesn't have that?*'

Quoting lines together – even the saddest in the show – reminded Kat just how good it felt to be with Safa.

'Esme is just gone. And nobody notices,' said Safa. 'Not

her family, not her friends, not even the guy who was going to propose to her that day. Now tell me . . . who has actually noticed that you're gone?'

She didn't know. She hadn't let herself face it. Now there was no choice, she saw that nothing had changed. If her absence had left any blank spaces behind, the world had filled them so easily nobody could tell the difference. The only person who seemed to remember was the creep who had made all this happen in the first place. She hated that it made her need him.

'So why not become somebody else?' said Safa, seeing the answer written on Kat's face. 'Somebody who has scores of friends, who is loved? Who *loves*? Somebody the world would miss.'

Kat wanted every one of those things, and in the last few days she'd been stupid enough to think she might have found it, at last. Now she knew she had been wrong, and she ran, knowing Safa wouldn't follow.

22

Refinement of the Decline

The message arrived on Wesley's phone when he was almost home. From Luke. He was almost too scared to open it.

did you nick it?

He stared at the words for a long moment, as if they were a code to decipher. *What are you talking about?*

the car got nicked. nobody else knew it was there. Tru is losing his shit

I swear, it wasn't me. I can't even drive!

It was a couple of minutes before a reply came. *it won't stop us. we'll find another way.*

Wesley started to type a response that further pled his innocence, but he realised it would only make him look guilty. Luke was wrong about one thing: there was one other person who could have known the car was there.

He turned away from home and hurried in the other direction.

*

Kat stood in the sitting room doorway as her dad slumped in front of the television, assignment papers littered across the carpet. The news was reporting on the trouble at the march.

'It's thought the attack was organised on the Facebook page of a far-right campaign group, with several posts calling for "retribution" against members of the march.'

Too tired to feel angry about it now. Instead she thought about what Safa had said. The world at large hadn't noticed Kat's absence, no, but she still didn't know about her family. It wasn't the first time Suzy had ignored her messages. She had seen less of Dad than usual, but he had tried to speak to her. There was nothing *conclusive*.

'Niko Denton, a prominent figure in the so-called alt-right, has denied involvement.'

Since arriving home she had swaddled herself in dressing gown and gloves, doing everything she could to hide the condition of her flesh. She peeled it all away now, leaving nothing but the sleeveless T-shirt and shorts underneath.

'Dad?' she said.

When he didn't respond, she forced herself to move closer.

'Dad,' she said. Not a question this time. A plea.

Eyes fixed on the TV, light reflecting in his glasses. Kat walked across the assignments, paper crackling under her feet like ice, until she was standing between him and the screen.

'Please,' she said, voice shaking now, the first hot tear streaking down her face.

His eyes focused, and her heart leapt, sure that he saw her. He stood, and Kat opened her arms, sure that he would embrace her. Instead, he turned towards the door.

'Kat?' he called over the noise of the television.

She darted in front of him. 'Dad, I'm right here.'

He shouted her name again, moving into the doorway to listen for a response. When none came he started to panic, hurrying to check the kitchen before returning to the hall. They were both crying now, neither able to comfort the other.

'Dad!' she shouted, reaching for him, the barrier holding her at bay. He rushed past her and up the stairs to throw open her bedroom door, cast around desperately, and then checked every other room in the house. It was only when he returned downstairs that the energy fell out of him. He sagged against the wall, and Kat watched helplessly as he sobbed into his hands.

'I've lost her. I've lost her.'

Something inside her broke, a rending as if her body would come apart. This was it, surely, the final straw that would complete the fade and make her disappear for good. She welcomed it. When she choked out another sob, found she was still there, she staggered past him, up the stairs and into her room.

Shuddering with tears, she tore the posters from the walls, tipped her books and films from the shelves and threw her collectibles to the floor, stamping it all under her feet. This had been everything Kat thought she was, and look what it had cost her. These last signifiers had to be destroyed.

She opened her computer and found the files for her

video game. Highlighted them all. There wouldn't be a chance to enter the game jam anyway. She might as well get rid of it now.

Delete. The files – countless hours of work – disappeared.

Cold fingers raised goosebumps on her skin, nerves still responding to her touch. She opened her phone camera, held it at arm's length and took a selfie.

There was no way to measure, no scale she could use to judge, but the photo made it clear: she was more faded than this morning. The colour of her skin had thinned, the shape of her body leaving less of an impression on the empty shelves, the newly bared walls that pushed through her from behind.

Stepping into another life had refined Kat's decline.

Heart drumming against her ribs, she remembered how whole she had been inside the boy. That must have taken something from her – joining with another person, even so briefly, had accelerated the fade.

Yet she didn't regret doing it. Safa was right: it was everything she had ever wanted.

Downstairs, the doorbell rang.

There was a light on in the house, and it gave Wesley the courage to walk to the front door and ring the bell. He didn't know what he would say, even when a shape grew larger in the foggy glass and the door opened, spilling warmth into the night.

'Hi, Mr Waldgrave,' he said. 'Is—?'

'I don't know,' said Kat's dad, voice shaking, his face

wet with tears. He backed away into the hall and slid down the wall to bury his face in his knees. Wesley edged uncertainly past and went upstairs alone.

The landing was dark, and he edged his way along to Kat's bedroom door. The shock of the room's destruction made him halt at the threshold. Books and DVDs littered the floor, shreds of posters clinging to the walls. The desk chair lay on its side, and an action figure crunched underfoot as he moved to right it. Her MacBook was open, screen aglow.

'You're here,' Wesley said, certain that it was true.

The only thing in the room apparently undisturbed was a small pile of sand-coloured gravel on the desk. He scooped it up and let the familiar stones play through his fingers. Gravel from the track that led to TrumourPixel's garage.

'And you were there,' he said, turning a slow circle to gaze around the room, hoping he might catch her in the peripheries of his vision. 'You stole the car. You're trying to stop them.'

If there was a response, he didn't hear it.

'I know it's weird I'm here, I just . . .'

Missed you. He couldn't bring himself to say it aloud.

The TV downstairs was loud enough to push through the ceiling, words too muffled to make out. Wesley forced a smile, hoped it didn't make him look insane.

'I needed somebody to talk to.'

He sat on the edge of the bed, leaving enough space that she could sit beside him, if she wanted.

*

Kat stayed by the door, as far from him as she could get. She had been frightened when she first found him there – her harasser, apparently able to enter her bedroom whenever he wanted – but with every word he spoke that fear was displaced by anger.

'I've got involved with some people I shouldn't have,' Wesley said, looking at his hands.

'You definitely shouldn't have, because they're Nazis,' answered Kat, even though she knew he wouldn't hear it.

'But it doesn't have to be a bad thing. Stealing the car hasn't stopped them, but we can do it together.'

Kat laughed bitterly. *'Together?'*

'I've been trying to find out what happened to Aaron Musley, the boy who disappeared before you,' said Wesley, speaking to the empty space beside him on the bed. 'I think he was trying to save himself from the fade by finding some connection to the world – something to live for. Maybe if you save Tinker . . . it might be enough to stop whatever is happening to you.'

Kat moved slowly to stand in front of him, stepping carefully across the debris of her life. There was that tug again, the yearning to slip inside his body. Except she didn't need that to know his true thoughts better than he did.

'You might know already, but I think you can . . . *go inside* people while you're fading. Temporarily.' He spoke as if the idea both thrilled and appalled him. 'Maybe if you can possess one of them or whatever when they attack Tinker, make them crash the car or let her get away. I don't really know how it works.'

'No, you *really* don't,' said Kat. Still, she wondered. Admitting he could be right meant admitting she needed him, and that made her sick. If it meant saving Tinker, she would have to swallow her pride.

Could it really save her? She looked around at the destruction of her room and knew she wanted to try.

'I won't do this for you,' she said to Wesley. 'I'll do it for Tinker. I'll do it so I can make it all up to Dad. I'll do it for myself.'

'Follow me to school tomorrow,' said Wesley, oblivious. 'I'll confront Luke and Justin, convince them I want to help, and find out exactly what they're planning. You'll hear it all and they'll never know. I'll be like a double agent. This is the only way I can give you inside information.'

'You're not giving me anything!' she shouted. 'If you really cared you would call the police and put a stop to this right now. I do need you, but not as much as you need me. I'm the only way you can stay friendly with your MRA mates without having to do the dirty work. You're not being brave. You're a coward.'

The look of determination, of triumph on Wesley's face as he scribbled his address on a scrap piece of paper made her want to reverse the fade just so she could smack him. How could he be so deluded and lost to convince himself he was doing the right thing? She lifted a hand towards him. One step, a moment of surrender to that seductive pull, and she could see for herself.

No. She stepped away at the same moment that Wesley got to his feet.

'There's somebody else we want to find to ask about

Aaron. A girl,' he said. 'But we don't know who she is. It must have been somebody he was close to – a friend or a girlfriend . . .'

Kat remembered what Safa had told her a couple of nights ago. She didn't want to help him, but it was clear now that the fade was accelerating. If he could find out more about what happened to Aaron, it might help her cling to herself for a little longer. She crossed the room to her laptop and began to type.

The light from the MacBook screen changed as Wesley moved to the door. Before it had simply been on the desktop, but when he returned to the desk an Instagram profile was waiting for him. A familiar young woman represented by a grid of selfies and modelling shots. The name at the top almost made him choke.

The girl who had come looking for Aaron, who he must have visited before the end.

'Selena Jensen.'

As soon as he was gone, Kat took out her phone and began writing a message to Safa.

You won't believe what just . . .

She stopped typing, staring at the blinking cursor. They had only just left each other, and already Kat missed her. She couldn't remember the last time she simply *had* to tell somebody something. She couldn't remember the last time she had somebody to tell.

And she had already lost her.

*

Wesley messaged Aoife on the walk home.

It's Selena. The girl who was looking for Aaron. He included the link to her Instagram profile.

Seriously?! came the reply. *There's no way she'll agree to meet us.*

She might if you mention Aaron's name.

Okay, I'll try! She signed off with a fingers-crossed emoji.

Wesley got home to find Dave playing with Evie in their room, shouts and giggles filling the flat, while Mum reclined on the short sofa with a damp cloth draped across her forehead. He felt like an actor walking onstage during the wrong scene.

'Rough day?' he asked, sitting across from her in the armchair.

Mum groaned as she levered herself upright. 'I took Evie to see that new Disney movie. They're so bright they always give me a headache. You could have come but I didn't know where you were. Evie was going nuts being cooped up here.'

'It's all right.' A thousand repeat viewings of *Frozen* had put him off Disney for ever. He looked around the bare walls of the front room, the tables with nothing on them but coasters and junk mail. 'Why don't we have any family photos out?'

Mum removed the flannel. 'We never have.'

'Yeah, but *why*?'

'I guess I got out of the habit of putting them up because we were in friends' houses,' she said. 'Plus

204

most of the photos we've got have Jordan and your dad in them.'

'It's like you're ashamed of the family we are now,' Wesley said.

'Of course not.' She patted the seat beside her, and he crossed to sit, letting her put an arm around him. 'I don't have a good reason for the photos, Wesley. But I'm proud of this family. We've been through a lot, and we're still here.'

He nodded, allowing himself to sink into her embrace. It made him feel like a child, and for once he was glad of it.

'I know there's been a lot going on, and I should have spoken to you about it sooner,' said Mum. 'Is there anything you want to talk about?'

The family was still there, after everything that had happened. They had clung on, but Wesley wanted to do more than that. He hated that the only way it could happen was to let somebody else take his place.

There was a lot more change to come. He had to show her that he was strong.

'I'm okay,' he said, choking down everything else he wanted to say. 'We should take some new family photos.'

'Of course,' said Mum. 'What's brought all this on, anyway?'

'I just think it's important that we keep memories,' he said. So even if he did lose his place here, there would always be something to remember it by.

23

Existential Stakeout

At the corner before he reached school, Wesley almost collided with an older boy blocking the pavement. He wore torn jeans and an orange T-shirt, and dark circles under his eyes suggested he hadn't slept.

'Excuse me, have you seen Kat Waldgrave?' he said, voice hoarse, as if he had been asking all night.

The question almost made Wesley laugh. 'I really haven't.'

The boy looked like he might cry. 'I'm sure she's here somewhere. I have to find her . . .'

Wesley thought immediately of Lukundo being drawn to Aaron's house after he had been inhabited by his missing friend. 'How do you know her?' he asked.

The boy looked pained. 'I don't. At least, I don't think I do.'

He must have been somebody Kat had inhabited. It *did* work. Wesley didn't know what strange connection brought the host in search of their faded passenger, but if he was searching for her here she had to be close by. Kat must have heard his plan, and followed him to school to carry it out.

After a moment's uncertainty, the boy followed Wesley to school, stopping finally to linger outside the gate.

In every lesson, Wesley couldn't stop glancing beside him, wondering if Kat was there, judging the little work he managed to scrawl out.

No shared morning classes meant he went looking for Luke and Justin at lunchtime. On the way to the canteen he ran into Aoife.

'Selena replied. You were right, as soon as I mentioned Aaron she agreed to meet us.'

'When?'

'Tonight. I haven't told the others yet.'

Wesley nodded. 'The sooner the better.'

He moved to walk past her, but Aoife stepped into his path to block him.

'I'm glad you've made us do this,' she said. 'It's made me rethink the whole thing. I think Robbie and Jae, too.'

'I'm glad,' he said, and kept moving before he had to think of a proper response. It embarrassed him to think Kat might have overheard.

The canteen was half-full when he arrived, and he spotted them at a table in the corner, wolfing down portions of lumpy chilli con carne. There were too many people here for them to turn violent, but their conversation would be masked by echoing voices and the smack of plastic trays on plastic tables.

'Let's do it,' he said, hoping Kat was still with him.

He was already talking before he took the seat beside them. 'I've been an idiot, okay, and I know I might have messed this up, but I've thought about it and I really want to—'

'Whoa, mate,' said Luke through a mouthful of chilli. 'Calm down. We were going to come looking for you.'

There was nothing violent in his tone. Wesley felt himself relax a little.

Luke pushed his tray away. 'We went too far the other night.'

A part of Wesley wished they hadn't quite got out of the way of that speeding car. Not enough to *kill* them, just injuries severe enough to keep them both out of action for a month or two. Problem solved.

'We believe it wasn't you who stole the car. You wouldn't even know how to drive it!' said Luke. 'And if you'd told anybody about it we'd probably know by now.'

Wesley kept quiet, trying to work out where this was going. He had expected to have to beg and plead to be let back into the gang. Instead they were being nicer to him than they ever had been before. Somebody was putting them up to this, and Justin's not-so-subtle elbow nudge to Luke's ribcage proved it.

'Look, I'm sorry, all right?' he said, clearly begrudging every word.

'We're sorry,' echoed Justin.

Wesley nodded, hoping it was enough of a reaction to keep them happy.

'It's dumb, getting this worked up over a prank,' said Luke. 'It's all just for a stupid video Tru wants to film.'

Wesley watched him closely. 'It really is just a prank?'

'Yeah, man. He's just taking it seriously because he wants Niko Denton to see.'

The smile on his face was fixed. Luke could probably convince somebody he wasn't a murderer while holding a severed human head.

'If I'm going to be involved, I need to know exactly what he's planning.'

Luke took a breath, as if he was fighting to keep calm. 'It's not as easy as that. Tru needs something from you to prove you're for real. We need another car.'

Wesley's stomach sank, knowing what would come next.

'You have easy access to more,' said Luke. 'We need you to steal one for us.'

'How am I supposed to steal from the dealership?' said Wesley.

'Get the keys off the new guy who's banging your mum,' said Luke, before remembering he was asking a favour. 'Her new boyfriend. He must trust you by now.'

'I just wash them.'

'So you know where the keys are kept, yeah?'

The lock box in the back office. 'I can't get to them.'

'You're saying there's no way?'

'I'd have to get his keys and—'

'All right, so that's what you do.'

'I don't know . . .' He could probably do it. The security at the dealership was basic. It might be the only way to find out the real plan so Kat could stop it.

Luke glanced around, as if assessing what he could get away with. 'Why do you think you have a choice? We let you in on the plan because we thought you could handle it. You don't get to be a pussy now. You owe us.'

'You don't want to make Tru unhappy,' said Justin. It sounded like he spoke from experience.

Luke hissed through his teeth, the sharp sound making Wesley meet his eye. 'He's right. We've already told you too much, and Tru doesn't want any loose ends. We've got all the evidence of what you did to Kat, and there are plenty of other things we can pin on you.'

An empty threat. It had to be.

Luke reached out and squeezed his shoulder hard. 'You help us get a car, and you're a legend, mate.'

Wesley glanced over his shoulder and swallowed hard. It was the only way. 'Okay.'

When Luke took his hand away he didn't seem pleased. He looked *relieved*.

'But you have to tell me what he's going to do with it.'

'We've been keeping track of Tinker on social media. Whenever she stays in a hotel or something she gets it for free as long as she posts about it, right?' Luke was clearly pleased with his cunning, nerves slipping away as he spoke. 'That means we'll know where she's staying before the convention, what route she'll take to get there. Everything. All we have to do is keep watch and pick her up when she's on the street.'

'And then what?'

Luke leaned back and smiled. 'I told you. Tru's going to film a video.'

It was simple enough that it might work. Simple enough that it could be stopped.

'Be at the dealership with keys tonight at two a.m.,' said Luke.

Wesley wished he could confirm that Kat had heard, that she understood what she needed to do. It might have stopped his hands shaking when he gave them a nod and left the table behind.

24

Down Will Come Baby

It hardly seemed fair that Kat could be invisible and have a stalker at the same time, but she had long since given up on the world playing by the rules. The boy followed her at a distance as she hurried away from school, always lagging slightly behind as if he was on the end of a slack length of string. Orange T-shirt. Torn jeans. Whatever power was drawing him here hadn't allowed him to change since she had stepped inside his body at the march.

The way he didn't see her was different now. Before, people seemed to know she was present but simply didn't care. Since fading further it really was as if she was invisible, as if the entire world was forgetting her.

At least his presence proved that it hadn't been a dream or hallucination. She really had inhabited him, if only for a few seconds. Perhaps some small part of her was left behind, enough to have quickened the fade and brought him in search of its parent.

It really *could* be the key to saving Tinker. Hide inside her body when they take her, cling on long enough to reach their hideout, and then . . . what? Break her chains and kung fu her way out of there? They certainly wouldn't be expecting it.

The boy was catching up. Kat increased her pace and took out her phone. There was only one person she could talk to about this.

Do you have somebody hanging around outside your house today?

Safa's reply was almost instant. *I WAS JUST MESSAGING YOU!!! Whistle woman is outside and she looks pissed. I think she wants revenge.*

Kat couldn't help but laugh. *It must be some side effect of what we did.*

It's CREEPY.

Glancing over her shoulder, Kat felt oddly fond of the boy. He remembered her, in his way, when almost nobody else did. She hoped she hadn't ruined his date.

It follows, she messaged Safa.

DON'T. Can you meet me in town? I wanna show you something.

No apology – not even any recognition – for what had happened at the march. Kat should have refused. Except she was hardly in a position to turn down company.

It was a welcome surprise to find the entire complement of the Lonely People waiting for him at the gates. Robbie wore a resistant expression, like he wanted to pretend he had been frogmarched there, but it wasn't fooling anybody.

'Thanks for coming,' Wesley said.

213

'You can stop thanking us,' replied Aoife. 'We want to be here.'

Apparently Selena had only agreed to meet them if it was somewhere away from her old home. They waited for a bus that would take them there and made their way to the back seats.

'I almost didn't come, Mr Delaney set us a thousand-word essay due *tomorrow*,' said Jae, as the windows rattled and the bus got under way.

'He always does that. He's a dick,' concluded Robbie.

'Mrs Rahimi is worse,' said Aoife. 'She makes everybody memorise poetry and gives the whole class five minutes detention for every line you forget. "The future is a grey seagull / Tattling in its cat-voice of departure".'

'What the hell is that?'

'I don't know, I memorise the lines and forget everything else.'

Wesley leaned back in his seat and focused on the passing street to smother a smile. It was the most mundane conversation, the kind that school kids all over the country must have been having. The kind of conversation shared between friends.

The square was quiet at this time of day, chairs and tables set up outside the pubs in defiance of the new chill on the air, nobody but smokers brave enough to use them. Just like before, Safa was leaning against the fountain, but the way she watched the people passing by was different now: hungry, appraising, a predator at a buffet.

The fade had accelerated in her as it had in Kat. From a distance she was indistinct, like haze from a hot road. A mirage of a girl.

'Hey,' she said when she spotted Kat's approach.

Oh, so it *was* going to be awkward. 'Hey.'

'We're going to get a bus.'

'Okay.'

They crossed to a stop at the edge of the square and stood in a silence so thick it would have broken the blade of a knife. It was so tempting to apologise, to say anything that would break this tension, but that wasn't Kat's responsibility. All she could do was wait.

'This is it,' said Safa.

A bus to the next town over, doors hissing open to let out an old man with a frame. They both jumped on, Kat tapping her card out of habit. Safa went straight upstairs to the top deck, and Kat was following when she spotted who occupied the bottom floor back seats. Wesley and the so-called Lonely People, laughing over some shared joke. The resentment she expected to feel at his apparent happiness didn't come. There was a vague satisfaction that he had taken her clue and it had kept him on the trail. Some part of her was even willing to feel happy that he might have found friends – she knew the importance of that more than anybody.

She went up to join Safa in the front seats.

'Man, this is hard without Siri,' said Safa, as soon as the bus was moving.

'What is?'

She grabbed and shook fistfuls of the air in frustration. 'Finding the right words.'

'Siri always gets it wrong.'

'Yeah, but she tries, bless her.'

Kat stayed quiet now, determined not to let Safa joke her way out of this.

'I guess I'm trying to say I'm sorry,' said Safa, toying with the nesting doll at her throat. 'I was a dick.'

'You *were* kind of a dick.'

'It's true what I said about struggling to feel as if anything matters, but I want you to know . . .' She squirmed in her seat, as if being this earnest was physically painful. 'You matter.'

Heart soaring, belly flipping, smile tugged open by puppet strings. 'Thank you. And you matter to—'

'No more!' said Safa, flapping her hands. 'I can't take it.'

'Okay, so where are you taking me?'

'It really is hard to explain,' said Safa. 'I just want you to understand everything.'

What they called the next town over was really part of the same urban sprawl. No clear border marked it except for a change in chicken shop names. Apart from a snarl of roadworks, traffic was light. They pulled up in the town centre less than twenty minutes later. Wesley and the Lonely People got off at the same stop and started along the high street.

'Well isn't that nice,' said Safa. 'I knew they never really wanted to fade.'

Watching them go, she almost sounded jealous.

They piled into the crowded Caffè Nero Selena had chosen as a meeting place and found her sitting at a table in the middle of the room, in plain view of the counter. She looked almost exactly as Wesley remembered, black hair scraped back into a high ponytail, eyebrows thin enough to have been drawn on. The only difference was a walking cane leaning against the table beside her.

She wasn't alone; a guy in a thick jacket that may or may not have hidden bulging muscles/gleaming knives/a machine gun sat close at her side and eyed them suspiciously as they approached, Aoife leading the way.

'Is it okay if we sit down?' she asked.

Selena looked between them, fingers dancing nervously on the rim of her coffee cup, and then nodded.

The cafe was busy enough that they needed to beg spare chairs from other tables. As soon as he sat opposite her, Wesley's leg began to bounce of its own volition. He had to keep telling himself he had only played the smallest of roles in the #SelloutSelena campaign, there was no reason he should feel guilty.

'I thought it probably wasn't safe to come alone,' said Selena, nodding to the bodyguard beside her.

'We understand,' said Aoife. 'You don't know us, and I got in touch out of the blue.'

'I don't speak to anybody from school any more. I would say it's a shame, but I wouldn't mean it.'

'There are still a lot of stupid rumours about what happened to you.'

Selena smiled at that. 'The truth isn't very exciting. Obviously I was in hospital for a while after it happened. My knee was badly damaged, and it needed some rehabilitation.' She tapped her fingers against the cane. 'And, you know, I still need counselling about the whole thing. It doesn't go away, just like that. But I don't want to let it ruin my life. I still get some modelling jobs, and I'm working with a charity on a campaign against online bullying.'

Wesley tried to hold his leg still. He imagined this was what it would be like to sit opposite Kat, without the fade to insulate him from her fury, only worse, because there would be no way he could pretend he wasn't entirely to blame.

'So, what did you want to talk about?'

'Um, I mentioned it in the message,' said Aoife. 'You knew Aaron Musley?'

Selena smacked a palm against her forehead. 'Right, of course. That keeps happening lately.' She turned to her bodyguard. 'It's okay, can you give us a few minutes?'

He left them alone to talk.

The high street was flatter and wider than home, the hooks of gentrification sunk a little deeper. Kat hadn't bothered to come here in years, and the greasy spoon cafe she'd always stopped at with Mum was now an artisan crêpery.

'Should we try and get something to eat?' asked Safa.

'Just show me.'

Along the high street, they passed phone shops and estate agents and upmarket clothes stores. A banner strung between lamp posts was advertising a Halloween market, whatever that meant. First the shops went fancy, then they tried to lure you out to them with extravagant events. It would be happening at home soon.

Safa led her to a Greek fast food place Kat hadn't known was there, though the stuttering light in its sign and the peeling letters in its window suggested it had been there a while.

'I told you I'm not hungry.'

'No, look inside.'

Past lunchtime, it was quiet inside the restaurant. The only customers at the white plastic tables were a balding man biting into a kebab and a young woman sitting close to the counter.

'What?'

Safa pointed to the woman. 'She's my Cradle.'

'We weren't together long, but I think we'd liked each other for a while,' said Selena, frowning as if she had to haul the memory across a great distance. 'He was the real reason I broke up with Gabriel because, you know, Aaron didn't treat me like shit.'

Wesley was still trying to wrap his head around the idea that anybody could have been with Selena and been unhappy with their life.

'When everything with the hashtag started to get out of control, Aaron told me he couldn't take it any more.' The group watched in silence while Selena pondered this. 'I couldn't blame him, you know? But at the same time it was *me* dealing with all this abuse. Nobody knew about us, and it wasn't like I had the option of just walking away from it all. It would have meant a lot if he had stood by me.'

Across the cafe, Selena's bodyguard watched them

closely. Wesley pressed a fist into his restless leg. He wanted to tell her what he knew about the campaign against her, the small part he had played within it. But what good would it do now? It couldn't change what had happened, and it might keep him from learning information that could save Kat.

'Do you know what happened to him?' asked Robbie.

She thought about this for a long moment. 'I knew he was gone, and I guess I never stopped to ask where. It was just the truth, you know? I used to think about him all the time, whether I was hating him or missing him like crazy. It got really intense one day, and then it just . . . stopped.'

Wesley leaned forward. 'But you didn't forget him?'

'How could I?' she said. 'After the message he left me.'

The young woman was reading a thick book propped up against the wall and making notes on a pad, a lock of dark, curly hair escaping her bun and falling across her eyes. A cup of coffee steamed beside her.

'You're going to choose her?' said Kat. 'After you fade for good?'

The woman glanced up at them and they both pretended to be studying the menu in the window, before remembering that it didn't matter.

'It's not just because she's gorgeous,' said Safa. 'The restaurant is family-owned and from what I can tell they all get on really well. She works here sometimes to help out, but she's studying full-time to become a therapist.'

Oh, the irony.

'How many times have you been here?' said Kat. 'To learn all this?'

Safa smiled. 'Thankfully I love souvlaki.'

It sounded too good to be true, and Kat thought of the suppressed *something else* she had felt when she inhabited the boy at the march. The rainforest inside him had not been as perfect as it seemed.

'You can't really know anything about her – not enough to become part of her *for ever*.'

'I know she's more than I'll ever be.'

Kat turned on her. 'You don't know that!'

'You wanted to know what triggered the fade in me,' she said. 'It wasn't any big moment. It happened the morning I woke up and knew – *knew* – that I couldn't go on as myself.'

There was an eerie calm about Safa now, as if being this close to her intended washed away any doubt. As if most of her was already gone. She checked her watch and looked away along the high street. Another young woman, big earrings jangling and an Afro like a halo around her head, was striding towards the restaurant. They stepped away to let her inside, and she passed, of course, without seeing them. The woman already inside the restaurant squealed and sprang to her feet, and they met between the tables, pulling each other into a kiss.

'Nobody will ever be that happy to see me,' said Safa, watching them dreamily as they broke apart, hands still clasped together between them.

I would, thought Kat. *I am.*

The first young woman gathered up her things and shouted a goodbye to whoever was in the kitchen.

They linked arms and left the restaurant, heading away between the shops. Safa moved to follow, but Kat turned in the opposite direction.

'You don't even want to try,' said Kat. 'What if these things will happen for us if we just wait?'

Safa took her shoulders and turned her to face an empty shop window, where only a hint of their reflections looked back. 'Some people hurt because of the things that happened to them,' said Safa. 'I hurt because of the things that didn't.'

Kat reached across and squeezed her hand. Live for long enough without hope and you'll believe that nothing can ever change for you. Maybe then you make it true.

Looking at the people scattered around the high street, it seemed impossible to pick any one she would want to become. It would be pot luck, best guess, hoping whoever she chose had their shit together as much as it looked.

She just had to hope it would never come to that.

'Let's go out tonight, scope out the local talent for you,' said Safa.

'I don't think I should . . .'

'Please, look,' said Safa, an edge to her voice now. 'I know you think stopping this attack will help you stay. If I can't convince you it's not worth it then I promise I'll stop bugging you. Just please don't leave me alone tonight.'

The façade had slipped again, and this time Kat was sure she glimpsed what was underneath. Doubt. Fear. Everything Safa had so ruthlessly hidden until now.

'All right,' said Kat. 'Let's paint the town invisible.'

One way or another, it would be the last time.

The picture on Selena's phone didn't make any sense. It showed bottles of ketchup and random sauces broken and spilled across a kitchen floor, colours running together into a soupy mess.

'What are we looking at?' asked Robbie.

Selena checked the screen before turning it back to them. 'You can't see it?'

'It just looks like your shopping bag broke.'

'There's a message written in it,' she said, pointing to the middle of the photograph. 'Like he used his fingers.'

Wesley squinted at the screen, like the words might make themselves known if he just concentrated, but he could see nothing there.

'It says *GOING NOW. LOOK FOR JOSEPH.*' She stared at the image. 'I've never shown anybody else before. You're not messing with me?'

They all shook their heads. If there was a message there, it was invisible to them.

'Call me old-fashioned, but couldn't he have used a pen and paper?' asked Jae.

'I think he tried. There were pens knocked off the side too.' Selena pointed to the corner of the photo, where biros and highlighters swam in the spilled condiments. 'It must have happened while I was home. I didn't hear anything, but when I saw it I realised he had been there. It felt like he'd been with me.'

That was how she was able to see the message. It

should have been invisible to her too, scrawled on another plane of existence, but Aaron had gone inside her to make sure it couldn't be missed. He had given her the power to see it. That's why she had gone looking for him at home, just like Lukundo had.

'*Look for Joseph*,' repeated Aoife. 'You think he wanted you to look after his little brother?'

Wesley straightened up so sharply that he banged his knee against the table. He couldn't believe he hadn't spotted it before now. Maybe the powers of the fade had hidden the truth from him. Lukundo and Selena had been drawn to Aaron's house because being inhabited made them need to be close to him. Just like that boy who had been searching for Kat. That meant that, even after he had disappeared, Aaron was still at the house. In one form or another.

'Thank you for meeting us,' he said, standing abruptly. The others confusedly followed.

'One last thing,' said Selena, as her bodyguard began to make his way back over. 'Can you tell me what really happened to him?'

There was no way she could really understand the truth, and even if she did she would soon forget. 'I think he's still around,' said Wesley, and left the cafe with the rest of the group in hot pursuit.

'What is it?' said Robbie, when they caught him half way up the high street.

'We were so focused on Aaron being gone that we never thought about where he *went*.' Wesley looked around at the people passing them, moving between shops or talking on their phones. It would be almost impossible to choose a Cradle, a lucky dip, even with the ability to sample a few before making a final decision. Unless you chose somebody you already knew. *'Look for Joseph.* He wasn't asking her to look after his brother. He was trying to tell her he chose his brother as his Cradle.'

They had spoken to Aaron, or whatever was left of him, a few days ago. They just hadn't known it.

25

Somebody Who Actually Cares

Wesley wanted to confront him immediately, but there was one more important thing to take care of first. Even as his shift at the garage was coming to an end, he couldn't stop glancing sidelong at the back office every opportunity he had. Legs aching with the effort of pumping up tyres, skin dry and tight from washing cars that didn't need it – nothing would take his mind from what he needed to do.

Tonight, he was going to steal a car. He just hadn't worked out how yet.

Dave sat at his desk, sorting out some paperwork from a sale earlier in the day. The lockbox on the wall behind him was open. It would be closed before they left, along with the office door. Wesley would only get inside if he had the keys.

He checked his phone, found a message from Luke.

see you 2am?

Yeah, he replied. No backing out now.

The next time his eyes slid sideways to the office he realised Dave was no longer at his desk.

'Good job on this one, sport.'

Wesley jumped out of his skin as Dave came around the car. 'Sport?'

'I thought it might be a cool nickname.'

'It's really not,' said Wesley, and they both smiled.

The car was a grey Vauxhall, almost aggressively nondescript and parked in the front row. It was currently Wesley's top target.

'You've really got a knack for this.'

It was hardly difficult, washing cars, but there was that warm glow of pride nevertheless.

'Thanks.'

'Everything all right?' said Dave, reaching out a hand to lean on the car before thinking better of it. 'You seem a bit on edge.'

Being outed as on edge only made him feel considerably more on edge. 'No, I'm just tired.'

'Is it cos of your brother being back?'

It was strange, having somebody ask him personal questions, especially one of Mum's boyfriends. It was even stranger being able to tell that he actually *cared*.

'I wish I could be glad that he's back,' said Wesley, wondering how much he should say, finding that he didn't care. 'I just think he broke the family apart in a way that means we'll never quite fit together properly again. I don't know if there's room for both of us.'

Or for you either, he didn't say.

Dave nodded, and now it was clearly him wondering if he should say what came next. 'I had a thought, about all of you. I've already talked to your mum about it, but it's only fair I ask you, too. You've done so much to look after her all these years.'

It was more than pride that Wesley felt now, a fragile luminescence he didn't know how to name. This was how it felt to be recognised, to have someone notice the efforts he had made. It almost made him miss what Dave said next.

'How would you feel about all of you moving into my place?'

There was genuine hope in Dave's eyes, making it clear this was something he really wanted to do and not the result of some misguided pity or demand from Mum. So when Wesley didn't answer straight away he began to talk faster.

'It's just an idea to get you and Evie away from that damp, out to a slightly nicer area. Not that I live in a palace, mind,' he said. 'It was just an idea.'

'No. I mean, I'm not sure.' Wesley hadn't even seen the place, but there was something tempting about the idea. If Dave's place didn't smell of bins it would be an upgrade.

But where they were now was *their* place. The first they had called their own since living in a long line of places they didn't belong. Instinctively, he knew that he wouldn't belong there either, that he would be handing Mum over, erasing everything they had been through. If he wasn't there to look after her, why was he there at all? She wouldn't need him any more.

And if things went south with Dave, and they had to start all over again . . .

'I'll have to think about it,' he said.

Although Dave looked disappointed, he didn't push it any further. He was so decent it was almost annoying.

'What about Jordan?' Wesley asked.

Dave sighed, like he'd made a decision he knew would come back to haunt him. 'We're going to talk about it. All of us. Speaking of which . . .'

He pointed to the road, where an Uber had just pulled up. Mum emerged from the back, throwing them a wave, leading Evie out after her. From the front, carrying a short stack of pizza boxes, came Jordan.

'There's my working boy!' said Mum, slipping between the cars to plant a kiss on Wesley's cheek, before doing the same to Dave.

'You make me sound like a rent boy,' he said.

Thankfully she wasn't wearing any rings, so the smack to the back of the head didn't hurt too much.

'I thought we were meeting you at home?' said Dave.

'You can drive us back, can't you?'

'Pizza is the best excuse to finish early.'

'Pizza!' said Evie.

Briefly, Wesley wondered if there might be a chance to sneak inside while they talked and pocket a set of car keys before anybody noticed.

'I hope you've worked up an appetite,' said Mum.

Dave smacked him on the back. 'He's a hard worker.'

Mum beamed, and there was the pride again, welling up like struck oil. He caught Jordan's eye, who had joined them with the pizzas, but looked away before he could catch his expression.

'Going cold,' said Jordan.

'Pizza!' reiterated Evie, jumping at the boxes.

While the others waited by Dave's car, Wesley watched him lock up: paperwork filed away, lockbox sealed, before closing the office itself. The keys went straight into the right pocket of his leather jacket.

When he joined them at the car, he found Jordan watching him, but it had to be paranoia that said he looked suspicious. Wesley pushed past him, almost unbalancing the pizzas, and closed himself in the front seat of the car.

26

Fake News Crocodiles

Wesley listened to the washing machine whirring in the kitchen, the bag of dirty laundry Jordan had produced as soon as they got home the surest sign of all that things between them were changing.

Sitting and squabbling over pizza together felt like being a family again, until he realised there was no *again*. They had never felt like a family. A unit. Anything whole. This might have been the closest they had ever managed.

There weren't enough seats for everybody in the front room. Wesley was on the floor while Mum and Dave sat wedged together on the sofa, Evie balanced between their laps. The armchair was taken by Jordan, separating him from the others, but he leaned over the arm while he told his story as if trying to be as close to them as he could.

'There was this guy in my hostel in Darwin who believed crocodiles are a hoax. Like, actually believed these five-metre killing machines were made up by the Australian government to attract tourists.' Jordan took a bite of pizza, cheese sticking between his teeth. 'So a bunch of us decided to take him out and prove him wrong.'

Dave covered Evie's ears, predicting the story was going nowhere good.

'We drive him to this billabong in the outback which is famous for having loads of crocs, so of course when we turn up there isn't one in sight. This guy starts ranting about how we're gullible idiots, how we've fallen for "fake news crocodiles", and he goes and stands right at the edge of the water.'

Wesley had never left the south of England, but even he knew that was a bad idea.

'Bear in mind they tell you never to go within five metres of any water like that because crocs can jump their body length. And I swear,' said Jordan, almost certainly meaning it was made up, 'this guy pulls down his pants and starts mooning the water.'

Everybody but Evie, ears still covered, had stopped eating, waiting rapt for what happened next. Wesley was no exception. He couldn't deny his brother's natural charisma, his ability to fit in and belong wherever in the world he put himself.

'He's shouting "come and get me, crocodiles!" and waving his pale arse, when all of a sudden there's this *ROAR* from the water and a crocodile the length of a car comes snapping at him.'

Mum jumped enough to send a piece of pepperoni flying across the room.

'Jeff!' called Evie.

'Was he okay?'

'Oh yeah, he was fine, the croc missed him.' Jordan leaned back in his seat. 'Except he literally shat himself.'

Everybody groaned.

'You were in Australia for almost two years,' said Mum, wagging what remained of her pizza slice. 'And *that's* the story you choose to tell us.'

'And over dinner,' added Dave.

'And that definitely, actually happened,' finished Wesley.

Jordan regarded him levelly. 'Don't tell me you don't believe in crocodiles either, bro?'

Wesley took a bite of pizza and stayed silent. It shouldn't be so easy for Jordan to come back into their lives. If anybody was paying attention, they would see he hadn't really changed, that he was just doing what he could to be accepted. If they let him, he would only do more damage, unravel everything they had achieved without him.

'So that's your best memory of Australia, is it?' he said. 'Nearly getting a guy eaten alive?'

Jordan's satisfied smile faltered. 'He was probably more alive in that moment than you've ever been, little bro.'

Nobody else seemed to acknowledge the barbed comment, reaching instead for the last few slices of pizza.

'Thanks for the food,' said Jordan, smiling broadly – too broadly – at Dave. The pact to never get friendly with any of Mum's boyfriends was well and truly broken. Jordan wouldn't do that without an ulterior motive.

'Pizza,' whispered Evie to nobody in particular.

Mum finished her slice, shifted Evie off her lap, and sat forwards. 'We need to talk to you about something.'

Wesley knew what would happen from there. They would agree to move into Dave's house, all of them, and Jordan would take his place, pushing him to the outside like always. The last year or more would no longer matter – if it ever had. Wesley would lose the last place he thought he belonged.

He glanced at the front door, where Dave's leather jacket was hanging. There was still a chance he could belong somewhere else. Everybody needs something to live for.

Pizza turned out to be the perfect accomplice, sending everybody to bed early to sleep it off. Wesley would have hours to claim the keys. Just as soon as he got Jordan out of the flat.

'Where are you staying?' asked Mum.

'Just with a mate,' said Jordan, putting on his shoes a little more slowly than seemed necessary.

A hesitation, Mum looking to Dave for encouragement before she spoke again. 'You can stay here tonight. If you want?'

Jordan smiled and nodded, and looked immediately to Wesley with a smile that spoke of triumph. Wesley glowered in return, betrayal sizzling in his belly.

'Night, bro,' Jordan said, as Wesley carried their sister to the bedroom.

Sleep didn't even seem like an option, and when his phone told him it was just after one a.m. he threw back the covers. Evie always slept like a brick, but he had already swept the floor clear of her toys and paints just in case he trod on anything to alert her. He eased the door open and peered out into the dark hallway. Next door Mum was snoring, but otherwise it was quiet. Wesley picked up his trainers and padded into the sitting room.

His brother was a long lump on the sofa, face down on the pillow, breathing noisily. Back when they had shared a room, there had been nights Wesley was frightened he might suffocate like that.

The boards squeaked under the thin carpet as he crept past him to the door. The jacket was still there, and Wesley reached into the pocket, gripping the keys hard so they wouldn't clink together.

Watching Jordan the entire time, he opened the latch and pulled the door open just enough to let his body through, before going out into the night.

27

Second-hand Kisses

The town centre was busier than usual, after-work drinkers getting caught up with those on a full-blown night out. Walking through them all felt different now. Kat could have reached out and *become* any one of them, shrugged their lives around her shoulders to try them on for size. She should be looking for one that fit, one she could soon call home. Despite her determination to redeem herself, it was still so tempting to experience it one last time, while she still had the power.

Safa stumbled on her heels for the tenth time since leaving the house. 'That's it,' she said, scooping them off and throwing them across the square.

'You'll get tetanus,' said Kat.

'By this time tomorrow there'll be nothing left to get tetanus.'

They had emptied Safa's wardrobe onto the bed to choose their outfits. While Safa chose a long, flowery dress she claimed to have never worn, Kat had quickly realised everything on offer was too short for her. They had raided her mum's wardrobe instead, and Kat wondered how long it would take for the strappy top and neatly ironed jeans to be missed.

A line of people shivered away from the door of a club on the far corner of the square. Automatically, Kat went to join the queue, before Safa sashayed past like a celebrity.

'We're under age,' she announced to the bouncers that flanked the door, before looking at Kat over her shoulder. 'The security here is a joke.'

Past the cloakroom, where the noise of the club was muffled, before they pushed through a set of double doors. Kat had never been to a club before. The music landed like a physical blow. It thumped in her chest, tickling her throat and making her want to cough. The air was hot, wet against her skin, like the rainforest inside the boy from the march. Flashing lights made her head spin.

She followed Safa to an open space against a wall overlooking a dance floor. It was probably still early for a club, but there were plenty of people dancing, more leaning against the walls or lounging at tables.

'What do we do now?' Kat shouted over the din.

Inside, Safa's confidence seemed to have dimmed. Whenever the lights swept through her she all but disappeared, making it seem as if she flashed in and out of existence. She looked around – the dance floor, growing busier by the second, the crowds at the bar, the queue for the toilet – and appeared lost.

'Are you going to do it again?' Kat shouted, gesturing to the people around them. They all tugged at her, inviting her inside. She remembered how good it had felt. The relief of escape.

Safa leaned close to her ear. 'I think I could without it tipping me over the edge. I can hold on. Until tomorrow.'

Tomorrow.

At least they had tonight. Kat could give her that.

'We're standing against a wall,' she said, as the music shifted to something faster, sending people running to the dance floor.

'So?'

'I bet this is exactly what we would do in a nightclub.'

A smile unfurled across Safa's lips, and she set off towards the dance floor, Kat following close behind. It was packed now, and they found a space for themselves near the middle.

'They say you should dance like nobody's watching,' said Safa. 'We'll never have a better chance.'

And she threw up her arms in time with the music, grinning wildly as her hair flew. Kat laughed and did the same, swinging her head and her hips, smiling so widely it hurt. The music was relentless, and the crowd jostled around them, pumping their fists in the air. The flashing lights seemed to obliterate Safa and remake her in jittery patterns.

The beat shifted, and the crowd began to jump, bouncing to the rhythm. The two of them moved as one, falling into time, bodies swaying closer. The last of Kat's self-consciousness withdrew. She jumped as high as she could, sweat already flying from her skin.

'Hey,' shouted Safa.

'Hey,' Kat replied, quiet enough that she may not have spoken at all.

'One last time.'

Safa spun away into a tight space between a group of girls dancing behind them. Without hesitation she slipped into the nearest body, sugar dissolving in water.

The newfound host kept dancing as if nothing had happened, smiling across at her friends. Kat eyed a young guy beside her dancing only with shuffling feet and arrhythmic nods of the head. The yearning was too strong. Tomorrow she would save herself. So why shouldn't she enjoy tonight? When Kat reached for him the barrier broke with ease. One last time. She took a breath as if going underwater.

Vertigo. The melee of the club muted.

There were two of her again. A proxy still in the club, another standing on a white sand beach with clear water lapping between her toes. Every grain of sand was warm, a memory, a feeling, on a beach that seemed to stretch for ever. She wanted to lie back and bury herself in the sand, armour herself with its possibility. Who might be watching him? Where might this night lead? This could be Kat's life, second-hand, if she chose it.

Except there was something else on the beach. A black shape of flotsam buried on the tideline. She waded towards it, feeling the energy emanating from it and the sand's determination to swallow it down. It was a box, just like she had seen in the rainforest, sealed tight but always threatening to leak.

In the club, the song changed again. A tempo shift sent ripples through the crowd. The guy – she, Kat – turned just enough to see Safa's host, and for a fleeting moment their eyes met. Kat watched as Safa stepped out of the girl's skin and burrowed deeper into the mass of bodies, slipping into another skin as the dancing intensified.

There was still a force inside her host trying to push her out, but she could hold on for longer if she wanted. Instead she let it evict her, emerging again on the dance floor, thrumming with energy. She gave chase to Safa, leaping into another body. It was so easy now, the resistance weakening with every transition.

A mountaintop, snow falling gently across a sweep of valley. Every flake was made of belonging, confidence, lightness, release. She caught them on her tongue, ignoring the looming black shape caught in a snowdrift.

When Safa switched again, she followed, bounding from body to body across the dance floor. A jungle, a yacht deck, a picnic blanket spread out in a park with gleaming skyscrapers on all sides. She couldn't get enough. It could all be hers, without the weight of *Kat Waldgrave* being attached to drag it all down.

And always the box, pushed out of sight, whatever lay inside a doomsday device ready to destroy it all.

Kat wanted to catch Safa out this time, switch first, get ahead of her in the chase. Close by were a boy and a girl dancing out of time to the music, arms draped over each other's shoulders, foreheads pressed together. Kat stepped out onto the dance floor and reached for the boy, just as Safa appeared and slipped into the girl. At the same moment the couple brought their lips together.

It wasn't her kiss, but *oh god* it was so close, and she sank into it as deeply as she could. Every inch of her body tingled, every nerve ending set ablaze, as surrogate lips nipped and opened, stubble scratched against skin. It said everything Kat had been unable to put into words, made her blind to whatever landscape was inside the boy. Pleasure sang through her. The pleasure of being noticed, of being seen by the only person who mattered. It was everything.

Except . . .

It wasn't her skin. They weren't her lips.

It lasted only seconds before it overwhelmed and bucked her out of his body, all thundering heart and sweaty skin. Safa appeared at the same moment, wide-eyed and breathing hard. Kat gasped at the sight of her.

'Look at you,' she said.

Safa glowed opaque, as if every star in the universe was lighting her up. The fade was gone.

Hardly daring to breathe, Kat lifted a hand and found it was solid, complete.

'Holy shit.'

The couple they had inhabited broke their kiss, and stared at them reproachfully. Others around them were looking too, looking right *at* them, sensing that something was wrong.

'They see us,' said Kat, hardly remembering they could probably hear her, too.

Safa's eyes gleamed with panic, and she tried to hide her face with her hands, before turning to push away through the crowd.

'Wait!'

As they ran for the exit, the colour drained from Safa's skin as the fade reclaimed its territory. A sensation of lightness, her body becoming untethered from the world just like that first day, let Kat know the same was happening to her.

By the time they burst out into the night, she was more faded than ever before.

28

Hijack

Nobody could possibly know what he was doing, but as he walked with hands buried deep in his pockets, stolen keys gripped in his fist, Wesley already felt like a criminal.

Every step towards the dealership made it more difficult to turn back. Made what he had to do more real. What was waiting for him if he went home with nothing? Jordan sleeping on the couch, the promise of a new life where Wesley had no place. Doing this wouldn't give him what he wanted, but it would give him *something*.

The streets were almost empty at this time of night, a few people noisily returning home from nights out. Paying him no attention at all. He reached the end of the road where he could turn towards Garden Hill, and shrank against some bushes as he thought he heard footsteps running past. Nobody there. His imagination trying to psyche him out and send him home. He turned the other way, only a few roads away from the dealership now.

More running footsteps, behind him this time. 'Hey!'

Wesley whirled around, tensed to run, until he realised it was Jordan.

'What the hell are you doing?' he said when he caught up, leaning on his knees to try and catch his breath.

'I couldn't sleep,' said Wesley, trying to hold his voice level.

'And Dave's keys are a cure for insomnia, are they?'

His brother hadn't been asleep after all. Wesley hissed through his teeth, irrationally angry, like he had been tricked. He spun away and started across the road, but Jordan followed close at his side.

'Tell me what you're doing.'

Head down, feet moving. He had to stay calm, couldn't let his brother get to him like he always did. 'Why should I?'

'Because I think you're doing something stupid.'

They hurried through a residential street lined with trees greyed by the cars parked now between them, petrified under LED street lights. On either side the houses were set close to the road, almost every window dark except where the phantom light of a TV flicked and shifted. Jordan didn't keep pushing for answers, but Wesley knew he wasn't going to leave it alone.

It was better this way, really. Jordan would be able to see first-hand how wrong he had always been about his little brother.

Another corner brought them close to the industrial estate, the dealership coming into view ahead.

'What are we doing here?' said Jordan.

A figure dressed in black lingered across the road

from the dealership. The sight of him made Wesley slow, before compelling himself to keep going. 'Not *we*,' he said.

'You don't have to do this.' Either Jordan had guessed, or he didn't need to.

'According to you this is exactly the kind of thing I should be doing.'

'I don't want you to do anything because of me.'

'You don't get to decide,' said Wesley. 'I have to do this. I have to.'

The waiting figure came across the road to meet them. It was Tru, hood pulled close around his face, his bulk only making him look more conspicuous in his black clothes.

'Who's this?' he said, lifting his chin at Jordan.

'My brother,' said Wesley, making sure his voice didn't shake. 'He's cool. You're cool, aren't you?'

Jordan held his eye for a long time – a challenge or a plea, he couldn't tell – and then nodded.

They moved between the cars towards the dealership office.

They ran, away from the square and through the streets, Kat always a few paces behind. Through streets and past people stumbling drunkenly home or simply out for late-night walks, until she realised where they were heading.

The hill was a dark rise against the sky. Safa finally stopped at the gate – lock broken for as long as Kat could remember – leaning against the Garden Hill sign but not breathing hard at all. In the darkness she was almost invisible. Maybe there was little need to breathe any more, hardly any body left to demand oxygen.

'You felt that,' said Kat, the last of the kiss's power idling inside her like a fallen petal.

Safa shook her head. 'It doesn't matter.'

'It brought us back. What if it means—?'

'This isn't Sleeping-fucking-Beauty!' Safa pushed the sign, the metal wavering. 'You don't get it – we can only feel like that if we join with somebody else. If it had just been me . . . the sooner we join our permanent Cradles, the sooner we can have that all the time. That's why I'm doing this.'

Kat touched her fingers to her lips. 'It was my first kiss.'

Safa exhaled, closing her eyes in something close to surrender. 'Mine too.'

The air was bitter in her lungs, but she wasn't cold. Every person she had entered inside the club had taken their piece of her, and away from the street lights there was no way to know what was left.

'Why are we here?' she said.

'I used to come here as a kid.'

Kat smiled. 'Me too.'

Without another word, they set off up the path to the top of the hill.

It all seemed too easy. There was no window to break, no cameras or security system to disable. Wesley simply unlocked the door, and pulled his sleeves over his hands to push it open.

'This is a shithole,' said Tru.

Wesley swallowed a reflex defensive response, instead crossing to the lockbox. He found the right key and opened it up. 'Too easy.'

He wouldn't let his jangling nerves show, not with Jordan standing in the doorway. This whole thing had turned into a performance, and Wesley needed to stay in character.

'You want something inconspicuous?'

'That's the idea,' said Tru, but through the security glass he had spotted the silver BMW. 'You got the keys for that?'

Wesley hesitated. 'It's not very subtle.'

'Yeah, but I bet it's fast.' Tru turned from the window, greed in his eyes. He leaned into the lockbox and snatched the BMW key with his gloved hand. 'You never know, we might need a quick getaway.'

'All right, whatever,' said Wesley, slamming the lockbox shut. He would do whatever it took.

Back outside, the alarm blipped as the doors whirred open. After that morning's sale the BMW had clear access to the road. Tru purred admiringly as he sank into the plush driver's seat. The engine started gently, belying its ferocity. Letting him take any of the cars was a betrayal, but letting him take *this* one was an insult.

Tru shut the door, slid down the electronic window and waved for Wesley to come closer. 'You can't tell anybody about this.'

'I won't.'

'No, I mean you *can't*. Anybody finds out about this – about *any* of this – you're just as guilty as me. You understand?'

One threat replaced with another. He wanted to ask if he would see them again. If the door was still open for him. Maybe he would never step through it, but to know it remained an option would still be a huge relief.

'Yeah, I understand,' he said.

The revving engine was impossibly loud, tearing open the night as it reverberated across the industrial estate. Tru grinned, a child with a new toy, guiding the BMW out onto the road and away. Wesley thought of Kat as he watched it go.

At the top of the hill they found the remnants of a bonfire, not more than a few days old, blackened earth ringed off by charred beer cans. Kat took in a view she hadn't seen since childhood. It was hardly spectacular: street lights tracing out the suburban sprawl that encircled the town centre, lights flashing on the cranes putting up blocks of flats nobody local would ever afford. This place had made her, but in the coming years it would likely change beyond recognition.

They sat a few feet back from where the bonfire had burned, both lifting their hands as if they could still feel its warmth.

'Are you scared?' asked Kat.

'Terrified.'

'You're good at hiding it.'

'That first time you inhabited someone, I thought that was it – you were gone for good and I was left here by myself.' Safa chuckled coldly. She reached for the locket around her neck and twisted it, the doll opening into top and bottom. Another smaller doll, the same but painted in different colours, nested inside. 'I've been selling you so hard on the fade so I don't have to do it alone. If I can convince you, I can convince myself.'

The second doll opened too, revealing a miniature third inside. Safa fumbled to close them up, as if her fingers were numb, and then stood the dolls in a row in front of her.

Kat lifted her hands to let the lights of the town shine through them. 'I don't want to experience everything second-hand for the rest of my life,' she said. 'I am *so* fucking confused about all of this, but whether I love you, have a stupid crush on you, or I'm just so confused by actually having a friend that I've mistaken infatuation for something more, I know that kiss was real. I know the connection we have – me and you – is real.'

'My dude, you're such a romantic.'

'You should stay here with me.'

Safa tilted her head towards her. 'What if neither of us gets to stay?'

'I'm going to save Tinker tomorrow,' said Kat. 'I think it'll bring me back.' What would it take to keep Safa here with her?

When the other girl took her hand it felt porous, as if their grips would pass through each other if they squeezed too hard. 'Let's just have tonight,' said Safa.

They sat together, close enough to be overlapping, until the sun began to rise.

'You shouldn't have done that,' said Jordan.

Wesley had to do it. For Kat. For himself.

'I bet you didn't believe I would.'

'I *hoped* you wouldn't,' he said, walking quickly back towards the office.

Wesley followed. 'What do you mean?'

The office door was still open, and Jordan set about wiping the door handle with his sleeves, before heading inside and doing the same to the lockbox. Finally, he turned to face his brother.

'You want to know the real reason Dad didn't want to see you?'

It felt like the ground was crumbling beneath Wesley's feet, and he took hold of the doorframe, immediately undoing Jordan's work. 'You said it was because he was ashamed.'

'That wasn't true,' he said. 'Well, not exactly.'

'So why?'

'You were too good for him, and he knew it. You always stuck with Mum and tried to make things better. He saw what he was taking from you, and he didn't want to do it any more. He wasn't ashamed of you. He was ashamed of himself.' Jordan reached past him to wipe the doorframe clean again, an excuse not to meet his eye. 'He told me he didn't want to mess you up, like he did to me.'

Wesley shook his head, sure that *this* had to be the lie. Nobody had ever thought he was good. 'You were his favourite.'

'Maybe that's true, little bro. But only because being around me didn't make him feel bad about himself.'

It was resentment, then, that had made Jordan act the way he did towards his brother. Had he always seen the way things were when Wesley hadn't? Everything that had brought him to this moment, right *here*, fell apart into a mosaic of pieces impossible to order. Jordan really did want to come home, to belong to something just as much as Wesley did. The future they had been offered only hours before could have worked.

And Wesley might have ruined it.

Jordan turned away from him, and reared back to kick the lockbox. The buckling metal was enough to shock Wesley back to the moment.

'We have to make this look like a break-in,' said Jordan. He kicked the lockbox twice more, opening enough of a gap that someone could realistically reach inside for the keys. They left the office, shutting the door behind them.

'Find a brick.'

Wesley found one in the mess of hubcaps and weeds that grew around the base of the office and handed it to his brother.

'Stand back.'

The edge of the brick easily broke the glass, shattering it onto the office floor to leave a jagged hole above the handle.

'Hopefully he'll think they managed to unlock it. I think that's the best we can do.'

Wesley nodded, numb and ashamed. 'Thank you.'

'It'll be all right,' said Jordan, squeezing his shoulder.

He could hardly meet his brother's eye. 'What if it's not?'

Jordan let out a long breath and gripped his shoulder a little harder. 'I'll think of something.'

29

Piss Off, Ghost

The walk home felt longer than usual, weighed down by the silence between them and the threat of the fast-approaching morning. Wesley was too busy going over the words that made a mockery of his memories, forced him to piece the last few years of himself back into a new picture that didn't make sense.

A maintenance train rumbled over the bridge as they reached the flats, startling pigeons out of a lineside tree.

'You never see milk floats any more,' said Jordan, apropos of nothing.

They stopped at the main entrance, Jordan's beat-up red car parked lopsidedly against the kerb.

'Don't tell anyone,' said Wesley, blocking the door.

'I'm not that thick. This isn't one of those *better to come clean* situations. We'll put his keys back and there's no way they'll think it was you.'

Tonight had changed something between them. The facts of their history hadn't altered – it would never be as easy as that – but Wesley was able to read it all differently now. It felt as if they could both lay a grudge to rest. Maybe they could learn to be part of the same future.

They went inside, quietly up the concrete steps and along the parade of doorways. At their door, Jordan stopped him as he inserted the key.

'The car,' he said. 'What was it for?'

Their relationship may have changed, but the truth would only make it harder to move forward from here. 'It doesn't matter.'

It was the only way to save Kat. The only way to save himself.

Inside, they returned the keys to Dave's jacket, before Jordan retired to the sofa. Everybody else was still asleep, snores from the next room and groggy murmurings from his little sister. Wesley joined them almost as soon as his head hit the pillow.

Kat approached home, determined to get a few hours sleep before turning supernatural vigilante.

'That would be a good TV show,' she muttered to herself as she walked up the path to her front door.

The keys passed through her hand when she tried to grab them. She tried again, but there was only the slightest resistance, like a needle puncturing skin, before the metal fell through her palm and jangled against the path. Nor could she retrieve them or grab the door handle.

'No, come on,' she said.

She threw herself at the door, expecting to phase straight through, but she somehow lacked the necessary weight and seemed to flatten against it, like a vampire without an invite.

The sky was being diluted with the pale light of morning. Kat held up her arms to it. The night's exertions had spread her too thin. *Like butter over too much bread*, she thought. It wasn't a lack of substance that plagued her now. It was a lack of plain *existence*.

Kat hurried away from the house. There was no way she could save Tinker in this state. Even if she was successful piggybacking to wherever TrumourPixel took her, she would have no way of cutting her bonds or fighting them off to escape. She would be just as helpless.

If only she could warn somebody, call the police or even leave a message for Tinker. If only somebody would hear. The anger churning inside her, the impotent rage, wasn't enough to bring back her physical form. It only made her feel more helpless.

The plan had to change. It should never have been left to her, and now it *couldn't* be.

Morning arrived in earnest as she made her way to Wesley's block of flats. With every step she expected to sink into the pavement, fall away into the Earth, and for the last of her pixels to be burned away to nothing.

She crossed the car park towards the front entrance, and as she did it clicked open. An older boy emerged, letting out a shivering breath in the cold. Kat hurried through the door behind him.

The boy fumbled in his pocket for some keys as he approached an old red car. As he found them, he seemed to think better of it and strode away towards the road instead.

Kat took the stairs up and found Wesley's front door. Nobody would be coming out for hours yet, so she settled on the concrete floor with her back flattened against the wall, only registering the idea of the cold but not its bite.

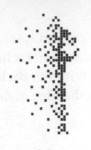

30

Dawn of the Final Day

Angry voices rattled Wesley awake, the kind of strained whisper that's supposed to be quiet but only carries more venom. He rolled over, sleep still dragging at the edges of his mind, and saw Evie sitting up in bed with the covers over her head.

'It's okay, Eves,' he said, though he wasn't sure it would be. He put his bare feet on the floor, crossed to poke his head into the hallway.

'I should call the police!' Dave's voice from the front room, his footsteps pacing across the floor.

'Please don't,' answered Mum. She sounded defeated.

There should have been more time before the missing car was discovered. Not that it would have made any difference. Wesley took a moment to find the courage to move. To go and find out if they had discovered the truth.

When he entered the room Dave stopped pacing, but hardly looked at him.

'What's going on?' So little sleep made it easy to affect grogginess, as if finding them like this was a surprise.

'Some people will take advantage of *anything* you offer them,' said Dave.

'A car was stolen from the dealership last night,' said Mum calmly. She was sitting in the armchair, half-dressed and pale.

The best thing Wesley could do was say as little as possible, until he worked out exactly what they knew. 'Somebody broke in?'

Dave turned on him and smiled mirthlessly. 'Oh, he tried to make it look that way. I went in early to finish that paperwork and found the window broken. He tried to make it look random, like I wouldn't know he nicked my keys!'

It felt like walking a tightrope, trying not to fall. Wesley arranged his face into as neutral an expression as he could, realising far too late who was missing from the room. 'Who?'

Mum exhaled. 'It looks like Jordan did it.'

Wesley swallowed, heart beating in his throat. 'How do you know?'

'As if that cack-handed attempt to disguise it wasn't enough, he put the keys back in the wrong pocket!' Dave lifted them out of his left jacket pocket. 'I always keep them in the right.'

The keys clattered together as he returned them to their correct place. Wesley dropped onto the sofa before his legs gave out. How could he have made such a stupid mistake? One lapse in concentration could have brought the whole thing down on his head.

'His car's still here too,' said Dave, pointing out of the window, before finally looking meaningfully at Wesley. 'He took the BMW.'

The hurt on his face made Wesley want to cry. He almost confessed, before he saw Jordan's bag still pushed into the corner and his clothes still drying on the radiator. He must have known he would take the fall. Wesley needed to speak to him as quickly as possible.

'I can work it off,' he blurted, looking between them.

'No, you can't,' said Dave, and it was unclear if he meant because it was impossible or because Wesley would never be trusted to work there again.

'Just don't call the police,' he said. 'Please.'

Dave ran a hand along his jaw, and then looked at Mum. 'I should – but I won't.'

Wesley sagged with relief. Until just a few hours before, ousting Jordan would have been the icing on the cake. Wesley knew better now. He hadn't fixed his family; he had only broken it further apart.

Kat had fallen asleep, propped against the wall, and only woke when the door shut behind somebody heading inside. She had missed a chance. There were raised voices inside now, some drama that would surely lead to another opening. This time she would be ready.

Nothing ached. No cold had found its way into her bones. Her body felt weightless, precarious, held together with little more than hope. She reached for her phone to take a final selfie, but couldn't grip it. There was no way to get in touch with Safa to find out if she was still there.

She looked at her hands. She had become Kat in draft form, a barebones briefing, the suggestion of a girl.

Too much had been taken from her. There was no way she could save Tinker alone. She needed to get inside.

As soon as he could get away, Wesley sent Evie to the kitchen for breakfast and grabbed his phone to send a message to Jordan. He couldn't think what to say, so simply told him everything that had happened in the hours since they'd got home.

The reply came almost instantly. *Don't tell them anything.*

But they're blaming you, Wesley wrote back, as if his brother somehow wasn't getting it.

They already think I'm the bad one, Jordan replied. *Let them.*

Beyond his room he heard Mum and Dave's last whispered argument, and then the door opening as Dave left. He froze, waiting to see if Mum would come to question him. Every guilty beat of his heart seemed like a thunderclap that would betray him to the world. Instead he heard the familiar sound of morning cartoons coming on, cereal being poured.

Wesley waited, his phone promising that Jordan was typing, pausing, typing again. Minutes passed before it arrived, but in the end it was only a few words long.

Let me know when the coast is clear and I'll pick up my stuff.

The door creaked ajar, but nobody came through. Wesley rubbed his thumb across the screen, as if it might uncover all the words left unsaid, and then shoved the phone into his pocket.

Kat stood inside the bedroom door, watching Wesley watch his phone, apparently waiting for a message that didn't come.

Not even he would see her now. Wilful blindness had long since caved into genuine obliviousness. While before it had made her feel safe, now it would only make more difficult what she needed to do.

'Wesley,' she said.

He put down his phone and leaned his head back against the wall, hearing nothing.

'Wesley!'

It was stupid to have hoped that out of anybody she might have been able to break through to him. She was still so *angry* with him, and always would be, but he hadn't forgotten her. There had to be a way to turn it to her advantage, force him into genuine action to stop the attack instead of relying on her.

'You remembered me enough to invade my room!' she said, trying to slam the door, finding that even with all her weight she couldn't push it hard enough to reach the frame. His laptop was closed, and she couldn't get enough purchase to claw it open, let alone try typing him a message.

'I can't stop them by myself!' she shouted, standing as close to him as she dared, hoping the words might somehow sink into his subconscious. 'You're the only other person who can help!'

In front of her, Wesley took a deep breath and stood. They were face to face now. There was one more thing to try. A last resort. The substance of his body plucked at what remained of hers, urging her inside. The idea disgusted her, but if she couldn't get his attention from out here, she would have to try another way.

A single touch was all it took. She shrugged him on without a fight.

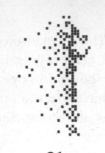

31

Kat's Cradle

A shudder wracked Wesley's body as he moved towards the door. Somebody walking over his grave. Probably guilt trying to hold him back, knowing the truth might spill out when he faced Mum. She was in the kitchen, packing a bag for Evie and lunch for herself.

'Can you take her to nursery today?' said Mum. 'I'm running late after all this.'

'Sure.' He was going to meet the Lonely People – his friends – to go and confront Aaron's little brother, but he could take her on the way.

'And can you come straight home, just in case Jordan comes back?'

It was unclear if she wanted the chance to talk him into staying, or if she was scared he would loot the place in their absence.

'I'm sorry, about your brother,' Mum said, zipping up the *Frozen* rucksack. 'I thought he'd . . .' She trailed off into a sad smile.

The guilt seemed to nag at the back of Wesley's brain, like voices on a radio turned too low. He felt *open*, his defences lowered. If he explained everything, maybe she would understand.

Except she was already gone, kissing him and Evie on the head on her way to the door.

The wind buffeted Kat, threatening to tear her fingers from the grimy, algae slick metal. The ocean, hulking grey and whipped white swelled on all sides, spray stinging her face. There was no sign of land, only the buoy to which she clung, swaying wildly in the onslaught.

The other part of her went with Wesley back into his bedroom, so calm on the surface, so different to the landscape she had discovered inside.

Below her, wedged onto a flat platform just above the seething water, she saw the same black box she had discovered sealed inside everybody else.

It was wide open.

A torrent of fear, loneliness and guilt poured from it, a storm that darkened the sky and riled the ocean. Every negative feeling that had been missing from her previous hosts took precedence here, swirling unchecked through Wesley's being.

No, it had all been inside those other people too. It had merely been suppressed. Kat had felt the same doubt and self-consciousness leaking from the boxes, pushed away and ignored but always threatening to escape. Those people, who seemed so confident, so normal, so capable of handling *anything*, felt all these things too. They just knew how to hide it. How to pretend.

Here, it all threatened to drown him. The desolation was so strong Kat wanted to bail out. It was too *familiar*. If somebody inhabited her, stepped into her internal landscape, they might find exactly this.

She understood him now, better than ever.

'Wesley,' she shouted into the wind, trying to project it into his brain. 'You have to hear me.'

Her other part watched him gather some of Evie's toys into a *Frozen* rucksack, no sign at all that he'd heard her.

'Help me! You're the only person who can! There's not enough of me left to stop them.'

Through the storm, a light blinked on the impossibly distant, shifting horizon. Some fragment of him had heard, but she still wasn't breaking through to his consciousness.

Painstakingly, she climbed down the metal strut as it pitched side to side, until she reached the platform. The wind was growing stronger, and water sloshed around her feet, soaking her legs. She pushed her aching hands under the box and heaved it to the edge. Empty, it was surprisingly light, yet sank under the water with hardly a splash.

It wouldn't change anything here. The wind was battering her now, trying to throw her into the waves. Where the box had been was an area of metal encrusted with hard, pale scum. She used her nails to scrape letters into it, a message she could leave behind inside him that might make him remember.

Kat was here.

As she carved the final letter, a sharp gust of wind swept her off her feet. She screamed as the grey water loomed, but by the time she landed it had become Wesley's bedroom carpet.

Another involuntary shudder made Wesley drop his shoes. He turned, expecting to find somebody behind him – he could have sworn he'd heard somebody shout his name.

'You all right in there, Eves?' he called through to the front room.

'Cartoons,' she called back through a mouthful of cereal, half of which would no doubt now be down her front.

The times he had been in Kat's bedroom felt like this – as if he was forgetting something right in front of his eyes, unable to find the solution to a puzzle that should be plain.

It was only his imagination, making up the world in a way he wanted to see. Nothing more.

Kat paced in front of Wesley while he sniffed some socks to determine their cleanliness and began to put on his shoes.

'Why won't you hear me?' she said.

He couldn't. He wouldn't. Wesley shoved his feet into his trainers without untying the laces and checked his phone again.

'You wanted to make a mark on the world at any cost, so you clung to the only community that would have you. Maybe you wouldn't make real friends, but it was better than nothing, right?' Kat said, anger overwhelming her. 'Except it was all false. It's nothing like real belonging. No community based on hatred or intolerance can offer that.'

There were no messages, and Wesley stood, zipping up the rucksack.

'You can't leave it up to me to stop them! It isn't fair. You have to take responsibility for what you've done.' She moved as close to him as she could stomach. 'If you don't hear me now, it's all over.'

He walked past her, and out of the room.

Wesley waited for his little sister to slurp the last of the sugary milk from the bottom of the bowl, and then he helped her with her shoes.

'You like going to nursery, right?'

She looked at him as if it was the stupidest question she had ever heard. 'Yes.'

'I'm just checking!' He pushed the last Velcro strap closed. 'I don't want you to think we're getting rid of you because you're a nuisance.'

'*You're* a nuisance.'

'Well *you* smell like a butt.'

Evie cackled, and let him put the rucksack on her back. He opened the front door, let her skip out onto the walkway, and closed it behind them.

Kat lay on the floor between the beds, wondering if she could stay there until it happened. Melt into the carpet like a stain. Maybe then Wesley would see her outline and remember everything that had happened.

No, she couldn't give up. She still had to find a way to stop the attack. There had to be a way to make him see.

There were paints on the table at the end of his sister's bed. What if it wasn't her he needed to see? Maybe the only way to make Wesley remember her, to make him take responsibility, was to introduce him to himself.

The paints were simple but plentiful, deployed mainly for the finger drawings that were scattered across the table surface and pinned to the wall, but they would do the job. Kat delved her hands into the colours, and although they dripped through her flesh and skin, enough clung on that she could make it work. Kat turned to the blank canvas of wall beside the bedroom door and began to paint.

32

The Girl Cut Out of the World

After dropping Evie at nursery, Wesley made his way towards school where he had arranged to meet the others. More than anything he wanted to return home, tiredness weighing heavy, practically demanding he turn around.

He checked the time. Only a few hours until the attack. If he went home he wouldn't be able to think of anything else.

It was a school day, so they had arranged to meet on the corner where they could intercept Joseph on his way there. Robbie was already waiting, inconspicuous in uniform as other students filed past.

'It's always a relief when I see any of you,' said Wesley, leaning beside him on a garden wall. 'I keep thinking one of you will disappear too and start this all over again.'

'What if you didn't even notice? There might have been more of us but we've already forgotten them for good.'

Wesley shook his head. It was too awful to think about.

'I never wanted to look for Aaron,' said Robbie.

'I thought finding the truth would scare us out of the idea. And I was right.'

'Is that a bad thing?'

Robbie hunched his shoulders, tucking his head down into the collar of his oversized school blazer. 'Focusing on the fade meant I didn't have to think about *why* I wanted it. That's why I kept doing all those stupid prayers and stuff.' He laughed. 'I even started doing them at home by myself.'

'What, all that *make us lonely* stuff?'

'I always knew it was stupid, but it was better than talking about feeling so wrong that I actually wanted it to work.'

They stood together in silence for a moment, watching the other students move past on their way to school, hurrying alone or dragging their feet in groups.

'Do you still want it?' asked Wesley.

'Sometimes.' Robbie swivelled his head to look up at him. 'But I'm starting to see that maybe being me doesn't have to be completely terrible.'

'Hey!'

They both turned to see Aoife and Jae hurrying towards them, glancing over their shoulders.

'Joseph is right behind us.'

Wesley lifted himself up from the wall. 'Let's find out how it ends.'

Kat had no choice but to go ahead and try to stop the attack by herself. It was due to happen in a couple of hours, and she couldn't wait around any longer for Wesley to come back. She couldn't just do nothing.

The people she had inhabited last night were waiting for her outside the flat. They didn't frighten her any more; she was overwhelmingly grateful to see them. She walked between them as they talked to each other, glanced anxiously up at the flat or where she had just stood, and thanked each of them for remembering her. The boy whose body she had borrowed for her first kiss was there, and she lingered beside him for a moment, resisting the pull that she thought might draw her inside for ever. She had sampled their lives, tried them on for size, if only for a moment. Every single one of them had been so tempting, was still so tempting. Except the world inside Wesley had shown her the truth. There was so much more beneath the surface than anybody could know.

Kat no longer wished to be anybody but herself; she only wished she still had the power to save herself.

It would take at least an hour to reach the convention centre. She ran, leaving the crowd behind, the lightness of her body making every step feel as if she was gliding. The morning was dull, a blanket of grey cloud seeming to mute the streets. The venue was beyond the other side of town. At least a lack of corporeal form seemed to mean she wouldn't get out of breath.

Still, as she skirted the town centre, a bus pulled up that she knew would take her close. While others tapped their cards, Kat jumped on through the middle doors and stayed close to the exit.

A few passengers were heading to the convention. Cosplay was a dead giveaway. The local old ladies and grumpy middle-aged men side-eyed a man in full

Dothraki costume, while near the front a little girl in a Pikachu onesie was chattering excitedly to a young woman dressed as a gender-swapped Goku from *Dragon Ball Z*.

Kat loved nerds *so much*.

The bus took a longer route, wending through a retail park before returning to the main road that all but passed the convention centre. Kat got off at the corner, carefully avoiding the cosplayers. Any contact might be enough to pull her inside, and her body might not survive any further dilution. She had to save it for Tinker.

The centre was an unsightly grey building that stretched an entire block. *WonderVerse Con* flashed in pixellated letters from a scrolling sign, queues already formed at the doors. There were costumes everywhere, as well as geek-themed T-shirts and tote bags. How had she never had the confidence to attend something like this? Everybody was being utterly themselves, and it was *celebrated*. If she was going to fit in anywhere, surely it would be here.

She stayed across the road to get clear of the crowds and walked the length of the street. There was no sign of any suspicious car. If their plan was to snatch Tinker as she made her way inside, they had to be close by.

At the next corner was another bus stop, more colourful visitors spilling out onto the pavement and streaming across the main road. What looked like a back entrance was just opposite, but it was too busy for any car to stop. Kat looked further, across the junction to a row of shops and takeaway restaurants. There was a delivery track between them, and there, poking out as far as it could without conspicuously blocking the pavement, was the front of a silver BMW.

They spread across the pavement to cut Joseph off before he could pretend not to see them and keep walking. He stopped in front of them and sighed.

'All right, but not here.'

Away from the school, back towards Wesley's house, they followed him in silence.

Finally, he said, 'So you've figured it out.'

'You should have just told us.'

Joseph kept walking, but more slowly now, as if he needed the steps to keep his brain working. 'How could I tell anybody? The whole thing is so strange, and there was no way I could know for sure. All I have is the *feeling* that he's here.'

The group gathered closer to him, almost tripping over each other's feet, as if they might somehow sense Aaron there. Maybe they needed to see – really *see* – this thing they had all thought they desperately wanted.

'Everyone else has forgotten him, or come as close to it as possible. But I *can't* forget him.' Joseph lifted a hand to his chest. 'At first I did whatever I could to keep his memory alive, but whenever I made Mum remember she got so upset. It's better if everybody else forgets. It's not like he's ever coming back. I just have to miss him by myself.'

'We remember,' said Aoife.

'Soon you won't, not now you don't need him any more.'

They were still walking, drawing closer to Wesley's

home, but the strange tugging on his body had shifted away from there, felt as if it was trying to lead him somewhere else. He did his best to ignore it.

'Here,' he said, handing back the family portrait he had taken from their house. 'I'm sorry I took it.'

Joseph looked at the photograph, rested his fingers against his brother's smiling face.

'Can you speak to him?' Wesley asked.

'It's not like he's inside my head pulling levers and pressing buttons to move me around,' said Joseph. 'I just know he's there, resting, not really a part of the world any more. He regretted letting this happen to him, so he went for the person that was most like him. And all I'm doing is letting him down. I mean, I'm glad he's not totally gone, but it's not fair either. I couldn't save him, and now I'm supposed to give him the kind of life he thought he was missing. I have to carry that burden because Aaron couldn't.'

Wesley thought of Kat, even now going alone to stop the attack. He had left her with that responsibility, but it was for her own sake. It was the only way to save her, to give her what Aaron couldn't find.

They stopped just short of the railway bridge that ran beside Wesley's block of flats. 'He appeared to me, at the end,' said Joseph.

Everybody gathered close. 'He did?'

'I think when he chose me, it meant I could see him. There was hardly anything left. He was . . . less than a ghost. Almost completely invisible. He tried to take my hand, but I just passed right through him. He didn't even have physical form any more.'

The tug on Wesley's body grew stronger, as if somebody was calling him from afar. He thought of the message Aaron had left for Selena, written in messily spilled food instead of with the pens that were right beside it. If the fade gradually took away their physical form, it would mean they were no longer able to hold anything, able to assert any will on the world. That's why he would have been unable to grip a pen, take his brother's hand one last time.

It would mean Kat would have no way to save Tinker.

Although the sight of the car made the beast in her chest thrash weakly – perhaps it too was fading out – it also made her angry. Their plan was so *basic*. They were nobodies, pathetic little boys playing vigilante for an empty cause propagated by more pathetic little boys behind their keyboards.

And it would work, if she couldn't do something to stop it.

Kat looked across the road again, and saw another car pulling up as close to the back entrance as it could manage. Tinker wouldn't have any entourage or security – she was famous, but still just a young woman who lived with her mum.

That oh-so-familiar pink hair emerged from the front passenger seat, and she waved goodbye to whoever had driven her before looking around for the right way to go. A couple of people spotted and immediately delayed her, asking for selfies.

Across the junction, the BMW began to move.

The gravity of it all left Kat's feet rooted to the spot for a moment. There was nothing she could do to stop it. She was powerless.

Passing Tinker and her small gathering of fans was a girl wearing a costume Kat recognised. A flowing white high-necked dress, almost like a Victorian nightie, worn with black biker boots, spiked gauntlets, and a perm that would make the '90s blush. Esme from *Doctor Backwash*, the girl cut out of the world.

Kat wouldn't let it happen to her. One way or another she would fight for this life that used to be hers.

The BMW joined the traffic heading towards the convention centre. There wasn't any time to think – Kat leaped into the road and ran.

The drivers couldn't see her, wouldn't do anything to avoid her. She gritted her teeth as she darted out of the path of one car, only to jump back as an overtaking moped almost mowed her down. Would it pass right through her if she was hit? It wasn't the time to find out.

Timing a gap between two cars coming the other way, she spotted the BMW cross the junction. It slowed down to draw up beside Tinker and the fans around her.

'Look out!' Kat screamed.

Nobody heard her – nobody could *fucking* hear her – and she sprinted for Tinker as the BMW stopped, back doors throwing open.

It happened in seconds. Two boys with their faces covered – Luke and Justin, it had to be – grabbed Tinker from behind and covered her mouth to keep her from screaming. Everybody around them stood frozen as she was dragged to the back door of the car.

Only Kat moved, flinging herself headlong and landing inside the other girl's body as the door slammed shut.

33

And My Axe!

Wesley ran away from the others without saying a word, under the railway bridge and towards home. It hadn't been tiredness calling him back; it had been Kat. She must have been at the flat, must have inhabited him, and she wouldn't do that unless it was urgent.

There was nobody outside the flats, only Jordan's car still parked by the entrance. Wesley ran upstairs and found that the front door was already open.

'Hello?'

Inside, Jordan had packed all of his still-damp clothes into carrier bags. He was leaning over the coffee table, and jumped at the sound, relaxing when he saw who it was. In one hand he held a pen for the note he'd been writing, in the other a small stack of bank notes.

'What's that for?' said Wesley.

'It's everything I saved when I was working in Australia. It won't cover the BMW, but . . .' He put the money neatly on the table. 'At least I won't leave you empty-handed this time.'

'You can't just go,' said Wesley. 'You wanted to come home.'

'I did.' Jordan signed off the note with an illegible squiggle. 'But maybe this is the best thing I can do for you. To make up for everything.'

For years, Wesley had wanted his brother to show him kindness. Now he was, Wesley wanted him to take it back.

There wasn't time for this. He pushed deeper into the flat. 'Was anybody else here?'

'You mean Mum or Dave? No, I made sure.'

Wesley rushed through to his bedroom. This was where he had felt light-headed. It had to have been where she had stepped inside his body. What had she been trying to tell him? He looked around the room but there was no sign, no telltale clue. It was only when he turned back towards the door that he saw it.

The mural covered the entire wall beside the door, an ocean of blues and greys and blacks, whipped into a storm by hurried, impatient finger strokes. Rising from the water was a narrow frame, tapering to a point where the shadow of a person clung to it for dear life.

Wesley recognised it . . . no, the painting recognised *him*.

Underneath the mural, scrawled in block capitals, were two words that unlocked everything.

SAVE YOURSELF.

His knees threatened to buckle, and he caught himself to sit on the edge of the bed. All at once he saw how much had been hidden from him: Kat standing in the school toilet as he searched for her on that first day; Kat watching him sit on her bed, talking back to him, telling him truths he would never have been willing to admit; Kat screaming at him, desperate for his help.

'What's wrong?' said Jordan, appearing in the doorway.

'Do you see that?' Wesley pointed to the mural.

Jordan moved inside the door. 'The wall?'

Nobody would see this message but him. Nobody else would understand it.

The attack might already have happened, and he knew Kat would not have given up trying to stop it. If she had gone with Tinker, she would be powerless to prevent whatever TrumourPixel had planned for her. Wesley had told himself the attack needed to happen so that Kat could intervene. A way to save herself. If she succeeded, she would save him too. What a burden he had put on her shoulders.

It was time for him to face up to everything he had done.

Somehow he knew exactly where Kat would be. It was as if a tiny piece of her was lodged inside him, and it would guide him back to her. This is what Lukundo and Selena must have felt when they went searching for Aaron.

'You have to drive me somewhere.'

Wesley ran for the stairs, and he heard his brother follow without question.

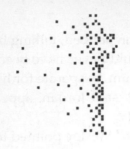

34

A Livestream

The storage unit's concrete walls reverberated with Tinker's rasping screams as she was dragged from the back of the car. One of her attackers clamped her legs, while another struggled to hook her flailing arms. A thick metal door had been closed behind them, and the unit was essentially a concrete box, so no sound would escape. They wrestled her to a metal-framed chair at the back of the space, where a couple of cardboard boxes were stacked. It took two of them to pin her down long enough to get handcuffs onto her wrists and wrap bike chains around her arms and legs.

Kat crouched behind the chair and tried to work out what to do next. The journey here had drained her to almost nothing. It had been so easy to stay inside Tinker and her internal landscape of a lush oasis at the heart of a sprawling desert. Even as terror whipped up stinging gusts of sand and jostled the box sunk deep in the clear water of the spring, shadows bubbling from under its lid, Kat had considered making the girl her Cradle. If she couldn't stop what was going to happen to Tinker, she could at least endure it with her.

There had to be a way. She couldn't give up.

'Gag her, for Christ's sake,' said TrumourPixel, approaching calmly like a factory supervisor.

One of them found a leather strap and levered it between her teeth, pulling it tight behind her head and tying it off.

'News is already spreading,' said Tru. In the car, they had taken Tinker's phone, and he was using it now to check her social media feeds. 'Told you we'd get an audience.'

The other two took off their masks. Luke and Justin, both smiling, sweating, jittering with nervous energy.

'Get them ready to tune in,' said Luke.

'I'm *doing* it,' said Tru through gritted teeth. 'She's logged in to every social media account, I can send a message from all of them.' He wagged a finger at Tinker. 'You should really do something about your security.'

While they were distracted, Kat crept behind the chair and reached for the keys that had been left on a shelf. Her fingers passed right through without even making them move. In the gloom of the unit, she could barely see her own hand.

'It's okay,' she whispered in Tinker's ear. The lie didn't matter if it couldn't be heard.

The three attackers moved clear of the area around Tinker, leaving her to tug at her bonds. Tears ran in dark tracks down her face and her pink hair stuck to the wet. Luke took her phone and pointed it at the scene.

'Ready?'

Tru, face still covered, nodded.

They were going to stream it all, Kat realised in horror. It would be broadcast to all of Tinker's subscribers and anybody else who visited her channel.

The livestream began, the phone aimed close at Tinker as she cried for help around her gag. Tru moved to stand over her, Luke stepping back to get them both in the frame.

'Welcome,' he said. For some reason it made Luke laugh. 'We promised we would retaliate if you continued to attack us. You didn't take us seriously.'

What enemy was he speaking to? Whatever enemy he had invented in his mind to justify his hatred, to turn it back on the world.

'You bitches, who spout your anti-male propaganda, need to learn that there are consequences,' he said, walking around the back of the chair, within inches of where Kat was helplessly crouched.

Tinker was trying to talk through the gag, a single repeated word that sounded like *please*.

'You try to emasculate us. You want to tear us down from our rightful place in the world and make us your slaves. Most of the world might be fooled, and that is why we who see the truth must fight back to realise our potential. We're going to send a message. And you can help us decide what it'll be.'

Again, Kat reached for the keys, willing her fingers to find a grip on reality. She managed to knock them to the floor, but from there no amount of concentration allowed her to pick them up. The chains, holding Tinker tight even as she struggled, passed clean through Kat's hands. She began to cry, roaring in frustration at her futility.

'There's a lot of people threatening us or telling us to stop,' said Justin, reading the livestream chat on his own phone. 'But there's a few actual ideas coming in.'

Holding the screen for Tru to see, Justin looked so relieved that it was working, that he had something to contribute.

'These are all great suggestions,' Tru said.

Kat fought the urge to be sick. People watching this live were actually egging them on. They had to think it was all a joke, a publicity stunt. Surely those people didn't believe it was real, didn't want to play any part in causing pain.

'Let's start with something simple.' Tru walked across to the cardboard boxes, and he leaned down to tear the tape from the top box. From inside he produced a pair of hair clippers. 'We'll get rid of this slut's pretty hair.'

He wielded the clippers like a pistol, laughing as he set them buzzing. Behind the camera Luke laughed too, wide-eyed as if he had never been so entertained, while Justin wiped sweat from his forehead. Tinker whined and gnashed, thrashing her shoulders uselessly against the chains.

From the floor, Kat watched in despair. She had let fear of being alive get the better of her, let herself fade away almost to nothing, and now it had stopped her from saving Tinker, of doing any good in the world. Kat squeezed her eyes shut in revulsion and shame.

A metallic bang rattled around the unit. The clippers ceased buzzing as they all turned to see the shutter behind them ripple slightly.

'It's nothing,' said Luke, but the shake in his voice betrayed him.

Another blow against the shutter, harder this time, followed by another and another. The plates of the metal clanked and roiled in angry waves.

'What the hell is that?' said Tru, pulling away from his captive.

Kat stood, a smile of hope breaking across her face at the sight of the bucking shutter. Somebody had come to help.

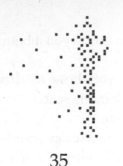

35

Life Buoy

They drove as fast as Jordan dared, the old car juddering and swaying as Wesley called directions and they swerved through traffic.

'How do you know where we're going?'

'I just do!'

Kat's presence was calling to him, a ship's light on his horizon, but there was no way he could pinpoint it yet. As they drove he had started to call the police, before realising he wouldn't know where to send them. All he could do was feel her presence growing closer and guide them towards it. Find Kat, and he would find the attackers.

'I should never have left,' said Jordan.

'At least you're here now.'

They ran through a red light, narrowly avoiding being side-swiped by a van. Its angry beeping fell quickly behind them.

'It was hard, being around after what Dad said.' Jordan gripped the wheel hard. 'I hated you for it. And if Dad thought I was the bad one, I was going to live up to it. I should have shown you a better way, but I didn't know it myself.'

'Did Dad show you how to drive like this?' said Wesley, pinned back in his seat.

'No, this was all me.'

Another corner, and Wesley shouted 'Here!' pointing to the fast-approaching entrance of a storage warehouse.

The car tremored as Jordan slammed the brakes, turning them onto the track between a long boulevard of outdoor units like oversized garages. Someone emerged from the office to yell at them, but they were past him in seconds.

'Which one is it?' said Jordan.

'Keep going.'

Wesley could feel her strongly now, close enough that he could run aground. Every unit looked the same, but he knew it was further down the track. Wesley braced himself to fight. They would be outnumbered, and people like Tru would fight back with everything they had. It didn't matter – he would do whatever it took.

'There!'

The track curved slightly before it ended. As they came around, Wesley saw they wouldn't be outnumbered after all. A small crowd of people was swarmed around the final unit. They beat their fists against the metal and tried to wrench it up from the ground.

'What the—?' said Jordan as he stopped the car.

The side door of the unit was flung open, and Luke and Justin came running out. The car doors blocked the track, stopping them short. Wesley didn't hesitate – he took advantage of Luke's surprise, tackling him hard and knocking the wind out of him.

'You're dead,' Luke wheezed, but Wesley pinned his arms to the ground so he couldn't fight back.

Jordan took down Justin without much of a fight. The crowd found the open side door and streamed into the unit.

'I'll call the police,' said Jordan.

Luke wriggled under Wesley's weight but couldn't get free. 'If you don't let me go, you'll go down for this too.'

'You're right,' said Wesley. 'And maybe it's exactly what I deserve.'

He lifted his head to look for any sign of Kat.

The crowd, all the people she had inhabited the night before, filled the unit and trapped Tru against the back wall, grabbing his arms so he couldn't fight his way out.

'Help her!' shouted Kat. Although nobody looked at her, the boy whose kiss she had stolen broke away from the group to retrieve the keys and began unlocking Tinker's bonds.

Kat had done it. She had stopped the attack, with a little luck and a lot of weirdness. The crowd had followed her here, as they always would, whether she was in danger or not. Maybe they had sensed something was wrong, or had simply heard enough to intervene. She thought of the protesters at the march who had run towards the attackers instead of away.

Lightheaded, Kat stumbled out of the unit. A car was blocking the track, Luke and Justin pinned to the ground by two other guys. Wesley and his brother.

He had received her message and come to help. Finally, he had done the right thing.

And now he looked right at her, mouth falling open with shock.

'You can see me?' she said.

His mouth closed, opened again, not finding any words along the way. Kat looked down at herself – she was every bit as faded as before. Stopping the attack hadn't had any effect. To him, she must have appeared as a ghost.

She was near the end, and that made her remember.

'Take my phone,' she said.

'Wha—?'

Moving closer, she jutted her front pocket at him. 'I can't hold my phone. I need to know if there's a message.'

The thralls were exiting the unit, leading Tru with them like a prisoner of war. Now he was caught the bravado was stripped away, and he looked on the edge of tears. Tinker stayed inside. There would be someone here to take care of her soon enough.

Seeing how outnumbered they were, Luke didn't try to take advantage when Wesley lifted a hand to take out her phone.

Kat told him the access code. 'Is there anything?'

'There's a message.' He looked up at her. 'It's from Safa.'

She wouldn't have been able to touch her phone either, but there was nothing to keep her from dictating to it.

'*I can't hold on any longer,*' Wesley read. '*I have to go to her.*'

Police sirens in the distance, growing closer.

'When was it sent?' said Kat.

'Only twenty minutes ago.'

If it hadn't happened yet, there was only one place Safa would go. Only one person she could need to find at the end of herself.

'Can you drive me?' she said to Wesley.

'My brother . . . but he can't see you.'

Indeed, Jordan was looking across at his brother – apparently talking to thin air – as if he had gone mad.

There were enough people there to hold all the attackers, and they took over gladly, faces fierce as they held the captives down. The police would be here any moment to take control.

Kat started towards the car. 'So *you* tell him where I have to go. I don't have much time.'

36

Revenant

Wesley could not stop staring at Kat in the rear mirror. There was something so unreal about her, the worn pattern of the backseat criss-crossing through her body. And yet with his memories unlocked he knew she had been there all along. So close to being forgotten, but not quite.

'The traffic's going to be a nightmare,' said Jordan.

'Just keep going,' said Wesley.

There had been no complaints from Jordan any step of the way, despite him being told almost nothing about what was happening. He was helping his brother without question. Wesley would remember it.

There was so much he wanted to say to Kat, but her eyes were glued to the window. Even if it felt like the right moment to talk, he didn't want to freak Jordan out any more by speaking to an apparently empty back seat.

Quickly, Wesley checked Twitter on his phone. 'The police found Tinker,' he said, so they both would hear. 'And it says they have three people in custody.'

Behind them, Kat blinked, but her eyes never left the window.

Five minutes from the centre of town, they hit traffic. Roadworks filled the air with noise and dust, and a long line of traffic snaked past in a fugue of exhaust fumes. Wesley opened his door and stepped out for a better view. 'It's solid all the way down.'

Jordan slumped down in his seat. 'We'll be here for hours.'

Wesley was about to sit back down when Kat spoke for the first time during the ride.

'Let me out.'

'Don't you want—?'

She scrabbled at the door, but her hands couldn't grasp the handle. 'Let me out!'

Wesley opened the door, and Kat ghosted past him. He watched her run into the traffic, and after a moment she was lost in the smoke.

The high street was busy, afternoon shoppers out in force. Kat knew exactly where Safa would be, and she fought her way through the crowds to reach the Greek restaurant near the end of the street.

At first she saw nobody outside, only passers-by. What if she was too late? Safa might have gone before Kat had a final chance to stop her. Just the thought of it made Kat feel like she would break apart like a dandelion in the wind.

She fixed Safa in her mind and looked again – properly *looked* – and the shape of a girl became clear. Safa stood opposite the restaurant in the middle of the street, eyes fixed on the people inside. Kat, oddly nervous, went to her.

'Hey,' she said.

Safa turned, smiled. 'You made it.'

For a long moment they simply gazed at what remained of each other. Kat held an image of Safa in her mind from the first day they met, the other girl rescuing her from exile in a school toilet, and it made her easier to see now.

'Sorry I'm late,' she said. 'I was busy stopping a terror attack.'

'You did it?'

Kat could hardly believe it herself. 'I did it.'

'My dude.' Safa's smile, fragile but true, quickly died. 'You're still faded.'

'That's because I need you to stay.'

'I think it's clear you don't need me.' Safa pointed inside the restaurant, where her chosen Cradle was at the same table as before, books spread across its surface. 'But I need her.'

'You *don't*,' said Kat, furious that she wasn't able to take the other girl's hands inside her own. 'You think you do. You think you're broken, but you're not. I realised what I was feeling whenever I was inside those other people. They look like they're living perfect lives, but it's a cover. Everybody is trying their best not to fuck everything up. They're all just as scared as you are. It takes everything they have to hide it.'

The girl inside the restaurant looked up from her work, talking to a man who was busy wiping down the counter. Kat wondered what landscape lay inside her; how well that distended black box would be hidden beneath it.

'It's not about being broken, or being bad, or not fitting in,' said Kat. 'You just have to find the people who allow you to be *you*.'

Safa shook her head. 'I never thought I would.'

Kat's whole body felt charged, every particle of her being humming with energy. If she could cling on hard enough, maybe she could force Safa back. She felt more real than she ever had, and she *willed* the other girl to feel it too.

'You did. You found me. And I found you.' Kat was beginning to cry, but she didn't care. She wouldn't wipe the tears away. 'You're the only person I've ever felt I could be myself with, without hiding anything. Without being ashamed. You made me happy to be me. We don't need to become anybody else – if we're together we can be *us*.'

There was hardly a face left to see, but she somehow sensed that Safa was smiling. 'Look,' she said.

Kat lifted her hands. They were solid again. Complete. She turned them over, saw the lines and blemishes and whorls of fingerprints she thought she had lost. She rubbed her fingers together, astounded by her skin's friction. Rubbed them up her arms, along her legs, pressed her fingertips to her face and laughed.

'I'm back,' she said. She was so *glad*. To stand here as herself, happy inside her reimbursed skin, was liberating beyond belief. She had fought to save herself, fought to *like* herself, and been rewarded.

Still that air of a smile. 'You sexy cow.'

'Now you.'

A tear traced the curve of her jaw, her skin fizzing

in its path, and Safa lifted the idea of a hand to dry it. 'I want to.'

Kat's heart leapt. 'I want you to.'

'You mean it? You would have me?'

Kat tried to find her eyes. 'If you want to stay with me, then *stay*.'

'I don't know if I can hold on.' Safa's body momentarily flickered out of existence, before sputtering back with frightened eyes as clear as day. She reached for Kat's hands, desperate to cling onto the world, but could find no grip. 'I'm scared, Kat. I can feel myself coming apart. I'm going and I can't stop it.'

'No!' Everybody else on the street could see her now, and the passing shoppers regarded her curiously or rushed their children past. She didn't care. 'You're too stubborn to let it happen if it's not what you want. You told me to fight for myself. Now you have to do it too. *Fight*.'

When they had first learned to step inside the lives of other people, it had been fuelled by thoughts of everything they felt they had got wrong in their lives. All the reasons they should be excused to leave themselves behind. Now Kat held tight to all the reasons she had discovered to stay.

'Remember singing "Mr Pretzel"?' she said.

Safa's form sputtered, reformed. 'And messing with Miss Jalloh's precious bell.'

'You put your thumb inside my mouth when I had brain freeze.'

'You dance like you're getting attacked by bees.'

A tear rolled down Kat's cheek as she smiled. 'Only

with you.' A steadying breath, before she lifted her hands in a final bid to reach for Safa's fingers . . .

And felt them graze her palm.

They both cried out in delight. Kat fumbled for a better hold, clutching Safa's hands inside her own. They grew firmer, friction seeming to throw sparks between their skin.

Kat held her eyes. 'Now come back to me.'

She pulled gently, as if guiding her back through a rent in the universe, and Safa coalesced in front of her. Colour rushed back into her skin, filled her lines and rounded her features, until she was complete again, emancipated from the void.

'It's good to see you,' said Kat.

They squeezed each other's hands – strong, unequivocal – as tightly as they could. In that embrace was a promise: that they would be there for each other, hold each other up, and never let the other forget they were wanted.

'You're stuck with me now, my dude,' said Safa.

Kat grinned. 'We're stuck with ourselves.'

Together, they were ready for it.

37

Season Three, Episode One

It had felt peculiar to leave each other after hours of sitting together on a bench in the middle of town, pressed tightly shoulder-to-shoulder and talking about ... nothing in particular, without the shadow of the fade hanging over them, knowing they had as much time as they could ever want.

Neither of them wanted to dwell on what they had almost lost. Instead, they read the news that Tinker had been rescued by a rather confused group of strangers, and three assailants had been arrested ('You are actually a frickin' hero,' said Safa proudly). Plans were hatched for an all-night *Doctor Backwash* marathon, before they pooled ideas for a new video game to replace the one Kat had deleted.

The bus journey home passed in contented silence, each knowing there was no rush to speak. They squeezed hands again before they parted, as if to confirm it had all been true.

Now Kat stood alone on her doorstep, frightened to go inside.

'Chances are he won't realise anything has changed,' she told herself, unsure if she believed it.

They had spent so much time wondering where the fade would take them that she had never considered what might happen if she came back. It felt like returning home from a long voyage after everybody thought her lost at sea.

Or maybe she was being a melodramatic butthole.

She put her key in the door, relishing the solid push and turn, and stepped inside.

'Hello?' she called.

Dad appeared from the sitting room, eyes glistening and jaw slack with disbelief. Kat smiled timidly and opened her arms.

He rushed forward and pulled her into a hug, wrapping his arms around his daughter as if he would never let her go. 'There you are,' he said, breath hot on top of her head.

Kat pressed her face into his chest and sniffed back a tear. 'I'm sorry, Dad.'

'It's okay. You're here now.'

'Yes,' she said. 'I'm here.'

38

A Cure for Apathy

Two weeks had passed before Wesley climbed Garden Hill, early enough that the rising sun smouldered on the horizon, and met Kat at the edge of the browning trees. The dewy grass was already clogged with fallen leaves.

What he had to say was far more than a fortnight overdue. 'I'm so sorry,' he said. 'For everything.'

When she had got in touch and asked to meet him there, he had almost been too ashamed to go. But he owed her this, and so much more besides. Now he was there, he couldn't keep the words from spilling out.

'I told my mum and her boyfriend about the car.' Wesley had never seen Mum look so disappointed, but it meant Jordan could come back. It gave them another chance to fix everything. 'And I told the police everything I knew about the attack. They might bring charges against me.' If that was what he deserved, he would accept it.

Framed by the trees, Kat hadn't even looked at him. They were separated by a wide patch of overgrown grass, and neither moved to close the gap.

'There's nothing I can say to make this right, but—'

'I know how you feel about yourself.' Kat turned to him, expressionless. 'Do you know what I did to you?'

Wesley shifted uncomfortably. The urge to find her, to be close to her, had dissipated soon after she had run away from the car, but the painting on his bedroom wall still gnawed at him in a way that felt similar. Like being caught naked. As if the contents of his soul had been spilled out in front of him.

'You went . . .'

'Honestly, I'm sorry for that,' she said. 'I couldn't see any other way.'

It humiliated him, that somebody had seen who he really was. That *she* had seen. It made him want to hide his face.

'That painting . . . is that what I look like inside?'

'More people than you'll ever know feel the same way you do.' Kat's expression darkened. 'It's no excuse for the way you acted. To be so . . . hateful.'

Wesley blanched at the word, stammered to defend himself, but Kat wasn't finished.

'Nobody would need to feel like that if we were kinder to each other. If we had more empathy.' She nodded, as if egging herself on. 'I've had to learn to be kind to myself. I can't do that if any part of me is taken up by hatred for you. You don't get to take anything more from me.'

'I wanted to help,' Wesley said. He had, hadn't he? 'I remembered you. Tried to keep you from fading.'

She fixed him with a look that filled him with shame. It was only when there was really no other choice that he had truly tried to help.

'You were scared for yourself. That's all. You don't deserve credit for doing what any decent person would have done sooner.' said Kat. 'I know what you've done for the other Lonely People, and I'm glad. Being kind is how you won't be forgotten. We have to stop the people who want us to hate.'

Wesley would do everything he could to make sure TrumourPixel was punished. To make amends to Mum and Dave. To welcome Jordan home. To be good to his new friends. It would be a start.

'Thank you,' he said.

'It wasn't my job to teach you.' Kat began to walk, feet pressing the sodden grass flat, past him and onto the path. 'I want you to remember me. But I never want to speak to you again.'

She moved away down the hill and left him behind, never once looking back.

Wesley waited there a while to watch the town below brighten and stir into life. Up here, he felt separate from the world. It spurred him to turn, and set off back along the path and home.

39

A Cautionary Tale
for the Lonely

The last time Wesley visited the flat it was almost empty. Their possessions had been transferred piecemeal to Dave's place, as many boxes as would fit into a car at once, until hardly anything was left. Wesley had volunteered to collect the final few himself, leaving them to get on with unpacking.

He had planned to walk around the place slowly and commit it to memory. It was supposed to feel romantic. The end of an era, etc. Instead he felt only an eagerness to leave it behind.

The bedroom smelled of paint. They had covered up the damp as best they could, though it still left an ominous shadow across the ceiling. The mural beside the door had been more easily hidden. Wesley ran his fingers down the wall. There was nothing of it left to see, but he would always remember it. A cautionary tale for the lonely.

Three boxes remained, mostly toys and other junk excavated from under the bed. Wesley stacked and heaved them awkwardly up, and staggered back to the front door.

'You said you didn't need any help.'

The boxes were taken from him one by one, Aoife insisting on carrying the heaviest while Robbie and Jae fought for the lightest.

'I was going to have a sentimental moment,' Wesley said. 'But then I decided against it.'

He locked the door and pushed the keys through the letter box. It was a relief, to hear them *thunk* on the other side. To walk away for the final time.

As they emerged from the main door, Buttnugget hopped up onto the wall and arched his back in invitation.

'Now *you* I am going to miss.' Wesley ran his fingers through the cat's soft fur, smiling as he immediately began to purr.

'You can come over and see my cat,' said Jae.

'Or we can trap this one in a box and run for it,' added Robbie.

It was only a fifteen-minute walk to Dave's flat. They took turns exchanging the boxes so one person could always have a break.

'Thanks for helping,' Wesley said, as they turned off the road. It was a taller block of flats, set back away from the street behind trees and a small playing field. Before they had even reached the car park he spotted three cats he would do everything in his power to befriend.

'It's nice here,' said Aoife.

'Yeah. It is.'

A battered red car was waiting near the main entrance, back seat piled with boxes. Its door opened to greet them.

'So you really *do* have friends,' said Jordan. 'Ready to go up?'

Wesley smiled. 'Let's do it.'

Even a year later, it was a little strange to have a full-length mirror where her posters used to be. Kat examined her costume: the white, high-necked dress wasn't exactly the right fit, and the boots barely made it past her ankles. There was absolutely no way she was giving herself a perm, so the slightly droopy wig would have to do.

'Esme,' she said to her reflection, pulling on a pair of studded gauntlets. 'You're back.'

Kat hoped her cosplay would at least be good enough that she wouldn't look stupid at the convention. Especially as she would be meeting so many new people there.

'You look amazing.'

Kat whirled around to find Safa outside her bedroom doorway, holding her arms wide to show off her costume.

'Oh. My. God.'

A full-body brown morph suit left only her face uncovered, and sewn into its front was an enormous, looping plushie pretzel with angry eyes and a gurning mouth. It made the costume so wide that she couldn't fit through the door.

'I thought you were joking!'

Safa shrugged, the entire pretzel rising and falling with her. 'I want to make an impression. And knock loads of people over by accident.'

'How many people are we meeting there?'

'At last count it was nine, if they all show up.'

In the last year, they had kept the All the Lonely People site running, but had stripped out the cryptic sixth-form poetry and instead detailed everything they had learned about the fade in a way that made it clear it was not to be aspired to. They had seen the effect that finding connection could have for the detached – for them, for Aoife and Robbie and Jae – and they responded to anybody who contacted the site to try and help them find it too.

They would be meeting some of them for the first time at the convention. Another gathering of the Lonely People, but for a different purpose now. The familiar panic awakened in Kat's chest, but with Safa beside her she had the power to fight it back into its corner.

'We're going to get stuck in traffic!' shouted Dad from downstairs.

Kat took out her phone. 'Let's take a selfie, while it's just the two of us.'

'Okay, but you're going to have to come out here.'

The photo was a disaster. The wig tickled Safa's nose and made her sneeze so that the pretzel covered half of Kat's face. It was perfect.

'We could just stay here and watch *Backwash* together all day,' she said.

Safa threaded her hands through the loops of the pretzel, and Kat took them in her own. They held onto each other – still there, still real – and then made their way downstairs.

Acknowledgements

It's always a little surreal when a story laboured over in the bedrooms and spare rooms of numerous homes, on cold benches in airports and hard beds in hostels, in simultaneously revelatory and despairing emails and notes to myself, becomes an actual *book*. There are many people to thank for that.

Thank you to Ella Kahn, who always believes in me and my work even when I am absolutely convinced it is as worthless as a doorbell on a gravestone.

To Sarah Castleton, who is the most ruthless, insightful, and empathetic editor I could ask for. As ever, this book is *so* much better for her work on it.

The whole team at Atom – Stephie, Olivia, Sophia, Maddie, and everybody else behind the scenes I don't see – is such a pleasure to work with.

This is my third published book, and during that time I've learned the value of having writer friends to moan at about, well, everything. Thankfully I have The Agency for exactly that (when we're taking a well-earned break from fighting ghosts together) – Non, Darran, Simon and Ashley, you guys are hashtag the best.

Barb, thank you for ensuring I was always up extra early to write, and thank you to Piggy for always arriving to cover my keyboard with hair and dribble at the exact moment I've found the motivation to actually start.

A huge thank you to all the writers, bloggers and

vloggers that have reviewed and supported my books, especially Nicola (@PrythianBworm), who possibly owns more copies of my second book than I do, and Zoe (@zcollins1994). Both are doing top work in the UKYA community.

And lastly, thank you to Hannah, who never quite knows if I'm telling the truth about what I'm writing until the book is published. The next one is about a dog in the Vietnam War . . .